Light 'n Lively Reads

for ESL, Adult, and Teen Readers

Light 'n Lively Reads

for ESL, Adult, and Teen Readers

A Thematic Bibliography

La Vergne Rosow

Illustrated by the Author

1996
Libraries Unlimited, Inc.
and Its Division
Teacher Ideas Press
Englewood, Colorado

LIBRARIES UNLIMITED, INC.
and Its Division
Teacher Ideas Press
P.O. Box 6633
Englewood, CO 80155-6633
1-800-237-6124

Library of Congress Cataloging-in-Publication Data

Rosow, La Vergne.
    Light 'n lively reads for ESL, adult, and teen readers : a
thematic bibliography / La Vergne Rosow.
    xxxvii, 343 p. 17x25 cm.
    Includes bibliographical references and index.
    ISBN 1-56308-365-5
    1. English language--Textbooks for foreign speakers--Bibliography.
2. High interest-low vocabulary books--Bibliography. 3. Readers--
Bibliography. I. Title.
Z5814.E59R67   1996
[PE1128]
016.4286'4--dc20   96-7084
                                                              CIP

In recognition of literacy volunteers everywhere, who give their time so others may know the joy of reading.

Contents

Unit 4—MYSTERY, SUSPENSE, AND HORROR— FOR THE FUN OF IT *(continued)*

Unit 5—LETTERS, LOGS, AND JOURNALS 63

Unit 6—PARENTING 77

Unit 7—SICKNESS, DEATH, AND DYING 99

Unit 8—RACISM, BIGOTRY, AND TOLERANCE 121

Preface

It was quite by accident that the first adult I ever taught made a miraculous transition from nonreader to reader in just a few months' time. Here was a man who had managed to get through the traditional California kindergarten-through-twelfth-grade system and a university degree program without ever having had his literacy level questioned. He was bright and personable, but he didn't know how to get ideas from marks in books or how to transform his ideas into marks on a page—until we worked together as tutor and student in a volunteer literacy program. I hadn't a clue why things had gone so well or if I'd ever be able to facilitate such a transformation again. Then there was another miracle. And another. Since that time, I've discovered that no miracle is necessary.

As a traditional teacher, I loved having a neat package of things that fit the curriculum, so that I could move masses of people efficiently from point 1 to point 2, and have them arrive lockstep at predetermined goals. But this didn't work, because not everybody arrived at the finish line. Education professionals from the cognitive camp tried to make me understand that the bell curve theory expects this. In many ways, again and again, I heard, "You've got to have a nice distribution in order to reflect the general population." But as an intuitive humanist, I did not like running a contest that had built-in losers. It felt unfair, as if I were taking in a fixed number of students on false pretenses, promising to teach everyone but really planning not to teach that bottom of the bell. And at the top of the bell, well—their parents flesh out the curriculum, don't they? Still, I was unprepared to do anything else. I had not even thought about my own philosophy of education, much less learned how to identify the various positions that entire institutions reflected.

Then I became a volunteer tutor for Literacy Volunteers of America (LVA). Starting with basic literacy and then teaching English as a Second Language (ESL) in a one-on-one format, I began to want a high success rate even more. With a student population of one, the teacher is in a win or lose situation. I had no theory base, but the LVA philosophy did support learner-centered methods. And in LVA if something did not feel comfortable to the tutor-student pair, they did not do it. Skills, drills, phonics in isolation, and rote memorization immediately took a backseat to legitimate language arts. My students learned, and quickly, too. But as I mentioned earlier, I did not have a clue as to why, and I wondered when it would all end. I went back to school to find out. At the University of Southern California I had the good fortune to take a language acquisition class from Steve Krashen. There I discovered "the affective filter" and "comprehensible input," two notions that effective teachers know intuitively but that often do not fit activities in artificially constructed curriculums. (The affective filter is the emotional barrier to learning. Comprehensible input refers to new information that is presented in small increments, so that the learner can absorb the new knowledge and relate it to what is already known.) I also began to consciously understand the power of reading.

Having gone through teacher education classes and tutor training classes without benefit of theory-to-practice connections, I started to realize that both formal and nonformal teacher preparation systems fail to give solid theoretical foundations to the people who need it most, the teachers who will be in the trenches. By *theory,* I hasten to explain, I simply mean the probable *reasons why things work or do not work.*

Meanwhile, I began teaching community college ESL and reading classes. One school actually maintained a fixed schedule, requiring, for example, all level A classes to be on the same workbook chapter at the same time. Instructors were monitored to assure synchronization with the curriculum. It was efficient, and some instructors enjoyed the freedom from lesson planning. The students, who got to know all the ropes of registration and test taking, required little attention once they were in the system. And quite a few who landed in my classes had been there for three, four, five, and six years without learning enough English to move on to regular community college classes. Suffice it to say that the monitored ESL classes were less than lively, except when I managed to rush through the workbook requirements and do some legitimate language acquisition work.

I experimented with materials like junk mail and journal articles, and once, when we were moved to a classroom used for landscape design during the day, we hit a cache of magazines that whetted many appetites for authentic literature. Though the students knew they were suddenly learning faster in my classes than they had in the past, I knew that as soon as I was out of the picture, they would be hard-pressed to identify what they needed to maximize their own language learning. Elsewhere, I continued to teach reading and writing to native English-speaking adults. Their experiences had often been on tandem tracks with those of the ESL students. Once they learned how to be obedient participants in a formal system, little was done to empower them or to help them move out of the system. It was then that I began to formalize my notion of teaching theory directly to the learner. Several hundred students later, I am here to tell you that students *like* knowing why the teacher is doing what she is doing, and they like being able to negotiate their experiences from informed perspectives. Indeed, my book *In Forsaken Hands: How Theory Empowers Literacy Learners* is a step-by-step guide to how I taught theory to children, teens, and adults (Rosow 1995).

The literature tells us that reading makes you smarter and that writing helps you think. Krashen has already collected that data and put it into a salient form in his *Fundamentals of Language Education* (1992) and *The Power of Reading* (1993). But getting adult learners engaged in reading that is both interesting and accessible, and then helping them to move into increasingly more difficult texts, takes more than just knowing that it is a good idea. Besides, in these times we are often faced with large, multiethnic classes, comprising students who possess a wide range of reading and writing abilities. Some are well read in their first, second, or even several languages and value literacy for its own sake. Some come from school systems that have taught them that the object of school work is to get a grade or a credit. Still others are preliterate and monolingual. And all may show up in the same adult education or community college classroom. Add to that the fact that populations are constantly shifting in the United States, and you have activities that used to work beautifully but now do not.

There is no overstating the energy required to address today's educational environment. Teaching requires as much fortitude and creativity as it ever has. And, although no one would argue the teacher's right to design lessons that fit the immediate students in the classroom, it is good to know that starting from scratch is not a prerequisite to our success, at least not with every student. (Though every student does have to show up for class and does have to participate in the program before a teacher can assume any responsibility for success or failure. Quality contact time is critical to students' success.)

There is no way for a teacher to externally motivate a student to undertake the amount of practice required for proficient reading. And those students who have managed to sidestep pleasure reading—or who have never discovered it—have all kinds of excuses for denying themselves the right to read for the fun of it. Here are some of the ways I help them learn to see this enjoyable activity as valid:

- To the young child who claims not to like reading, I say: "You need to hear lots of stories before you know which are the good books and which ones are boring. In fact, it takes about 5,000 stories to really learn what's good. Little kids who like to read learned to read by having someone read to them every day and every night at bedtime. Little kids who don't like to read need somebody to read to them a lot. I will read some of my favorites to you, so you'll see why I like them."

- To the teenager who says reading is boring or that it is hard to comprehend, I say: "If you get bored sometimes, that's just a sign that your brain wants something more interesting to do. That's a sign of intelligence. Certainly you won't remember words that bored you. I'm willing to bet you don't remember boring people or boring movies either. But if you are very interested in something, you'll be able to pay attention. To comprehend what you read, you need to read interesting things. We'll start with me reading samples of things to you, so that you can hear how the author intended it and can concentrate on finding things you really like. When we discover what interests you, I will help you find a lot of easy readings to get started with. Once you read a lot of easy stuff about something, you'll know the words you need to move on to even more interesting things. But first, I will read to you."

- To the English-as-a-second-language or English-as-a-foreign-language student who claims that English grammar is much more difficult than that of other languages, I say: "Yes, I keep hearing that. Linguists learn about grammar rules from the ways that people talk and write. They have discovered that there is no end to the new rules that keep popping up in English. And even though finding those rules and learning about them is their life's work, they can never get it all. Certainly you don't think you have to compete with them.

  "Native speakers don't learn all the rules of grammar before they start to speak. Indeed, children rarely think about rules of grammar during the first five or six years of study. Neither do they learn one rule at a time. By being exposed to all the grammar rules *in use*, children acquire ways of applying them. But, how do they get that exposure? For the spoken language, they get it in communicative situations. In the literate home, parents provide higher-level vocabulary, grammar, and early writing lessons by reading stories to the child, so the child hears how written language is put on the page for years before trying to do it. And, of course, the high level of grammar used in long written sentences exposes that child to complex rules, without ever naming a single rule. Yet, the listener starts acquiring them, naturally. Over time, the child makes the transition from being read to to reading independently, starting, of course, with the things heard over and over at home. But you're all grown up, so what's to be done? Well, let me share with you some of those stories that introduce the native speakers to our language. And I'll give you something native speakers get in literate homes all over America several times a day and every night. I'll read to you."

- To the adult who is caught in the grind of trying to memorize all the rules of spelling and punctuation, I say: "There are a few spelling and punctuation rules worth knowing. We can list them on less than a page and you can keep them handy for use when you need them. Of course, many computers have programs that will help you correct those things too. (I have found it curious that adults who have trouble with spelling and other writing-related tasks often think that having a personal spelling list or other reference tools around is cheating. Who has taught them such ideas? Why? It is not cheating to help yourself do what you want to do.) First I want to point out that you will never be able to spell every word you can say. Your spoken vocabulary is always ahead of your written one. So don't dwell on what you can't do. Once you've acquired the basic survival vocabulary and the basic words you need at work, you won't hear many new words. Nor will you read them in ads or at work. You'll increase your vocabulary and spelling by pleasure reading. That's why well-read people sound different from people who don't read. But you were talking about spelling. When you see a word that you have heard but never seen before, you'll notice that it is either spelled the way you thought it would be or that it is surprising. Sometimes you may want to underline it in your book or even keep a little list of words you are interested in. But even if you do neither, over time, the more you read, the better your spelling will get and the more likely you are to notice punctuation you haven't paid attention to before. So follow along as I read to you. And when you want to, we'll stop and discuss the words and punctuation you find interesting."

- To the parent of young children who claims not to have time to read for pleasure, I say: "Your children need to see you reading for your own pleasure. They will learn how to behave by what they see you do. If they see you looking at beautiful picture books with interest, they will know that grown-ups in their family value beautiful books. If they see you writing notes to others in the family, they will learn that this family communicates in literate ways. The more you read in the presence of your children, the better it is for them. And when you share a good book with a child, you are teaching the child that literacy is about being loved and cared for. Meanwhile, your own vocabulary and knowledge base will be growing, making you better able to assist your child in school and giving you the language to communicate with your child's teachers. Reading for pleasure gives you the power of language. But you need help finding things to get started with, so I will read some things to you."

- To the person who is working ten- and twelve-hour shifts who claims not to have time to read for fun, I say: "You are probably so tired you don't even have the energy to listen to the news at night. What is more, you hardly have time to talk with your family and you pride yourself in self-sacrifice for them. I understand that. But consider the impact on your loved ones when they understand that you are so proud of yourself that you've decided you deserve 20 minutes of uninterrupted quiet time each day. If improving your spoken and written language is a priority for you, there are two things you can do that will bring visible change in just 30 days.

  1. Read for pleasure just ten minutes a day. That means taking something to work and reading for ten minutes during your break or at the end of your lunch period. It can be a magazine or a collection of short stories or a joke book. But remember that frequency is very important. Do it every day.

  2. After you read, write something down in a notebook. It does not need to be about what you read, but it will reflect the new words, spelling, grammar, and punctuation that is still swimming in your head from your pleasure reading. Always write the day and the date at the top of the page. You will see significant change in just thirty days. And you'll be reading faster. I guarantee it.

> But, first you need to know what to read. It's not that easy finding something that is both interesting and promises to be easy enough to handle when you're under pressure at work or are very tired. So let's start by my reading to you. That way you can just relax and listen and judge for yourself about the content and quality."

- To the engineer who has managed to escape academic writing by making a career choice that requires no writing—until now, I say: "I have worked with many engineers who were bright people, but who were traumatized over their writing very early on. Unwilling to be badgered and humiliated, and wanting to achieve at something, they turned to more technical language use. That, in turn, robbed them of exposure to good leisure reading materials, the very thing they needed to show them how good writers express themselves. So all they ever read were technical materials and simple instruction passages. Later they were limited to workplace writers who, like themselves, had never discovered what good writing looked like. But we can change that starting now. Tell me what you'd do if you weren't in a technical field and I will read to you about possibilities."

- To the teacher who says students have to have "the basics," I say: "I quite agree. Knowing that ideas and good times come from books is surely basic. Knowing the rhythm and flow of spoken and written language is basic. Understanding the connections between ciphers on book pages and sounds of language is surely basic. Knowing how good writers put their ideas down on paper is basic to being able to write well. Not coincidentally, the adults with whom I've worked—the ones who could not get meaning from text, even when they were smart enough to do many other things very well—consistently lack one basic element: a memory of being read to for pleasure as children. Isn't that interesting? And all of the above-mentioned basics come from being read to. So, if we are to begin at the beginning of any literacy program, we must first read to our students. Yes, regardless of age, I always read to my students."

Reading to students is a basic form of language instruction. For young children, for teenagers, for adults, for senior citizens, for native speakers of English, and for new speakers of English. Reading to students is the most effective way to introduce good things to read. Lots of good things to read—things the student considers highly interesting—are key to letting voluntary practice start. But what to read remains a question.

There is so much to read, and yet the right stuff is so difficult to find. And it takes so much time to ferret out things students will enjoy from the morass of unsellable texts. Where is a list of books that will serve a diverse population from a wide range of abilities, and different levels of English language speaking? What if some of those people have a lot of time to read and others are just getting interested in books? Where is there a guide to things that a teacher or tutor can read to students of any age that will whet the appetite for more? 'Tis here.

References

Krashen, Stephen. *Fundamentals of Language Education*. Torrance, CA: Laredo, 1992.

———. *The Power of Reading: Insights from the Research*. Englewood, CO: Libraries Unlimited, 1993.

Rosow, La Vergne. *In Forsaken Hands: How Theory Empowers Literacy Learners*. Portsmouth, NH: Heinemann, 1995.

Acknowledgments

Thanks first to my editors, Tama Serfoss, Kim Dority, Steve Haenel, who thought of many details, and to Shannon Graff, editorial assistant, Kay Minnis, typesetter, and Stacey Chisholm, author relations/acquisitions at Libraries Unlimited. Thanks also to Sue Mendizza for leading me to *Chicken Soup for the Soul*, Julie Holder for the *Letter from Home*, and Pamela Fisher for commemorative stamp information. To many in the book business, including Randy McDonald of Sandcastle Books; Mike and Ida Cahill; Judy Nelson; Jonelle Allen of Scholastic Book Fairs; and countless helpful people at Crown Books and Barnes and Noble. To the reference and children's librarians at the Huntington Beach Public Library, Mariner's Library, Newport Beach Library, and Garden Grove Library; Clare DiFelice of the Beaumont Library District; and Al Bennett of the California State Library, for help with finding books, information about books, and ideas about ways of collecting them. To Rose Saylin, Sue Berman, and Linda Light for moral support; Ruth Colvin, the visionary who opened the doors of literacy volunteering to me and many thousands of others; Gayle Miller, Trudy LeClair, and other Kappans who have opened their classrooms and their libraries to me; Rich Littlefield for insights into real estate tests; Dick Evans and Robert Rosow for general guidance; David Loertscher for the concept of this book; Steve Krashen for regular shipments of quality data; Steve Posner for a wealth of quality writing; David Eskey for good counsel; and to my son Paul who carefully stepped over stacks of books on his way to the refrigerator.

I remain indebted to the volunteer tutors in the Beaumont, California, literacy program, who have given me insights into which books worked well with their students and why; and to the adult learners in Beaumont and in my workplace literacy classes who shared their ideas about many of the books in this collection. I am also indebted to my Phi Delta Kappa colleagues who have led me to people who led me to more wonderful books for all ages. There have also been the teachers who have taken time to present at reading and language conferences and have been most eager to share their discoveries of great books.

It is difficult to know where to draw the line in saying thanks, but I must add one more group—the people I've found in the aisles of book stores, the little kids who can tell exactly why a book is good, the parents and grandparents who know which things must be read again and again, and the teachers who are always there, spending their own funds to make reading accessible to their students—ever-struggling to level the playing field for students in underfunded schools.

It takes a lot of people to identify a good long list of books. I'm grateful to all of them.

xix

Introduction

Who Is This Book For?

The unit introductions and annotations in this book describe some of the ways I address my adult basic literacy students, English as a Second Language (ESL) students, remedial and reluctant child readers, and their families. You may ask how we can deal with both native speakers and nonnative English learners, and both adult and child learners, at once—with the same methods and literature. From my philosophical perspective, it is all language arts. We are starting at the English language level of the learner and helping that learner find ways of acquiring more language proficiency. When we view our field as language arts, unnecessary and limiting walls melt away, and the theoretical notions that serve learners well in ESL classes will serve learners equally well in reading and writing. Using comprehensible input, or providing students with only as much information at one time as can be readily absorbed and connected with what they already know, is consistently effective, no matter how old a learner is, or whether or not the learner is a native speaker of English. The influence of learner interest on comprehension is an undeniable influence in any language. Background knowledge building is essential for success with complex text every time.

This book is written to assist both the learner and teacher in locating high-powered reading materials. The concepts presented here are both leading edge and thoroughly field tested. In my students—adult and children—I've discovered an untapped capacity to critically address teaching practice, making these students an excellent resource for improving my teaching. But the only way to include the learners in meaningful decision making about practice is to teach them what the teacher knows. If you are a parent or a tutor, read this book aloud to your child or student and discuss the possibilities as you go. If you are a new reader, know that I am talking with you about your learning; sometimes I will address you directly, and rely on your teacher, parent, or tutor to read the message to you.

This approach is learner centered and learner empowering. It will provide you with connections between theory and practice. It will offer ways of employing cooperative learning in large classes. And it will give you ready reference to reading materials on adult and family-oriented themes that flow from easy reading to advanced literature. This book offers suggestions for where to find current readings on the topics and also suggests dialogue and writing activities that can accompany the readings. Each thematic unit has an annotated bibliography to allow you to collect items from the library, bookstore, and flea market.

Because of the widespread need to address large classes, I will do this most of the way through the book. With the exception of cooperative learning groups, the methods discussed here can work for adult and child learners whether they are being tutored one-on-one, are receiving special small group reading or language treatment, or are members of large classes.

Reading Aloud

Before we can read, we must know what good reading sounds like. When the teacher reads aloud, powerful things happen. The students relax and just enjoy the story; hear the written language well presented; and acquire vocabulary, sentence structure, and writing style, without trying.

Whether they are university graduate students, literacy volunteers, community college ESL or reading students, or basic literacy students, I read to my learners, both child and adult. While I was a doctoral student at the University of Southern California, two world-renowned professors demonstrated to me the power of story. David Eskey, who has set up English language programs around the world, uses colorful storytelling almost every class period to make his most important points memorable. Steve Krashen, world-renowned linguist, reads Spiderman comics to his graduate students—not because they can't do it for themselves, but because being read to is the best way to lower the affective filter (the emotional barrier to learning) and make way for important messages to enter the brain. Sure, there is some initial surprise when I begin to read to my adult students, but there is never a complaint.

Too often I have been in discussions that show people have mixed up reading and being read to. Parents and teachers report that they read to their students, when in reality they are making the student perform every other sentence or every other page. That is not being read to. Being read to means letting the student enjoy the delights of hearing good reading, stopping along the way to discuss what has been read, being free to ask that something be reread or clarified. This process occurs naturally with the young child in a literate parent's lap. For the student who never received that basic support of literacy, the teacher must introduce it. There is no call for performance from the listener, except when the listener needs to participate and then only briefly.

Listening to someone read gives the learner quality input. Seeing words in context—such as following along, looking at posters with pictures, studying record albums, book jackets, fast food signs, and other environmental print—helps give text with meaning connected to it. In addition, being read to illustrates to students how the rhythm and flow of written language sounds. It takes a lot of quality input before output is reasonable. Students reading aloud, writing, and answering comprehension questions are all output. Being read to is the first and strongest way a learner of any age learns the relationship between the sounds of the language and symbols on the page. Hearing what good reading sounds like gives quality input.

Many read-aloud passages can be found in the "Book Chapters and Strong Passages" section in each unit.

Reading Materials Groups

The categories or units in this book are, to some extent, arbitrary. They are loose judgments of what will be easy for a new reader or entry-level ESL student to comprehend and what will be more difficult. Simple sentence-length and word-size ways of looking at readability have not given me the information I need for selecting readings for individual students, though they do offer a general way of measuring difficulty. But it is impossible to know what kinds of experiences a person has already had that will support comprehension without interviewing that particular person. That is the beauty of one-on-one tutoring: lessons can be completely individualized. It also makes a case for cooperative learning groups, as students within the groups begin to make reading recommendations to one another. But with large classes—which the lower levels of adult basic education (ABE), literacy, and English as a Second Language tend to be—the teacher is faced with trying to establish ways of helping students help themselves improve language arts skills. As international reading expert Frank Smith has pointed out in his book *Insult to Intelligence: The Bureaucratic Invasion of Our Classrooms* (1988), we learn to read by reading. The more we read, the better we get at it. And in the process, we learn about the things that make up written language.

Strategies for Teaching Reading

Love Notes

First a word about love notes. Each time a student stands up in front of the entire class, whether to introduce a classmate or to promote a book, the payoff is that everyone in the class must then write a love note to the speaker. The informal notes must use traditional date, greeting, closing, and signature; must say something positive about the presentation; and must ask a question. The recipient is not obliged to respond to the mail—that would be punishment—but often notes continue to flow back and forth unmonitored. This is teacher liberation. There is no feedback requirement on writing you do not see.

Individualized Instruction

When I am working with students, I provide each with individualized attention. I use many techniques to individualize learning, including interest surveys, taped feedback, literary clubs, written letters of support and feedback, and making connections with the community.

Interest Surveys

Based on the results of an interest survey, I bring in reading materials (and, at the higher levels, reading lists) for individual students. A newspaper article, a cartoon, an Ann Landers column, a reprint from a professional journal, or a recipe can open an informative dialogue between teacher and student.

Taped Feedback

Cassette tapes are my way of giving students who can't yet read written comments personal instruction. The student gives me a blank cassette tape and the original of something he or she has written, but keeps a photocopy. I return the tape but not the original paper. I read through the paper on tape, making suggestions for changes. My speed and elaboration depend upon the level of the student. If an ESL student, I may take into account vocabulary that is readily mistaken for something else, and I spell out words that the nonnative student may have never heard. However, monolingual students who are nonreaders also have limited vocabularies, so I take care to discuss any mixed metaphors or literary forms in comprehensible language. In both cases, I employ theoretical terms we have covered in class. For example, I might tell a student that I do not want to drive up his affective filter—his emotional barrier to learning, often caused by stress—or I might invite the student into a literacy club (discussed in the next section).

Literacy Clubs

In *Insult to Intelligence* (1988), international reading expert Frank Smith introduces the metaphor of literacy club membership to show how to foster a sense of belonging in a particular group. He first used the term "literacy club" to indicate a set of attitudes about one's right to act like a literate person. Because learning is a social process, Smith argues that a person must be "invited" into this club, with the potential for becoming a successful member, before an attempt at learning will occur. This invitation signals to the learner that the tutor will support the learner, encourage success, and not ridicule the learner's attempts.

Written Feedback

Letters from the teacher or tutor to students always do wonders. They make the student feel like an individual while providing valuable reading practice. This usually nets written responses from students.

Written responses to students' personal journals take a lot of time, and I only do this a couple of times a semester. However, students often jump the gun by presenting their journals ahead of schedule and more frequently than required. Although my remarks may be brief, I might make a note promising to bring in a special reading or suggesting that the student look up a given book.

Personal responses to group journal entries reach a much wider audience. The group journals never leave the classroom except via the teacher, and they are available as high-interest reading during class. Anyone may make entries and anyone may respond. That frees the teacher to make entries that will sell ideas to the entire class in an informal, low-stress format. Or to put it another way, the teacher's entries offer comprehensible input under low affective-filter conditions.

Community Connections

Make arrangements to connect the learners with other instructors or professionals in the community. This can create a lot of self-confidence on the part of the learner without a tremendous amount of output on the teacher's part.

Cooperative Learning

A person in my class may belong to a variety of groups. Initially, I encourage the self-selection of four group mates (making a total of five) based first on ethnicity, then on gender. The more diversity in experience and perspective, the more interesting the group, the greater the communication challenges will be, and the higher the potential for learning. To facilitate the first self-selected group, I list categories of native language and/or ethnicity on the board, and then have each student write his or her name under the appropriate heading. After that, I allow volunteers to select group members for their "home groups" based on the lists. The next step is for each group to decide on a meaningful group name. These home groups are responsible for each other's well-being, collecting handouts for absent members, and helping other members select good reading materials from classroom collections.

Of course, if most of the class is from a single ethnic group, it may be more difficult to find obviously diverse groups, but the challenge remains to create learning clusters that will foster discovery. Even if students have seemingly similar backgrounds, they may create a group that fosters discovery. For example, one group of Hispanic students named itself "The Conquistadors," without knowing the historical implications of the word. Researching their group name became their research task for the rest of the semester, and they made a series of presentations that were far more elaborate than anything I ever would have assigned.

Later I call for regrouping based on research topics (yes, research starts at level 1 for native and nonnative speakers alike), special interests, hobbies, favorite authors, or the like. And it is interesting how intercultural connections naturally emerge as students start trying to develop their own common themes. My motive is to keep students interested in the work so that literacy and language accomplishments are by-products of the process.

In every grouping, each person should learn the first and last name of each person in their group and be able to locate each member's homeland on the map. To broaden the friendship base and language-use experience, I assign each student to interview a classmate and write an introduction to that person, then introduce the new friend to the class. Usually I ask them not to choose members of their home group for this exercise. In this way, a wealth of questions is generated that can then be applied to home group members under less pressing conditions. And if this kind of informal interviewing begins in the first, or home, group, it continues on its own in subsequent groups, and that fosters student retention, language learning, geography, history, and intercultural communication.

Classroom Library

Maintaining a library is easier said than done in situations where the teacher must move from room to room or school to school. The cost can be high and the toll on the back awesome. Having said that, let me add that I have had success under these circumstances by providing the following:

- Endless supplies of discarded magazines from the library. They are just left out in the open on a table. If students wish, they can even take them home. And when that happens, I credit myself with fostering a high interest in reading.

- A large cardboard box with magazines, old *TV Guides*, and used paperback books. Identify the box clearly on the outside so that custodians do not discard it and other classes invade it less often.

- A secured file cabinet with a cache of magazines, paperbacks, reference books, *TV Guides*, and children's literature. This arrangement allows the teacher the spontaneity needed to help individual students and small groups at the moment of need. It still gets expensive, and I have learned not to supply books that I cannot replace. A lot of my paperbacks come from a used bookstore.

- Environmental print, such as maps, posters, and signs posted on the walls. Environmental print is a marvelous informal teacher, the simple messages shout "Look at Me!" and compel the student to "read the world" of the classroom every day. In the process, they acquire spelling and vocabulary without conscious studying. I've noticed that when I do dictation that uses words on the walls, students frequently look up to double-check themselves, intuitively knowing where to find the word. That's a sure sign that they've been reading the walls, even though no one ever assigned them.

- Publishers' book posters from conferences. They are free and support a print-rich environment. Sometimes libraries also receive more of one poster than they can use—ask for them.

One-Minute Promotions

At any time during the semester, students are at liberty to promote a book they have found particularly interesting. In one minute or less, the student makes a sales pitch to the class, telling briefly what the book is about, the title and author, the difficulty of the vocabulary, and any other salient issues. There is no deadline for doing these. Sometimes five or six students sign up to promote, other times none. When a student is in a silent period,[1] and unwilling to perform in front of the class, demanding a performance would serve only to drive up the affective filter for everyone in the room. When a student is ready and eager to speak, the positive outcomes are the reward; no artificial motivators are required.

Readers Theatre

Readers theatre is reading aloud for entertainment purposes. It is an excellent way to reinforce both content and language skills in a low-stress format. It does not require any special props or costuming, though they can certainly be present. The necessary ingredients are the following:

A reader or several readers.

An audience of one or more people who know that this is a sensitive performance.

A text that the reader or readers have practiced a lot. It may be published text or something the reader has written.

A place where the reader faces the audience and reads for entertainment purposes. To prepare for it, the reader must practice the piece until it feels comfortable.

For the teacher to demand that students read aloud before they have a chance to practice is unkind and nets much poorer results than they could give under appropriate circumstances. It also drives up the reader's affective filter and bores the audience, twice pointless—though many adult students can recall this nonsense going on in their early school years. Readers theatre is a celebration of literacy, an event to be enjoyed by all participants.

Research Presentations

- Individual reports can be given whenever a student completes a research project. The report is written as an abstract and includes sharing the most valuable sources of information.

- Research panels may be groups of students working on exactly the same topic or on related topics. Seated at the front of the class, they present the results of extensive, in-depth reading.

Field Trips

Trips to used bookstores and the library allow students to find personally interesting materials while working within the whole-class format. At a used bookstore, each student is encouraged to select both a fiction and a nonfiction book for sustained silent reading (SSR; see page xxx). In the library, the tours (for both adult and child learners) always end in the children's section, where each person is to find three books that are both easy and interesting.

Although students from literate homes are comfortable with children's literature, others may not be inclined to seek out such pleasure-reading material voluntarily. Before the library tour, I review the value of reading things that are easy and interesting. I also explain that many of our idiomatic expressions and culture comes from children's literature. For some, that is enough of a sales pitch. However, there are usually some who need more exact instructions to be able to walk out of the library with children's literature. Here are a handful of assignments that I've found allow teens and adults to take the plunge:

- Select three books at different difficulty levels and identify the ways in which they might be used to teach children.
- Select three books on different topics and describe when they might be used to teach adults.
- Select two fiction books and one nonfiction book that give useful information. Identify what age student would most benefit from the information.
- Select three books and compare the blurb or jacket information with what the book actually gives the reader.
- Select three picture books and rate them according to how well the pictures support comprehension.
- Select three books and identify which would be best for teaching new vocabulary to the class.
- Select three books of international legends or folklore. Compare the lessons taught by the stories.
- Select three books that would help you teach history, science, or math.
- Select three books at different levels that would be appropriate for bedtime reading.

Notice that the assignments call for opinions, not right or wrong answers. What is important is that the reader develop critical analysis skills.

As always, I am right there to help students test a few passages to make sure the selections are reasonable and to help students understand that simply touching a book does not mean you are stuck with it. My students never get enough of these excursions. Weekly class evaluations frequently include requests for more teacher-led trips to book sources. But it is not necessary to follow through on every such request. Librarians and bookstore owners report extensive sightings of my students long after an event.

The follow-up is to have the students report on their books to the home group. This can lead to a variety of discussion topics. (This is not a test to see if the entire book was read; if the book is worthwhile to the reader, it will get read. If it is interesting, it will be understood.) Once the reluctant reader has begun to read books for meaningful activities, the chance of real pleasure from reading is high, too. In cooperative groups, the average number of books discussed is fifteen, giving the uninitiated a chance to learn about other books before returning to the library.

Guest Speakers

Guest speakers provide a wealth of learning events before, during, and after the actual visit. If the speaker has written anything (such as poetry or a book) or provided brochures on a topic (such as political issues), has a special agenda (such as a public service), or is a future teacher who wants to observe, there are pre-visit activities that afford language and literacy learning opportunities. Have the class read the material ahead of time, if possible, have them develop a list of possible questions, or have them do some research on the speaker's topic.

After the presentation, have students write thank-you notes. These notes are legitimate, authentic writing activities. Also, encourage the students to discuss the speaker and the information provided and researched in their collaborative groups.

Authentic Texts

There are a great many so-called simplified or adapted texts on today's ESL and literacy markets. Such books and anthologies often display the names of famous authors but deliver washed-out, poorly constructed counterfeits. The unpleasant result is that students who are ill prepared to recognize this deception may find the chopped-up sentences and uninteresting word choices not only boring but more difficult to comprehend than the original text. As a result, they may feel they have read and not enjoyed an author they have never met at all. This disempowers the learners and can cause them to mistakenly believe that they just do not appreciate quality literature. Further, it models poor writing. There is so much quality reading material available at all levels that to foist such fodder off on unwary adults is not only damaging to their self-images but also a serious waste of their precious reading time. Students must be taught to look for signs of text tampering. Words like *modified* and *abridged* and phrases like "adapted for ESL" or "rewritten for new readers" should forewarn the adult learner that something has been changed. Conversely, the term "complete and unabridged" is a positive sign. If there is any question about the authenticity of a text, the adult student is advised to select something else to read.

Quality input begets quality output, and the adult reader does not want to acquire literacy habits that are anything less than those enjoyed by good readers and writers. If the work of one well-known author is too difficult to read in its original form, the authentic state, it should be set aside until later.

How unfortunate it is to see the gutsy dialogues of Jack London and the innuendo of O. Henry scraped from their story lines, leaving mere skeletal remains for unwary readers. And the abridged works of John Steinbeck are a blasphemy against the literature of our time. Those bankrupt little story shells are a waste of the trees cut down for their paper. They should bear warning signs: *Caution! This text was not written by the author named. It may misrepresent quality language use and does not reflect the way the named author wrote.*

Note that retellings of old tales are quite another matter. In storytelling and literate homes around the globe, the fables of Aesop have been part of bedtime, campfire time, sick time, well time, child/parent time, and sibling time for thousands of years. No matter what the native language, Aesop has been there. First told for adult audiences in an oral culture, the tales were about 300 years old before they were first written down. Now they appear in nearly every known written language. This is a powerful connection for students of English. After I read a fable such as "The Lion and the Mouse," "The Fox and the Grapes," or "The Dog in the Manger" aloud to a multicultural class, I like to ask if the students have heard it before. How old were they? In what country or language did they first hear the tale? Such reminiscing can lead to a discussion that cuts across ethnicity and generations and teaches geography at the same time.

Sustained Silent Reading (SSR)

Whether in a large class, workplace program, or individual tutoring session, I use the first fifteen minutes of each session for sustained silent reading. In my classrooms, a stack of teacher-selected materials includes magazines of all sorts discarded from the local library (*People, Time, Redbook, Ladies' Home Journal, Life, Omni, Popular Mechanics, GQ, Sports Illustrated, National Geographic, Newsweek,* etc.), children's books, research articles, and other things that may appeal to both zealous readers and those who forgot to bring anything to read to class. In keeping with the research that caused SSR to become so popular, this is free voluntary reading (FVR). Students select their materials. There are no tests, no reports, and no other accountability. This frees a student to relax, read, and reread passages or to sample text at will, building good reader strategies that might have been discouraged during the early school years of many adult learners. Methods and materials opinion surveys at semester's end often indicate that my students value SSR as a major contributor to vocabulary development.

Book Trading

Once students promote a paperback book to the class, they have a ready market for its resale. Often, however, underlined words and marginal notes make the previously inexpensive books invaluable. In my classes, students are encouraged to write titles and authors of available books on the chalkboard, but by mid-semester most students have waiting lists for their works by popular authors such as Judy Blume, Sonya Friedman, Judith Krantz, and David Viscott. And the Sweet Valley High series quickly becomes cult literature.

Newspapers

My favorite Southern California newspaper is the Sunday edition of *The Los Angeles Times*. Because of the variety of topics and difficulty levels, it has something for almost every adult learner. The editorial section often offers good illustrations of points of view. The business and sports sections allow students to build background knowledge unavailable on television news. The TV schedule also connects television and literacy. The book review section offers real-life book critiques that employ the kinds of critical thinking we want to engender (as opposed to the low-level thinking summaries many have come to know as book reports). The letters to the editor vary considerably in quality and content, offering many reading, discussion, and writing opportunities. *The Los Angeles Times Magazine* almost always offers both strong fiction and well-written nonfiction pieces. And the travel section gives a wealth of information about the world, exchange rates, temperatures, and other adult-level topics. One Sunday *Times* can supply many weeks of meaningful reading, writing, and speaking activities. However, with wonderful results, I have used it as the class text, requiring each student to buy the Sunday edition each week.

Homework

I have two standing rules for all students:

1. Read for pleasure for a minimum of ten minutes per day. More is better.

2. Write in your journal for a minimum of ten minutes after you read. The new vocabulary, sentence structure, and style will be fresh in your brain, and you will write better.

Dos and Don'ts

- Do read aloud to adult students—often—just for the fun of it.
- Do teach reading and language acquisition theory to students.
- Do provide the theoretical justification for classroom practice.
- Do provide students with actual research results, so they can make informed decisions.
- Do provide a wide range of reading materials in the classroom.
- Do lead, not send, students to places where they will find appropriate reading materials.

- Do help students select materials that are personally interesting and intellectually challenging.

- Do give time for students to read for pleasure during class.

- Do help students understand that talking about reading they have done is a way of thinking out loud that will facilitate retention.

- Do help students understand that what they read greatly influences what they are able to write.

- Do help students understand that reading will improve spelling, vocabulary, syntax, grammar, and writing style.

- Do help every student understand that reading is pleasurable and that they are good at it and getting better.

- Do help students understand that reading is about making meaning, not barking sounds well. If there is no comprehension, there is no reading.

- Do help students understand that questioning text and challenging the author's motives is common among critical thinkers.

- Do help students see that there are many kinds of literature and that it is okay to love some and loathe others, even if the instructor feels just the opposite.

- Do warn students against the pitfalls of manipulated or simplified texts.

- Do pay attention to the kinds of reading students pursue and encourage them to move ahead in the same topic or genre.

- Do have students keep a log of their reading, so they can see the progress they have made. The log is part of the student's portfolio.

- Don't demand that students read aloud when they have not practiced.

- Don't create stress around reading.

- Don't argue about whether or not a student should like a particular book or story.

- Don't destroy pleasure reading by testing for comprehension.

- Don't destroy confidence by demanding book reports on books the student does not find worthwhile.

- Don't mislead students by substituting simplified, abridged, manipulated or otherwise mutilated texts for authentic reading materials.

How to Use the Readings:
A Guide for Guiding Students

When asked how to use collections like this for the adult and family populations that I usually work with, two approaches come immediately to mind:

- Breadth. Reading everything they can at a level that is easy for them will allow students to build a lot of background knowledge on a wide range of topics quickly. It will reinforce vocabulary through multiple uses from different perspectives. And it will teach syntax, grammar, and spelling in the process. This approach will be particularly useful to a person who is going to face standardized tests with random readings or other language-related tasks.

- Depth. Encouraging students to start with easy books on a topic that interests them will allow them to develop background knowledge and vocabulary needed for more difficult reading in that subject area. If students focus on one topic, they will be able to read challenging material on that topic within a surprisingly short time. So, going through all the picture books on the single topic, all the Thin Books, then all the Challenging Books will establish an informational and language base to support further study and discussion. This approach will be of value, for example, to a person who is about to take a science class and wants to get familiar with the language of that field.

Obviously, reading things that are interesting to you will be better than forging ahead in books you cannot concentrate on. Interest is key to reading success. If you cannot remember what you just read, and you are under no particular stress, it may be that you need to find something else to read.

Helping learners understand how to use books for their own best language development will liberate them to take charge of the process. That liberates the teacher, too.

The thematic units in this book have afforded various groups of students a wealth of language and literacy experience. However, not all readings in a unit are appropriate each time. Feel free to pick and choose. And when you cannot find something in your collection, substitute, improvise, or ignore. If your experiment works well, write me about it. I would love to hear about your variations on the themes or ideas for new themes.

Kinds of Reading Materials

First Readers and Picture Books

First Readers are books that have many pictures or photographs to support comprehension. These books generally have large print, a lot of open space, and very little text per page. Most importantly, they have illustrations that carry a wealth of information that fosters comprehension and retention. However, learning to read the pictures is not an automatic part of learning to decode books. Indeed, while working with Arthur, a fourth-grader who had never been read to, I discovered he was not even looking at the detailed pictures in the Dr. Seuss book *The Cat in the Hat*. As soon as Arthur was taught to use the pictures before trying to figure out the printed words, his comprehension improved.

Still, some books have a poor picture-text relationship. In one class I visited recently, the children were broken into ability groups, each group using books from a different collection. The high-level readers got to choose from a bin filled with colorful, well-written picture books, the kind that you might give a teacher friend as an anniversary or birthday gift. The stories were interesting, and the pictures provided lots of additional information. The poorest readers and the nonreaders got only simple booklets, mostly with black-and-white drawings, sketches, or symbols that bore little or no relationship to the words on the page. In some cases, the picture that should have supported a word did not appear until the following page! In others, the pictures actually gave misinformation about the text. The teacher did not work with the readers individually. An aide, who had no reading education—not even at an in-service—called each child up for "individualized reading." That is to say, the child was required to read to the aide from a book the child had taken home to practice with parents.

The best reader in the class had already heard all of the books in the good reader bin because both his parents read to him every night and had purchased all the books on the teacher's good reader list. The poorest reader in the class could not get through the booklet she had had at home for several weeks already. The aide explained that it was difficult to get cooperation from the child's home. Besides that, she suspected the mother did not even know how to read. Suffice it to say that in that classroom, the poor readers had a difficult time escaping the low reading group.

By the time poor readers reach adulthood, they will have lost track of the inequities they have experienced and may just believe that they are not smart enough to read. If they land in a class where the teacher reads good stories aloud, however, or if they have tutors who read to them from beautiful books like those used for the high-level readers in this first-grade class, they will begin to comprehend how much joy there can be in books. The picture books recommended here will compensate for a lot of missing language arts education.

But not all books in this "First Reader" section will be picture books. They may also be books with large print and easy vocabulary that can be understood by a new reader or someone just learning English. The only way to be sure if a particular book fits a particular learner is to try it.

Thin Books

Thin Books are just that—not many pages. Though the language used in all of the books I have selected is clear and well written, the Thin Book vocabulary can usually be navigated by low and low-intermediate learners.

The affective filter, or the wall of feelings that goes up when the learner is under stress, tends to be lower when the student sees that this is not a big book. It looks easier, and, indeed, it is generally easy to get through. Although some Thin Books do not cover information as well as more challenging texts, other Thin Books deliver content quite effectively.

Challenging Materials

Challenging Materials are just that. They are often written in small typeface and have condensed content. There is a much higher ratio of text to graphics, and sometimes no graphic support at all, though in some cases there are extensive pictures. The Challenging vocabulary makes little, if any, attempt to support comprehension by restating information in a variety of ways and uses the most specific vocabulary possible. This material can be extremely interesting to the person who already has background knowledge on the topic or in the vocabulary being used. So, for the student who just cannot get enough of a topic, or for the teacher with students at many levels, Challenging texts are suggested as one part of the collection.

Book Chapters and Strong Passages

From time to time, I have pulled out a single chapter that relates specifically to the thematic unit. And occasionally there is a passage that drives home an important point. There are also simple references to the topic in a larger work about an entirely different subject. These selections have a variety of purposes:

- They can be read aloud to a single student or a large class to introduce a topic. In some cases, a passage is so poignant or well-written that it is called out as a "read aloud."

- They can be used as discussion starters. We know that talking about reading reinforces comprehension. Also, having something important and stimulating to talk about will foster more language in cooperative groups.

- They may provide just the citation needed by a student who is developing research skills.

- They are good reading in and of themselves and might be used to fill time between assignments or during sustained silent reading.

- A student trying to figure out what to read might munch through these selections as a readings sampler.

Newspaper and Magazine Articles

The newspaper and magazine articles are intended as suggestions for the kinds of articles you will want to look for in available periodicals rather than as specific prescriptions. It is quite likely that wherever you are, your library has unique selections that I would never see. Likewise, I may be reading a newspaper or magazine that seems easily available, but that you have never actually had your hands on. Also, many libraries are limited in the numbers of periodicals they can house. An excellent magazine may have to be discarded to accommodate new material. So, if you can call up the articles I suggest, by all means use them. If not, just use the summary information for ideas about what you can locate.

Unit-Specific, Need-Specific, or Unique Selections

In some units I suggest reading materials that are not an exact fit with the general groups of readings outlined here. These materials will have a title that alerts you to their contents.

Other Events and Supplements

At the end of the thematic unit there may be a variety of suggestions for extending the interest and maximizing the benefit of the time you spend collecting materials. Following are some ideas that could apply to almost any thematic unit, though the kinds of literature or support materials will vary.

Teachers also can use student activity suggestions from the following list:

- Writing to authors for more information or just to say thanks

- Writing to historical locations for more information

- Looking for articles on the topic in newspapers and magazines

- Drawing pictures and writing captions

- Collecting posters and exhibiting them

- Collecting maps and exhibiting them

- Designing topic-related posters (combining art and language)

Note

1. The "silent period" is a phenomenon often observed when a new kid arrives on the block unable to speak the language. The child may not offer a peep for six months, then suddenly start to talk in whole sentences. The question comes up, "Why didn't you say something sooner?" Obviously there had been plenty of time when speaking would have improved the child's circumstances, but he or she simply couldn't. During the silent period, the language learner is getting the input that is essential before output can be produced. The needs of a learner in a silent period—whether child or adult, though it's more difficult for an adult nonnative speaker to maintain a silent period—should be respected. The more stress attached to language performance during the silent period, the more difficult fluent language use will be to achieve.

References

Krashen, Stephen D. *Fundamentals of Language Education.* Torrance, CA: Laredo, 1992.

Rosow, La Vergne. *In Forsaken Hands: How Theory Empowers Literacy Learners.* Portsmouth, NH: Heinemann, 1995.

Smith, Frank. *Insult to Intelligence: The Bureaucratic Invasion of Our Class-rooms.* Portsmouth, NH: Heinemann, 1988.

———. *Reading Without Nonsense,* 2d ed. New York: Teachers College Press, 1985.

The Arts

Unit 1

Books about artists and art forms and books using art as part of the communication process are all part of this unit. Though I am not attempting to cover the spectrum of art in the contemporary world, this unit does provide a progressively more complex set of readings that the creative student or one interested in the arts will enjoy.

Because I have found that art projects greatly facilitate language development activities, this unit is heavily biased toward the visual arts area, particularly illustrated books. That is not an oversight. It is a push to get the language arts learner to connect literacy with personal creativity—a natural connection that good readings may help solidify.

As in all the other units, reading aloud to students will help them sense the rhythm and flow of written language about a topic of high interest. For example, the relationship between sound and symbol—the connection between printed text and the sound it makes in English—will naturally appear during the time the teacher is reading aloud either in class or on an individual student's cassette tape, when the student is free to listen and follow along. And just listening without even seeing the text will teach the student the rhythm and flow of written language. Written language *sounds* different from spoken language. That means reading aloud to ESL and native speakers of English teaches them writing. Reading them classics teaches them classical writing style. Reading them folktales teaches them storytelling. Reading them poetry teaches them the language of poets. When you read to your student one-on-one, you give a very personal gift. When you read aloud to the class, everybody wins.

First Readers and Picture Books

1. *All of You Was Singing.* An Aztec creation song retold by Richard Lewis, with art by Ed Young. New York: Aladdin, 1991. Arts focus: Illustration.

The pictures build from simple to complex as from the water everywhere emerge the earth monster, serpents, and finally the planet as we know it, with every part singing. This could serve as an inspiration for classroom art, collage, or oil pastel creations.

2. *Animalia.* Graeme Base. New York: Harry N. Abrams, 1986. Arts focus: Illustrations.

Animalia is my all-time favorite alphabet book. Each letter is illustrated with one or two pages of exquisite illustrations filled with objects beginning with that letter. This is the ultimate lesson in phonics, alliteration, and imagination. It is definitely suitable for adults. I know, having given it to many friends for birthdays and anniversaries. Some of the pages offer delights for specific thematic units presented here. For example, "Myths, Legends, Fables, and Fairy Tales," Unit 3, will benefit from the "Diabolical Dragons Daintily Devouring Delicious Delicacies." On the same page you will find dice, dropping things, a dictionary, a diamond, a doll, and a decanter. Ingenious Iguanas and Wicked Warrior Wasps will likely do well in a natural science unit but may belong with critters and creatures, too. The Vulture Ventriloquist might also be advised to stay in the creature collection. No matter what unit it ends up in, if you leave this book around, it will be studied for its content and loved for its wonderful illustrations.

3. *The Armadillo from Amarillo.* Lynne Cherry. San Diego, CA: Harcourt Brace Jovanovich, 1994. A Gulliver Breen Book. Printed with environmentally sensitive materials. Arts focus: Research.

Starting with a postcard written in Amarillo, Texas, the armadillo begins a trek that first opens to a breathtaking spread of San Antonio bluebonnets in full bloom. Having lived there and seen them, I can tell you that Cherry has transplanted this sensational gift of nature right inside this book. Postcards run tandem to rhyming text where, for several pages, the armadillo discovers the wonders of endangered species' habitats and the vastly varying landscapes of Texas. In search of a bird's-eye view, the armadillo hitches a ride on the back of an eagle. The two eventually connect with a spacecraft, which gives them and us a perspective on where we are and how we look from outer space. The real and whimsical join to make important statements about our relationship with this planet and the grand scheme of things. On the last page are author's notes.

4. *Brother Eagle, Sister Sky: A Message from Chief Seattle.* Paintings by Susan Jeffers. New York: Dial Books, 1991. 1992 Abby Award winner. Arts focus: Ink drawings colored with wash and dyes.

The words of Suquamish and Duwamish Chief Seattle, delivered in his native tongue during negotiations with settlers for land rights in the nineteenth century, are translated here and interpreted with inspirational colored ink illustrations that fill every page. "How can you buy the sky?" he begins, as he slowly recounts the stories of the universe as told to him by his mother, father, and grandfather. If we are all part of a grand system of life, how can one claim ownership of another? When the book is finished, there is a stunning sense that Seattle continues to hope for a more reasonable treaty than the one his broken people had to accept during the time that he lived. There is so much to think about in this giant picture book that it is difficult to assign categories. It is philosophy, logic, wonder, spirituality, honor, memory, respect, dignity for all, and unity. The best use for this book may just be to let it be—in the learning environment, in the home, on the table, in the chalk trough. Then perhaps the many-layered messages will have time to unfold without shocking the viewer who may not yet be at peace with the Earth.

5. *The Ever-Living Tree: The Life and Times of a Coast Redwood.* Linda Vieira. Illustrations by Christopher Canyon. New York: Walker, 1994. Arts focus: Research by author and illustrator; collaboration.

This is just the history of the world—all over the world—during the life of a California redwood. The book opens to a two-page spread that tracks a tree across time, from prehistory to 2,500 years of age. A human figure is provided for comparison to a 300-foot tree. All that before you get to the first page. The Greeks, North American Indians, the Chinese, Jesus of Nazareth, George Washington, the American Revolution, space flight, and national park campers pass in and out of time as the tree continues to grow. Vieira is a summer docent in a national park where the big trees are a main attraction. This immersion in the lives of the trees gave her the background to write about them in the present and the curiosity to find out what had gone on during the lifetime of one of these giants. She told me that just standing on the spot where a scattering of saplings had sprung from a fallen ancient one caused her to ask these questions. Canyon has never been to California, but, according to Vieira, his research for his illustrations was so thorough, she, as a park docent, could not tell that from his artwork. In this collaboration, artist and illustrator did not meet.

6. *The Great Kapok Tree: A Tale of the Amazon Rain Forest.* Lynne Cherry. San Diego, CA: Harcourt Brace Jovanovich, 1990. A Gulliver Breen Book. Arts focus: Research. Printed on recycled paper, dedicated to the memory of Chico Mendes, "who gave his life in order to preserve a part of the rain forest."

Exquisitely illustrated, this book is an irresistible lead-in to a unit on rain forests, the planet, ecology, or geography. The text is well supported by drawings of animals that live in the Amazon and loaded with adult-level information. Inside the front and back covers are world maps showing rain forest regions around the globe.

7. *How to Hide a Crocodile, and Other Reptiles.* Ruth Heller. New York: Grossett & Dunlap, 1994. Arts focus: Illustration.

Heller's poetic style and beautiful, realistic drawings join with a thorough understanding of her subject to give the reader a lot of scientific information—almost incidentally. Meet a crocodile, matamata, green tree snake, python, iguana, chameleon, and gecko. Now you see them, now you don't.

8. *How to Hide a Polar Bear, and Other Mammals.* Ruth Heller. New York: Grossett & Dunlap, 1994. Arts focus: Illustration.

Words like camouflaged, snowshoe hare, patches, dappled, deer, disappear, zebra, silhouette, leopard, sunshine, lion, mane, sloth, algae, thrive, hostile, detection, and predator come up as natural extensions of Heller's compelling rhymes. The colored drawings give strong meaning to words that can hardly be forgotten, once the book has been read aloud.

9. *How to Hide an Octopus, and Other Sea Creatures.* Ruth Heller. New York: Grossett & Dunlap, 1992. Arts focus: Illustration.

As with Heller's other picture books, the illustrations make this a visual delight. And the rhyming text propels the reader through words like sargassum fish, grotesque, bizarre, creatures, urchins, barnacles, and anemone. Scientific tidbits are served a few words at a time amid powerful pictures that assist comprehension.

10. *If You Were a Writer.* Joan Lowery Nixon. Illustrated by Bruce Degen. New York: Aladdin, 1995. Arts focus: Writing.

"Melia's mother was a writer," and as she tells her little girl what a writer would do to get ideas, to get started, to get a reader's attention, the reader learns about these things, too.

11. *Kites Sail High: A Book About Verbs.* Ruth Heller. New York: Grossett & Dunlap, 1988. Arts focus: Illustration.

With rarely more than a dozen words per page, Heller's exquisite illustrations demonstrate the meanings of individual verbs and then ease the reader into an understanding of tense forms. It is an ideal introduction to verbs for adults and also one they can take back to their children to enjoy and to teach. Any teacher or tutor who has gotten rusty on the parts of speech will appreciate this and the companion books (see entry 26) of Heller's monumental and well-done work.

12. *The Man Who Planted Trees.* Jean Giono. Wood engravings by Michael McCurdy. Afterword by Norma Goodrich. Chelsea, VT: Chelsea Green, 1985. Arts focus: Engravings.

Here is a story of hope with a message that one person can make an incredible difference to our planet. A widower in his forties seeks a solitary life in a barren and deserted expanse of land. By methodically planting trees that are suited to the natural elements, over time he manages to restore life and even a change in atmosphere for miles and miles. It is not his land, nor does he know who owns it. He is just doing what he feels is right and is rewarded by making a difference. First published as a short story in *Vogue* in 1954, under another title, this first-person narrative sounds absolutely believable. The language is simple and the story compelling. The afterword gives an overview of Giono's productive storyteller's life, with summaries of several intriguing tales, and may cause the reader to think, "I could do that." The address and phone number of environmental group Global ReLeaf are provided at the end of the book.

13. *The Middle Passage.* Illustrated by Tom Feelings with an introduction by Dr. John Heinrick Clarke and a map of the most common routes rendered by Anita Karl/James Kemp. New York: Dial Books, 1995. Arts focus: Art appreciation; storytelling; drama; creative expression; research; map illustration.

Feelings describes the evolution of his idea for this text-free book: "[M]uted images flashed across my mind. Pale white sailing ships like huge white birds of prey, plunging forward into mountainous rising white foaming waves of cold water, surrounding and engulfing everything. Our ancestors, hundreds of them locked in the belly of each of these ships, chained together like animals throughout the long voyage from Africa toward unknown destinations, millions dying from the awful conditions in the bowels of the filthy slave galleys." So goes the description of conditions for human beings during the Middle Passage across the Atlantic Ocean—now exposed in a graphic form that is beyond words. Feelings said it took him nearly twenty years to create it. Indeed, it required over 200 years. When I first saw a few of the galleys of this picture book, I was shaken, awestruck, speechless—the close-up faces, the distant views of mystical ships, the cutaways into their holds. Dignity, agony, fear, and wonder rush across the pages. Feelings researched his topic in traditional academic fashion and as an ethnographer, going to live in Ghana. It is impossible for me to imagine an educational theme that could not somehow employ this monumental work. It is clearly among the most important creative achievements in American history.

14. *Northern Lights, the Soccer Trails.* Michael Arvaarluk Kusugak. Art by Vladyana Krykorka. Toronto-New York: Annick Press, 1993. Ruth Schwartz Award. Arts focus: Illustration.

Adoration of mother for child and child for mother, a ride on a canoe on a sled pulled by dogs, sickness and the death of a parent, soccer played with a caribou skin ball, and the northern lights are experiences the reader gets through a sensitive tale of one Inuit girl. The beautiful and detailed colored drawings are supplemented by beaded items that reflect symbolism emerging from the text. On the back cover is a summary of the aurora borealis, known on Baffin Island as "Soccer Trails." It is believed that these lights are deceased loved ones playing soccer in the sky.

15. *The Nutmeg Princess*. Richardo Keens-Douglas. Illustrated by Annouchaka Galouchko. Buffalo, NY: Annick Press, distributed by Firefly, 1992. Arts focus: Illustration.

The bold and brilliant colors of the Caribbean isle of Spice, Grenada, tantalizingly speckle about three-fifths of this beautiful book. The text appears in solid little chunks, almost as if trying to stay out of the way of the pictures. Even so, there is enough text to give an interesting tale. Because the language is not easy, I suggest this first be introduced as a read aloud rather than turned over to the new reader or ESL student. Following is an introduction to the language of Keens-Douglas: "There were sapodillas, mangoes, bananas, star-apples, sugar-apples, guavas, oranges, sousops, and plums, just to name a few. And when these fruits were in season, she would go into the land and pick them and load them onto her donkey-drawn cart."

16. *Rechenka's Eggs*. Patricia Polacco. New York: Philomel Books, 1988. Reading Rainbow selection. Arts focus: Picture-book illustration.

Here is a mystical story of connections—between humans, animals, and a universal goodness. It is also about the cycle of life. Old Babushka's main reason for living is winning first place in the painted egg contest each year. She also cares for hungry and wounded animals.

17. *A River Ran Wild*. Lynne Cherry. San Diego, CA: Harcourt Brace Jovanovich, 1992. A Gulliver Breen Book. Arts focus: Research.

This exquisitely illustrated, authentic history of a river belongs in every classroom. Most of the two-page spreads have a full-page drawing opposite two or three easy-to-read, large-print paragraphs surrounded by small illustrations. Inside the front and back covers are maps that contrast New England in the 1500s with the same in the 1900s.

18. *Smoky Night*. Eve Bunting. Illustrated by David Diaz. San Diego, CA: Harcourt Brace, 1994. 1995 Caldecott winner. Arts focus: Collage.

The horror of a world gone mad, as riots break out in the streets, begins a series of dramatic incidents that cause a young boy, an old woman, and their pets to reach a level of understanding that could not be achieved during a time of peace. Richly textured collages of glass, wrappers, trail mix, and other found objects make this book a visual wonder. This series of highly textured collages, combined with Chagall- and Picasso-type cartoon paintings, is an extraordinary demonstration of how collage can be incorporated into a balanced art curriculum. The illustrations support the text page by page. This is a fine read aloud, especially for adults (I know, because the author read it to an audience I was in), and it is a book all will want to revisit.

19. *Sophie.* Mem Fox. Illustrated by Aminah Brenda Lynn Robinson. New York: Harcourt Brace, 1994. Arts focus: Illustrations with acrylics, dyes, and house paint on rag cloth.

Sophie loves her grandpa, who is always ready to play with her until one day— . The simple,funeral illustration shows Grandpa in his casket. Then there is grief. Mem Fox—consistently powerful.

20. *The Spice Alphabet Book: Herbs, Spices, and Other Natural Flavors.* Jerry Pallotta. Illustrated by Leslie Evans. Watertown, MA: Charlesbridge, 1994. Arts focus: Illustrator's research.

This is one of the most information-intensive Pallotta books yet. Though the format appears to offer the traditional young child's ABCs, this is loaded with adult fare. Almost incidentally paper-clipped to the G page is an index card with Grandma's Molasses Spice Crisps recipe. The Q page gives the historical use of quinine for malaria during the construction of the Panama Canal. There is also an inset map showing the Canal Zone. The last page is solid with tiny print, presenting other bits of information that the artist found but could not fit into the book proper.

21. *The Star-Spangled Banner.* Illustrated by Peter Spier. New York: Dell, 1992. Arts focus: Full-color illustrations; watercolor.

This is a must-have for every American home. Each exquisite two-page illustration demonstrates the meaning of a single line of the national anthem. A brief, interestingly written profile of the nation in the throes of the War of 1812 gives readers a sense of the people, places, and terrible struggle that framed the poem that would become a famous song. A map of the war zone gives a clear idea of where the author, Francis Scott Key, was during this moment of glory and inspiration. A copy of the original hand-written text is opposite the map. And there is a two-page spread showing many historical U.S. flags. The lyrics are set to music on one page, for the pianist in our midst. This large paperback looks like a children's book and is, indeed, a Reading Rainbow selection, chosen for the PBS children's book reading program, but it has value to every adult interested in U.S. history. I have found it useful for both ESL students and adult new readers.

22. *Tar Beach.* Faith Ringgold. New York: Crown, 1991. 1992 Caldecott Honor Book and 1992 winner of the Coretta Scott King Award for Nonviolent Social Change. Arts focus: Picture-book illustration; artist biography.

A quilt and drawings illustrate this dream come true. Part of the dream is that the little girl's dad will not have to worry about the racism that excludes him from the union and access to work. Part of the dream is that she will wear the bridge with the lights like a diamond necklace. On the last page, Ringgold's autobiography includes the progression from an actual quilt that had the story written around the edges to the design for this book.

23. *Three Gold Pieces: A Greek Folk Tale.* Retold and illustrated by Aliki. New York: HarperCollins, 1994. Arts focus: Illustration.

Consistent with Aliki's other works, the illustrations are a surprising delight in themselves. Here the story may seem demeaning—a poor man enters a work contract of ten years' duration without ever asking the terms of his employment.

Then he ends up paying his employer all of his earning for three bits of advice. As the story continues, however, the advice turns out to be of considerable value to the main character. The implications of this old tale can lead to current life comparisons and questioning of messages sent through text.

24. *Thunder Cake*. Patricia Polacco. New York: Philomel Books, 1990. Arts focus: Picture-book illustration.

Fear and the courage to keep going are the themes for a book with beautiful, detailed colored drawings. Grandma helps the young child address her fear of thunder. Though Polacco draws from her family's Russian folk history, this is a universal story.

25. *Tough Boris*. Mem Fox. Illustrated by Kathryn Brown. San Diego, CA: Harcourt Brace, 1994. Arts focus: Picture-book illustration.

Almost traditional watercolor illustrations give meaning to the single line of prose on each two-page spread. There is a thirty-one-word vocabulary for the entire book—though this is not to say they lack meaning, not to say they are simple words. The story deals with stereotyping, sadness, grief, and death.

26. *Up, Up and Away: A Book About Adverbs*. Ruth Heller. New York: Grossett & Dunlap, 1991. Arts focus: Illustration.

Not only does this book explain what an adverb is, it also addresses syntax: "Before an ADVERB answers 'When?' it always answers 'Where?' " Consistent with Heller's rhyming information delivery system, this little book delivers all kinds of information, gently, rhythmically, and with incredible illustrations. One two-page spread has a map of Africa, Asia, and the Indian Ocean. Why? So you can find the answer to "WHERE in the world is Timbuktu?" My students praise every book they see from this series, which is still in progress.

Note: Each of Heller's scientific books is supported by a content expert who helps the artist make her picture books palatable science.

27. *Wilfrid Gordon McDonald Partridge*. Mem Fox. Illustrated by Julie Vivas. Brooklyn, NY: Kane/Miller, 1985. Arts focus: Picture-book illustration.

This is an extraordinary example of how text and pictures give meaning together. The lad with the long title name has an active, fun-filled life visiting his next-door neighbors, residents of an old people's home. We are not told he is poor; we just see the markings within the illustrations, just as we see the emotions of the residents of the home. Even so, the tale is about memory loss and the importance of having something to think or care about. It is about the contrast between youth and age. It is about valuing human beings. For any age reader, of any culture, this is a powerful book.

Thin Books

28. *Always to Remember: The Story of the Vietnam Veterans Memorial*. Brent Ashabranner. Photographs by Jennifer Ashabranner. New York: Scholastic, 1988. Arts focus: Conceptualization; sculpture; environmental art; architecture.

This clear accounting of the historical and emotional roots of the United States' involvement in the Vietnam War gives many details about people affected by it. Wounded in action and witness to the deaths or wounding of over half his company, veteran Jan C. Scruggs came home to a legacy of shame for having gone to war. One night, after seeing the movie *The Deer Hunter*, he was driven to make a memorial of substance to the effort and suffering that had transpired. It would have the names of all those men and women lost in the Vietnam War. This dream became an obsession that led to a nationwide competition, with 1,421 designs submitted and judged without names or identification of any kind. The Wall, entry number 1,026, by 21-year-old Yale student Maya Ying Lin, was selected. The daughter of Chinese immigrants was to make a profound contribution to the art and history of America. The commission of the work, the actual construction of this massive project, the work of the young artist to protect the aesthetic integrity of her design in the face of political interests, and the fruition of this monument make testimony to attitudes about art in contemporary America. There is a read-aloud section under "Book Chapters and Strong Passages" in this unit.

29. *Beethoven Lives Upstairs*. Barbara Nichol. Illustrated by Scott Cameron. New York: Orchard Books, 1993. Arts focus: Music; illustration.

This is almost a picture book. In a compelling exchange of letters, a young boy and his uncle discuss the public reputation and personal habits of the great musician who has moved into the home of a young widow and her three children. The balance of letters between adult and child, with an occasional note from the boy's mother, makes this an appropriate book for new readers of any age. The fictionalized story is based on historical facts that give insight not only into the genius of Beethoven, but also into the stresses of a hearing-impaired, creative soul. The story might make good reading on its own; however, this book offers more—emotionally charged oil paintings that illustrate the circumstances in young Christopher's house. This is a good easy reader for units in this book on the "Arts," "Letters, and Journals," and "Tolerance."

30. *Bull Run*. Paul Fleischman. Woodcuts by David Frampton. New York: Scholastic, 1993. Arts focus: Illustration.

Simple, telling maps make up the first two pages, one depicting the existing states and their positions in the Session, the other a close-up of the Eastern Theater of the Civil War, where the Battle of Bull Run took place. At the end, a two-page spread shows two maps of the battle scene, morning on the left, afternoon on the right. One by one, in isolated vignettes, as though reporting to an unseen interviewer, fictional characters tell their stories of hearing about war, getting ready for the battle, heading off, and how the battle occurred—the tragic discovery that war is not a game. The momentum of this series of reports builds so subtly that the reader does not realize what has happened until it is done. Each speaker has a personal icon woodcut. This creative illustration approach to a novel book format gives a fresh feel to the old topic of war.

31. *Elvis Presley: The King*. Katherine E. Krohn. Minneapolis, MN: Lerner, 1994. Arts focus: Music.

This is a grass roots musician's story told in plain language, particularly valuable for the new reader of modest roots or for a memory of the 1950s, when Elvis began his rise to stardom. You will not find an index, and the table of contents is not very informative, but the little book on Elvis the Pelvis, born in Tupelo,

Mississippi, in 1935, tells the great American success story in a unique way. Humble beginnings, disappointments, a teenage romance, hopes of big-time recordings, broken promises and a broken marriage, drug addiction, and death at his prime, all combine to make this a legend that has not ended. "On the day Elvis Presley died, every florist in Memphis ran out of flowers," Krohn says.

32. *A Fire in My Hands: A Book of Poems.* Gary Soto. New York: Scholastic, 1990. Arts focus: Poetry; poets.

Before each poem in this book, Soto tells the circumstances of its coming to life. The simple language and universal messages will make connections for both new and seasoned readers.

33. *The Friendship.* Mildred D. Taylor. Pictures by Max Ginsburg. New York: Dial Books for Young Readers, 1987. Arts focus: Pencil illustration.

In fifty-three pages, the telling of one incident on a summer afternoon in 1933 gives the reader an up-close view of how racism in Mississippi influenced the behavior of people who would otherwise be friends. The story is told from the perspective of a young girl. The matter of how one person addressed another led to an incident that made the social inequities obvious. This language issue is joined by the dialects of the characters. Clear, readable text is only part of this powerful little book. Full-page pencil illustrations give yet another dimension to the story and support the descriptions with realism and detail. Here is both a social study and an art collection.

34. *I Was a Teenage Professional Wrestler.* Ted Lewin. New York: Scholastic, 1993. Arts focus: Illustrator, special interest.

A glossary of wrestling lingo and wrestling holds fills the last three pages of the book. Many may want to start there. Though the book has an ample supply of photographs of known, unknown, and colorful wrestlers from the 1950s and 1960s, there are also drawings and paintings by the author, who used wrestling to pay the rent while he attended the Pratt Institute. This split life allowed him a unique place among artists and wrestlers. In this autobiography, Lewin, now a professional illustrator, begins recounting the fun times he and his brothers had as children when their father took them to the fights. It was a father-son occasion that set the course for Ted. He also recounts stories about wrestlers who lived in his house and how they spent their time outside the ring—none, that he could recall, ever read. This is an interesting read, whether you are a sports fan, art enthusiast, or neither.

35. *Life Doesn't Frighten Me.* Poem by Maya Angelou. Paintings by Jean-Michel Basquiat. New York: Stewart, Tabori & Chang, poem copyright 1978, illustrations copyright 1993. Arts focus: Paintings; poetry.

Seeming to be a children's picture book, this collection of illustrations and ideas suddenly shocks the senses with the kinds of things that really frighten us all. Oil pastels, gouache, acrylics, and collage give the illusion of children's art; and the rugged, haphazard-looking type font looks like children's writing, but they combine to convey a level of sophistication that calls for rereading, rereading,

rereading. At the end are two-page biographies of the author and the illustrator. They are interesting reading in themselves and promise insights into the lives of two artists who made a mark beyond the expected. Angelou's call to everyone to "read everything possible, be it African-American, European, Latin, or other literature—but, especially Shakespeare," makes this even more appropriate for adult new readers. The drug death at an early age of the artist, whose works send the reader on an emotional roller-coaster ride, makes this an even more important book for people concerned about the influence of illegal drugs on our lives. Each of us lost when this young man stopped making art. The poem qualifies as either a read aloud or a First Reader, but it requires discussion.

36. *Lives of the Musicians: Good Times, Bad Times (and What the Neighbors Thought).* Kathleen Krull. Illustrated by Kathryn Hewitt. San Diego, CA: Harcourt Brace, 1993. Arts focus: Musicians and music; cartoons and historical research.

Antonio Vivaldi, Johann Sebastian Bach, William Gilbert and Arthur Sullivan, Erik Satie, Scott Joplin, Wolfgang Amadeus Mozart, Johannes Brahms, Clara Schumann, Ludwig van Beethoven, Charles Ives, Frederic Chopin, Igor Stravinsky, Stephen Foster, Peter Ilich Tchaikovsky, Giuseppe Verdi, Woody Guthrie, George Gershwin, Nadia Boulanger, and Sergei Prokofiev are introduced via full-page, full-color, documentary-style cartoons that tell a great deal about the musician, even before the name is known. Birth and death information and a three-line summary of the artist's life let the reader gather more hard data than several minutes searching through an encyclopedia might net. Two and a half pages of spirited text gives the inside information about the person and uses quotes. "Musical Notes," with details that must not have fit into the story, end each presentation. For those who want more information, the back of the book includes "Musical Terms," "Index of Composers" (some lives crossed paths), and "For Further Reading . . . And Listening." Any of these featured stories would make good read alouds (see entry 58 in "Book Chapters and Strong Passages").

37. *Lives of the Writers: Comedies, Tragedies (and What the Neighbors Thought).* Kathleen Krull. Illustrated by Kathryn Hewitt. San Diego, CA: Harcourt Brace, 1994. Arts focus: Authors and literature; cartoons and historical research.

Murasaki Shikibu, Miguel de Cervantes, William Shakespeare, Jane Austen, Hans Christian Andersen, Edgar Allan Poe, Charles Dickens, Charlotte Bronte, Emily Bronte, Emily Dickinson, Louisa May Alcott, Mark Twain, Frances Hodgson Burnett, Robert Louis Stevenson, Jack London, Carl Sandburg, E. B. White, Zora Neale Hurston, Langston Hughes, and Isaac Bashevis Singer are summarized in a Hewitt cartoon and then demographically described by Krull. After that a fun-filled or tragedy-torn tale of survival as a creative being is told in two and a half pages or so. This is excellent SSR fare for the new reader on the Thin Books level. "Bookmarks" gives further details that Krull thinks you might enjoy. Readers might read one each day for SSR and learn everything they ever wanted to know about these folks. But Krull takes no chances. After a page of literary terms and an index of writers, the last page offers "For Further Reading . . . And Writing." Any of these essays could serve under the "Book Chapters and Strong Passages" chapter for read alouds (see entry 59).

38. *Mermaid Tales from Around the World.* Retold by Mary Pope Osborne. Illustrated by Troy Howell. New York: Scholastic, 1993. Arts focus: Illustrations.

A full-page, full-color illustration signals the mood and opening of each new tale; a decorative icon signals each story's close, making this handsome book interesting to look at, even before the reading begins. Osborne's retellings are brief and offer detail-free summaries of passages that might otherwise be considered inappropriate for young readers. This issue of style could lead to dialogue with adult writers about how audience influences content. The author uses simple vocabulary most of the time, and most of her sentences tend to be short but not choppy. The last page has a bibliography that could lead readers on a research project to find other variations on the theme or other versions of the same tales. Inspiration for the retellings comes from France, Canada, the Aegean Sea, Ireland, Russia, Nigeria, Japan, England, China, India, Persia, Arabia, Germany, and Denmark. There are readings for author, art, and art writing under "Book Chapters and Strong Passages" (see entry 60).

39. *Mojave.* Diane Siebert. Paintings by Wendell Minor. New York: Thomas Y. Crowell, 1988. Arts focus: Poetry; illustrations.

Written in the first person, that person being the Mojave Desert, this poem gives an "inside" perspective of the desert's interactions with rivers, windstorms, time, lakes, tumbleweeds, lizards, birds, rats, hedgehogs, cactuses, mustangs, miners, ghost towns, burros, seasons, butterflies, coyotes, and bighorn sheep. There is a tremendous amount of vocabulary in this seemingly brief poem, but the rhyming couplets and complete sentences facilitate comprehension and assist prediction. This is, as with most rhymes, an easy way to present the concepts of phonics—in process. Scientific information is also dispensed casually, for example,

> Here, silvery mirages dance
> Among the prickly cactus plants
> Whose spines and bristles help them thrive
> Where weaker plants could not survive.

Can you see how the pronunciations of "dance" and "plants" compel the reader into a phonetic awareness that a phonic rule would be hard-pressed to convey? At the same time, the reader learns that the "spines and bristles" serve a scientific purpose. Large-print, easy-to-follow text on the left is supported by clear, realistic, full-page illustrations on the right. This is a First Reader poem and a great read aloud.

Challenging

40. *California Missions: The Earliest Series of Views Made in 1856: The Journal & Drawings of Henry Miller: Account of a Tour of the California Missions and Towns 1856.* Santa Barbara, CA: Bellerophon Books, 1987. Arts focus: Journal illustrations.

Here is a first-person history, written in creative story form and illustrated by the same hand. Good for high intermediate and advanced students.

41. *Children of the Dust Bowl: The True Story of the School at Weedpatch Camp.* Jerry Stanley. Illustrated with historical photographs. New York: Crown, 1992. Arts focus: Documentary photography.

This book briefly describes how agricultural jobs in the Dust Bowl states declined by 400,000 between 1930 and 1940, when "nearly 50 percent of Oklahoma's farms changed hands in bankruptcy court sales" and a mass of displaced and starving people headed for California. The historical documentary photographs include the famous Dorothea Lang portrait of a newly widowed migrant mother and many other black-and-white images that give a stark portrait of homeless people in the wake of the Great Depression. This small book is a case study in documentary photography.

42. *Creepy Classics: Hair-Raising Horror from the Masters of the Macabre.* Edited by Mary Hill. Illustrated by Dominick R. Domingo. New York: Random House, 1994. Arts focus: Illustrations on paper.

The quality art in this book makes it a double treat. Dramatic charcoal illustrations maximize the power of black and white, casting dark shadows, reflecting underlighting, and shocking the eyes with sudden contrast.

43. *Ellis Island.* Wilton S. Tifft. Foreword by Lee Iacocca. Chicago: Contemporary Books, 1990. Arts focus: Documentary photography.

This is an oversized picture book with a rich collection of documentary photographs illustrating every chapter. Copies of passports, baggage tags, and architectural drawings also give a sense of reality to a distant time in U.S. history. Close-up shots of individuals, herds of people on the deck of a ship in harbor, and remarkable documentation of ethnic dress make this well worth the time of any student of documentary photography.

44. *The Golden Mean, in Which the Extraordinary Correspondence of Griffin & Sabine Concludes.* Nick Bantock. San Francisco: Chronicle Books, 1993. Arts focus: Collage; ink drawing; 3-D; tempera.

The last of a trilogy, this book also has exquisitely decorated postcards, envelopes, and writing paper. And it provides a sense of informal writing as the typed parts have hand-corrected typos here and there. The mystery of this unusual pair of correspondents compels the reader through vocabulary that would never show up in an elementary workbook but would certainly be useful to the adult new reader or writer. Deputation, do-gooders, busybodies, orchestrated, cronies, and precise are all found in the short first paragraph of the letter Griffin wrote to Sabine on September 18. Par Avion, Air Mail, Special Delivery, Japan Air Lines, Carte Postale, Via Aerea, Per Luchtpost, and Amnesty are offered as part of the mail-opening process. Consider the impact of discovering words from your native land in a beautiful book. This trio, including *Griffin & Sabine* (entry 45) and *Sabine's Notebook* (entry 50), belongs in any adult unit on geography, art, illustration, letter writing, or sociology.

45. *Griffin & Sabine: An Extraordinary Correspondence.* Nick Bantock. San Francisco: Chronicle Books, 1991. Arts focus: Collage; ink drawing; 3-D; tempera.

As an art piece alone, this book is a wonder to behold. The haunting correspondence between two artists is made more disturbing by the fact that one of them does not know who the other is. Letters and postcards from around the world are laid bare for the reader who dares to enter this surreal world. I have had students with no expressed interest in correspondence suddenly start writing letters after experiencing this book. See also *Sabine's Notebook* (entry 50) and *The Golden Mean* (entry 44).

46. *Hey! Listen to This: Stories to Read Aloud*. Edited by Jim Trelease. New York: Penguin Books, 1992. Arts focus: Writers; writing.

Known for his *Read-Aloud Handbook*, here Trelease gives two or three pages of background on an author, then an excerpt from a book or an entire piece. This work is Challenging because of the absence of pictures, white space, or other devices for aiding comprehension. However, the background information on the writers and literary works will provide a super launching pad for students who are just discovering the research process. As in the book you are holding now, in *Hey! Listen to This* there is enough information that students can write a short research paper about literary works or authors before making that trek into the library stacks. Because this is written for the adult audience, the approach may not be great reading below the fifth-grade level. Yet the parent or teacher can use the information to build background knowledge before reading to a child or student of any age. Every few pages you will encounter a great read-aloud passage for some unit.

47. *I Dream a World: Portraits of Black Women Who Changed America*. Brian Lanker. Foreword by Maya Angelou. New York: Stewart, Tabori & Chang, 1989. Arts focus: Documentary and portrait photography; artists.

This oversized book has 167 pages of American history. On one side of each two-page spread is a full-page black-and-white museum-quality photographic portrait of a famous African-American woman; on the other is a biographical sketch and interview, detailing her place in history. The birth date appears just below the name, and a narrow column gives an overview of her contributions to society. There are several politicians, literary figures, and artists whose stories belong in a variety of units in this bibliography. As a text for portrait photography, this is full of notions of how to capture the subject through the lens. Some of the portraits are close-up shots, showing every pore and wrinkle; others back up to show a room or musical instrument; still others let an entire city form the backdrop for the woman photographed. Reading these brief, well-written passages with students then discussing the photographic treatment of the subject can provide meaning-filled analysis and new insights.

48. *Letters from the Sand: The Letters of Desert Storm and Other Wars*. U.S. Postal Service. Washington, DC: GPO, 1991. Arts focus: Commemorative stamps; photography; children's art.

Some reproduced in clear type, some in the original handwriting, these letters and postcards document the history of the United States during wartime. Diary entries, children's art, stamps, and historical photographs support the text, which takes the reader on the same emotional roller-coaster rides that the writers themselves experienced. Seldom is the Spanish-American War (1898–1899) covered in such detail. "The letters from Vietnam were just too sad to read," an adult new reader told me. So much pictorial support is in this high-interest book that it does not really qualify for the Challenging category, yet the vocabulary and writing variety offer a lot of quality input not found elsewhere. There are actual commemorative stamps in the collector editions of this book.

49. *The Life of Sir Arthur Conan Doyle.* John Dickson Carr. New York: Carroll & Graf, 1976. Arts focus: Writing.

This story is as entertaining as the life of Sherlock Holmes reported by Dr. Watson. A devout spiritualist, Sir Arthur Conan Doyle reflected that belief system in his life, as well as the notion that one might communicate with the dead.

50. *Sabine's Notebook, in Which the Extraordinary Correspondence of Griffin & Sabine Continues.* Nick Bantock. San Francisco: Chronicle Books, 1992. Arts focus: Collage; ink drawing; 3-D; tempera.

Exotic envelope, stationery, and stamp designs, supplemented by random sketches along the margins, make this book as visually enticing as the first of the series. The envelopes offer vocabulary words like confidential, personal, express, proof, special, and checked. See also *Griffin & Sabine* (entry 45) and *The Golden Mean* (entry 44).

51. *The Ultimate Dinosaur, Past-Present-Future.* Edited by Byron Preiss and Robert Silverberg. New York: Bantam Books, 1992. Arts focus: Illustrations—realism, surrealism, color.

This book offers a mix of science and fiction through scientific essays and enthralling science-fiction short stories. The clear type is set in a magazine format that supports the reader. Though the text might not look Challenging at first blush, the scientific names of plants, animals, and periods serve to slow the reader down, but never to a full stop. It is illustrated with a mix of pen and ink drawings and full-color paintings that document the history of the dinosaur through time—past, present, and future. It is informative, entertaining, and a wonderful picture-book adventure. An appendix supports the scientific reader who wants to get a clear timeline of land and animal distributions during the days of the dinosaurs.

52. *Witness to an Era: The Life and Photographs of Alexander Gardner: The Civil War, Lincoln, and the West.* D. Mark Katz. New York: Viking, 1991. Arts focus: Documentary photography.

This is an oversized picture book and an extraordinary portrait of an artist's life. Gardner documented the Civil War, made numerous photographs of President Abraham Lincoln as well as the conspirators to Lincoln's assassination. Pictures of all of these are in the book. There are also reproductions of letters and other handwritten documents, complete with scratch-outs and editing, of the Civil War era. The running commentary and captions bring to life this part of American history more effectively than does any other picture book I have seen. In addition, the issues of battlefield agony, racism, slavery, intrigue, crime, and punishment are brought to the fore. This is an excellent book just for page-turning dialogue. It is also well written.

53. *Wouldn't Take Nothing for My Journey Now.* Maya Angelou. New York: Random House, 1993, pages 445–49. Art focus: Essays: In need of illustrators.

This is a collection of philosophical essays—most only a page and a half long, all thought-provoking. It makes a good read aloud or SSR collection. The complexity of thought, not the sentence structure or vocabulary, makes this text Challenging. If each essay was illustrated—somehow, I do not know how—it could be a picture book.

Book Chapters and Strong Passages

54. "Educating a Special Child." In *Hey! Listen to This: Stories to Read Aloud*. Edited by Jim Trelease. New York: Penguin Books, 1992, pages 44–45. Arts focus: Research for writing; the creative process.

In this passage we learn of the impact that one person can have on societal attitudes across time. It also supports the use of journals. During a visit to America in 1842, when he visited Laura, a blind, deaf, and mute girl, Charles Dickens was surprised to learn that her Boston doctor had taught her to read and write. At the time, such children were societal discards—locked away, hidden, shamefully kept from human interaction. Dickens recorded the discovery of Laura's remarkable learning ability in his journal, which was eventually published. Forty years later, the mother of Helen Keller read about the incident and was inspired to find a teacher for her disabled daughter. The search for information about Laura, the source of this inspiration, led Edith Fisher Hunter to write *Child of the Silent Night*; an excerpt, "A Room Without Windows or Doors," follows this historical account in the Trelease book.

55. "The Fisherman and His Wife." Brothers Grimm. In *Jamestown Heritage Reader*. Book C. Providence, RI: Jamestown, 1991, pages 12–88.

This retelling of the classic tale is illustrated with detailed ink drawings that show the conditions of poverty and wealth through which the simple couple progress. This story makes excellent readers theatre fare, just by letting readers take the parts of the Fish, the Fisherman, and the Wife. The rest of the story can be read by the narrator.

56. *Jamestown Heritage Readers*. Books A–F. Edited by Lee Mountain, Sharon Crawley, and Edward Fry. Providence, RI: Jamestown, 1991.

This is a beautiful anthology of classic and popular fiction and nonfiction. Stories have the illustrations as they appeared with the reproduced version of the story, many quite remarkable. The books are identified by difficulty level, A being easiest, F most difficult. But these letters are really only guidelines. It is interesting to note that some selections in book D are easier for adult new readers than some in book C, for example. Books B, C, and D have been most popular among my adult learners. By the time they get to book F, I suggest they belong in the regular library collection. Though most of the selections are in their authentic state, some vocabulary has been manipulated. I recommend teachers look at the end of the acknowledgments to see which stories are still in the original state and just use those. Though some of the changes may be minimal, the task of figuring out which changes modify the writer's style is probably too time-consuming. The teachers' guides for this series are quite rich, giving background information on authors, illustrators, and, occasionally, historical bits. Every page of text, in the readers themselves and the teachers' guides, is graced by a wide decorative border, an added delight.

57. "Little Blue Engine." In *Where the Sidewalk Ends*. Poems and drawings of Shel Silverstein. New York: HarperCollins, 1974, page 158. Arts focus: Poetry response.

This is a spoof of the famous Watty Piper story of the "Little Engine That Could." This poem is a fantastic, dramatic read aloud. I have used this incredible collection of poems in many different ways with adults and children. It was popular as a community college ESL text and has provided a wealth of material for readers theatre events, too.

58. *Lives of the Musicians: Good Times, Bad Times (and What the Neighbors Thought)*. Kathleen Krull. Illustrated by Kathryn Hewitt. San Diego, CA: Harcourt Brace, 1993.

Any of the musicians' stories make good read alouds. For more information, see "Musical Terms," "Index of Composers" (some lives crossed paths), and "For Further Reading . . . And Listening," in the back of the book. All of these make *Lives* a wealth of musical information that may whet the appetite for more. See entry 36 in "Thin Books" for more details.

59. *Lives of the Writers: Comedies, Tragedies (and What the Neighbors Thought)*. Kathleen Krull. Illustrated by Kathryn Hewitt. San Diego, CA: Harcourt Brace, 1994.

Any of the writers' lives make good read alouds. Poetry could be introduced by the story of Edgar Allan Poe, pages 32–37. See entry 37 in "Thin Books" for more details.

60. *Mermaid Tales from Around the World*. Retold by Mary Pope Osborne. Illustrated by Troy Howell. New York: Scholastic, 1993.

- Passage for Art: *Artist's Note*, pages 81–83. Here the artist discusses his intellectual progression from one style to another for the book. Howell tells how other artistic influences caused him to change his ideas about media and subject treatment.

- Passage for Art and Writing: *Author's Note*, pages 78–80. Here Osborne gives background details on the selections and makes it clear that hers are but part of a long line of retellings. More detail is given in entry 38 "Thin Books" above.

61. "A Note from the Author." In *The Dark Way: Stories from the Spirit World*. Told by Virginia Hamilton. Illustrated by Lambert Davis. San Diego, CA: Harcourt Brace Jovanovich, 1990. Arts focus: Writing.

This one is a read aloud. This storybook qualifies as Challenging reading. In the arts unit, the writer's message is of special interest. Virginia Hamilton shares her personal and professional connections with the selections of this book in her introduction. Any writer, writing student, or would-be writer will gain inspiration from this beautiful account of why this book was written.

62. "Oranges." Gary Soto. In *A Fire in My Hands: A Book of Poems*. New York: Scholastic, 1990, pages 23–24. Arts focus: Poet; poetry; background for the work.

Easy, honest telling lets the reader relate to the twelve-year-old boy who comes up short on money for the ten-cent candy selected by his "date." The resolution to this conflict in just a handful of words leaves everybody celebrating.

63. "The Pied Piper of Hamelin." A European folktale retold by Joseph Jacobs. In *Jamestown Heritage Reader.* Book C. Providence, RI: Jamestown, 1991, pages 67–75. Arts Focus: Illustration; writing; poetry; inspiration. Easy reading.

An inexplicable swath of misfortune raced through all of Europe, leaving death and destroyed lives behind. Rats later proved to be the main culprit. The Pied Piper tale recounts an actual event in which the children of one small town were wiped out. I like linking this story, which has been retold in many different styles, with the companion poems "The Pied Piper of Hamelin" by Robert Browning (see entry 64) and the Shel Silverstein poem "The One Who Stayed," in *Where the Sidewalk Ends.* In the two companion poems, we can see how history and the work of other artists affect our own creative efforts.

64. "The Pied Piper of Hamelin: A Child's Story." Written for and inscribed to W. M. the Younger, by Robert Browning. In *The Complete Works of Robert Browning, with Variant Readings & Annotations,* vol. III. General editor Roma A. King, Jr. Athens: Ohio University Press, 1971. Arts focus: Poetry research; scholarly study of poetry. See pages 249–59 and the editors' notes, pages 384–86.

This long poem is written in rhyme and is fun to read aloud. I consider it Challenging because it is quite long and uses many archaic words and phrases that could trip the ESL student or new reader. But the footnotes at the bottom of each page make finding definitions easy, and it is possible to just skip along reading without looking up anything and get a nice, bouncy, though depressing story. The editors' notes offer a lot of scholarly information in plain English. For example, there is debate over what Browning's source for this old tale was. It gives July 22, 1376, as the date of the actual incident. And the notes explain that this poem was written for a sick child who loved to draw, so Browning asked the sequestered youngster to illustrate it for him.

65. "Poems." In *Fables for Our Time and Famous Poems Illustrated.* James Thurber. New York: Harper & Row, 1983, pages 75–128. Arts focus: Satirical illustration; artist and illustrator collaboration (posthumous).

At the end of his book of essays, Thurber has a series of famous poems set to his own, satirical illustrations, causing the reader to view the familiar texts with fresh eyes. Thurber's attention to Henry Wadsworth Longfellow; Charles Kingsley; Sir Walter Scott; Alfred, Lord Tennyson; A. E. Housman; Rose Hartwick Thorpe; John Greenleaf Whittier; Leigh Hunt; and Thomas Dunn English provides an avenue of expression for the artist that might otherwise be overlooked—illustrating the familiar and giving it new life.

66. "Questions and Answers About Poetry." Gary Soto. In *A Fire in My Hands: A Book of Poems.* New York: Scholastic, 1990, pages 60–63.

Before each poem in this book, Soto tells the circumstances of its coming to life. At the end of the book are several insightful questions and answers about this autobiographical work.

67. "Robin Hood at the Archers' Contest, a Play." In *Jamestown Heritage Reader*. Book D. Providence, RI: Jamestown, 1991, pages 132–45. Arts focus: Theatre; oral reading.

Though they could be adapted for children, the six speaking parts are for adults in this romantic adventure play adapted from the English legend. After hearing it read by his tutor, a man in the Beaumont, California, literacy program insisted his wife attend his next lesson to read the part of Maid Marian. Subsequently, the new reader read the piece at a readers theatre event. Can you see how being read to and practicing in a fun-filled way leads to confidence about the reading process? There is no need for costuming at a readers theatre, but the clear line drawings do give ideas for simple things a reader might do to set the mood. This book has big, easy-to-read print.

68. "Staying Alive." David Wagoner. In *Survival!* Lexington, MA: D. C. Heath, 1995, pages 22–27. Arts focus: Fine art as illustration; poet's background.

Illustrated by the surrealistic black-and-white images of M. C. Escher, Wagoner's poem plods along, almost presuming that you are in the woods and in need of instructions on how to stay alive. The poetic form gives just a few words per line, but the vocabulary includes trusting, calming, deciding, hiding, watching, uncanny, and unidentifiable. It is a great read aloud and also lends itself to readers theatre treatment. On page 27, a one-paragraph biography of the author makes it clear that he knows his subject.

69. *The Story of Mexico: La Historia de Mexico en Español y en Ingles*. Nancy Conkle, Eric Tomb, Donna Neary, Elena Lopez, and Diane de Avalle-Arce. Santa Barbara, CA: Bellerophon, 1991. Arts focus: Muralists; line drawings; coloring book.

In coloring book format, this bilingual book—a paragraph in Spanish with the same in English—opens to the Aztec calendar. Then a series of short, single-read passages bounces through the history of Mexico and the names behind it, names like Quetzalcoatl, Moctezuma II, Hernan Cortes, Antonio de Mendoza, Juana Ines del Cruz, Don Agustin de Iturbide, General Vincente Guerrero, Emperor Maximilian, his wife Carlotta, and Presidents Juarez and Cardenas. Also included are modern artists who have given Mexico an international reputation: Diego Rivera, Jose Orozco, David Siqueiros, and Frida Kahlo. Though the passages are brief and the pictures supportive, the very new reader will have difficulty. The ESL student who reads even minimally in Spanish will love this book. I have used it in workplace, literacy, and ESL classes. During SSR, just as does a picture book, it allows Latinos a chance to connect with literature and history in empowering ways.

70. "A Story Rescued from the Ashes." In *Hey! Listen to This: Stories to Read Aloud*. Edited by Jim Trelease. New York: Penguin Books, 1992, pages 227–29. Arts focus: Story background; creative person's need for support.

An eighth-grade dropout, child of poverty, further impoverished by the Great Depression, Wilson Rawls was so fearful of ridicule that he burned all of his writings before his wedding so his new wife would not see them. At her insistence, he rewrote *Where the Red Fern Grows*, now viewed as a great American dog story.

71. "The Tortoise and the Hare." In *Fables for Our Time and Famous Poems Illustrated*. Written and illustrated by James Thurber. New York: Harper & Row, 1983, pages 60–61. Arts focus: Writer response to writer.

This is a perfect follow-up to the traditional Aesop fable. It demonstrates how one writer is inspired by another. Thurber simply tells the story as it would logically occur, should such a race take place. As a readers theatre event, the two fables played out, traditional first and Thurber second, make excellent fare for children and adults.

72. "The Vision of Maya Ying Lin." In *Always to Remember: The Story of the Vietnam Veterans Memorial*. Brent Ashabranner. Photographs by Jennifer Ashabranner. New York: Scholastic, 1988, pages 35–43.

Though the entire book is worthwhile reading, this chapter is profound read-aloud material and can foster dialogue on many topics. It is not surprising to learn that the artist was driven by a well-developed personal philosophy. She is quoted as saying, "A memorial shouldn't tell you what to think, but should make you think."

73. *The World Almanac and Book of Facts 1995*. Edited by Robert Famighetti. Mahwah, NJ: Funk & Wagnalls, 1995. Statistics of many sorts offered in narrative and column format.

Do you want to know who is spending money on the arts and how much? "Arts and the Media" starts on page 300 and continues for thirteen information-intensive pages. This book might be viewed as an encyclopedia you can hold in your hand.

Newspaper and Magazine Articles

The Los Angeles Times and *The New York Times* offer vast collections of movie, theatre, dance, art exhibition, and event reviews. Draw on these inexpensive professional opinions for contemporary reading materials. Both arts-specific and general interest magazines can give a wide assortment of readings on high-interest topics. The following are just samplings and may serve as idea prompts, if they are not readily available to you.

74. "The Andalusian Dog." L. S. Klepp. *Entertainment Weekly*, March 8, 1991, pages 50–51.

This is a book review of volume 1 (1881–1906) of John Richardson's projected four-volume *A Life of Picasso* (New York: Random House, 1995). "Richardson sensibly sees the sign of emerging genius not in the precocious, workmanlike early sketches and paintings but in the fledgling artist's stunning capacity for concentration and hard work—from the beginning, Picasso was possessed." Klepp observes that the "brilliantly illustrated book" is also in "a geographical and cultural landscape."

75. "Collectors: Tables with Dragonfly Legs." Christie Brown, *Forbes*, January 16, 1995, pages 101–4.

Though much of the article reads like a decorator's promotion, there is intriguing content here for the adult who is interested in antiques or investments.

"Collectors will not find many bargains. Over the last decade, prices have risen about 30 percent. A famous dragonfly table by Galle now brings $25,000 to $30,000, up from about $20,000 in 1984." It would be interesting to track this kind of information across time and other magazines, such as *Architectural Digest*, if students are interested. The reading, though not simple, may prove compelling to the right readers.

76. "Stones' Missal." Fred Goodman. *Entertainment Weekly*, March 8, 1991, page 7.
    In just a few paragraphs Goodman summarizes the Rolling Stones' song "High Wire" about Operation Desert Storm, and the controversy the song stirred because of its content "in time of war."

Other Events and Supplements

In an arts unit, the teacher can have students do any of the following:

- Design certificates with colorful markers.
- Write to authors for more information or just to say they appreciate the work.
- Write to museums, galleries, and old theatres for more information.
- Look for articles on the arts topic of choice in newspapers and magazines.
- Draw pictures and write captions.
- Draw responses to illustrations or other representational art.
- Draw responses to written works.
- Write poems to art pieces.
- Collect art event and book posters and exhibit them.
- Make a collection of theatre and art event programs.
- Visit a museum and write a review of the exhibit.
- Critique a new movie or play.
- Photograph public art in isolation and with people and animal interactions.
- Create a catalogue of local public art.
- Create a collage of artists' names found in newspapers, magazines, and promotional materials.
- Create a readers theatre script (see page xxvii of the introduction for a description of readers theatre).

Sports

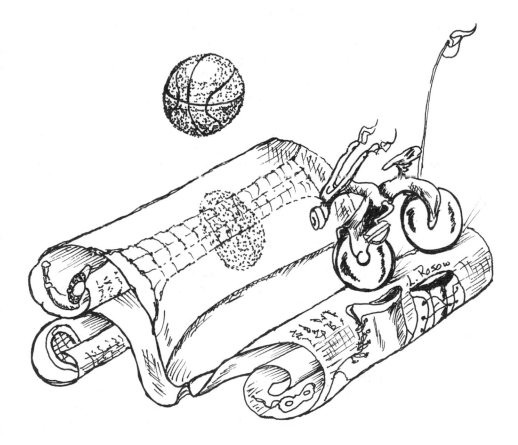

As this book goes to press, I continue to search for more good readings featuring girls and women in sports traditionally played by boys and men. We still have a long way to go. It seems unfair to eliminate good stories that feature only one gender, just because there are no counterparts. Conversely, the message that is sent by allowing this incredible imbalance is that it is okay. It is not. The argument may come up that adults will know girls should be encouraged to play any game they choose, but I have found that all too frequently we accept the world we have as the way the world is supposed to be. I really do believe we can create a better world, one with equity and harmony and truly open opportunities for all. But first we need to recognize that we do not have such a world now.

Literature, the kinds of things we read, has a great deal to do with how we think. Reading is a powerful shaper of individual thoughts. Although this is a collection of imbalance, in it are some fine reads for those who are grappling with language development. And to the person selecting material for adults and families, I suggest you attempt to create a spirit of equity through dialogue and questioning. Perhaps drawing attention to imbalance will inspire the writers you are nurturing to help set the scales right. We really can all be much better than we are.

For the sports fan, though many exciting news accounts appear across the land each season, there seems to be a shortage of great writing come book time. It is almost as though the sports writers forget their play-by-play enthusiasm when they enter the arena of thirty pages. This again could be the subject of dialogue, inspiring today's students to become tomorrow's authors.

First Readers and Picture Books

77. *Baseball's Awesome Hitters*. D. L. Arneson. Racine, WI: Western, 1992
     This is a gold mine of short readings. Thirty baseball legends are featured via small portrait, full-page action shot, and a well-paced biography. Listen to this motivational spot: "Mickey Charles Mantle was born in Spavinaw, Oklahoma, on October 20, 1931. His miner father had played semiprofessional baseball. He did not want his son to work in the mines, so from the time he was five, Mickey was coached to be a switch-hitter. He became the greatest switch-hitter in baseball history" (page 51). The story of Lou Gehrig, pages 36–38, speeds past his life until after college, gives statistics on his competition with Babe Ruth, and provides a full paragraph on the mysterious disease that was to take his life. This particular passage might be used to build background knowledge for subsequently more difficult stories on Gehrig.

78. *Northern Lights, the Soccer Trails*. Michael Arvaarluk Kusugak. Art by Vladyana Krykorka. Toronto-New York: Annick Press, 1993. Ruth Schwartz Award.
     Adoration of mother for child and child for mother, a ride on a canoe on a sled pulled by dogs, sickness and the death of a parent, soccer played with a

caribou skin ball, and the northern lights are experiences the reader gets through a sensitive tale of one Inuit girl. The beautiful and detailed colored drawings are supplemented by beaded items that reflect the symbolism emerging from the text. On the back cover is a summary of the aurora borealis, known on Baffin Island as "Soccer Trails." It is believed that these lights are deceased loved ones playing soccer in the sky.

79. *A Picture Book of Jesse Owens*. David A. Adler. Illustrated by Robert Casilla. New York: Scholastic, 1992.

Important dates are chronicled on the last page, starting with the birth of J. C. Owens on September 12, 1913. Later, a teacher, misunderstanding J. C., wrote Jesse in her roll book and permanently changed the name of the boy who would grow to be a world-class runner. The chronology ends with his death from lung cancer on March 31, 1980. Even as the grandson of a former slave won Olympic victories that honored his country, he was forbidden the right to live where he chose or ride in the front of the bus. Adolf Hitler, too, had shown disdain for the man with black skin and refused to shake hands with him. It was generations later before U.S. President Gerald Ford and then President Jimmy Carter attempted to set right the wrongs cast on this American.

80. *Play Ball, Amelia Bedelia*. Peggy Parish. Pictures by Wallace Tripages. New York: Scholastic, 1972.

When told to tag a player from the opposing team, Amelia looks through her purse, locates a tag, and hangs it on the bewildered boy. So it goes through all of the unfamiliar—to Amelia—language of baseball. Great illustrations assist comprehension. This series of books is popular with adult new readers and English as a Second Language learners.

81. *Playing Right Field*. Willy Welch. Illustrated by Marc Simont. New York: Scholastic, 1995.

Each two-page spread of this picture book has two to four lines of text that are perfectly aligned with the charcoal and watercolor drawings. The story is one known firsthand to many, that of being the least able and last chosen for some sport. So it was with Willy Welch each Saturday as he waited to be sent to his traditional spot in right field where there was little to do except watch the dandelions grow. There is a cassette tape of the author singing the text as he accompanies himself on the guitar. When I played the tape and shared the book in a workplace English communications class, one man was inspired to share his recollections of such a fate in Mexico. This simple human tragedy is one that will strike a universal chord.

82. *Teammates*. Peter Golenbock. Illustrated by Paul Bacon. San Diego, CA: Harcourt Brace Jovanovich, 1990.

This is a simple picture book of baseball, racism, and how one manager, Branch Rickey of the Brooklyn Dodgers, and two players, Jackie Robinson and Pee Wee Reese, started revolutionary change.

Thin Books

83. *Ask Dale Murphy.* Dale Murphy with Curtis Patton. Introduction by Furman Bisher. Chapel Hill, NC: Algonquin, 1987.

Every coach and parent should have a chance to read this tender, thoughtful, insightful, and inspirational book. It began as a newspaper column by the same name. The format is questions from young fans, in bold type, answered in half-page essays on the topic, making it great SSR reading. The question "Do you have trouble unwinding after a game? Sometimes I can't sleep and I'm just in Little League—Billy Taylor, 11" is answered in several paragraphs that end with the following: "My main advice to Little Leaguers is to enjoy the game and have fun. It's good to be excited and have butterflies in your stomach. But if you haven't had a good time, it's not worth it" (pages 85–86). There is a Strong Passage for coaches and parents in that section (see entry 102 in "Book Chapters and Strong Passages").

84. *Baseball's Greatest P-I-T-C-H-E-R-S.* S. A. Kramer. Illustrated by Jim Campbell with photographs. New York: Scholastic, 1992.

Drawings and photographs of pitching action support the large, easy-to-read text, high interest for any person who loves baseball.

85. *Better BMX Riding and Racing for Boys and Girls.* George Sullivan. Illustrated with photographs and diagrams. New York: Dodd, Mead, 1984.

The addresses of the American Bicycle Association and National Bicycle League are provided for anyone wanting more information about racing rules. A glossary that tells what MAG wheels are and the meaning of RAD and radical is a good place to start. Action photos and graphic illustrations of motion curves support the instructions on racing and how to win. Selection of handlebars and what to wear are only part of the racing hopeful's instruction list.

86. *The Home Run Kings: Babe Ruth . . . Henry Aaron.* Clare Gault and Frank Gault. New York: Scholastic, 1974.

Two baseball greats are here. George Herman "Babe" Ruth learned to be a tailor while acquiring pitching skills. Henry "Hank" Aaron broke Babe Ruth's hitting record. The two stories are told in easy-to-understand prose with chunks of photos in the middle of each.

87. *I Want to Tell You: My Response to Your Letters, Your Messages, Your Questions.* O. J. Simpson. Boston: Little, Brown, 1995.

The title describes most of the content of this easy reader with photographs. Anyone intrigued by the trial, the murders, or the reactions of people of all ages to this very public event will find something to read in this book. Even before the infamous Ford Bronco freeway chase and the controversial verdict, the fact that Simpson was NFL's Most Valuable Player in 1975 and inducted into the Pro Football Hall of Fame in 1985, coupled with his post-athletic career as commentator, movie actor, and product promoter, means this is a high-profile person about whom many sports fans will have a lot of background knowledge.

88. *I Was a Teenage Professional Wrestler*. Ted Lewin. New York: Scholastic, 1993.

A glossary of wrestling lingo and holds fills the last three pages of this book. Many may want to start there. Though the book has an ample supply of photographs of known, unknown, and colorful wrestlers from the 1950s and 1960s, there are also drawings and paintings by the author, who used wrestling to pay the rent while he attended the Pratt Institute. This split life allowed him a unique place among artists and wrestlers. In this autobiography, Lewin begins recounting the fun times he and his brothers had as children when their father took them to the fights. It was a father-son occasion that set the course for Ted. He also recounts stories about the wrestlers who lived in his house and how they spent their time outside the ring—none, that he could recall, ever read. This is an interesting read, whether you are a sports fan, an art enthusiast, or neither.

89. *Know Your Game: Baseball*. Marc Bloom. New York: Scholastic, 1991.

Before starting this book you may want to skip through the "Baseball Talk" glossary on page 62. It will familiarize you with words like dugout, strikeout, umpire, warm-up, hook slide, and good eye. Here is a how-to book that sounds like your best buddy is showing you the ropes. "Imagine pitching a no-hitter in your first Little League game. That's what California Angels pitcher Jim Abbott did when he was learning baseball skills as a young athlete. Abbott went on to star in high school and college. He also pitched the U.S. to victory in the 1988 Olympic Games before moving up to the major leagues" (page 15). So explains your friend who assures that missing a ball or two is no reason to give up. There are few illustrations and the large type solidly fills the pages, leaving the reader to figure out meaning. But the conversational style is inviting, especially to a person already interested in the great American pastime.

90. *Know Your Game: Soccer*. Marc Bloom. New York: Scholastic, 1990.

This book has about the most persuasive and informative sections on nutrition I have seen. Comparing the body to a car's engine, the author explains how what you put on your pizza, for example, can either rev you up or slow you down. Regarding the game, there are clear little graphics to show how described moves should look. And discussions of gear, rules, and teamwork are salient. Though the author generally avoids reference to gender, on page 42 he suggests there are high school soccer teams for boys and girls, and on page 50 he says they should do the same exercises. Nonetheless, all the athletes in his "Soccer's Greatest Stars" section, pages 43–46, are males, and the cover photo shows two boys engaged in the game. I am including this easy reader despite the gender bias, because I could not find an easy soccer reader with a balance of male and female players, even in the photographs. In an effort to provide another approach to gender balance, I have been combing newspapers for shots of girls playing soccer. No luck. The teacher may want to open discussion about gender equity in sports in general and soccer in particular.

91. *Like Father, Like Son: Baseball's Major League Families*. Sarah Gardiner White. New York: Scholastic, 1993.

It is not just fathers and sons; many familial relationships emerge in this entertaining assortment of high-profile sports names. It is a well-written book with a few nice black-and-white photos.

92. *Lou Gehrig: One of Baseball's Greatest.* Guernsey Van Riper, Jr. New York: Macmillan, 1986.

This large-print paperback is one of a series on childhoods of famous Americans. The story starts with the dilemma of a young boy who is ridiculed for being fat. It also addresses the pain of racism expressed against children with German surnames when President Wilson declared war against the German government. This clearly written story is a good, fast read.

93. *The Martial Arts Almanac.* Ngo Vinh-Hoi. Illustrated by Neal Yamamoto. Los Angeles: Lowell House Juvenile, 1995.

Large print, clear illustrations, lots of short passages, and information on a whole host of martial arts make this a fascinating read even to the person who has no interest in taking a class. But for those who have such an interest, there is a list of the best martial arts training films and how to locate a school. And there are surprises like, "The most famous martial artist ever was . . . Elvis Presley? That's right!" (page 19).

94. *Martina Navratilova.* Jane Mersky Leder. Mankato, MN: Baker Street Productions, 1985.

This is the story of the rise and fall and rise again of an early-achieving tennis champ, Martina Navratilova of Czechoslovakia, who has had a roller-coaster lifestyle with triumphs and tragedies every year. Weight loss, political shifts, and the freedom afforded when she moved from communism to the United States, all wreaked havoc on this ambitious young woman. Because of her parents' love of skiing, she learned to ski just after learning to walk and showed great promise. "When she was three, Martina's parents were divorced. She seldom saw her father after that. 'He wasn't a real family man, and he was very emotional,' she said. Her father died when she was nine years old. Years later she learned that he had killed himself" (page 7). Documentary photos speckle this story in easy-to-see type. The sentences are simple and meaningful for a nonnative speaker of English.

95. *More Weird Moments in Sports.* Bruce Wever. Designed and illustrated by Howie Katz. New York: Scholastic, 1983.

This book is perfect for sustained silent reading. It has two or more complete stories on every page.

96. *The Official Freebies for Fans: Something for Nothing or Next to Nothing!* Editors of *Freebies* magazine. Chicago: Contemporary Books, 1994.

This book is loaded with ideas on how to get mail into your life. A short paragraph introduces the source of reading materials, such as where to write for twenty celebrity addresses for the cost of a long, self-addressed envelope, and how to join the Gilligan's Island Fan Club. Another section gives addresses of fan clubs, baseball teams, hockey teams, football teams, basketball teams—you name it in sports. There is a list of names and addresses of places you might go. And the book also has a lot of things you can buy for under $5.

97. *1001 Fascinating Baseball Facts: Facts, Records, Anecdotes, Quotes, Lore, and More.* David Nemec and Pete Palmer. Lincolnwood, IL: Publications International, 1994.

Here is everything you need to know about baseball but thought you already knew. A brief history of the game is followed by myriad small chunks of information in well-written, sometimes spell-binding prose, supported by historical and current photographs, documentary statistics, and lists. This is a wonderful SSR library item and can be used to bring sports fans of all ages into the world of reading.

98. *The Story of Babe Ruth, Baseball's Greatest Legend.* Lisa Eisenberg. New York: Dell, 1990.

A lightweight paperback with large print and wide margins, this biography is an easy-to-read tale of poor, small town boy makes good. It is about a child who spoke only German at home and learned English from his friends on the street. It describes Ruth as one of eight children, only two of whom survived. It tells about a young boy who was truant more often than not, began drinking alcohol at the age of ten, could barely read or write, and who was finally sent to a school for incorrigibles. Then the story begins to detail the boy's baseball development. Though the book is a compelling overview of Ruth's life, it does not go into great detail, leaving room for more in-depth reading from other sources.

99. *The World Series: The Great Contests.* Richard J. Brenner. Syosset, NY: East End, 1994.

Nine action-packed stories with all-time famous names make this a lively addition to the sports fans reading collection.

Challenging

100. *Great Upsets of the NFL.* Richard Kaplan. New York: Random House, 1972.

Ten notorious changes of fate are documented with fast-paced reporting and historical newspaper photographs. There are quite a few two-page spreads of solid type, but the reading is good and the vocabulary will encourage a new reader to keep going: "Mistakes had cost Detroit dearly in the first half. Now it was San Francisco's turn to stumble. Tittle fumbled on his 27-yard-line, and Bob Long of the Lions landed on the football. You could see renewed life blossom all along the Detroit bench. Maybe the game wasn't over yet" (page 75). To find out what happened between Detroit and San Francisco, you have to read the book.

101. *The Mick, an American Hero: The Legend and the Glory.* Mickey Mantle with Herb Gluck. New York: Jove, 1985.

Here is a fun read, even if you are not a sports fan. It is simple telling in the words of the baseball legend himself. It reads like he is talking to you, the interviewer, in the locker room. He discusses tough negotiations, in spite of the fact that lots of ballplayers make more per year than most Americans earn in a lifetime. "I remembered a conversation with Claire Ruth during an Old-Timers' game. I was standing by the rail of her box seat telling her I wished I could've seen the Babe play. Mrs. Ruth set me straight. 'Get what you can while you're on top' and after a long pause, 'Babe was pushing to take over as Yankee manager, knowing he'd only have another year or two left as a player. When it came down to dollars, Mickey, they handed him the pink slip. Two lousy lines notifying him that he was unconditionally released.' I never understood it. He was the greatest drawing card in the history of baseball and owner Jake Ruppert tossed him aside like an old shoe." The first five pages of chapter 18 (pages 148–58) tell about big-time negotiations for pay that moved the Mick from $7,500 to $65,000. Included are career stats and a scrapbook of memorable photos.

Book Chapters and Strong Passages

102. "Adult Coaches and Children." In *Ask Dale Murphy.* Dale Murphy with Curtis Patton. Introduction by Furman Bisher. Chapel Hill, NC: Algonquin, 1987, pages 21–23.

Though this entire book (reviewed under "Thin Books," entry 83) is an assemblage of good short passages, this section provides plain talk about sports and the relationships young people have with their caretakers: "I received a letter the other day from a twelve-year-old child involved in athletics who complained about his coach yelling at him." The heart-sent, common-sense messages about the impact sports has on youths can open the floor to discussion about values and consequences.

103. *The Groucho Letters: Letters from and to Groucho Marx.* New York: Simon & Schuster, 1967.

In a letter written on March 21, 1960, comedian Groucho Marx remembers a St. Patrick's Day parade from his youth when he, as a spectator, yelled to the recently defeated boxing champ Jim Jeffries a question about the match that so riled the fighter that the big man seriously offered to leave his carriage and kill Marx on the spot (page 269).

Short Passages for SSR

104. "Black Hair." In *A Fire in My Hands: A Book of Poems.* Gary Soto. New York: Scholastic, 1990.

A Mexican boy sits in the bleachers, rooting for the one person on the team who looks like him. As a youth, Soto was no good at sports, and he has written this poem in memory of his good times as a spectator.

105. *The Guinness Book of Records,* 1995 ed. Edited by Peter Matthews. New York: Bantam Books, 1995.

The cover reads, "The unmatched, authoritative collection of world-class facts, figures, and feats from around the globe, completely revised with all-new photos and features." An entire section on sports and games begins on page 510. One short offering begins, "The batter with the career strikeout record is Reggie Jackson, who struck out 2,597 times in twenty-one seasons with four teams," page 526, and continues to give action-packed information in the next two sentences. There are interesting, adult topics on every sport in this book, available in short passages. And they are loaded with useful, everyday vocabulary written in clear, modern English. This is an SSR dream come true.

106. "Jay Johnstone." In *Eccentrics.* Henry Billings and Melissa Billings. Providence, RI: Jamestown, 1987, pages 24–26.

"From 1966 to 1984, Jay Johnstone played major league baseball for eight different teams." *Eccentrics* is one of a series of books with high-interest short passages for adults. I have used them successfully with ESL and adult new readers. My only complaint about the series is that often more text space is devoted to tests and skill activities than to the good reads the series authors have proven they can write. This softcover booklet has twenty-one stories about eccentric people.

107. *1001 Fascinating Baseball Facts: Facts, Records, Anecdotes, Quotes, Lore, and More.* David Nemec and Pete Palmer. Lincolnwood, IL: Publications International, 1994.

Two- and three-paragraph, high-interest passages abound, as do many small information boxes with just a couple of trivia-loaded sentences. There are lots of statistics, too. This is a great book for a new reader or new English speaker who loves that game.

108. "Roberto Clemente: A Duty to Others." In *Heroes: 21 True Stories of Courage and Honor*. Providence, RI: Jamestown, 1985, pages 106–8.

Heroes is one of a series of books that offer three-page, adult-level topics written in a compelling newsmagazine format. This story is about a Latin American baseball hero. The bad news is that this series provides tedious skills and drills at the end of each story, inconsistent with the goals of reading for interest and pleasure.

109. "Terry Fox and the Marathon of Hope." In *Heroes: 21 True Stories of Courage and Honor*. Providence, RI: Jamestown, 1985, pages 42–44.

Heroes is one of a series of books that offer three-page, adult-level topics written in a compelling newsmagazine format. This inspiring story is about a marathon runner with one artificial leg.

110. *The World Almanac and Book of Facts 1995*. Edited by Robert Famighetti. Mahwah, NJ: Funk & Wagnalls, 1995.

The attack on figure skater Nancy Kerrigan and other current sports issues are presented in fast-action, information-intensive passages you can read in just a few minutes. Statistics of many sorts are offered in narrative and column format. This book might be viewed as an encyclopedia you can hold in your hand.

Newspaper and Magazine Articles

111. "Derby Is More Than Just a Race." Andy Mead. *The Orange County Register*, May 7, 1995, Sports section, pages 1, 7.

The subheading reads "Horse Racing: From interesting names to poetry, the Run for the Roses has meaning for its fans." The story is a string of testimonials from people who care about the Derby in highly personal ways. One woman, whose homesick parents expected her to be born on the day of the Derby, was named Derby even though she was three weeks overdue.

112. "He's a Riot—That's No Bull!" *National Enquirer*, July 16, 1991, page 18.

The *National Enquirer* is one of the best high-interest, easy-reading formats for adults that I know of. My students are always delighted when I bring one to class, and they sometimes start reading the tabloid in grocery lines as a result. There are usually big pictures to support the text, and this story is no exception. It is about a Spanish matador who created a riot in Madrid when he entered the ring and then suddenly decided not to fight.

113.   "Memories of Shoeless Joe Jackson Happy Ones." Associated Press report. *The Orange County Register,* May 7, 1995, Sports section, page 9.
    A lifetime fan of Jackson, Jack Thompson is writing a book about one of baseball's most famous natural hitters. The article tells of memorabilia that include a photograph of Thompson as a barefoot child, being treated to ice cream by the baseball legend. The article is loaded with nostalgic memories, including the trick of mixing peanuts in your Coke during games. If this issue of the *Register* is not in your collection, and your local paper did not use this AP story, do not worry. There are similar offerings in Sunday papers across the land. Just go to the sports section and shop around.

Other Events and Supplements

For sports enthusiasts there is little more likely to foster good writing than sports-related activities. Not everyone will want to do everything, but that's horse racing!

- Record your favorite sports announcer in action. Imitate one performance.
- Write to a sports writer asking how a person enters the profession.
- Collect baseball or basketball cards.
- Compare statistics between teams.
- Write for freebies.
- Look up birthplaces of sports figures.
- Write to ball parks for more information.
- Save newspaper and magazine articles on an incident, and watch the story change over time.
- Write a letter to the editor about the changes or inconsistencies you see in articles over time.
- Collect cereal box stories.
- Make a collage of newspaper pictures of sports figures. Write a story about the collage.
- Write a series of stories featuring little-known or amateur sports figures.
- Create a little book about "the underdogs."
- Develop a multisports dictionary.
- Collect commemorative stamps with sports themes. Write about them.

Myths, Legends, Fables, and Fairy Tales

Unit 3

The romance of superhuman feats, of people transformed to things, of things transformed to treasure has a wondrous quality that attracts humans of all ages. And down through the ages many tales have been retold in ways that suit the times, so a happy ending may become a twisted bit of luck, or a wise old man may become a clever young girl in a modern edition. But stories that are handed down usually have some lesson or message imbedded in such a way that they can be enjoyed from the cradle to the grave. Still, not all "old" stories are particularly old. Ancient tales can spring from anywhere to satisfy any need.

And speaking of needs, for the new reader or new speaker of English there are increasing numbers of books addressing one part of an epic or one strange phenomenon. Then, once the background knowledge has begun to solidify, the reader can move on to more in-depth retellings of familiar tales or access a breadth of materials by spreading out within a genre. Consider for a moment the power of just looking at the Diabolical Dragons in Graeme Base's *Animalia*. Dramatic pictures can delight and feed the imagination. Dialogue will also encourage broad thinking about the mythological creatures. Then consider the First Reader *Saint George and the Dragon*, discussed below. After learners extend their language and information base of dragon knowledge, more readings involving this mythological creature might follow.

First Readers and Picture Books

114. *The Adventures of Spider: West African Folk Tales*. Retold by Joyce Cooper Arkhurst. Illustrated by Jerry Pinkey. New York: Scholastic, 1964.

Have you been wondering how the world got wisdom? Would you like to know how the spider got a thin waist or became bald? Perhaps you want to know why there are spiders on your ceiling. The answers to these important questions and more are found in these short, well-written, and well-illustrated stories. Each tale has a lesson or two. For parents, there are ways of entering notions of common sense and greed, without direct reference to children. For teachers, there are avenues for comparing values on a global level.

115. *Aesop's Fables*. A new translation by V. S. Vernon-Jones, with an introduction by G. K. Chesterton. Illustrated by Arthur Rackham. New York: Avenel Books, n.d.

This is a facsimile of the 1912 edition. Sometimes with two or even three to a page and sometimes a single fable running a couple of pages long, these witty stories about human nature provide both quick reads and dialogue boosters.

116. *Aesop's Fables*. Retold by Ann McGovern. Illustrated by A. J. McClaskey. New York: Scholastic, 1963.

Fables nearly 3,000 years old are retold with clarity and spunk in just a few words by master storyteller Ann McGovern. Traditional morals are incorporated into the last line of the fable, and simple drawings provide a lot of context for the reader. I have used this book with both new readers and ESL students. It is always well received. Often ESL students from literate homes have heard the tales in their native languages.

117. *All of You Was Singing*. An Aztec creation song retold by Richard Lewis. Art by Ed Young. New York: Aladdin, 1991. Picture book.

The pictures build from simple to complex as from the water everywhere emerge the earth monster, serpents, and finally the planet as we know it, with every part singing. This could serve as an inspiration for classroom art, collage, or oil pastel creations.

118. *Anansi the Spider, A Tale from the Ashanti*. Retold and illustrated by Gerald McDermott. New York: Holt, Rinehart and Winston, 1972.

This is another author who so admires the trickster Anansi that he has decided to retell a story, too. The language used by McDermott has a bouncy, rhythmical beat, not traditional English syntax. His simple, block-style illustrations make everyone think, "I can do that!" McDermott thoroughly researches his characters and gives them the personalities and physical characteristics that reflect their origins. He is currently working on a series of trickster tales.

119. *Animalia*. Graeme Base. New York: Harry N. Abrams, 1986.

Animalia is my all-time favorite alphabet book. Each letter is illustrated with an exquisite spread of one or two pages of illustrations filled with objects beginning with that letter. This is the ultimate lesson in phonics, alliteration, and imagination. It is definitely suitable for adults. I know, having given it to many of my friends for birthdays and anniversaries. Some of the pages offer delights for specific thematic units. This unit will benefit from the "Diabolical Dragons Daintily Devouring Delicious Delicacies," on the same page as dice, dropping things, a dictionary, a diamond, a doll, and a decanter. Ingenious Iguanas and Wicked Warrior Wasps will likely do well in a natural sciences unit but may belong with critters and creatures, too. The Vulture Ventriloquist might also be well advised to stay in the creature collection. No matter what unit it ends up in, if you leave this book around, it will be studied for its content and loved for its wonderful illustrations.

120. *Borreguita and the Coyote*. Verna Aardema. Illustrated by Petra Mathers. New York: Scholastic, 1991. Picture book with cassette dramatization by Blanca Comacho.

Poor little lamb Borreguita is doomed, sure to be eaten sooner or later by big, arrogant Coyote. Later, it turns out, for Borreguita bargains for more time and finally outwits the predator completely. On the cassette this simple Mexican folktale is dramatized by Blanca Comacho, who is accompanied by the music of Richard De Rosa. There are many fine Scholastic storybooks with accompanying cassette recordings that may be purchased separately. I have kept a collection of them available as a personal lending library. They model good reading. They model correct pronunciation. They are almost as good as being read to by a loving parent.

121. *Chanticleer and the Fox*. Adapted from Geoffrey Chaucer's *Canterbury Tales*. Illustrated by Barbara Cooney. New York: Harper & Row, 1989. 1959 Caldecott Medal winner.

The wealth of detailed and whimsical scratchboard illustrations of the landscape, people, and rooster Chanticleer are matched by beautifully written text. Chaucer would have reveled in the words chosen to update his Old English tale. Here is just a sample, just part of the description of fine Chanticleer: "For crowing there was not his equal in all the land. His voice was merrier than the merry organ that plays in church, and his crowing from his resting place was more trustworthy than a clock. His comb was redder than fine coral and turreted like a castle wall, his bill was black and shone like jet, and his legs and toes were like azure." As you can see, this is not simple language, but it belongs in the First Reader section because just a few readings by the teacher will place this fine text into the heart and mind of the listener.

122. *Chicken Sunday*. Patricia Polacco. New York: Scholastic, 1992.
        Friends who happen not to be the same color must call on wit and wisdom to create the Easter they intend to share.

123. *Demeter and Persephone, Homeric Hymn No. 2*. Translated by Penelope Proddow. Illustrated by Barbara Cooney. Garden City, NY: Doubleday, 1972.
        Just a few words per poetic line make a long and complex tale easy to get through. And in the end, you understand why spring comes and why it goes again. "Translator's Note" at the end of the book explains the origins of this story and gives detailed information on the "Cast of Characters and Places." This could well be interpreted for readers theatre. Though the story is about adults, the illustrations would supply ample inspiration to children who might want to try it as well. This would be an excellent study of comparison with the two other Persephone books in this unit (see entries 133 and 149). Together they will allow a group of students to see how the same tale may be told in different ways, even with different details, and how the same story may have either complex or quite simple language, as is the case here.

124. *Festival of Freedom: The Story of Passover*. Retold by Maida Silverman. Illustrated by Carolyn S. Ewing. New York: Simon & Schuster, 1988.
        Sanctuary becomes a place of slavery for the Israelites when they are forced to live under the rule of a pharaoh who will not even yield to plagues. The book tells of Moses' mother setting him in rushes to prevent the child from being killed and of the pharaoh's daughter finding him and raising him as her own. Years later, the burning bush and the parting of the Red Sea are added to Moses' list of miracles. The book also gives detailed instructions on the Seder and recipes for Haroset.

125. *The Frog Prince Continued*. Story by Jon Scieszka. Paintings by Steve Johnson. New York: Puffin Books, 1991.
        The traditional fairy tales of Hansel and Gretel, Cinderella, Snow White, Sleeping Beauty, and the Frog Prince take on an adult reality as the Frog Prince and his suburbanite bride discover the unpleasantness of having novelty replaced by familiarity. After reading the traditional tales, the adult reader will be refreshed and amused by the unexpected honesty of this tale. A surprise ending is the frosting on the cake for a book loaded with everyday language and soap opera attitudes.

126. *Hiawatha's Childhood*. Henry Wadsworth Longfellow. Illustrated by Errol Le Cain. New York: Puffin Books, 1984.
        This excerpt from the famous legend written by Longfellow is graced with incredibly beautiful illustrations. The word pictures drawn by the wise old grandmother Nakomis are revisited in full color and imagination by Le Cain. Magical and legendary explanations for everything in nature are passed to the grandchild,

who drinks up the legacy. There are so many applications for this perfect pairing that I am hard-pressed to think of any unit that could not use it somehow.

127. *Lon Po Po: A Red-Riding Hood Story from China.* Translated and illustrated by Ed Young. New York: Scholastic, 1989.
      A clever tale of a wolf, little girls, trickery, and wit is presented in just a few lines per page with wonderful pictures.

128. *The Man Who Could Call Down Owls.* Eve Bunting. Illustrated by Charles Mikolaycak. New York: Macmillan, 1984.
      This is a picture book with haunting, surprising pencil drawings of owls. It is also a storybook of a man with mystical healing powers, his apprentice, and an assassin who wanted those powers. The languages of owls, forests, caring, teaching, and values each emerge from a seemingly simple picture book. For these discussions, it stands alone. It also works well as a companion book with Jane Yolen's *Owl Moon,* detailed in "Parenting," Unit 6, entry 315.

129. *Northern Lights, the Soccer Trails.* Michael Arvaarluk Kusugak. Art by Vladyana Krykorka. Toronto-New York: Annick Press, 1993. Ruth Schwartz Award.
      Adoration of mother for child and child for mother, a ride on a canoe on a sled pulled by dogs, sickness and the death of a parent, soccer played with a caribou skin ball, and the northern lights are experiences the reader gets through a sensitive tale of one Inuit girl. The beautiful and detailed colored drawings are supplemented by beaded items that reflect the symbolism emerging from the text. On the back cover is a summary of the aurora borealis, known on Baffin Island as "Soccer Trails." It is believed that these lights are deceased loved ones playing soccer in the sky.

130. *One-Minute Favorite Fairy Tales.* Shari Lewis. Illustrated by Benton Mahan. New York: Doubleday, 1985.
      These really are retold stories you can read in just one minute, and the illustrations are fun to look at. Though in one minute Lewis does not give much detail, the stories let you introduce the adult learner to a vast number of tales in a short period of time. That means the learner will have enough background knowledge to launch into regular bedtime stories with children.

131. *One-Minute Greek Myths.* Shari Lewis. Illustrated by C. S. Ewing. New York: Doubleday, 1987.
      Lewis did not simplify the texts when she whittled these twenty classics down to one minute each. Nor did she try to hide the necessary. Consider Hercules: "When Hercules was only a few minutes old, someone dropped two nasty snakes into his crib in order to kill him" (page 42). So, although the language is quite adult, the Ewing illustrations are imaginative, colorful two-page spreads that support the text pleasantly. There is a pronunciation guide to get you through the names.

132. *The Peopling of Australia.* Percy Trezise. North Ryde NSW 2113, Australia: Angus & Robertson, 1990.
      This Aboriginal story of creation gives the history of the world in a few well-illustrated pages.

133. *Persephone and the Pomegranate: A Myth from Greece.* Kris Waldherr. New York: Dial Books, 1993.

Charming illustrations and a nicely told tale present this old story in a readable form.

134. *The Rajah's Rice: A Mathematical Folktale from India.* Adapted by David Barry. Illustrated by Donna Perrone. New York: W. H. Freeman, 1994. Picture book.

This tale has been retold in a variety of forms. Here a young girl, bather of the king's elephants, uses her love of numbers to learn and her love of elephants to open the door to change for her impoverished village people. By using a numbers trick, she gets all of the rajah's rice from him. At the end of the book, a chessboard is used to graphically illustrate the power of two.

135. *The Rough-Faced Girl.* Rafe Martin and David Shannon. New York: Scholastic, 1992.

This is a retelling of an Algonquin Indian "Cinderella" story with illustrations that convey all kinds of human qualities—good and evil. The disfigured girl finally gets a chance at happiness. Though there are several solid paragraphs on some pages, the drawings push comprehension along.

136. *Saint George and the Dragon.* Adapted by Margaret Hodges from Edmund Spenser's *Faerie Queene.* Illustrated by Trina Schart Hyman. Boston: Little, Brown, 1984.

Like vignettes seen through latticework, the colorful drawings brighten every page of this wonderful tale. The Princess Una, the Red Cross Prince, and even the mighty dragon look splendid as the details of the prince's battles yield progress, little by little. And finally, in service to the Fairy Queen, the prince becomes Saint George of England.

137. *Sleeping Ugly.* Jane Yolen. Illustrated by Diane Stanley. New York: Scholastic, 1981.

This is a tongue-in-cheek return on every sickeningly sweet fairy tale you have ever heard. With just a few words per page and great illustrations, the absurdity of women's helplessness, beauty on the outside, kissing frogs, love at first sight, and magic spells all come to fore.

138. *Something from Nothing.* Adapted from a Jewish folktale by Phoebe Gilman. New York: Scholastic, 1992. Picture book.

Grandpa is a tailor whose first loving gift to little Joseph is a blanket. Over time, Joseph outgrows his baby blanket, which Grandpa remakes into a jacket, which Joseph outgrows, and Grandpa remakes into a vest. And so it goes until nothing is left, nothing, everyone tells the boy. But Joseph knows how to make that gift of love into one more thing—a story. This is a story of faith, family, and the power of positive thinking, passed from one generation to the next.

139. *Strega Nona's Magic Lessons.* Story and pictures by Tomie dePaola. New York: Scholastic, 1982.

Strega Nona is a wise old woman with mystical, magical powers that everyone wants to learn. And that is where the complications start. Tomie dePaola's humorous illustrations take up most of the space and push meaning into the text.

140. *The Tale of the Mandarin Ducks*. Katherine Paterson. Illustrated by Leo Dillon and Diane Dillon. New York: Scholastic, 1990.

Mysterious paintings fill each magical page, as the story unfolds of abusive power and greed and of a mandarin drake who returns goodness with mercy.

141. *Tales of Pan*. Mordicai Gerstein. New York: Harper & Row, 1986.

The comical, whimsical illustrations make this a fun book just for page turning. Nothing serious about the great gods here. And Gerstein's storytelling makes the wealth of information in the stories just sort of tumble off the page and into your lap. Did you know that Pan invented panic? He was also responsible for the first eclipse. And his pranks led to the conditions that cause Mount Aetna to rumble and spew fire and smoke to this day. Though this book is found in the children's section of the library, it is guaranteed to be a popular one among adults who are interested in mythology.

142. *Three Gold Pieces: A Greek Folk Tale*. Retold and illustrated by Aliki. New York: Harper Trophy, 1994. Picture book.

As with Aliki's other works, the illustrations are a surprising delight in themselves. Here the story may seem demeaning—a poor man enters a ten-year work contract without ever asking the terms of his employment. Then he ends up paying his employer all his earning for three bits of advice. As the story continues, however, the advice turns out to be of considerable value to this main character. The implications of this old tale can lead to current life comparisons and questioning of messages sent through text.

143. *The Three Little Wolves and the Big Bad Pig*. Eugene Trivizas and Helen Oxenbury. New York: Scholastic, 1993.

This funny turnabout might be quite a downer if the pig, who terrorized the sweet little wolves, did not suddenly experience a change of heart.

144. *The Tree of Life: The World of the African Baobab*. Barbara Bash. San Francisco: Little, Brown, 1989.

The legend of this oddly shaped tree, the animals that call it home, friend, or food, and the cycle of life that runs from rain to rain are presented with scientific detail and storyteller craft. The detailed watercolors are full of visual information and delights as well.

Thin Books

145. *Favorite Greek Myths*. Retold by Mary Pope Osborne. Illustrated by Troy Howell. New York: Scholastic, 1989.

Each myth starts with a beautifully done full-page illustration, which is followed by about three pages of text. There is lots of white space, and the language is pretty easy to get through most of the time. However, the text is not simplified, and some spots have a significant number of large, uncommon words. Starting on page 71, "Gods, Goddesses and Mortals" are listed, with short descriptions of their familial relationships. They are followed on page 75 with a glossary, "Modern Words with Greek Origins." Did you know that cereal comes from the goddess of grain, Ceres? There is also a helpful index.

146. *Folktales, Timeless Tales.* Retold by Tana Reiff. Illustrated by Cheri Bladholm. New York: New Readers Press, 1991.

These retold tales from around the globe are familiar and fun to read, although the style suffers from an attempt to write down to the level of a new reader. Cheri Bladholm's clear, detailed illustrations are entertaining in and of themselves and help to push the stories along. A cassette tape by Reiff offers less than stellar reading, but her clear pronunciation is popular with ESL students.

147. *Her Stories, African American Folktales, Fairy Tales, and True Tales.* Told by Virginia Hamilton. Illustrated by Leo Dillon and Diane Dillon. New York: Blue Sky Press, 1995. 1995 Laura Ingalls Wilder Award.

Here is a mix of true, not true, and maybe true stories by and about African American women and their benefactors. At the end of each tale is Hamilton's best account of the tale's historical origins. The Dillon acrylic paintings are a delight unto themselves.

148. *Mermaid Tales from Around the World.* Retold by Mary Pope Osborne. Illustrated by Troy Howell. New York: Scholastic, 1993.

A full-page, full-color illustration signals the mood and opening of each new tale; a decorative icon signals each story's close, making this handsome book interesting to look at, even before the reading begins. Osborne's retellings are brief and offer detail-free summaries of passages that might otherwise be considered inappropriate for young readers. This issue of style could lead to dialogue with adult writers about how audience influences content. The author uses simple vocabulary most of the time, and most of her sentences tend to be short but not choppy. The bibliography might lead readers on a research project to find other variations on the theme or other versions of the same tales. Inspiration for the retellings comes from France, Canada, the Aegean Sea, Ireland, Russia, Nigeria, Japan, England, China, India, Persia, Arabia, Germany, and Denmark. There is a Cyclops and sea nymph story under "Book Chapters and Strong Passages," entry 161.

149. *Persephone and the Springtime: A Greek Myth Retold.* Margaret Hodges. Illustrated by Arvis Stewart. Boston: Little, Brown, 1973.

Your first visit here should be spent just turning the pages and drinking up the illustrations. Such enchanting and colorful ink drawings grace each page of this book I was tempted to put it under picture books. I did not because it has too much text to fit in that category. But it is well-written text that tells the story of Persephone, who is abducted by Pluto and taken to live under the sea. The rest of the story explains why we now have only six months of lovely weather on Earth.

Challenging

150. *The Dark Way: Stories from the Spirit World.* Told by Virginia Hamilton. Illustrated by Lambert Davis. San Diego, CA: Harcourt Brace Jovanovich, 1990.

Twenty-five eerie tales with illustrations that build terror in the reader's soul are followed by historical notes on the legends' origins. Hamilton makes no attempt at simplifying her text. Her vocabulary is Challenging and her style compelling. These stories are read alouds that will teach writing style to the listeners.

151. *The Frog Princess and Other Tales.* Illustrated by Nikolai Ustinov. New York: Doubleday, 1987.

Can you believe that there is a logical, reasonable excuse for the drought that covered the earth about a hundred years ago? Well, once you've read "The Rain Maiden," you'll know. Each turn of the page of this enchanting collection reveals wonderful pictures.

152. *Heroes & Monsters of Greek Myth.* Bernard Evslin, Dorothy Evslin, and Ned Hoopes. Illustrated by William Hunter. New York: Scholastic, 1967.

Myths of demigods Perseus, Daedalus, Theseus, and Atalanta, and fables of Midas and Pygmalion are told in clear, well-written text. Each story has one delightfully fanciful black-and-white drawing on the first page. On page 109 is a chart of "Roman Names for Greek Gods," followed by three pages called "Mythology Becomes Language," giving a list of words from the myths that are now in the English language. Perhaps we have already faced the fact that echo came from the story of Narcissus and Echo, and martial comes from the Roman god of war, Mars. But how about cloth, panic, and fortune? Yes, these and many more common English words are traced to their mythological roots at the end of the book.

153. *Norse Mythology A to Z.* Kathleen N. Daly. New York: Facts on File, 1991.

"Reader friendly" describes this more-than-an-alphabet book or encyclopedia. The author provides an introduction with names of gods to get you started, a detailed index at the end, and many copies of illustrations to entertain you along the way. Though the material is complex, and the many unusual names slow the reader, this Challenging book is interesting and information-intensive. It is excellent sustained silent reading fare, as the passages are quite short and can be read at random. Take Day, for example: "The son of NIGHT and her third husband, DELLING. ODIN set Night and her son, Day, in the sky to ride around the world, bringing darkness and light at regular intervals. Day's horse was SHINING MANE (SKINFAXI) whose golden glow lighted up the earth. (See 'Night and Day,' under CREATION)." Following several paragraphs on runes (that which is secret), samples from several runic alphabets are shown to convey the similarities and differences among English, Norse, and Germanic runes.

154. *Star Wars, from the Adventures of Luke Skywalker.* George Lucas. New York: Ballantine Books, 1976.

Adventure and drama are played out in a fast-moving text that has enough uncommon English words to qualify it for the Challenging category. Added to that is the author's invented vocabulary. There are many great read-aloud passages, making this book a candidate for a serial presentation of teacher reading for, perhaps, ten minutes of each session. A chunk of color photographs from the movie are not needed but add to the entertainment.

155. *The Ultimate Dinosaur: Past-Present-Future.* Edited by Byron Preiss and Robert Silverberg. New York: Bantam Books, 1992.

This book offers a mix of science and fiction through scientific essays and enthralling science-fiction short stories. The clear type is set in a magazine format that supports the reader. Though the text might not look Challenging at first blush, the scientific names of plants, animals, and periods serve to slow the reader down but never to a full stop. It is illustrated with a mix of pen and ink drawings and full-color paintings that document the history of the dinosaur through time—past, present, and future. It is informative, entertaining, and a wonderful picture-book adventure. An appendix supports the scientific reader who wants to get a clear timeline of land and animal distributions during the days of the dinosaurs.

Book Chapters and Strong Passages

156. "Gabriel-Ernest." Saki. In *Creepy Classics, Hair-Raising Horror from the Masters of the Macabre*. Edited by Mary Hill. Illustrated by Dominick R. Domingo. New York: Random House, 1994, pages 17–26.

"Gabriel-Ernest" could be true. There are many indications that a Pan-like creature managed to pass itself off as child to a lonesome woman, but in the end, a child is missing and the foundling is gone, and there are questions.

157. *History's Big Mistakes*. Adam Bowett. Illustrated by Chris Mould. London: Belitha Press, 1994.

The legend of labyrinth-builder Daedalus, who invented wings for himself and his son, Icarus, so they might escape from the prison the father had built, is on pages 8 and 9. The story of the Trojan Horse is quickly told on pages 26 and 27. The way in which pictures and text support each other makes this book a candidate for a space between "Picture Books" and "Thin Books" sections. A glossary is made even more useful as all of the words defined there are highlighted in the main text. The witty, running stories are interesting and easy to read, with lots of space devoted to incredibly humorous cartoons. Little bits of additional information are offered in small boxes on nearly every page. Each two-page spread tells of another historic foible. Strong passages occur in every section.

158. *Lost Star: The Story of Amelia Earhart*. Patricia Lauber. New York: Scholastic, 1988.

This is the incredible story of a woman who always seemed to have a philosophical response to what others might view as adversity. Historical photographs accompany this well-told tale. Pages 100–102 offer an interesting mythological passage, telling of the naming of her plane and the odd coincidence that the star known as Amelia was lost just as the namesake had been. It was a toss-up for me whether to go Thin Books or Challenging on this one.

159. "Magic." In *Where the Sidewalk Ends*. Poems and drawings of Shel Silverstein. New York: HarperCollins, 1974, page 11.

"Magic" is an eight-line poem about imaginary creatures.

160. "The Medusa." In *The Dark Way: Stories from the Spirit World*. Told by Virginia Hamilton. Illustrated by Lambert Davis. San Diego, CA: Harcourt Brace Jovanovich, 1990, pages 43–48.

This myth explains in human terms how this horrid creature wreaked havoc on mortals and gods alike. Then the author's comment shares the Greek and Roman roots of the myth. There is more detail under "Challenging," entry 150.

161. "The Sea Nymph and the Cyclops." In *Mermaid Tales from Around the World*. Retold by Mary Pope Osborne. Illustrated by Troy Howell. New York: Scholastic, 1993, pages 12–16.

This Greek tale quickly conveys love, indiscretion, spitefulness, revenge, and absolution—quite a lot for just three-and-a-half pages of text. The organization and style make this a good introduction to Cyclops, Greek myths, or human nature and psychology. More detail is under "Thin Books," entry 148.

162. "The Tortoise and the Hare." In *Fables for Our Time and Famous Poems Illustrated*. James Thurber. New York: Harper & Row, 1983, pages 60–61.

This is a perfect follow-up to the traditional Aesop fable. It demonstrates how one writer is inspired by another. Thurber simply tells the story as it would logically occur, should such a race take place. As a readers theatre event, the two fables played out, traditional first and Thurber second, make excellent fare for children and adults.

163. "The Unicorn." In *Where the Sidewalk Ends*. Poems and drawings of Shel Silverstein. New York: HarperCollins, 1974, pages 76–77.

In terrible grammar, Uncle Shel traces the absence of unicorns on Noah's ark. I have used this incredible collection of poems in many different ways with adults and children. It was popular as a community college ESL text and has provided a wealth of material for readers theatre events, too.

164. "The Unicorn in the Garden." In *Fables for Our Time and Famous Poems Illustrated*. James Thurber. New York: Harper & Row, 1983, pages 64–66.

This is a spoof on the mythical unicorn and a person's right to believe in it. It is also about marital relationships. Women and men in my community college ESL classes have given this little story rave reviews. It connects with the universal and inevitable moments of discord between long-married people. Thurber's language is by no means simplified. It is culture- and content-laden, great writing, supported by Thurber's iconoclastic little ink drawings.

Magazine Articles

165. "Hidden Monsters." Karen Ehrlich and Lee Speigel. Painting by De Es Schwertberger. *Omni*, January 1983, pages 108–13, 120.

Bigfoot, lake monsters, including Nessie of Loch Ness, and other strange creatures of the planet are the subject of this true-life treasure hunt report. *Omni* magazine is always Challenging vocabulary, but the subject matter is high interest and the writing is top quality.

166. "The Mystery of the Lost Patrol: This Time, the Bermuda Triangle Gives One Back." Tom Post with Spencer Reiss. *Newsweek*, May 27, 1991, page 25.

"It was vintage Twilight Zone," opens the story of a plane discovered under 700 to 900 feet of water off the coast of Florida. While searching for more traditional treasure—Spanish galleons—a salvage team spots what appears to be the remains of a vanished Flight 19. Even so, the evidence is not conclusive, and some of the details do not quite match up.

Other Events and Supplements

Consider, for a moment, how much of our day-to-day lives are influenced by myths, legends, fables, and folktales. Many expressions have their roots in some childhood tale. Others are steeped in legend. The following ideas are jumping-off spots for projects your students may decide to try. What matters is that the participants are allowed to stop when their interest does. Have students do any of the following:

- Readers Theatre. For details see Readers Theatre in the introduction on page xxvii.
- Play out a short mythological passage and record it on video. This activity can be particularly refreshing when original, not store-bought, costumes and props are created from available materials.
- Write a new episode in mythological terms, based on a headline news story.
- Collect pictures of sculptures or paintings of mythological entities and list the features of the mythological creatures.
- Write captions for collected pictures of mythological creatures and beings.
- Find pictures of dragons from around the world and across time.
- List everything you can think of about a dragon.
- Design your own dragon.
- Look for articles using mythological terms in newspapers and magazines.
- Page through the Yellow Pages and other advertising-laden books to find logos and other identifying items, such as wing-footed Mercury, that feature mythical vestiges.
- Design a personal mythological logo that relates to family fables or folklore.
- Write the story of the logo.
- Create a classroom totem.
- Invent an unusual noise and write its mythological origin.
- Write the autobiography of a mythological or legendary figure.
- Change a fairy tale to fit modern times.

Mystery, Suspense, and Horror—For the Fun of It

Unit 4

For the person already intrigued by the unknown, these readings may lead into increasingly more advanced literature. I have found that students who have books from a variety of these categories may start with something too difficult, but they can use the beautiful pictures in the First Readers as an excuse to move into works they can read quickly and easily. This is not just good for self-esteem. It also allows the student to read more and, therefore, acquire more vocabulary and grammar from the context. I cannot overstate the value of having a large, easily accessible book collection. That, coupled with a teacher who reads to the students, will foster language and literacy development.

Mystery and suspense stories go just one step further. They foster intellectual risk taking, especially when the reader has been taught to stop, ask questions, and speculate along the way.

First Readers and Picture Books

167. *Flight: The Journey of Charles Lindbergh*. Robert Burleigh. Illustrated by Mike Wimmer. Introduction by Jean Fritz. New York: Philomel Books, 1991.
Fritz's firsthand account of hearing about Lindbergh's triumphal flight across the Atlantic connects much of this story with the lives of adults who are struggling against difficult odds. Fritz was a child in Shanghai, China, listening to her mother read of the twenty-five-year-old's lonely flight, an adventure of worldwide importance. Wimmer's graphic paintings make a wondrous journey in themselves as they show the story from multiple perspectives—Lindbergh's feet on the ground, the farewell scene, in the cockpit, under the plane at sea, in a dense fog, and from the cockpit looking down at the Eiffel Tower at night, just to name a few. The story is written totally in the present tense—you are there; it is 1927. "In the airfield's hangar, he tells the story of his flight to the other pilots: The cramped cockpit, the aloneness, the long, long night. Meanwhile, unknown to Lindbergh, newspaper headlines all over the world are beginning to blazon the news: AMERICAN HERO SAFE IN PARIS!"

168. *The Headless Horseman Rides Tonight: More Poems to Trouble Your Sleep*. Jack Prelutsky. Illustrated by Arnold Lobel. New York: Greenwillow Books, 1980.
Now here is an eerie collection of read-aloud poems that will entertain and intrigue any age reader.

169. *Hershel and the Hanukkah Goblins*. Eric Kimmel. New York: Holiday House, 1985.
Unbelievably strange illustrations propel a tale of a master of bluff. Here is a great read aloud. When I took a collection of good books for my graduate students to investigate, a group of them sat rapt as one read it to them.

170. *The Man Who Could Call Down Owls*. Eve Bunting. Illustrated by Charles Mikolaycak. New York: Macmillan, 1984.
This is a picture book with haunting, surprising pencil drawings of owls. It is also the story of a man with mystical healing powers, his apprentice, and an assassin who wanted those powers. The languages of owls, forests, caring, teaching, and values each emerge from a seemingly simple picture book. For these

discussions, it stands alone. It also works well as a companion book with Jane Yolen's *Owl Moon*, entry 315.

171. *More Stories to Solve, Fifteen Folktales from Around the World*. Told by George Shannon. Illustrated by Peter Sis. New York: Beech Tree, 1991.
   This is the sequel to *Stories to Solve . . .* and is presented in the same format, except some stories are longer. The first part has the story riddle. The second has the solution. The third has an illustration of the solution. These are fun, fast reads often with mathematical and scientific solutions.

172. *More Two-Minute Mysteries*. Donald J. Sobol. New York: Scholastic, 1971.
   These mysteries, by the author of *Encyclopedia Brown*, pose a problem in a page or a page and a half and then give the solutions upside down on the last page of the story. It is a tough call as to whether these two Sobol books belong with First Readers or in Thin Books with the 1963 Encyclopedia Brown mystery, entry 185. The actual story length seems to have made the difference in this unit—these being mostly shorter than the 1960s version. But if you find yourself making a firm decision otherwise, I would like to hear what it is and why.

173. *The Mystery of the Missing Red Mitten*. Steven Kellogg. New York: Puffin Books, 1992.
   Simple line drawings contribute to the reader's comprehension, as the missing mitten becomes the subject of a mystery.

174. *Old Devil Wind*. Bill Martin, Jr. Illustrated by Barry Root. New York: Harcourt Brace, 1993.
   This book usually shows up in independent bookstores around Halloween. The rich, full-page illustrations support a rhythmic, playful, predictable text that is loaded with common, everyday vocabulary needed by adult and child alike. I have used it as a readers theatre story for a large group and have seen new readers connect with it in one-on-one tutoring, too. Suspense is built as the broom and flickering candle fill the air with smoke and strange noises.

175. *One Fine Day*. Nonny Hogrogian. New York: Aladdin, 1971.
   It all begins when a fox is caught stealing and loses his tail. What will he do to get it back? This predictable text will lead the reader all over the countryside before revealing the answer. Adults and children love this book. The pictures are supportive enough that a new reader can hear it once and then read it to others.

176. *The Polar Express*. Chris Van Allsburg. Boston: Houghton Mifflin, 1985.
   The rich, full-page illustrations are almost a story in themselves, but the strange little bell left by a spirit makes for a lot of dialogue. Though this book is usually around at Christmas time, it makes wonderful reading any time of year. Sometimes it is packaged with a cassette-taped version.

177. *Stories to Solve, Folktales from Around the World*. George Shannon. Illustrated by Peter Sis. New York: Beech Tree, 1985.
   Fourteen tales of wit and mystery are presented in a three-page format. The first page has the story riddle. The second has the solution. The third has an illustration of the solution. These are fun, fast reads.

178.   *This Is the House That Crack Built.* Clark Taylor. Illustrated by Jan Thompson Dicks. San Francisco: Chronicle Books, 1992.

Using the rhythm and meter of the traditional children's rhyme "This is the house that Jack built," this richly illustrated little book tells the story of cocaine— from drug baron to the innocent crack baby born to the addicted mother. At first the story seems easy enough, then the momentum builds. I used to reserve this for adults only. No more. Every reading program should have a copy.

179.   *The Three Little Wolves and the Big Bad Pig.* Eugene Trivizas and Helen Oxenbury. New York: Scholastic, 1993.

This funny turnabout might be quite a downer if the pig, who terrorized the sweet little wolves, did not suddenly experience a change of heart.

180.   *Two-Minute Mysteries.* Donald J. Sobol. New York: Scholastic, 1967.

These one-and-a-quarter page mysteries have the solutions printed upside down on the second page. Although some have clearly logical answers, others call for presumptions the reader may not be likely to make or "correct" grammar clues that are seldom heard in everyday conversation. Although some readers will enjoy the chase, most of these mysteries are better used in small groups or in a one-on-one discussion with the tutor. Occasionally, words are hyphenated at the end of the line, making reading and comprehension more difficult.

Between Picture Books and Thin Books

The following trilogy leads the reader into a mysterious world of intrigue, beauty, drama, and suspense. They are pop-up books for grown-ups.

181.   *The Golden Mean, in Which the Extraordinary Correspondence of Griffin & Sabine Concludes.* Nick Bantock. San Francisco: Chronicle Books, 1993.

The last of the trilogy, this book also has exquisitely decorated postcards, envelopes, and writing paper. It also provides a sense of informal writing, as the typed parts have hand-corrected typos here and there. The mystery of this unusual pair of correspondents compels the reader ahead through vocabulary that would never show up in an elementary workbook but would certainly be useful to the adult new reader or writer. Deputation, do-gooders, busybodies, orchestrated, cronies, and precise are all found in the short first paragraph of the letter Griffin wrote to Sabine on September 18. Par Avion, Air Mail, Special Delivery, Japan Air Lines, Carte Postale, Via Aerea, Per Luchtpost, and Amnesty are offered as part of the mail-opening process. Consider the impact of discovering words from your native land in a beautiful book.

182.   *Griffin & Sabine: An Extraordinary Correspondence.* Nick Bantock. San Francisco: Chronicle Books, 1991.

As an art piece alone, this book is a wonder to behold. The haunting correspondence between two artists is made more disturbing by the fact that one of them does not know who the other is. Letters and postcards from around the world are laid bare for the reader who dares to enter this surreal world. I have had students who had no expressed interest in correspondence suddenly start writing letters after experiencing this book. Art and psychology units should include this book, but the trilogy also offers an adventuresome way of entering world geography.

183. *Sabine's Notebook, in Which the Extraordinary Correspondence of Griffin & Sabine Continues*. Nick Bantock. San Francisco: Chronicle Books, 1992.

Exotic envelope, stationery, and stamp designs, supplemented by random sketches along the margins, make this book as visually enticing as the first of the series. Meanwhile, the envelopes offer vocabulary words like confidential, personal, express, proof, special, and checked.

Thin Books

184. *The Curse of King Tut's Tomb: A History Mystery*. Jay Montavon. New York: Avon Books, 1991.

A timeline from 4241 B.C. to A.D. 1939, floor plans of the tomb and burial chamber, historical photographs of the ill-fated boy king and his equally ill-fated exhumer, and well-written history with speculation about the macabre coincidences—too many of them—combine to make this small book a compelling read. This History Mystery is part of a series of true stories that have kept my adult new readers and ESL students rapt. They also make great read alouds.

185. *Encyclopedia Brown, Boy Detective*. Donald J. Sobol. Illustrated by Leonard Shortall. New York: Bantam Books, 1963.

Boy wonder Encyclopedia Brown has exceptional observational skills and is able to solve mysteries just by paying attention. Each of the ten stories in this volume is just a few pages long, and, in most cases, the reader must follow directions to locate the page where the solution to the mystery is spelled out. These mysteries are good brain twisters, the language is clear and modern, and the search for the crime solution offers a chance to get useful instructions in the process. There is a series of these books, so if a person enjoys the style, refills are available. They may also serve as a precursor to Sir Arthur Conan Doyle's Sherlock Holmes mysteries. They make good SSR or lunch break reading.

186. *Even More Tales for the Midnight Hour*. J. B. Stamper. New York: Scholastic, 1991.

Each of these thirteen stories of horror is around ten pages. There are no pictures to support comprehension, and the vocabulary could not be called simple. But the stories are good.

187. *Figs and Phantoms*. Ellen Raskin. New York: Scholastic, 1974. 1975 Newbery Honor Book.

This is fine writing, with high interest, and contains enough daily readings to get the new reader through a couple of weeks of leisure reading times—or more.

188. *The Giver*. Lois Lowry. New York: Houghton Mifflin, 1993. 1994 Newbery Medal Award.

In clear, everyday English, Lowry unfolds a strange tale of a controlled society that has no access to literature and no right to critical thinking. Only one person in the community is permitted knowledge of a time when the weather was not the same and skin colors were different. Genetic engineering and daily doses of drugs prevent nearly everyone from stepping over the line that causes them to be "released." This intriguing story, focusing on one young boy, promises hours of leisure reading and thought-provoking dialogues.

189.   *Harry Houdini, Master of Magic.* Robert Kraske. New York: Scholastic, 1973.
      The intriguing, true story of a master escape artist is told in simple language with easy-to-understand dialogue. Occasional historical pictures are included. How he accomplished the amazing feats he performed for thirty-three years remains a mystery.

190.   *Lives of the Writers: Comedies, Tragedies (and What the Neighbors Thought).* Kathleen Krull. Illustrated by Kathryn Hewitt. San Diego, CA: Harcourt Brace, 1994.
      Certainly Poe is an easy choice here. Not all the characters in this book had horror-filled lives, but it is difficult to get along in the creative world without a good deal of suspense and drama. Murasaki Shikibu, Miguel de Cervantes, William Shakespeare, Jane Austen, Hans Christian Andersen, Edgar Allan Poe, Charles Dickens, Charlotte Brontë and Emily Brontë, Emily Dickinson, Louisa May Alcott, Mark Twain, Frances Hodgson Burnett, Robert Louis Stevenson, Jack London, Carl Sandburg, E. B. White, Zora Neale Hurston, Langston Hughes, and Isaac Bashevis Singer are summarized first in a Hewitt cartoon and then demographically described by Krull. After that a fun-filled or tragedy-torn tale of survival as a creative being is told in two and a half or so pages. This is excellent SSR fare for the new reader who has entered the Thin Books. "Bookmarks" give further details that Krull thinks you might enjoy. Readers might read one each day for SSR and learn everything they ever wanted to know about these folks. But Krull takes no chances. After a page of "Literary Terms" and an "Index of Writers," the last page offers "For Further Reading . . . and Writing." Consider using these stories to develop mysteries about famous figures. Start with things you did not find here and start listing questions. Also see entry 223 under "Strong Passages" below.

191.   "Lonna and Cat Woman." *Her Stories, African American Folktales, Fairy Tales, and True Tales.* Told by Virginia Hamilton. Illustrated by Leo Dillon and Diane Dillon. New York: Blue Sky Press, 1995. 1995 Laura Ingalls Wilder Award.
      A love triangle is complicated by a she-vampire, a violent, tantrum-throwing she-vampire, who attracts the police. And if you want to know the rest you have to read the story. A full description of this book of historic tales is in Unit 3, entry 147.

192.   *Lost Star: The Story of Amelia Earhart.* Patricia Lauber. New York: Scholastic, 1988.
      This is the incredible story of a woman who always seemed to have a philosophical response to what others might view as adversity. A read-aloud passage begins on page 16, as Amelia "Meely" headed for a school poetry reciting contest. Along the way, she stopped to visit a horse she sometimes rode and discovered it unfed and without water. Disregarding her dress and school schedule, she missed the contest to care for the horse. "But, she told her favorite teacher later, she didn't mind. She was glad to know the poem and had fun learning it.

That was what counted, not the prize," page 17. This notion of learning for learning's sake may prove an inspiration to those who are discouraged by test scores and other extrinsic rewards. Eventually, Earhart became an enthusiastic pilot, determined to do what had never been done before. In the process, she vanished from the face of the Earth. Historical photographs accompany this well-told tale. Pages 100–102 offer a mythological passage, telling of the naming of the plane and the odd coincidence that the star known as Amelia was lost, just as the namesake was. It was a toss-up for me whether to go Thin Books or Challenging on this one. Many of my students have become intrigued with this story. There are a number of books on Amelia Earhart, each with slightly different details, so a person might want to read a variety of titles on the subject.

193. *More Scary Stories to Tell in the Dark.* Collected from folklore and retold by Alvin Schwartz. Drawings by Stephen Gammell. New York: J. B. Lippincott, 1984.

This book and several others by Schwartz show up in bookstores around Halloween each year. In one-and-a-half to three pages, an eerie tale unfolds to trouble students' SSR time. There are twenty-eight tales. Starting on page 83 are author's notes, giving more detail about the phenomena in the book.

194. *More Stories to Solve: Fifteen Folktales from Around the World.* Told by George Shannon. Illustrated by Peter Sis. New York: Greenwillow Books, 1994.

Here is a new twist on problem solving. In about two pages and three illustrations, a puzzling human event is presented. On the next page comes "How it was done," in which the solution to the puzzle is told. At the end of the book are the author's notes on where he first encountered each tale. This story hunt makes an entertaining read in itself.

195. *Mummies and Their Mysteries.* Charlotte Wilcox. New York: Scholastic, 1993.

At the start of the book is a metric conversion table. At the back is a helpful glossary. In between, a world tour by mummy finds awaits— Egypt, Peru, the Far East. Old mummies and new are discussed and their photographs shown for close inspection. Some mummies are bundled up, some gift-wrapped, others just lost and then found. All have tales to tell about their times, lives, and deaths.

196. *The Mystery of Chimney Rock, Choose Your Own Adventure #5.* Edward Packard. Illustrated by Paul Granger. New York: Bantam Books, 1979. 121 pages—but not consecutive!

"You're the hero of the story! Choose from 40 possible endings" are the instructions on the front cover. Instructions at the bottom of each page tell you to go on to the next page or decide about going to page X or page Y, depending on what you, as the lead character, would do. Easy-to-follow, everyday dialogue and prose are supported by clear ink illustrations every two or three pages. Though the books were originally written for young teens, I have found many adults enjoy the game of "surviving" these plots. And, yes, if you like one, there are many, many more.

197. *The Mystery of Pony Hollow.* Lynn Hall. Illustrated by Ruth Sanderson. Champaign, IL: Carrard, 1987.

There is something powerful between a girl and her horse. It cannot be put into words, not even by the pragmatic young heroine of this story. Panda is occupying the same stall as did the lead male Oberon, imported from Ireland forty years earlier. Sarah discovers a mysterious connection between her own horse, the one who first occupied their common stall, and an old man brought to look after the ponies of the ranch. The name of the colt, strange noises from a long-shut hut, and an old groom moving in and out of consciousness make this story at once believable and incredible. Though the primary character is young, I cannot imagine an adult putting this story down once the reading is begun. At first blush, this looks like a stock youth mystery. It is not. It is a mystery and ghost story with a twist of the macabre, offering strange options to a crime of passion between trainer and horse forty years before.

198. *Scary Stories to Tell in the Dark.* Collected from folklore and retold by Alvin Schwartz. Drawings by Stephen Gammell. New York: Scholastic, 1981.
    This collection features short stories—about two pages each—making it an excellent SSR or lunch hour item. It almost qualifies as a First Reader and is a great read aloud for those few minutes at the start or end of a lesson or when things have gotten a little boring.

199. *The Secret Is Out: True Spy Stories.* Teri Martini. Illustrated by Leslie Morrill. New York: Avon Books, 1990.
    These short, true stories are each about ten pages long, including a couple of illustrations. They are good reading.

200. *Stonewords: A Ghost Story.* Pam Conrad. New York: Scholastic, 1990.
    Here is a nice, chilly read with generally common vocabulary.

201. *Who Dunnit? How to Be a Detective in Ten Easy Lessons.* Marvin Miller. New York: Scholastic, 1991.
    There is a new unit every two pages, making this a good SSR choice. Page 8 shows how to set up a ruler code. And pages 42–43 show how to set up codes using the push buttons on the phone pad. On page 44, learn how to convert a watch into a compass. The skills needed for solving crimes range from using rulers to solving puzzles to analyzing handwriting.

202. *Who Shot the President? The Death of John F. Kennedy.* Judy Donnelly. New York: Random House, 1988.
    When I first took this book into my entry-level ESL class, I did not think the cover would attract enough attention to get it picked up. It was borrowed, read, reborrowed, passed around the class, and finally was completely falling apart, carried in and out in a plastic bag. This true mystery story, delivered in simple language and printed in a large typeface, has proven one of my all-time most popular books for all levels of ESL and literacy.

203. *A Woman's Place.* Linda Grant. New York: Charles Scribner's Sons, 1994.
    It is a compellingly written, modern adventure about sexual harassment in the computerized workplace. The heroine, Catherine Sayler, is a private eye who risks her own life to uncover a multitude of crimes, including murder. The

language is tough-minded, almost a tongue-in-cheek mockery of the old guard whodunits, but the vocabulary and dialogues and first-travel reports make this so easy to follow, I've put it in the "Thin Books," though it's more than 200 pages.

204. *The World's Most Famous Ghosts*. Daniel Cohen. New York: Minstrel Books, 1989.

Every couple of pages there is a full-page photo or a collection of photos and illustrations to help set the mood. Though the language is not Challenging, it contains a wide assortment of content-laden words like seance, psychic, and assassin. These ten ghost tales are good read-aloud stories or SSR offerings.

205. *You Be the Jury: Courtroom IV*. Marvin Miller. New York: Scholastic, 1991.

Reading this book requires problem-solving skills as readers decide which clues to accept and which pages to turn to next. Then they turn the book upside down to get answers. Fingerprint analysis, water flow study, counterfeit versus genuine dollar bill recognition, map study, and invoice reconciliation are just a few of the skills needed to get to the bottom of the crime. There are good illustrations throughout, but this is not a simple read. Some of my students love the challenge, and others think it is a frustrating puzzle.

Challenging

206. *Buried in Ice: The Mystery of a Lost Arctic Expedition*. Owen Beattie and John Geiger. New York: Scholastic, 1994.

A chronology of the search for the Northwest Passage begins in 1508 and moves through the centuries until an expedition out from 1903 to 1906 completes the passage by boat. A 1984–1986 expedition discovers the remains of the 1848 Franklin Party, theretofore missing. It seems "lead poisoning from food tins played a role in the expedition's disastrous end." Each chapter is supported by historical photos, paintings, illustrations, and artifacts. The high-level text is well written. A glossary at the end is most intriguing.

207. *Into the Mummy's Tomb: The Real-Life Discovery of Tutankhamun's Treasures*. Nicholas Reeves. New York: Scholastic, 1992.

Though the photographs of the art, expeditions, and mummies are exquisite and informing, the graphics are detailed and clear, and the organization of this Thin Book is logical and easy to follow, I have put it under "Challenging" because the language is just that. However, there is a well-done glossary, and the picture captions are relatively easy to follow. This book has history, adventure, science, and even an instruction page on how mummies were made. It is loaded with facts and makes a great conversation starter.

208. *Jurassic Park*. Michael Crichton. New York: Ballantine Books, 1993.

This is science fiction, well-researched science fiction, with loads of thought-provoking insights into old questions about dinosaurs and modern ones about DNA. It would be a great read aloud for any language arts setting.

209. *A Murder Is Announced*. Agatha Christie. New York: Berkley, 1978.

It is an invitation to a murder, an open invitation in the personal column of the *Gazette* that proves irresistible to everybody who is curious or has nothing much to do on Friday, October 29—that means everyone who's anyone. So it is a mischievous game for the entire community at Little Paddocks—until the lights go out. This is not a simple murder mystery. Nor is it simple reading. But for the person attracted to puzzles, intrigue, and problem solving, Miss Marple offers many entertaining moments.

210. *The Pearl.* John Steinbeck. New York: Bantam Books, 1947.
    A read-aloud passage starts on page 112: "It was an old and ragged moon, but it threw hard light and hard shadow into the mountain cleft, and now Kino could see the seated figure of the watcher on the little beach beside the pool." The passage continues to build a tense, suspense-filled game between Kino, who owned the Pearl of the World, and the men who would kill anyone to get it. The passage ends on page 115: "And then Kino stood uncertainly. Something was wrong. . . . Tree frogs and cicadas were silent now . . . and he knew the sound—the keening, moaning, rising hysterical cry from the little cave in the side of the stone mountain, the cry of death." Steinbeck's beautifully written descriptions are complemented by his simple, straightforward use of words. Students who would not be expected to understand this level of prose have become avid readers when introduced to *The Pearl*.

211. *Spies of the Revolution.* Katherine Bakeless and John Bakeless. New York: Scholastic, 1962.
    Strange messages, codes, and surreptitious goings-on filled the days of the Colonies' revolution against England. Here are the details of the Boston Tea Party and other lesser-known events. Consider the simple mapmaker: "As it was Sunday, the two disguised officers dared not leave their lodging. Anyone walking the streets during church services was likely to be arrested. The two men kept out of sight till sunset, the end of the Puritan Sabbath. After that, secure in the early February dusk, they walked freely about the town, seeing what they could see. Then they went out on the hills sketching, and returned safely to their lodging. It was presumably one or the other of these two spies who made the plans for a camp and fortifications on Chandler's Hill, outside Worcester. The plans were found later after the British evacuated Boston" (page 13). This is not easy reading, but the stories offer rich entertainment and call to be read again and again.

212. *The Strange Case of Dr. Jekyll and Mr. Hyde.* Robert Louis Stevenson, unabridged. Mineola, NY: Dover, 1991.
    Mystery, suspense, drama, and romance make this timeless tale as good a read as it was when written in 1885. Stevenson's straightforward writing style lets the student of English and the new reader navigate a classic with ease.

Challenging Short Story Collections

213. *As War with Germany Threatens, Sherlock Holmes Takes the Stage for His Last Bow.* Sir Arthur Conan Doyle. London: Penguin Books, 1981.
    The work of mastermind Holmes is recorded in the journal of his dear friend and colleague in crime intrigue, Dr. Watson. If you do not find this Holmes, find another one. The words written in the first half of the twentieth century remain testimony to the power of intense research and careful observation. The master

detective knows something about everything and picks up clues from the most common and remote corners. The vocabulary in these mysteries is Challenging. Though skipping and guessing will work much of the time, little by little, the words that readers skip become their own.

214. *Creepy Classics: Hair-Raising Horror from the Masters of the Macabre.* Edited by Mary Hill. Illustrated by Dominick R. Domingo. New York: Random House, 1994.

Dramatic charcoal illustrations and a glossary help readers through words such as sepulcher, which may not be in the 1990s vocabulary, and aid comprehension of these timeless tales. Each selection is prefaced by a brief historical statement, a biography of the author, and an introduction to the circumstances under which the tale first came to light. W. W. Jacobs, Saki, Robert W. Service, Guy de Maupassant, M. R. James, William Shakespeare, Bram Stoker, Edgar Allan Poe, Sir Arthur Conan Doyle, and Mary Shelley are showcased here. This is a fine introduction to many fine authors through a brief encounter. With any luck, the reader will find one or two that rate further pursuit. Meanwhile, these tales offer short passages that can fill the minutes between this and that—and then keep your mind off everything else for hours. Artists will enjoy the illustrations that maximize the power of black and white, casting dark shadows, reflecting underlighting, and shocking the eyes with sudden contrast.

215. *The Dark Way: Stories from the Spirit World.* Told by Virginia Hamilton. Illustrated by Lambert Davis. San Diego, CA: Harcourt Brace Jovanovich, 1990.

Twenty-five eerie tales with illustrations that help build terror in the reader's soul are followed by historical notes on the legends' origins. Hamilton makes no attempt at simplifying her text. Her vocabulary is Challenging and her style compelling. These stories are read alouds that will teach writing style to the listeners.

216. *Famous Tales of Mystery and Horror.* Edgar Allan Poe. Mahwah, NJ: Troll, 1980.

Horror and intrigue are the trademarks of this author's work, and here are five of his famous stories to trouble sleep. The text is Challenging and full of innuendo. Some of my adult ESL students have found Poe an avenue into the world of leisure reading.

217. *Great Short Works of Joseph Conrad.* Joseph Conrad. New York: Harper & Row, 1967.

This volume contains seven stories and a biography of Conrad. The power of Conrad's writing comes, in part, from honest storytelling. His descriptions and the emotional reactions and attitudes of his characters convey real people. Even so, the stories in this collection are by no means easy reading. It is the content that drives the reader on. One good way to ruin a Conrad story is to demand a report on it or a reaction paper. One way to work with the text is to let a self-selected group of readers meet to reflect on the passages they find memorable.

218. *Great Short Works of Mark Twain.* Mark Twain. New York: HarperCollins, 1967.

Twenty witty stories offer a month of good reads for coffee breaks.

219. *The Life of Sir Arthur Conan Doyle.* John Dickson Carr. New York: Carroll & Graf, 1976.

This story is as entertaining as the life of Sherlock Holmes as reported by Dr. Watson. A devout spiritualist, Doyle believed that one might communicate with the dead.

220. *The Raven and Other Poems.* Edgar Allan Poe. New York: Scholastic, 1992.

Classic Poe in an easy-to-carry-to-lunch paperback is guaranteed to upset any meal and make one late getting back.

221. *Stories by O. Henry.* O. Henry. New York: Tom Doherty, 1988.

Here is the master of surprise endings. O. Henry's stories enchanted thousands across America when he first began running these serially. Now you need not wait at all. Just leap from one good read to the next. However, O. Henry's language is not simple. This collection should be offered to the high-level ESL or relatively advanced reader. The alternative, of course, is to read these stories aloud, allowing time to discuss language and plot, before unveiling the ending.

Book Chapters and Strong Passages

222. "The Bloody Tower." In *The World's Most Famous Ghosts.* Daniel Cohen. New York: Minstrel Books, 1989, pages 16–28.

This is the tale of a whole collection of folks who died in the infamous Tower of London. This book is on the Thin Books level.

223. "Edgar Allan Poe." In *Lives of the Writers: Comedies, Tragedies (and What the Neighbors Thought).* Kathleen Krull. Illustrated by Kathryn Hewitt. San Diego, CA: Harcourt Brace, 1994, pages 32–37.

This is excellent SSR fare for the new reader who has begun reading Thin Books. More detail is under "Thin Books," entry 190.

224. "George Kaufman: Keeping Fit." In *Eccentrics.* Henry Billings and Melissa Billings. Providence, RI: Jamestown, 1987, pages 36–38.

This story tells of a man who was a successful writer in spite of what might have been a disabling terror of germs. *Eccentrics* features twenty-one stories about eccentric people.

225. *Ghosts, Hauntings and Mysterious Happenings.* Phyllis Raybin Emert. Illustrated by Jael. New York: Tom Doherty, 1990.

There are twenty-seven spell-binding stories of the unexplained in this easy-to-carry little book. ESP, dousing, premonitions, and ghostly sightings, all reportedly true, offer the reader a full story in five to fifteen minutes. The vocabulary is not simple, but the writing is direct and easy to follow.

226. "Heart of Darkness." In *Great Short Works of Joseph Conrad.* Joseph Conrad. New York: Harper & Row, 1967, pages 210–92.

This story is delivered primarily in simple, first-person testimony, in which one man relates details of a journey into the depths of his time. One Strong Passage about discarded slaves, left to die beneath the trees, begins on page 225 with "I avoided a vast artificial hole somebody had been digging on the slope" and ends on page 226 with a description of a dying man who seemed to the narrator less than human: "He lapped out of his hand, then sat up in the sunlight, crossing his shins in front of him, and after a time let his wooly head fall on his breast-bone."

227. "The Human Experiment." In *Aliens & UFOs*. John F. Warner and Margaret B. Warner. Providence, RI: Jamestown, 1984, pages 130–32.

The strange phenomenon of "missing time" is just one thing members of the Davis family have in common with others who have encountered UFOs.

228. "Judicial: Legislation and Litigation." In *The Guinness Book of World Records 1995*. New York: Bantam Books, pages 435–38.

This section begins with the "Most inexplicable legislation," which is a passage in Scottish infamy. It is heartening to note that Americans are not the only ones who can write English beyond comprehension. More interesting may be a brief accounting of the "Greatest mass arrest," 15,617 to be exact, which took place in 1988 with a group of demonstrators at the Korean Olympic Games in Seoul. The extremes of wills, wrongful arrests, alimony and divorce suits, and trial attendances are covered in short passages here. The next section, "Crime," pages 438–45, covers assassinations, murders, lynchings, poisonings, thefts, kidnappings, bank frauds, maritime frauds, and even the last public hanging. This is high-interest, low-stress material, perfect for leisure reading time.

229. "Justice and Injustice." In *I Want to Tell You: My Response to Your Letters, Your Messages, Your Questions.* O. J. Simpson. Boston: Little, Brown, 1995, pages 85–99.

The title describes most of the content of this easy reader with photographs. Anyone intrigued by the trial, the murders, or the reactions of people of all ages to this very public event will find something to read in this book. The letters and Simpson's responses are written in easy-to-read language. The mystery and trial enthusiast is sure to have a great deal of background knowledge to support comprehension of this book. Of particular interest is this chapter, but the entire book may become part of the "record" for the reader.

230. "The Killer Bees Are Coming!" In *Phenomena*. Henry Billings and Melissa Billings. Providence, RI: Jamestown, 1984, pages 24–26.

Here is a phenomenon that has been increasingly on our minds for several years now.

231. "Lincoln's Ghost." In *The World's Most Famous Ghosts*. Daniel Cohen. New York: Minstrel Books, 1989, pages 1–15.

President Lincoln's is not the only ghost haunting the halls of the White House. This story gets progressively stranger with each page.

232. *Mysteries of People and Places*. Phyllis Raybin Emert. Illustrated by Jael. New York: Tom Doherty, 1990.

Tales about Egyptian pyramids, Stonehenge, and the Bermuda Triangle are among the two- to four-page stories from around the globe found in this collection. An eerie illustration accompanies each tale. The type is fairly small and so is the book.

233. "The Pied Piper of Hamelin: A Child's Story." Written for and inscribed to W. M. the Younger, by Robert Browning. In *The Complete Works of Robert Browning, with Variant Readings & Annotations*, vol. III. General editor Roma A. King, Jr. Athens: Ohio University Press, 1971, pages 249–59, editors' notes pages 384–86.

This long poem is written in rhyme and is fun to read aloud. It is under the Challenging heading because it is quite long for a poem and uses many archaic words and phrases that could trip the ESL student or new reader. But the footnotes at the bottom of each page make finding definitions easy, and it is possible to just skip along reading without looking up anything and get a nice, bouncy, though depressing story. The editors' notes offer scholarly information in plain English. For example, there is debate over what Browning's source for this old tale was. It also gives July 22, 1376, as the date of the actual incident. And the notes explain that this poem was written for a sick child who loved to draw, so Browning requested that the youngster illustrate it for him. The editors also suggest what might have led to the disappearance of the children in the mountain. Consider having students speculate on the actual events and come up with solutions to the disappearance.

234. *The Raven and Other Poems*. Edgar Allan Poe. New York: Scholastic, 1992.

These are the famous, macabre, and lamenting works of a master storyteller. Any one of these selections would make a great read-aloud introduction to this unit or an inspiration boost to those grappling with the task of writing about the unthinkable realities of life. Poe's inspiration, after all, came from his most unhappy experiences.

235. *Ripley's Believe It or Not! Strange Coincidences*. New York: Tom Doherty, 1990.

Believe it or not, in 1990, at a double wedding in Patan, India, the brides had such heavy veils they were married to the wrong men—and the village elders declared final the matches made in error. This and many other adult topics are covered in this quite portable, thoroughly illustrated, SSR book.

236. *Ripley's Believe It or Not! Weird Inventions and Discoveries*. New York: Tom Doherty, 1990.

Believe it or not, this little paperback has one to three inventions per page! Did you know the first passenger elevator was lowered and raised by hand? The first picture of a bicycle appeared with an angel riding it in a stained-glass window—200 years before the invention of the bicycle? Living in Taiwan is a 6,000-year-old cypress tree? The idea of the safety pin was sold for only $400? There are even more surprises in this great trivia collection. The print is quite large for most, not all, and there are illustrations for everything.

237. *Stranger Than Fiction: Weird Stories and Ghostly Happenings*. Martin Walsh. New York: Scholastic, 1979.

Bigfoot, the Loch Ness monster, and Lincoln's dreams become reality in these eight- to ten-page tales. This is great read-aloud fare.

238. "The Triangle of Fear." In *Phenomena*. Henry Billings and Melissa Billings. Providence, RI: Jamestown, 1984, pages 48–50.

Mysterious disappearances and crashes in the sea just southwest of the tip of Florida have baffled scientists for many years. A map of the infamous Bermuda Triangle is on page 48.

239. *UFO Encounters.* Rita Golden Gelman and Marcia Seligson. New York: Scholastic, 1978.
A mix of fact and rumor, each chapter is a good read for the UFO enthusiast—and the skeptic. The text is straightforward but well laced with high-level words. Photographs and diagrams show up intermittently, not unlike the topic of discussion. Intermediate ESL and new readers at the Thin Books level will enjoy this during SSR.

240. "Voodoo Magic." In *Phenomena.* Henry Billings and Melissa Billings. Providence, RI: Jamestown, 1984, pages 30–32.
For the people who believe in voodoo, there are psychological explanations of how mind over matter can be hazardous to your health. Yet this short story goes beyond the scientifically explainable.

241. "The Wild Boy of Aveyron." In *Phenomena.* Henry Billings and Melissa Billings. Providence, RI: Jamestown, 1984, pages 18–20.
"He was found digging for vegetables in the garden of a tanner who lived near Aveyron, in southern France." *Phenomena* has high-interest short passages for adults. I have used it successfully with ESL and adult new readers. My only complaint is that often more text space is devoted to tests and skill activities than to the good reads the authors have proven they can write. This softcover booklet has twenty-one stories about incredible phenomena.

242. *Witness to an Era: The Life and Photographs of Alexander Gardner: The Civil War, Lincoln, and the West.* D. Mark Katz. New York: Viking, 1991.
This oversized picture book is an extraordinary portrait of an artist's life. Gardner documented the Civil War, made numerous photographs of President Abraham Lincoln, and photographed the conspirators to Lincoln's assassination as well. Pictures of all of these are in the book. The photograph of young Private William Johnson (June 20, 1864) dangling from the gallows and the accompanying text on page 76 tell of extreme punishment used against a black man who attempts to "commit an outrage on a white woman. Considerable importance was given to the affair, in order that the example might be made more effective. Johnson confessed his guilt, and was executed . . . in plain view of the enemy." There are also reproductions of handwritten documents, complete with scratch-outs and editing, of the Civil War era. The running commentary and captions make this part of American history more real than does any other picture book I have seen. And the issues of battlefield agony, racism, slavery, intrigue, crime, and punishment are brought to the fore. This is an excellent book just for page-turning dialogue. It is also well written.

243. "The Year Without a Summer." In *Phenomena.* Henry Billings and Melissa Billings. Providence, RI: Jamestown, 1984, pages 10–11.
Extraordinary weather conditions like those experienced in 1816 have not been documented before or since.

Newspaper and Magazine Articles

244. "Case History." Jim Newton. *Los Angeles Times Magazine.* June 27, 1993, pages 10–14, 34–35.

The Rodney King story had many side events that made for great suspense. There was a trial for the officers who had committed the beating that was captured on video. Then another. At every stage of the game there were conflicts, polarization, and, in Los Angeles, the constant threat of another riot. "Seven A.M. Saturday morning, April 17, Judge Davies conceded, was 'an unusual time to convene a court session.' But there had never been a session quite like this one. Fear set the schedule. Police and sheriff's deputies were on full alert, National Guard troops were in their armories, federal agents ready to deploy" (page 35). Here is a fast-paced, compellingly written, real-life suspense drama. The language is neither simple nor pretentious. It would make a great teacher read aloud and class discussion. Consider the impact of small groups taking different sides and generating questions—for the police and for the victim. Groups could represent the police, the victim, the victim's family, the man with the video camera, a victim of a drunken driver, and a victim of a high-speed chase.

245. "Hidden Monsters." Karen Ehrlich and Lee Speigel. Painting by De Es Schwertberger. *Omni,* January 1983, pages 108–13, 120.

Bigfoot, lake monsters, including Nessie of Loch Ness, and other strange creatures of the planet are the subjects of this true-life treasure hunt report. *Omni* magazine is always Challenging vocabulary, but the subject matter is high interest and the writing is top quality.

246. "The Mystery of the Lost Patrol: This Time, the Bermuda Triangle Gives One Back." Tom Post with Spencer Reiss. *Newsweek,* May 27, 1991, page 25.

"It was vintage Twilight Zone," opens the story of a plane discovered under 700 to 900 feet of water off the coast of Florida. While searching for more traditional treasure—Spanish galleons—a salvage team spotted what appeared to be the remains of vanished Flight 19. Even so, the evidence is not conclusive and some of the details do not quite match up.

247. "Teddy: The Power, Not the Glory: Presidential Hopes Drowned on a Dark Night in Chappaquiddick." In "The Kennedy Scandals," *Globe Special.* Edited by Michael J. Irish, 1991, pages 28–32.

One of the most publicized deaths of recent decades came in 1969, when Mary Jo Kopechne, 29-year-old secretary to powerful U.S. Sen. Ted Kennedy, was discovered drowned in his car in the shallow waters near Dike Bridge in Massachusetts. No autopsy was ever allowed, and Kennedy waited nine hours to report the accident. Questions about this incident dashed all hopes of a try for the presidency and continue to surface as the story ferments.

Other Events and Supplements

For a readers theatre event, consider a mock trial. First write the script as a class. Then read the parts. Or if you are working one-on-one, how about writing an interview between reporter and witness, mother of the accused and a radio host, or prosecutor and victim. Readers theatre is an excellent way to reinforce content and language skills in a low-stress format. It does not require any special props or costuming, though they can certainly be present. See the introduction on p. xxvii for general instructions on readers theatre.

Teachers may want to suggest any of the following as student activities:

- Write to mystery authors for more information or just to say thanks.
- Write to historical locations where unusual events occurred for more information.
- Look for articles on local mysteries in newspapers and magazines.
- Draw pictures of mysterious locations and write captions.
- Collect posters of local or national mysteries and exhibit them.
- Collect maps of crime scenes or historical mystery sites.
- Collect clues from a local crime scene and write stories about the clues.

Letters, Logs, and Journals

Unit 5

There are many published examples of personal correspondence and journal keeping, offering us a chance to look right over someone's shoulder and into his or her personal life. It is intriguing. And it provides comprehensible input on a variety of topics. As adults read, they are discovering form and format that will transfer back to their writing. This genre also shows how the writer solves certain problems that do not occur in other forms. For example, correspondence between two people builds on the background knowledge each has, based on prior communication or experience. They can say more with less than they could in, say, an essay.

Though several of the books cited in this unit could be delightful read alouds, with the exception of the few short passages identified below, I suggest using contemporary letters for the read-aloud part of this unit. For example, if last week you read aloud a newspaper article on a controversial issue, there may be a letter to the editor that is equally sensational this week. Read that letter aloud and discuss it.

First Readers and Picture Books

248.   *The Armadillo from Amarillo.* Lynne Cherry. San Diego, CA: Harcourt Brace Jovanovich, 1994. Printed with environmentally sensitive materials.

Inside the front cover is a map of Texas with postcards, suggesting the theme to come. Starting with a postcard written in Amarillo to his cousin in Philadelphia, Sasparillo, the armadillo from Amarillo, begins a trek that first opens to a breathtaking spread of San Antonio bluebonnets in full bloom. Having lived there and seen them, I can tell you that Cherry has transplanted the sensational gift of nature right inside this book. Postcards run tandem to rhyming text where, for several pages, the armadillo discovers the wonders of endangered species habitats and the vastly varying landscape of Texas. In search of a bird's-eye view, the armadillo hitches a ride on the back of an eagle, and the two eventually connect with a spacecraft that gives them a look at where we are and how we look from outer space. The real and whimsical join to make important statements about our relationships with this planet and the grand scheme of things. On the last page are interesting author's notes. Inside the back cover is a series of "photographs" of the places the adventurous armadillo has been. The postcard vehicle is a great one for writing short passages—summarizing big ideas and getting them down on paper. Here we graphically see that there is a wealth of information that supports the short passage on the postcard.

249.   *Dear Children of the Earth, A Letter from Home.* Schim Schimmel. Minocqua, WI: NorthWord Press, 1994.

Surrealistic paintings mix animals of land, sea, and air in brilliant illustrations of each passage of the letter from Mother Earth. It begins, "I am writing this letter to ask for your help. Do you know who I am? I am the planet, earth. But I am much more than just a planet. I am your Home." In gentle, powerful language the letter provokes thought about questions. "Tell me, my children where will the animals live when my forests are all gone? Where will the whales and dolphins swim when my oceans are too dirty to live in? And where will the birds fly when my sky is poisoned?" This is an open letter to all the children of the Earth about the fate of our home.

250. *The Jolly Postman, or Other People's Letters.* Janet Ahlberg and Allan Ahlberg. Boston: Little, Brown, 1986.

The Jolly Postman rides his bike though story land, delivering letters to and from the occupants of fairy tales that are old and familiar to the literate, English-speaking and -storytelling world. Each letter has its own envelope, allowing the reader to remove the contents for close inspection. This is a super chance to read a lot of other people's mail. The type comes in all sizes, mostly from large to extra large. A great deal of background knowledge is required for the reader to fully understand all of the implications in, for example, a letter to Mr. Wolf from the attorney representing Little Red Riding Hood on behalf of her grandmother. However, even to the unprepared, the postmarks, inserts, and clever, contemporary illustrations support comprehension as they entertain through this unusual format. As you'll see later in this section, this format is gaining in popularity. Obviously written for children, this is a gift book to be appreciated by every teacher of any level on your list.

251. *A Letter to Amy.* Ezra Jack Keats. New York: HarperCollins, 1968.

Colorful collage and acrylic illustrations lead the reader through pages of understanding that have only one or two lines of text each. This story of a little boy who wants his letter to be a surprise expresses strong emotion with few words.

252. *Letters from the Past.* Virginia Henkel. Illustrated by Bruce Luxford. Peton, New Zealand: Nelson Price Milburn, 1989.

Young Jessica discovers an old box of letters in her great-grandmother's attic. They reveal a correspondence between her great-grandmother Elly, who grew up in Wellington, New Zealand, and her pen pal, Grace, of London, England. Documenting personal and global events between December 1910 and June 27, 1912, these letters from the past offer high-interest reading, history, and geography connections through simple text.

253. *The Prince Who Wrote a Letter.* Ann Love. Illustrated by Toni Goffe. New York: Child's Play International, 1992.

This is not a book of letters, nor does it even have the kinds of letters this unit is about. Indeed, the prince in this book was being instructed in the old-fashioned parts-to-whole way that had him learning the letter "a" first, "b" second, and so on, instead of learning to write his most important word, Paul, first. Perhaps that explains the other out-of-date events that led from a simple statement to rumor to a near war between kingdoms. The surprise-ending story is lively, and the vocabulary includes exclaimed, school, hurried, pleased, opposite, something, sensible, secretly, eavesdrop, exactly, happened, kitchen, conversation, husband, alarmed, dungeon, seize, immediately, ruffian, battlements, muskets, particularly— well, you get the idea—this is not simplified language. But nestled in the heart of a funny, timeless theme, and supported by full-color illustrations that fill every page clear to the edge, this is comprehensible input. Read this once to your adult new reader, discussing it as you go, and that adult will be ready to take the book home to invest in family literacy. But, because it does not have a letter in it, you may still wonder why it is in this unit. This is a book *about* a letter—one that was misunderstood—one that nearly started a war—one that was never written.

254. *The War Began at Supper: Letters to Miss Loria*. Patricia Reilly Giff. Illustrated by Betsy Lewin. New York: Delacorte Press, 1991.

Miss Loria, a beloved student teacher who has moved away, is the addressee of most of the letters from the students in Mrs. Clark's elementary school class. Concerns about the Persian Gulf War manifest in many ways among the young writers, whose simple prose makes easy reading about difficult subjects. Even the new reader will be able to use this book during SSR. Each letter is short enough to allow completion of a unit during one sitting.

Thin Books

255. *Ann Landers Speaks Out*. Ann Landers. Greenwich, CT: Fawcett, 1975.

This collection of letters to and from one of America's favorite advice columnists provides high-interest, adult-level dialogue in short, easy-to-understand passages. There are books like this published every few years, and some libraries have collections of them. Used bookstores and swap meets also are good places to look for older editions. Comparing letters and responses with ten or twenty years between can open the floor to a lot of culture-specific dialogue. They are great for SSR, and some serve well as read-aloud attention getters, for many topics are addressed in Landers's work.

256. *Beethoven Lives Upstairs*. Barbara Nichol, Illustrated by Scott Cameron. New York: Orchard Books, 1993.

In a compelling exchange of letters, a young boy and his uncle discuss the public reputation and personal habits of the great musician who has moved into the home of a young widow and her three children. The balance of letters between adult and child, with an occasional note from the boy's mother, makes this an appropriate book for new readers of any age. The fictionalized story is based on historical facts that give insight not only into the genius of Beethoven, but also into the stresses of a hearing-impaired creative soul. The story might make good reading on its own; however, this book offers more—fine, emotionally charged oil paintings that illustrate the circumstances in young Christopher's house. This is a good easy reader. It almost passed as a picture book.

257. *The Best of Dear Abby*. Abigail Van Buren. Kansas City, MO: Andrews & McMeel, 1981.

Here is a collection of letters written to the newspaper lovelorn and life-problems specialist. She opens the book with a long autobiographical letter, telling how she and her identical twin sister, Ann Landers, grew up, entered the same profession, were estranged, and finally reconciled. It is a whirlwind accounting that is sure to prove interesting to twins of any age and to many people who are not getting along with their siblings—of any age. For this "Dear Readers" letter, the book is worth opening. After that comes advice to others. She does not give her responses in letter form but answers most collections of the same problem in general terms. The letters are, in most cases, short and easy to understand.

258. *Dear Mr. Henshaw*. Beverly Cleary. Illustrated by Paul O. Zelinsky. New York: Dell, 1983.

This book begins with a second-grader's one-line letter to his favorite author, and his response to the author's flip answer starts a long-term pen pal relationship between the two. Eventually, the boy uses his letter format to move into his own diary, documenting his life as the only child in an impoverished and eventually broken home. The straightforward, simple writing is believable, given the main character's age and experiences. Set in contemporary California, the day-to-day situations strike a chord with many new readers and provide basic language for ESL students.

259. *The Golden Mean, in Which the Extraordinary Correspondence of Griffin & Sabine Concludes*. Nick Bantock. San Francisco: Chronicle Books, 1993.

The last of the trilogy, this book also has exquisitely decorated postcards, envelopes, and writing paper. It provides a sense of informal writing, as the typed parts have hand-corrected typos here and there. The mystery of this unusual pair of correspondents compels the reader ahead through vocabulary that would never show up in an elementary workbook but would certainly be useful to the adult new reader or writer. Deputation, do-gooders, busybodies, orchestrated, cronies, and precise are all found in the short first paragraph of the letter Griffin wrote to Sabine on September 18. Par Avion, Air Mail, Special Delivery, Japan Air Lines, Carte Postale, Via Aerea, Per Luchtpost, and Amnesty are offered as part of the mail-opening process. Consider the impact of discovering words from your native land in a beautiful book.

260. *Griffin & Sabine: An Extraordinary Correspondence*. Nick Bantock. San Francisco: Chronicle Books, 1991.

Anyone who was able to digest *The Jolly Postman* (see entry 250) will consume *Griffin & Sabine*. As an art piece alone, this book is a wonder to behold. The haunting correspondence between two artists is made more disturbing by the fact that one of them does not know who the other is. Letters and postcards from around the world are laid bare for the reader who dares to enter this surreal world. I have had students who had no expressed interest in correspondence at all suddenly start writing letters after experiencing this book.

261. *I, Columbus: My Journal, 1492–1493*. Edited by Peter Roop and Connie Roop. Illustrated by Peter E. Hanson. New York: Avon Books, 1991.

A prologue gives a historical setting and some background on Columbus, how he came to be a seaman, his pitch to Queen Isabella and King Ferdinand on how profits from the trip that incidentally led to America would support their efforts to acquire Jerusalem, and his gratitude as he set sail on August 3, 1492, on an adventure beyond his own imaginings. Then his own prologue references India, the prince known as Great Khan, and Columbus's pledge to keep a log of his experience on the seas. The log itself is a translation made from Columbus's copy of the log he ultimately presented to Queen Isabella. Inside the front cover is a map of Columbus's voyage to the New World, though he never knew it as such, and inside the back cover is a map of his trek home. This is easy reading, filled with adventure and history. Columbus also spells out the day of the week and the month of the year, just as my students do in their own journals, though

Columbus places the number of the date before the name of the month, in the European style. This practice helps students learn to spell and write with ease the days and months in a meaningful process.

262. *I Want to Tell You: My Response to Your Letters, Your Messages, Your Questions.* O. J. Simpson. Boston: Little, Brown, 1995.
    The title describes most of the contents of this easy reader with photographs. Regardless of your stance on the crimes, the accused, or the need for so much press coverage, the fact is that this is a literacy-background-building epic with tremendous potential. It is almost impossible to find an American today who is not familiar with this subject. And the support materials are in every major magazine and newspaper. That means the teacher can readily find readings at all difficulty levels and may engage new readers in the search process. Anyone intrigued or annoyed by the trial, the murders, or the reactions of people of all ages to this public event will find something to read in this book.

263. *Letters from a Slave Girl: The Story of Harriet Jacobs.* Mary E. Lyons. New York: Charles Scribner's Sons, 1992.
    Inspired by the autobiographical letters published by the adult Harriet Jacobs, Lyons creates fictional letters to Jacobs's deceased mother, father, and other relatives to convey the historical events from 1825 to 1842 and the personal imaginings, triumphs, and tragedies of a slave girl who grows up as she strives to gain her freedom. This fictionalized biography is based on true events from the life of Harriet Jacobs. The final section, "Harriet: The Rest of Her Story," takes us from 1842 to 1852 in a narrative of the freedom fighter's life. The black Southern dialect of the slave girl begins to show the influence of white mistresses with whom she has extended contact. Jacobs was taught to read but learned writing on her own initiative. It is presumed that she used discarded account books for writing paper during this period when handmade paper was expensive and slaves were forbidden by law to read or write. This book is a powerful telling of one woman's experience as a slave. Gender issues, human rights, civil rights, and the Civil War are addressed through this first-person accounting of suffering, courage, and hope.

264. *Letters from the Inside.* John Marsden. Sydney, Australia: PAN, 1991.
    This is a chilling series of letters between two teenage girls, one on the "outside" and one incarcerated for a crime the nature of which isn't immediately revealed. Anyone who has ever been imprisoned or who has a loved one in prison will connect with this story. There are no pictures, the type is not large, and it does not have a happy ending, but this is a one-night read. This is a viable part of your social studies, geography, and psychology units, as well.

265. *Love Letters.* Harriet Coret. New York: New Readers Press, 1990. Sundown series.
    There are only a few actual letters in this story of a young woman who, at first, must rely on a friend to read her mail to her. But the story of evolving literacy through high-interest subject matter sells this theoretically sound practice in a concrete context. This book has gotten positive reviews from several of the women I have worked with. If a person likes this book, there are probably others by the same author in this series that will be valuable reading material.

266. *My Side of the Mountain*. Jean Craighead George. New York: Dutton, 1959. 1969 George G. Stone Center for Children's Books Recognition of Merit Award, 1960 Newbery Honor Book, ALA Notable Book, Hans Christian Andersen International Award.

Well-deserving of all its awards, this is the story of a runaway boy who manages to survive in the wilderness. He chronicles his adventures in his journal and does little drawings of some of the natural elements he discovers. This is an intriguing story of survival and discovery. The first-person, simple language makes this a rich storehouse of comprehensible vocabulary.

267. *The Official Freebies for Fans: Something for Nothing or Next to Nothing!* Editors of *Freebies* magazine. Chicago: Contemporary Books, 1994.

This book is loaded with ideas on how to get mail into your life. A short paragraph introduces sources of reading materials, such as where to write for twenty celebrity addresses for the cost of a long, self-addressed envelope and how to join the Gilligan's Island Fan Club. Another section gives addresses of fan clubs, baseball teams, hockey teams, football teams, basketball teams—you name it in sports. There is a list of names and addresses of places you might go. And the book also has a lot of things you can buy for under $5.

268. *Pedro's Journal: A Voyage with Christopher Columbus, August 3, 1492–February 14, 1493*. Pam Conrad. New York: Scholastic, 1991.

There really was a ship's boy named Pedro at the helm when the *Santa Maria* ran aground, but we do not have his actual writings—if, indeed he was able to read and write. But here is the next best thing, a work of the imagination—what Pedro might have written had he engineered the disaster at sea. Each entry in this fictionalized diary has a large month and date and easy-to-read text. Well researched pencil drawings throughout offer historical information in themselves. This story details one young man's adventure on the high seas with Christopher Columbus and encounters with various tribes of Indians. Though the author denies all connections to the authentic assumptions of how the *Santa Maria* was sunk, one plausible scenario detailed is, in which the homesick ship's boy causes the disastrous loss. This is a compellingly written journal. Use this in U.S. and world history units, too. Note: For more details on the actual shipwreck and an exquisite illustration of it, see *Westward with Columbus: Set Sail on the Voyage That Changed the World*, by John Dyson, described in "U.S. Citizenship," Unit 16, entry 949.

269. *Sabine's Notebook, in Which the Extraordinary Correspondence of Griffin & Sabine Continues*. Nick Bantock. San Francisco: Chronicle Books, 1992.

Exotic envelope, stationery, and stamp designs, supplemented by random sketches along the margins, make this book as visually enticing as the first of the series. Meanwhile, the vocabulary on the envelopes offers words like confidential, personal, express, proof, special, and checked.

270. *The Secret Diary of Laura Palmer*. Jennifer Lynch. New York: Pocket Books, 1990.

The cover states that this is "a Twin Peaks Book as seen by Jennifer Lynch." This book is purported to be the actual diary of the fictional television series character. Carefully dated from July 22, 1984, to October 31, 1989, each entry in

Laura's diary reveals the inner thoughts and daily life of the deceased young woman. At the end of the diary, there are undated entries and pages torn out. Dedicated as she is to making regular confessions in writing, Laura Palmer uses language that is simple and direct, making it easy reading with contemporary input.

271. *Sheldon & Mrs. Levine: An Excruciating Correspondence.* Sam Bobrick and Julie Stein. Los Angeles: Price Stern Sloan, 1994.

This is a wildcat parody of Nick Bantock's carefully planned Griffin & Sabine trilogy. The format of open letters between Sheldon and his mother exposes a tense relationship with which every adult will connect. This is also a smorgasbord of informal mail possibilities: postcards, postcards written on index cards, notebook paper, a card, recycled package material, a telegram, wallpaper, and an occasional offering of more traditional formats. And as the primary characters bounce from New York to Georgia to California, there is an obvious opportunity for using a U.S. map. Meanwhile, psychologists and social scientists will definitely connect with the conditions laid bare by this dueling duo. But the biggest value of this book is in the writing class, where students get a contemporary look at how a parody can be committed.

272. *A Wall of Names: The Story of the Vietnam Veterans Memorial.* Judy Donnelly. Illustrated with photographs. New York: Random House, 1991.

This seemingly simple account of the Vietnam War Memorial moves progressively from the impact of the war on teenage soldiers, inhuman encounters with the elements of war in a swamp, the killings in the United States of peace protesters, veterans' return home, the memorial design controversy and compromise, to letters and gifts left at The Wall. Documented with photographs taken in the United States and Vietnam, this American perspective of "The Most Hated War" wrenches the heart while teaching about a piece of history that is too often simplified. Of special interest may be the fact that the winning design for the memorial was done as a school assignment and earned only a grade of "B." The large typeface is easy to read, and the photographs support this emotionally charged account.

Challenging

273. *Anne Frank: Beyond the Diary: A Photographic Remembrance.* Ruud van der Rol and Rian Verhoeven. Translated by Tony Langham and Plym Peters. Introduction by Anna Quindlen. New York: Viking Penguin, 1993.

Just as the title suggests, this book goes beyond the diary, into the world and the plight of those whose lives were on the brink of terrible change. Photographs of victims and villains, newspaper clips, artifacts, maps, letters, journals, a story begun by Anne Frank, and simple, fact-filled captions make this chronicle a detailed journey into a period that will mar the image of humankind for all time. This book should be read in conjunction with the diary. (See *The Diary of a Young Girl*, entry 276.)

274. *Between Ourselves: Letters Between Mothers & Daughters 1750–1982.* Edited by Karen Payne. Boston: Houghton Mifflin, 1983.

There are 400 pages of solid text containing the letters referenced in the title, diary entries, and biographical introductions to the writers. Death, prisons, mental hospitals, racism, women's suffrage, suicide, wars, and much more are discussed between authors usually intending audiences of no more than one. Though none of this is easy reading, the format offers a high-interest view into the perspective of women who were not expected to seek the spotlight. This book provides honest reports for the study of history, parenting, sociology, psychology, and literature. An index helps you connect with a variety of themes.

275. *California Missions: The Earliest Series of Views Made in 1856: The Journal & Drawings of Henry Miller: Account of a Tour of the California Missions and Towns 1856.* Santa Barbara, CA: Bellerophon Books, 1987.

Here is a first-person history, written in creative story form and illustrated by the same hand. Good for high intermediate and advanced students.

276. *The Diary of a Young Girl.* Anne Frank. Translated from the Dutch by B. M. Mooyaart-Doubleday. Introduction by Eleanor Roosevelt. New York: Modern Library, 1952.

The impact of this diary as a historical document must be fostered with each new generation of readers. It is so easy to lose track of war's human impact unless some single story makes the details real. That is what this young girl's diary of the Holocaust does for those who cannot remember. Roosevelt's introductory words give weight to the notion that this is a book that must be read. "Written by a young girl—and the young are not afraid of telling the truth—it is one of the wisest and most moving commentaries on war and its impact on human beings that I have ever read. . . . [H]er diary tells us much about ourselves and about our own children." This edition has a brief passage written in Anne Frank's own pen. This is a history book, a coming-of-age book, a storybook, all under one cover. (See also *Anne Frank: Beyond the Diary*, entry 273.)

277. *Family of Strangers.* Susan Beth Pfeffer. New York: Bantam Books, 1992.

Letters to family members and friends, short essays, a last will and testament, and transcripts of dialogue between the main character and her parents, psychologist, and imaginary boyfriend, Tim, comprise the text of this book, written from the perspective of the troubled teenager, Abby. Though the format allows short reading periods to be self-contained, Abby's vocabulary is well developed and complex enough to warrant classification in the Challenging category. This book demonstrates how letters to a friend, never meant to be mailed, can serve as a diary. This is a good, contemporary story that deals with many of the problems faced by two-career families as well as substance abuse and interpersonal relationships. It gives enough mature material to serve well in language and literacy settings for adults as well as youth. The dialogue that emerges from the situations described can be stimulating not only for formal education but also for family discussions.

278. *The Groucho Letters: Letters from and to Groucho Marx.* Groucho Marx. New York: Simon & Schuster, 1967.

Tongue-in-cheek, teasing, and sometimes even serious, Marx responds to television shows of his friends (and it seems not friends?), opponents, news articles, and actual mail. I always thought of Marx as that funny talk show host from the early days of television. Now I know that he was one funny writer, too. In these letters, he discusses the possibilities of being unemployed and the impossibilities of accepting invitations to tea 3,000 miles away. He makes it his business to set things straight; for example, he assures that one Miss Bankhead is, in real life, a shy and retiring type who leads a sedentary existence, pining away for a quiet little farm where she might have peace and quiet. In addition to his offerings about famous folks, there are exchanges with them. For example, in a series of letters between Marx and author E. B. White, the two discuss the unlikelihood of their ever meeting face to face. In most cases the exchanges are in understandable language; however, some of it borders on strong—in yesteryear's terms—and the topics are generally human—in Marx humor terms. Still, there are references that current readers may not recognize, and some letters employ atypical forms— F. Allen, for example, uses no capital letters. So I am reluctantly putting this book in the "Challenging" section, in hopes that many will find little chunks of it appropriate for linking with Thin Books and even First Readers. The one thing the book lacks is an index. As it is not the kind of work I am able to read from front to back, I have found and lost many treasures that would be nice to reference here. But sometime during your leisure reading time or SSR period, you will find them and you will laugh just as I have and will again. This book is a read and reread.

279. *The Holocaust.* Abraham Resnick. San Diego, CA: Lucent Overview Series, 1991.

In 128 pages with wide margins, the author chronicles the events and emotions of the years from 1933 to 1945. An easy-to-follow glossary is followed by a list of organizations to contact and their addresses.

280. *Letters from the Promised Land: Swedes in America, 1840–1914.* Edited by H. Arnold Barton. Minneapolis, MN: University of Minnesota Press for the Swedish Pioneer Historical Society, 1975.

This period of the greatest migration from Sweden to the United States is discussed through immigrants' letters and diaries and travel accounts by Swedish visitors. Religious persecution, language difficulties, economic strife on both sides of the Atlantic, and the difficult first six months are all detailed in these documents. There are several particularly telling passages: Foul air, cramped quarters below deck, putrid water, moldy and wormy food that was often in short supply, sickness, and death were standard during the eight- to ten-week voyages. This is so much like the slave transport and the experiences of poor Irish and Vietnamese and Cambodian boat people that it bears comparative analysis in the classroom or tutoring situation, particularly for ESL students. Note the first paragraph on page 14. Poor crops in Sweden from 1867 to 1869 are discussed on page 139. Illiteracy, spelling deficiencies, and the mixing of Swedish and English in letters are covered in a letter of complaint to the editor of *Hemlandet* from the Swedish postmaster S. M. Korling, who adds that addresses are often so incomplete that letters must be opened to find out who should receive them. Even then, if the letter is unsigned, it must be passed from hand to hand until someone recognizes the handwriting or contents (pages 140–41). Language acquisition is addressed on pages 196–97 in a letter of April 10, 1888, to Sister Lotten. The letter explains what we now call the Silent Period in 1888 terms. The young writer says, "[I]t is hardest the first half year as long as you can't manage with the language, but if you only can happen to find decent folks to work for it goes well and good humor is something wherever you go." About 1902, another letter details how satisfaction with America parallels language acquisition. That is, the immigrant experience begins with overwhelming homesickness that evolves into a love of the new country as English becomes more a part of the immigrant's life (page 290).

281. *Letters from the Sand: The Letters of Desert Storm and Other Wars.* U.S. Postal Service. Washington, DC: GPO, 1991.

Some reproduced in clear type, some in the original handwriting, letters and postcards document the history of the United States during wartime. Diary entries, children's art, stamps, and historical photographs support the text, which takes the reader on the same emotional roller-coaster rides that the writers themselves experienced. Seldom is the Spanish-American War (1898–1899) covered in such detail. "The letters from Vietnam were just too sad to read," said an adult new reader. So much pictorial support is in this high-interest book that it does not really qualify for the Challenging category, yet the vocabulary and writing variety offer a lot of quality input not found elsewhere. There are actual commemorative stamps in the collector editions of this book.

282. *The Living Lincoln: The Man, His Mind, His Times, and the War He Fought, Reconstructed from His Own Writings.* Edited by Paul M. Angle and Earl Schenck Miers. New York: Barnes & Noble, 1992.

This is a book of the letters, speeches, and journals that document the history lived by a literate man. Annotations help create a context for these one-sided communications. The entire book is worth study. If any part of it was published in booklet form, perhaps with illustrations, it would qualify as a Thin Book or even, for some parts, a First Reader. Lincoln's style was forthright, honest, and to the point. There is no wondering what he meant. Three short letters to his stepbrother, on behalf of his loving stepmother, deserve special note in "Book Chapters and Strong Passages," entry 290.

Other extraordinary letters are to Horace Greeley on March 24, 1862, to Maj. Gen. George McClellan on March 31 and April 9, 1862, and on June 9, 1863, to his wife concerning their son's pistol and a disturbing dream Lincoln had.

283. *Witness to an Era: The Life and Photographs of Alexander Gardner: The Civil War, Lincoln, and the West.* D. Mark Katz. New York: Viking, 1991.

This is not a book of letters, logs, and journals. However, the bits that are in it make it a poignant addition to such a unit. This is an oversized picture book and an extraordinary portrait of an artist's life. Gardner documented the Civil War and photographed President Abraham Lincoln as well as the conspirators to Lincoln's assassination. Pictures of all of these are in the book. There are also reproductions of handwritten documents, complete with scratch-outs and editing, of the Civil War era. See page 70 for the photographer's caption for a photograph of a dead Confederate soldier, page 109 for a handwritten note alerting the photographer that President-elect Lincoln was expected, and page 159 for a War Department memo, dated April 27, 1865, authorizing the autopsy of John Wilkes Booth. The running commentary and captions make this part of American history more real than does any other picture book I have seen. And the issues of battlefield agony, racism, slavery, intrigue, crime, and punishment are brought to the fore. This is an excellent book just for page-turning dialogue. It is also well written.

Book Chapters and Strong Passages

284. "Carpe Diem!" Alan Cohen. In *Chicken Soup for the Soul: 101 Stories to Open the Heart and Rekindle the Spirit*. Edited by Jack Canfield and Mark V. Hansen. Deerfield Beach, FL: Health Communications, 1993, pages 46–50.

   A simple card can make a great deal of difference—to the sender. This is about personal courage and reaching out—just doing what you really want to do.

285. "Educating a Special Child." In *Hey! Listen to This: Stories to Read Aloud*. Edited by Jim Trelease. New York: Penguin Books, 1992, pages 44–45.

   In this Challenging passage we learn of the impact that one person can have on societal attitudes across time. It also supports the use of journals. During a visit to America in 1842, when he visited Laura, a blind, deaf, and mute girl, Charles Dickens was surprised to learn that her Boston doctor had taught her to read and write. At the time, such children were societal discards—locked away, hidden, shamefully kept from human interaction. Dickens recorded the discovery of Laura's remarkable learning ability in his journal, which was eventually published. Forty years later, the mother of Helen Keller read about the incident and was inspired to find a teacher for her disabled daughter.

286. *How to Reach Your Favorite Sports Star*. Larry Strauss. Chicago: Contemporary Books, 1994.

   Birthdays, vital statistics, sports stats, and brief biographies and photos of forty-six men and women athletes are available in a fast, easy-to-follow format. Because each two-page spread is a separate feature, this book is catalogued under "Book Chapters and Strong Passages."

287. "In Response to Executive Order 9066: All Americans of Japanese Descent Must Report to Relocation Centers." Dwight Okita. In *Survival!* Lexington, MA: D. C. Heath, 1995, pages 70–71.

   In a short letter from a fourteen-year-old girl, the U.S. government is told of a white girl's reaction toward her Japanese-American best friend. "You're trying to start a war," she said, "giving secrets away to the enemy. Why can't you keep your big mouth shut?" This is a work of fiction about a historical event. It is on a Thin Book level. A paragraph about the author explains that his parents were interned in a World War II relocation center set up for 120,000 Japanese Americans. An aerial view of schoolgirls in a relocation camp accompanies the text.

288. "Keeping in Touch." In *How the White House Really Works*. George Sullivan. New York: Scholastic, 1989, pages 14–27.

   Though no letters are reproduced, a collection of calling cards illustrates how Presidents Eisenhower, Johnson, Reagan, and Nixon responded to some of their constituents' mail. Exactly what goes on in that giant house that belongs to all Americans is the subject of this book, which takes you on a whirlwind tour, introducing you to a few of the famous residents and the fourth-floor Correspondence Office, giving a look at the games people who live there have played and the guards who protect the people and things of the White House. This book humanizes one part of the president's life.

289. *Letters from a Slave Girl: The Story of Harriet Jacobs*. Mary E. Lyons. New York: Charles Scribner's Sons, 1992.
   A read-aloud passage concerning literacy: "We know that she had to conceal her literacy from her master. 'One day,' she recalled in *Incidents in the Life of a Slave Girl*, 'he caught me teaching myself to write.' We also know that she received notes and poems from friends. Since writing was forbidden, it is likely that she responded to them in secret" (page 136).

290. *The Living Lincoln: The Man, His Mind, His Times, and the War He Fought, Reconstructed from His Own Writings*. Edited by Paul M. Angle and Earl Schenck Miers. New York: Barnes & Noble, 1992.
   Three letters identified as Shelbyville, November 4, 1851; Shelbyville, November 9, 1851; and Springfield, November 25, 1851, show the concern Lincoln felt when his stepbrother proposed taking advantage of their widowed mother's land, selling it so that she would receive little income (pages 146–48). This is a book of the letters, speeches, and journals that document the history lived by a literate man. There is more detail under "Challenging," above.

291. "Service with a Smile." Karl Albrecht and Ron Zenke, Service America. In *Chicken Soup for the Soul: 101 Stories to Open the Heart and Rekindle the Spirit*. Edited by Jack Canfield and Mark Victor Hansen. Deerfield Beach, FL: Health Communications, 1993, page 224.
   Two letters can make us rethink our attitudes about attitudes. Here is a wake-up call.

292. *USKids History: Book of the American Revolution*. Howard Egger-Bovet and Marlene Smith Baranzini. Illustrated by Bill Sanchez. New York: Little, Brown, 1994.
   The Joseph Palmer letter (page 47) and the details of its composition (pages 46 and 47) are an interesting piece of history. Most of this book is written either from a child's perspective or about a child of the period. And some of the text seems to have been written down to make the words and sentences shorter, ironically making comprehension less likely. Even so, there is a lot of interesting information in the book, and it is worth making available to the would-be citizen.

293. *The War Began at Supper: Letters to Miss Loria*. Patrician Reilly Giff. Illustrated by Betsy Lewin. New York: Delacorte Press, 1991.
   Michael's letter of Tuesday, February 5 (pages 41–42), makes a profound read aloud. (See entry 254 under "First Readers.")

Other Events and Supplements

Having a collection of letter-based books spread out during a special promotion time (a week or a month) can foster a heightened awareness of how many different forms they can take. Add to that a collection of junk mail letters, bound in a looseleaf notebook and there is a definite real world connection. Even though students may be concentrating on writing or reading when I am talking, I encourage notewriting between students. It is a fabulous way of fostering high-interest practice that the teacher will rarely be asked to correct. And it's quieter than whispering.

- Bring letters to class from friends or relatives and read passages aloud.
- Write a letter to someone you have not seen for a long time.
- Write a letter to a historical figure, asking questions that are not answered in the available literature. It is okay if the person is no longer alive.
- Write to a special interest group in your city or county.
- Write to a politician. Share the response.
- Write a letter to someone you will never see again but wish you could.
- Pretend you are a parent of someone on the front page of the newspaper. Make a diary entry about your child.
- Find out if there is a local exhibit of letters you can see.
- Find out if a local autograph or letter collector will come in and share some of the collection favorites.
- After a field trip to a zoo, aquarium, or animal park, write a letter to an animal from the perspective of another animal. If you cannot arrange a field trip, use copies of *Ranger Rick* and *National Geographic*.
- Find samples of famous authors' writings and exhibit them.
- Collect letters written by members of your family and make a family letters album.
- Keep a daily journal.
- Get a pen pal by trading letters between classrooms, through a special interest magazine, or by writing to a veteran's hospital. Many immobile people want outside contact.
- Write a letter to your favorite movie or TV personality.
- Agree with a friend to take on famous personalities and correspond from that perspective.
- Leave love notes for people who have done little things you like.
- Design postcards and exhibit them.
- Collect letters to the editors of newspapers and magazines.
- Compare the letters to different sections of the newspaper.
- Collect Dear Ann Landers columns and other newspaper letters for the lovelorn.
- On the wall or bulletin board post open letters on your take of what has happened in class or at home.

Parenting

Unit 6

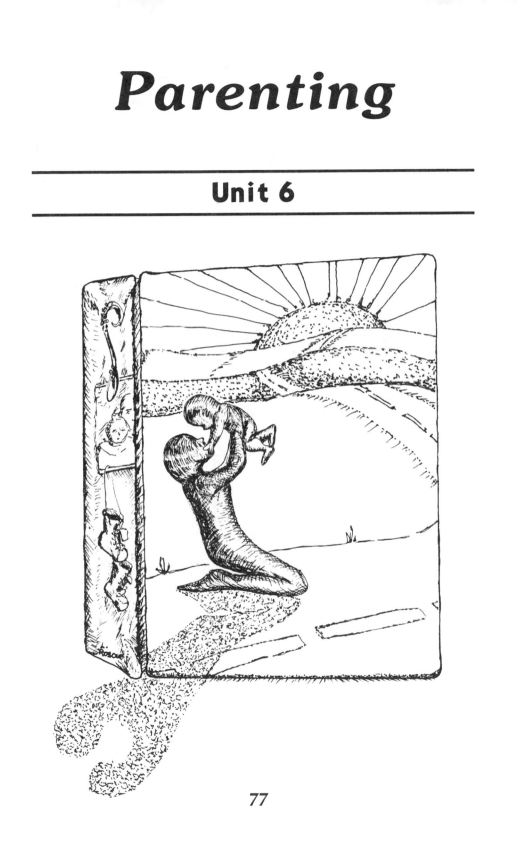

Certainly many of the fine books on child-rearing offer the parent a lot of useful ideas. Many of our own peers are products of well-followed instruction books. Yet such outcomes were the result of many hours of study on the part of parents who had time to study and the language and literacy skills to pursue that work—hard work.

Meanwhile, there are few easier ways of conveying parenting skills than through the humor and good tellings of other people's stories. Consider how much easier it is to tolerate the behavior of our friends' offspring; after all, we will not be held accountable for the little disasters. Children's literature often presents the essence of human behavior in simple, obvious actions and words. So it is not surprising that the children presented in books by our favorite authors can be easy to take—and understand. Often these children teach us that human frailties are only human. And sometimes their stories convey universal truths and unshakable values.

The readings in this unit are set up to help the parent consider children and parents from an objective point of view. That includes discovering the differences between one age level and another and identifying what things really matter and what things do not matter at all. In these few pages, only a trace of the available literature for this theme can be presented. But it is hoped these selections will open the door to yet another way of getting help with that most important and difficult of human tasks—parenting.

First Readers and Picture Books

294. *The Adventures of Spider: West African Folk Tales.* Retold by Joyce Cooper Arkhurst. Illustrated by Jerry Pinkey. New York: Scholastic, 1964.

Have you been wondering how the world got wisdom? Would you like to know how the spider got a thin waist or became bald? Perhaps you want to know why there are spiders on your ceiling. The answers to these important questions and more are found in these short, well-written and well-illustrated stories. Each tale has a lesson or two. For parents, there are ways of entering notions of common sense and greed, without direct reference to children. For teachers, there are avenues for comparing values on a global level.

295. *Alexander and the Terrible, Horrible, No Good, Very Bad Day.* Judith Viorst. New York: Aladdin, 1987.

This little book is one of a series written from the perspective of an ornery young redhead who is having a difficult time getting through the growing-up years. Girls and boys relate to him. Parents do, too. In this particular book, Alexander is contemplating migration to Australia.

296. *Alexander and the Wind-Up Mouse.* Leo Leoni. New York: Pantheon Books, 1969.

A little mouse longs to become a mechanical mouse, so he will be loved like the one given to the boy of his house. He takes a long journey to find the magic rock that will give him the key to happiness. Leo Leoni has written many thoughtful, message-laden stories, some with wonderful content about seasons, science, or tolerance. But this little story about self-appreciation is among my favorites. You may also be interested to know that Pam Perkins, director of the International Reading and Learning Center of Chapman University in Orange, California, has created "What Is Reading?" a video program for teaching about the reading process. In it a child reads the entire text of *Alexander and the Wind-Up Mouse* as Perkins listens. A group of Chapman graduate students then evaluates the reading performance. After that, the child retells the story in her own words. The results are, to say the least, surprising. Perkins's program is set up to be done in a group setting of parents, reading teachers, or others who are developing an interest in the teaching of reading. I think that is the best environment, too. We used it as part of our tutor education program when I was at the library in Beaumont, California. The workshops were run by literacy volunteer Anita Rowley. There we saw people absolutely change their minds about the reading process. Well, a couple got angry and left before the video was finished—no change there. But those who stayed for the follow-up discussion not only gained a clear understanding of why we never correct a reader during performance, but also found out about a powerful little book.

297. *Alexander Who Used to Be Rich Last Sunday.* Judith Viorst. New York: Aladdin, 1987.
   In this episode, young Alexander is having a difficult time hanging onto his money. It is a story that allows people to talk about the problems surrounding finances for kids and adults.

298. *Babushka Baba Yaga.* Patricia Polacco. New York: Philomel Books, 1993.
   Suspicion, intolerance, bigotry, and fear keep the unusual-looking old Baba Yaga from the loving relationships she needs—until she devises a cover-up.

299. *The Bracelet.* Yoshiko Uchida and Joanna Yardley. New York: Philomel Books, 1993. Picture book.
   "Emi and her family weren't moving because they wanted to. The government was sending them to a prison camp because they were Japanese-Americans. And America was at war with Japan. They hadn't done anything wrong. They were being treated like the enemy just because they looked like the enemy. The FBI had sent Papa to a prisoner-of-war camp in Montana just because he worked for a Japanese company." The year was 1942, and the U.S. government had taken action against some of its own innocent citizens—men, women, and children. Emi had gotten a bracelet from her best friend, a keepsake to remember her by until they met again—if they ever would. Dialogue between parent and child might be about:

- leaving friends

- values—what counted . . . to the child . . . to the parents? Is it possible for a symbolic item to really make a big difference in a child's ability to cope with stress?

- keepsakes—some people cherish them, others think they're silly. Why?

300. *Brother Eagle, Sister Sky, A Message from Chief Seattle.* Paintings by Susan Jeffers. New York: Dial, 1991. Picture book. 1992 Abby Award winner.
   Here is an illustration of the importance of lessons taught at an early age. Though the storytellers may be long gone, the power of meaning-filled dialogue

can support the adult in need of eloquence. The words of Suquamish and Duwamish Chief Seattle, delivered in his native tongue during negotiations with settlers for land rights, are translated here and interpreted with inspirational colored-ink illustrations that fill and cover every page. "How can you buy the sky?" he begins, as he slowly recounts the stories of the universe as told to him by his mother, father, and grandfather. If we are all part of a grand system of life, how can one claim ownership of another? When the book is finished, there is a stunning sense that Seattle continues to hope for a more reasonable treaty than the one his broken people had to accept during the time that he lived. There is so much to think about in this giant picture book that it is difficult to assign categories. It is philosophy, logic, wonder, spirituality, honor, memory, respect, dignity—for all, and unity. The best use for this book may just be to let it be—in the learning environment, in the home, on the table, in the chalk trough. Then perhaps the many-layered messages will have time to unfold without shocking the viewer who may not yet be at peace with the Earth.

301. *Chanticleer and the Fox*. Adapted from Geoffrey Chaucer's *Canterbury Tales*. Illustrated by Barbara Cooney. New York: Harper & Row, 1989. 1959 Caldecott Medal.

The wealth of detailed and whimsical scratchboard illustrations of the landscape, people, and rooster Chanticleer are matched by beautifully written text. Chaucer would have reveled in the words chosen to update his Old English tale. Here is a sample, just part of the description of fine Chanticleer: "For crowing there was not his equal in all the land. His voice was merrier than the merry organ that plays in church, and his crowing from his resting place was more trustworthy than a clock. His comb was redder than fine coral and turreted like a castle wall, his bill was black and shone like jet, and his legs and toes were like azure." As you can see, this is not simple language, but it belongs in the "First Reader" section because just a few readings by the teacher will place this fine text into the heart and mind of the listener. We see craftiness and learn much from this old tale.

302. *The Day of Ahmed's Secret*. Florence Parry Heide and Judith Heidi Gilliland. Illustrated by Ted Lewin. New York: Scholastic, 1990.

Rich watercolors fill each page to the edge with the faces and scenes of the Cairo marketplace, the great desert by the Nile, and the young Ahmed, who delivers heavy bottles of fuel to homes around the city. As he drives his donkey cart, Ahmed recalls the words of wisdom shared by his father during the times when they rode together, before Ahmed was strong enough to carry the fuel by himself. "Hurry to grow strong, Ahmed. . . . But do not hurry to grow old." As Ahmed makes his rounds, the reader gets a travel tour through the ancient city. On this day, too, Ahmed has a wonderful secret, one that is revealed to his family at the end of the book.

303. *Fly Away Home*. Eve Bunting. Illustrated by Ronald Himler. New York: Clarion Books, 1991.

This first-person story told by a preschool-age boy details activities of a homeless father and son who live in the airport. The child expresses anger and jealousy toward people who are meeting at the airport and then going home together. His only source of hope comes from a little bird that is stranded in the airport for days before finally finding an open door and flying away home. Supported by realistic watercolor drawings, this high-interest text is an easy reader. The contemporary subject provides a backdrop for dialogue and can be used as a prewriting stimulus.

304. *The Giving Tree.* Shel Silverstein. New York: Harper & Row, 1961.
This little picture book shows the metamorphosis of a relationship between a boy and his tree. Or, perhaps, a boy and his mother. Yet it could be between humankind and nature. Or humankind and the environment. At each stage of his life, the boy-man returns to the tree to take away more. And the tree is always happy to give. This is an emotion-filled book, one I have never been able to finish reading aloud. It does open many doors. As with many other classics, there are often copies in used bookstores. I always buy them for my students.

305. *Hiawatha's Childhood.* Henry Wadsworth Longfellow. Illustrated by Errol Le Cain. New York: Puffin Books, 1984.
This excerpt from the famous legend written by Longfellow is graced by incredibly beautiful illustrations. The word pictures drawn by the wise old grandmother Nakomis are revisited in full color and imagination by Le Cain. Magical and legendary explanations for everything in nature are passed to the grandchild, who drinks up the legacy. There are so many applications for this perfect pairing that I am hard-pressed to think of any unit that could not use it somehow.

306. *I'll Always Love You.* Hans Wilhelm. New York: Crown, 1985.
Love and saying "I love you," death and the grieving process are conveyed in just a handful of simple colored drawings and a few lines of prose. Here less is enough to keep the reader in tears for hours and thinking long, long after.

307. *If You Were a Writer.* Joan Lowery Nixon. Illustrated by Bruce Degen. New York: Aladdin, 1995. Picture book.
"Melia's mother was a writer," and as she tells her little girl what a writer would do to get ideas, to get started, to get a reader's attention, the reader learns about these things, too.

308. *Just Plain Fancy.* Patricia Polacco. New York: Dell, 1990.
To wish for something fancy was to risk being shunned in the Amish community where Naomi and her little sister Ruth lived. Then one day Naomi found a very strange egg outside the chicken hut . . . and it was still warm. The actual interaction of caretakers and children is played down, but this little girl's need to have something special also reflects a need to have an adult she can trust with her true thoughts and feelings.

309. *Koala Lou.* Mem Fox. Illustrated by Pamela Lofts. San Diego, CA: Voyager, 1988.
Koala Lou feels kind of forgotten by his mom, who is quite busy with much younger babies. He sets out to prove himself a champion tree climber just to win the admiration of his mother. This simple fantasy sets the stage for discussions of conditional and unconditional love.

310. *Life's Little Instruction Book: 511 Suggestions, Observations, and Reminders on How to Live a Happy and Rewarding Life.* H. Jackson Brown, Jr. Nashville, TN: Rutledge Hill Press, 1991.

This little book—just a little bigger than a postcard—began as a collection of ideas the author wrote down for his son, who was leaving home for the first time. In my classes, it has proven an SSR gold mine and has inspired dialogue, essays, love notes, and incredible interest in reading. Each page has one or more brief bits of advice like the following: "Be wary of people who tell you how honest they are. Avoid negative people. When playing games with children, let them win. Pay your bills on time. Turn off the television at dinner time. Respect your children's privacy. Knock before entering their rooms. Drink eight glasses of water every day. Respect tradition. Don't worry that you can't give your kids the best of everything. Give them your very best. Don't say you don't have enough time. You have exactly the same number of hours per day that were given to Helen Keller, Pasteur, Michelangelo, Mother Teresa, Leonardo da Vinci, Thomas Jefferson, and Albert Einstein. Live your life as an exclamation, not an explanation. Avoid sarcastic remarks. Just to see how it feels, for the next twenty-four hours refrain from criticizing anybody or anything." These are not the best; they are just random samples from a wealth of ideas. ESL, adult new readers, elementary school kids, and others find reading and rereading this simple, thought-provoking book quite pleasurable.

311. *Love You Forever.* Robert Munsch. Toronto: Annick Press, 1986.

Here is a life cycle book about a mother and a son who finally trade places. I used to give this to any friend who had a preteen or teenage son. Now I just give it to mothers and sons in general and occasional others, too. But to this day, I am unable to read it aloud. I do not know if anyone can.

312. *Maggie and the Pirate.* Ezra Jack Keats. New York: Scholastic, 1979.

Maggie's family lives in a broken-down school bus. It would seem her parents have no way of giving her anything special, but there is a tiny cricket cage her father has crafted just for Maggie. It is more valuable than it might seem. Maggie has friends who hang out with her and try to help her find her pet cricket when the Pirate kidnaps it. In the resulting turmoil, the cricket is killed. On the surface, Maggie appears quite poor. But then you meet the Pirate.

313. *The Man Who Could Call Down Owls.* Eve Bunting. Illustrated by Charles Mikolaycak. New York: Macmillan, 1984.

This is a picture book with haunting, surprising pencil drawings of owls. It is also a storybook of a man with mystical healing powers, his apprentice, and an assassin who wanted those powers. The languages of owls, forests, caring, teaching, and values each emerge from a seemingly simple picture book. For these discussions, it stands alone. It also works well as a companion book with Jane Yolen's *Owl Moon* (see entry 315).

314. *On the Day I Was Born.* Debbi Chocolate. Illustrated by Melodye Rosales. New York: Scholastic, 1995.

Here is the celebration of life by an entire family. On the day I was born, says the firstborn child, "my daddy held me up to the heavens. He said, 'Behold the

only thing greater.' " Pictures of caring family members, each identifying with the
new babe, support the dozen or so words on each two-page spread.

315.　*Owl Moon*. Jane Yolen. Illustrated by John Schoenherr. New York: Philomel
Books, 1987. 1988 Caldecott Award.

A father and daughter take a long walk in the snow to find an owl, one who
appears at a special time of the moon. Actually finding the owl is secondary to
this long, peaceful, caring, gentle walk in the woods, one that an author might
remember as an adult. This book is accompanied by a cassette tape, read by the
author. Community-college ESL learners praise this book and tape.

A very different owl story, one that also takes place at night, is Eve Bunting's
The Man Who Could Call Down Owls, noted above and detailed in "Myths, Legends,
Fables, and Fairy Tales," Unit 3, entry 128.

316.　*The Paper Bag Princess*. Robert Munsch. Toronto: Annick Press, 1980.

Having lost her castle and clothing to a fire-breathing dragon, a princess is
left with nothing to wear but a paper bag. The brave and intelligent girl undergoes
hardship and danger to save her charming prince. But when she rescues him, he
complains about her appearance. Values, self-esteem, male-female relationships,
and the importance of thinking things through before judging are imbedded in
this well-illustrated, funny, imaginative story.

317.　*Pink and Say*. Patricia Polacco. New York: Philomel Books, 1994.

Two very young teenagers get caught up in the treachery of the Civil War,
Pink with a black unit, Say with a white. Their stories join as the black man takes
time to save the life of his fellow soldier, dragging him home to be doctored. Say
is overcome with awe when he discovers Pink can teach him to read, a skill
forbidden slaves and obviously not the birthright of the poor white. Pink's mother
is as caring of her son's friend as she is of her own child and pays dearly for it.
This is an American history book, a parenting book, a literacy issues book, a social
science cornerstone, and much much more. Warning: This book cannot be read
aloud without drawing many tears from all present.

318.　*The Prince Who Wrote a Letter*. Ann Love. Illustrated by Toni Goffe. New York:
Child's Play International, 1992.

The prince in this book is being instructed in the old-fashioned parts-to-
whole way that has him learning the letter "a" first, "b" second, and so on, instead
of learning to write his most important word, "Paul," first. Perhaps that explains
the other out-of-date events that lead from a simple statement to rumor to a near
war between kingdoms. But nestled in the heart of a funny, timeless theme, and
supported by full-color illustrations that fill every page clear to the edge, this is
comprehensible input. Read this once to your adult new reader, discussing it as
you go along, and that adult will be ready to take the book home to invest in family
literacy. Dialogues might address single questions like:

- What would have happened if the Prince had been asked to talk about his
  day, his learning, his letter?

- How does it feel to have everything blown out of proportion?

- Do episodes like these last a lifetime for the child in question?

319. *Rechenka's Eggs*. Patricia Polacco. New York: Philomel Books, 1988. A Reading Rainbow selection.

Here is a mystical story of connections—between humans, animals, and a universal goodness. It is also about the cycle of life. Old Babushka's main reason for living is winning first place in the painted egg contest each year. She also cares for hungry and wounded animals.

320. *Smoky Night*. Eve Bunting. Illustrated by David Diaz. San Diego, CA: Harcourt Brace, 1994.

The horror of a world gone mad, as riots break out in the street, begins a series of dramatic incidents that cause a young boy, an old woman, and their pets to reach a level of understanding that could not be achieved during a time of peace. Richly textured collages of glass, wrappers, trail mix, and other found objects make this book a visual wonder. The illustrations support the text page by page. The way in which a fearful child expresses his suspicion of a neighbor and her cat and then comes to recognize her as a fellow human—and her cat as a creature that purrs, just as his does—illustrates that attitudes can change, and that it is okay to rethink and reevaluate our prejudices. In this simple, nonjudgmental book, Bunting demonstrates how personal growth can evolve. This is a fine read aloud, especially for adults. I know, because the author read it to an audience I was in. It is a book all will want to revisit. You may be interested to know that Bunting's powerful story emerged, in part, from her own naive expression of prejudice toward a teacher during World War II. Sometimes personal change takes a long time, indeed.

321. *Something from Nothing*. Adapted from a Jewish folktale by Phoebe Gilman. New York: Scholastic, 1992. Picture book.

Grandpa is a tailor whose first loving gift to little Joseph is a blanket. Over time, Joseph outgrows his baby blanket, which Grandpa remakes into a jacket, which Joseph outgrows, and Grandpa remakes into a vest. And so it goes until nothing is left, nothing, everyone tells the boy. But Joseph knows how to make that gift of love into one more thing—a story. This is a story of faith, family, and the power of positive thinking, passed from one generation to the next.

322. *Sophie*. Mem Fox. Illustrated by Aminah Brenda Lynn Robinson. New York: Harcourt Brace, 1994.

Sophie loves her grandpa, who is always ready to play with her until one day— . The simple funeral illustration shows Grandpa in his casket. Then there is grief. Mem Fox—consistently powerful.

323. *Spotted Owlets*. Victoria Miles. Illustrated by Elizabeth Gatt. Victoria, B.C., Canada: Orca, 1993.

Here is a small-format booklet with realistic illustrations and just a few lines of text per page. Those pages convey the struggle for survival of brother and sister owlets, the physical limitations of the young creatures, their family life, and habitat.

324. *The Story of Ferdinand.* Munro Leaf. New York: Puffin Books, 1964.
Many of us remember this wonderful little book from our own childhoods. It is about Ferdinand the bull, the original pacifist, who preferred smelling flowers to fighting people. The language is simple, the pictures supportive, and the message of nonviolence compelling. You may be interested to know that Scholastic now has a cassette tape dramatization of the story that uses sound effects and music to further the entertainment value of this story.

325. *Strega Nona's Magic Lessons.* Story and pictures by Tomie dePaola. New York: Scholastic, 1982.
Strega Nona is a wise old woman with mystical, magical powers that everyone wants to learn. And that is where the complications start. Strega Nona's response to the transgressions of her immature sidekick model a firm and caring parental response in which the punishment fits the crime. Tomie dePaola's humorous illustrations take up most of the space and push meaning into the text. There is a series of Strega Nona books with different humorous situations yielding her typical mature attitude. After all, she may have been at this for centuries.

326. *Sweet Magnolia.* Virginia Kroll. Illustrated by Laura Jacques. Watertown, MA: Charlesbridge, 1995.
In celebration of her sixth birthday, Denise is sent to visit her grandmother, a wildlife rehabilitator who lives in the swamps where she cares for injured creatures until they can be returned to their natural environment. The text is by no means simple, and there is a full page of it opposite each full-page illustration, but the mix of text and pictures promises to support comprehension and provide high- interest material. During the visit, Denise learns that to own an animal does not have to mean keeping it locked up. And that a keepsake from nature need not mean the destruction of another life. The reader gleans what is perhaps an equally important message about family. Denise is adored by her mother, grandmother, and older sisters, but that adoration is expressed in ways that convey strength and responsibility. There are many ways this small, powerful book might be used— environmental issues, geography, art, creatures and insects, plants, science, but the messages about family caused me to offer it here.

327. *The Table Where Rich People Sit.* Byrd Baylor. Pictures by Peter Parnall. New York: Macmillan, 1994.
This book was introduced to me by Donald Graves, when he read it aloud to an audience of several hundred at the 40th International Reading Association Conference in Anaheim, California. Need I add that most of the attendees were adults—reading teachers and interested others. After the reading there was silence and tears. Had I known about this incredible book sooner, it might have been the cornerstone for a values unit. It makes an excellent, gentle discussion starter on dollar values—on abstract things.

328. *Tales of Pan.* Mordicai Gerstein. New York: Harper & Row, 1986.
The comical, whimsical illustrations make this a fun book just for page turning. Though the midwife who delivered Pan ran screaming from the house when the goat-legged infant appeared giggling and snickering, his father, Hermes, was delighted with the son who also had two little horns and a small beard.

Hermes immediately snatched the babe and ran off to show his little boy to the other gods, none of whom cared for the smell of goat. Clearly the value of the child to the parent can be inspired by this phase of the book. And the short chapters allow the teacher to read single-purpose chapters over a number of lessons. Over time, not unlike a child of the terrible twos, young Pan caused all manner of chaos around him. With the advent of a loud noise, he invented both the word and the condition called panic. His relentless habit of falling in and out of love opens up the possibility of discussions on adolescence. Eventually, Pan moved away, as all offspring's parents would have them do. He even married and had an ornery little kid himself. So the cycle began anew, and the reader can make strong connections concerning heredity. Parenting, however, is not the only content of this storybook. Gerstein's storytelling makes the wealth of mythological information in the stories just sort of tumble off the page and into your lap. Pan, you see, was responsible for the first eclipse. And his pranks led to the conditions that cause Mount Aetna to rumble and spew fire and smoke to this day. Though this book is found in the children's section of the library, it is guaranteed to be a popular one among adults as well.

329. *Tar Beach*. Faith Ringgold. New York: Crown, 1991. 1992 Caldecott Honor Book, 1992 Coretta Scott King Award.
     A quilt and drawings illustrate this dream come true. Part of the dream is that the little girl's dad will not have to worry about the racism that excludes him from the union and access to work. Part of the dream is that she will wear the bridge with the lights like a diamond necklace.

330. *Three Gold Pieces: A Greek Folk Tale*. Retold and illustrated by Aliki. New York: HarperCollins, 1994. Picture book.
     Consistent with Aliki's other works, the illustrations are a surprising delight in themselves. Here the story may seem demeaning—a poor man enters a work contract of ten years' duration without asking the terms of his employment. Then he ends up paying his employer all of his earning for three bits of advice. As the story continues, however, the advice turns out to be of considerable value to this main character. The implications of this old tale can lead to current life comparisons and questioning of messages sent through text.

331. *Thunder Cake*. Patricia Polacco. New York: Philomel Books, 1990.
     Fear and the courage to keep going are the themes of a book with beautiful, detailed color drawings. Grandma helps the young child address her fear of thunder. Though Polacco draws from her family's Russian folk histories, this is a universal story.

332. *Tough Boris*. Mem Fox. Illustrated by Kathryn Brown. San Diego, CA: Harcourt Brace, 1994.
     Almost traditional watercolor illustrations give meaning to the single lines of prose on each two-page spread. There is a thirty-one-word vocabulary for the entire book—though this is not to say the words lack meaning, not to say they are easy words. The story deals with stereotyping, sadness, grief, and death.

333. *Uncle Jed's Barbershop*. Margaree King Mitchell. Illustrated by James Ransome. New York: Scholastic, 1993. Picture book.

This is a story of hope, a beloved relative, tenacity, a dream deferred and fulfilled, segregation, poverty, and the power of a positive model. This is a simply told story of a man who proved it is never too late to start over and never too late to succeed.

334. *Where the Wild Things Are*. Maurice Sendak. New York: Harper & Row, 1963.

This is the story of imagination and the wild behavior it produces in Max, about four years old. Dressed in his wolf suit, he threatens to eat his mother up! Nonplussed, she sends him to bed without supper. Max falls asleep and dreams of extraordinary wild things that, of course, worship him and love him. But in the end, he has to go home, where he discovers his dinner waiting on the table next to his bed. This is a grand read-aloud book, a wonderful way of seeing the punishment fit the crime, and a fine way of opening the door to dialogue about what really matters and what is to be expected from a young child.

335. *Wilfrid Gordon McDonald Partridge*. Mem Fox. Illustrated by Julie Vivas. Brooklyn, NY: Kane/Miller, 1985.

This is an extraordinary example of how text and pictures give meaning together. The lad with the long title name has an active, fun-filled life visiting his next-door neighbors, residents of an old people's home. We are not told he is poor, we just see the markings within the illustrations, just as we see the emotions of the residents of the home. Even so, the tale is about memory loss and the importance of having something to think or care about. It is about the contrast between youth and age. It is about valuing human beings. For any age reader, of any culture, this is a powerful book.

Thin Books

336. "Animals and 'Mothering.' " Chapter Ten. *Mysteries of Animal Intelligence*. Sherry Hansen Steiger and Brad Steiger. New York: Tom Doherty, 1995, pages 51-56.

This little paperback is chock-full of short passages that will serve well during SSR. The "Mothering" chapter is so loaded with incredible stories I'm tempted to just quote them all here. There is a mother cow who tracked down her calf that had been sold to a farm seven miles away, an elephant that served as a midwife to her elephant friends, and a mother chicken who, when given a few duck eggs in with her own, knew to lead the ducklings to water when it was time for them to learn to swim. Another mother hen knew to scratch up pupae from an ant nest for her guinea fowl hatchlings, who would have perished had she only provided the kind of food she fed her natural chicks. How do these parents know what to do? That is a scientific mystery. But for those who are convinced that they have an outstanding pet, there is an animal IQ test at the back of the book.

337. *Are You There, God? It's Me, Margaret*. Judy Blume. New York: Dell, 1970.

This coming-of-age book is a perfect parent-child read aloud. It will open doors for the young teen or preteen to ask sensitive questions without the parent seeming to be introducing the topic. Teenage newcomers are enthralled with this story. So are Native Americans, Vietnamese generals, Hispanic mothers, and people of mixed heritage. The easy, conversational style reflects the way young Americans talk. Margaret and all other Blume characters give my students vocabulary and ways of speaking that are much appreciated. This has become a stock item for my ESL classes, and I have used it for parent-child literacy as well. If you like this book, you are in luck. Judy Blume is extremely prolific. Furthermore, her books are often available in used bookstores.

338. *Ask Dale Murphy*. Dale Murphy with Curtis Patton. Introduction by Furman Bisher. Chapel Hill, NC: Algonquin, 1987.

Every coach and parent should have a chance to read this tender, thoughtful, insightful, and inspirational book. It began as a newspaper column by the same name. The format is questions from young fans in bold type that are answered in half-page essays, making it great SSR reading. The question "Do you have trouble unwinding after a game? Sometimes I can't sleep and I'm just in Little League.— Billy Taylor, 11" is answered in several paragraphs that end with the following: "My main advice to Little Leaguers is to enjoy the game and have fun. It's good to be excited and have butterflies in your stomach. But if you haven't had a good time, it's not worth it" (pages 85–86). There is a Strong Passage for coaches and parents in that section. (See "Book Chapters and Strong Passages," entry 355.)

339. *Charlotte's Web*. E. B. White. Illustrated by Garth Williams. New York: HarperCollins, 1990. 1953 Newbery Honor Book.

Few stories are both suspenseful and heartwarming in the way that the story of Charlotte and her friends is. On the chance that you have neither read nor been told this tale of ingenuity in the face of great peril, I will not go into detail. Suffice it to say that this book tells of friendship and danger and proves that tenacity and the power of positive thinking can change the course of history. This is a wonderful read-aloud book for parent to child, teacher to student, in each case with long time-outs for discussion of what has happened and what might happen next. This teaches that reading is a reflective, thinking process, not a linear one. It also teaches the good reader the strategy of predicting. What is important is not that the readers guess correctly what is coming up. What is important is that they think ahead, predicting the possibilities. This process teaches, among many things, the notion that there may be many solutions to a problem, many good answers to a question. Speaking of thinking beyond, looking at the author as a human who uses literacy in ways other than book writing can foster in learners the idea that they, too, may become literacy users and writers. To that end, I recommend taking a look at a short series of letters between E. B. White and Groucho Marx, found on pages 131–33 in *The Groucho Letters*, Simon & Schuster, 1967. (See entry 278 in Unit 5.)

340. *Dogsong*. Gary Paulsen. New York: Bradbury Press, 1985. 1986 Newbery Honor Book.

Russell Susskit's mother ran off with a white man many years before and his father has offered little more than shelter from the elements in their humble cottage. The fourteen-year-old Alaskan attempts to learn something of life from his surrogate grandfather, Oogruk, but receives a lesson in death, instead. Death, the old way, with dignity and conscious participation. He also receives a legacy into manhood as he rides into the wilderness with the old man's dogsled. During that journey he falls heir to a pregnant woman-child who has fled the ridicule of her villagers, preferring death to a life of humiliation over her sin. Russell does all he knows how to provide sustenance for himself and his newfound charge, but eventually realizes that neither he nor she are equipped to deal with adult matters brought on by her pregnancy. Multiple layers of parent/child relationships and cross-cultural values hold opportunities for read alouds, dialogues, small group and panel discussions. Paulsen's simple language makes his compelling insights accessible to the developing reader as well as the ESL student.

341. *The Family Under the Bridge*. Natalie Savage Carlson. Pictures by Garth Williams. New York: Scholastic, 1986. 1959 Newbery Honor Book.
    The setting is France in the wintertime, and the hobo Armand has been adopted by some orphaned children who have taken over his spot under the bridge. These new responsibilities are changing his life.

342. *The Giver*. Lois Lowry. New York: Houghton Mifflin, 1993. 1994 Newbery Medal winner.
    In clear, everyday English, Lowry unfolds a strange tale of a controlled society that has no access to literature and no right to critical thinking. Only one person in the community is permitted knowledge of a time when the weather was not the same and skin colors were different. Genetic engineering and daily doses of drugs prevent nearly everyone from stepping over the line that causes them to be "released." This intriguing story, focusing on one young boy, promises hours of leisure reading and thought-provoking dialogues.

343. *I Was a Teenage Professional Wrestler*. Ted Lewin. New York: Scholastic, 1993.
    A glossary of wrestling lingo and wrestling holds fills the last three pages of the book. Many may want to start there. The book has an ample supply of photographs of known, unknown, and colorful wrestlers from the 1950s and 1960s, plus drawings and paintings by the author, who used wrestling to pay the rent while he attended the Pratt Institute. This split life allowed him a unique place among artists and wrestlers. In this autobiography, Lewin recounts the fun times he and his brothers had as children when their father took them to the fights. It was a father-son occasion that set the course for Ted. He also describes the wrestlers who lived in his house and how they spent their time outside the ring—none, that he could recall, ever read. This is an interesting read, whether you are a sports fan, art enthusiast, or neither. Note: For a sample of Lewin's artwork, see *The Day of Ahmed's Secret* under "First Readers and Picture Books," entry 302.

344. *Journey*. Patricia MacLachan. New York: Dell, 1991.
    Eleven-year-old Journey tries to comprehend why his mother has just deserted him and his sister Cat. And long before, their father vanished without a trace. True, the children get occasional packets of money from their mother—sent without love notes or return address. And they are fed and clothed by his mother's parents, sharing what appears to be a normal life on their grandparent's farm. But when Journey happens to be at a friend's house as the dad kisses everyone in the room goodbye—including Journey—the boy realizes he can't recall ever being kissed before. That thought lingers. Written from the boy's point of view, the

language is simple, yet charged with the feelings of a deserted, introspective human, slowly edging towards truth and emotional maturity. An uninvited stray cat moves into Journey's room, becoming the much needed confidant of both Journey and his grandmother—a beautiful opener for discussions of pets and their value to those who have them. Grandma has warned not to name any animal you don't want to look after. Though every page is solid text—no pictures unless you count the photographs described by Journey—and the setting will be unfamiliar to readers from an urban environment, this qualifies as a first reader, a moving story, and a great real aloud, too. This little book is loaded with stopping points, places that would cry out for dialogue among adults or children . . . of any age, from any culture.

345. *Lafcadio: The Lion Who Shot Back*. Shel Silverstein. New York: Harper & Row, 1963.
      A lion cub is orphaned when hunters kill his mom. Over time he develops fear and then a love for the power of the gun he finds. He goes to the big city and becomes the thing he abhors. At last he tries to return to the tall grassland of his youth. This beautifully written book is a parable for racism and bigotry. It provides so much room for discussion between parent and child or teacher and student or among adults in small discussion groups that I cannot begin to list the ways in which it has contributed to my work with adults, teens, and young children. It is easy to read, has humorous cartoon illustrations, and messages, messages, messages.

346. *Missing May*. Cynthia Rylant. New York: Dell, 1992. 1993 Newbery Award.
      Summer can't remember ever being loved. She was traded from relative to relative after her mother died and finally settled in with Uncle Ob and Aunt May. Now May has died and Ob has sunk into a depression that threatens to orphan Summer once again.

347. *The Missing Piece*. Shel Silverstein. New York: Harper & Row, 1976.
      Though this is truly a picture book, it is under "Thin Books" because it is quite thick with unnumbered pages. It looks like a novel. The surprise comes when you find only one line of text per page, sometimes no text. There are incredibly simple line illustrations and a powerful message about being your own person. Every adult I have shared it with has loved it. Even so, the ensuing dialogue is never predictable. It gives different messages to different people. I use it as a gift for birthdays, breakups, moving from home, getting a new job. For anniversaries I combine it with the companion piece, *The Missing Piece Meets the Big O*, by Shel Silverstein, Harper & Row, 1981.

348. *My Dad Lives in a Downtown Hotel*. Peggy Mann. Illustrated by Richard Cuffari. New York: Scholastic, 1973.
      The impact of a family breakup on school behavior, the sense of isolation a child feels when first confronted with disharmony between his parents, the need to talk about troubles with someone who will not condemn the victim, and the fear of the actual breakup of the household are told in the child's own words: "What's got into you today, Joey?" his teacher asks. "Running around, shoving into everyone! You'd better stay in here til you feel you can behave yourself. And

then come out." His teacher closes the closet room door. "I looked around. I felt like knocking over everything in the stupid supply room. Ripping the posters off the walls. Busting my fists through the volleyball nets. Throwing the equipment all over the place. But then I figured, what was the sense. It would only make Miss Clifford trouble. And it wasn't her fault that my dad had walked out on my mom and me last night" (page 1). On page 65, he tells about "Our Time," a period during dinner when they have agreed to just talk about "Things." "Sometimes these are just regular things, you know—about homework. Or what color to have the bathroom painted because the guy in the apartment above ours let his bathtub overflow and it spoiled all the paint on our bathroom ceiling and walls. And sometimes we talk about—I mean things that are hard to talk about. Like—you know, divorce and all that stuff." Then he talks about isolation and the agony of keeping his terrible secret. "At first I didn't mention anything about it to anyone. I mean, my dad living downtown in that crummy hotel. Him walking out on us and all. I felt—ashamed. Even though the whole thing wasn't my fault, maybe people would think it was." But one day when he and a schoolmate are riding the bus, "for some reason, I found myself spilling the whole works to Pepe," who responds, " 'So what?' Yeah, he didn't bat an eye. 'Lots of kids got no dad living in the house,' he said. 'There's this little kid used to tell everyone his dad got killed in a car crash. But one day when we was playing dominoes on his front stoop, he tells me, "You know, man, maybe my dad got kilt and maybe he didn't. I'll never know, 'cause I never even seen him once. I don't even know who he is!" And then this little kid laughed and laughed. We both did.' " But divorce and broken homes are no laughing matter. Neither are the tensions children are forced to carry around when they have terrible secrets to bear. This is a powerful book, a quality parent-child read aloud, even if no divorce is in their lives, and a compellingly told story for all ages.

349. *Red Dirt Jessie*. Anna Myers. New York: Walker, 1992.
   "My sister Patsy is dead," opens the first chapter. Jessie, her little brother H.J. and her mother are the survivors on the dirt poor Oklahoma farm. Jessie's father, though officially alive, has dropped into such despair that he seldom looks at anyone and never speaks. The Dust Bowl has left the family with nothing and that is why there wasn't money enough for Patsy's medical treatment. The guilt has robbed Jessie of yet another family member, but she is determined that she is going to get her father back.

350. *Sarah, Plain and Tall*. Patricia MacLachlan. New York: Harper Trophy, 1985. 1986 Newbery Medal.
   This is a touching story about family relationships and people in general. The simple, direct letters written among the people who were contemplating becoming a family are remarkable exercises in truth. Everyone is involved in selecting the stepparent and stepchildren.

351. *So Much to Tell You*. John Marsden. New York: Fawcett Juniper, 1987. Australia's 1988 Book of the Year Award.
   Awful secrets, a family torn apart over domestic discord, and a young woman's wish to be normal again, thump out a spell-binding story of parental neglect and worse through the first-person accounting conveyed in fourteen-year-old

Marina's journal entries. There is so much to discuss about parenting as a result of this book, I cannot suggest it for any other unit. It is a read aloud, a silent read, and a possible readers theatre source.

Challenging

352. *Death Be Not Proud: A Memoir.* John Gunther. New York: HarperPerennial, 1989.

The book opens with the John Donne poem that inspired the title. Gunther's son, Johnny, was struck down by a cancerous brain tumor when he was only seventeen. This book is his father's memorial to the courage and tragedy of that young man's life and death.

353. *The Red Pony.* John Steinbeck. New York: Penquin, 1965.

Set in California is this tale of a boy's turmoil as he is faced with too much responsibility and fails—a failure that ends in the death of a beloved animal.

354. *Who's Afraid. . . ? Facing Children's Fears with Folktales.* Norma J. Livo. Englewood, CO: Teacher Ideas Press, 1994.

Fears of being lost, of losing a parent, of being blind, of wetting in class, of school, of being caught in theft, of being suspected of lying, of being sick or hospitalized, of dreams.

"Many a timid child has been terrorized by an intimidating adult who says, 'I could eat you up' as they pinch the child's cheeks. We have seen this child-eating idea in 'Hansel and Gretel' and the 'Basket Woman.' But a look at children-eating monsters would not be complete without Baba Yaga. . . . Yes, the messages of these folklore characters are scary and cruel, but there seems to have been a place for bogeymen throughout the ages. Children can learn to cope with dangers through these stories" (page xxvii). In her thoughtful book on using literature to assuage children's fears, Livo also opens the doors for adults to talk about fears, many of them the same as children's, many left over from unresolved issues in childhood. The book introduces a topic, offers folktales that reflect these universal concerns, and then offers ways of discussing the issues of the past and present. At the end of each unit are a bibliography and a reference list with full citations.

Book Chapters and Strong Passages

355. "Adult Coaches and Children." In *Ask Dale Murphy.* Dale Murphy with Curtis Patton. Introduction by Furman Bisher. Chapel Hill, NC: Algonquin, 1987, pages 21–23.

"I received a letter the other day from a twelve-year-old child involved in athletics who complained about his coach yelling at him" (page 21). The heart-sent, common sense messages about this and other concerns regarding the impact that sports can have on youths open the floor to discussions about values and consequences. (For more detail, see entry 338 under "Thin Books.")

356. *Ann Landers Speaks Out.* Ann Landers. Greenwich, CT: Fawcett, 1975.

This collection of letters to and from one of America's favorite advice columnists provides high-interest, adult-level dialogue in short, easy-to-understand passages. Letters from parents about their children, children about their parents, and neighbors about both give reflections on our times. There are books like this published every few years, and some libraries have collections of them. Used bookstores and swap meets also are good places to look for older editions. A chance to compare letters and responses with ten or twenty years between can open the floor to a lot of culture-specific dialogue. These books are great for SSR, and some serve well for read-aloud attention getters, as there are many topics addressed in Landers's work.

357. *The Best of Dear Abby*. Abigail Van Buren. Kansas City, MO: Andrews & McMeel, 1981.
Here is a collection of letters written to the newspaper lovelorn and life problems specialist. She opens the book with a long, autobiographical letter telling how she and her identical twin sister, Ann Landers, grew up, entered the same profession, were estranged, and finally reconciled. Sibling rivalry is an intriguing and important topic for the parenting unit, and here, gone public, is one of the most notorious cases—with a happy ending. This letter is a whirlwind accounting that is sure to prove interesting to twins of any age and to many people who are not getting along with their siblings—of any age. For this "Dear Readers" letter, the book is worth opening. After that comes advice to others. She does not give her responses in letter form but answers most collections on the same problem in general terms. The letters in most cases, are short and easy to understand.

358. "Bopsy." Jack Canfield and Mark V. Hansen. In *Chicken Soup for the Soul: 101 Stories to Open the Heart and Rekindle the Spirit*. Edited by Jack Canfield and Mark V. Hansen. Deerfield Beach, FL: Health Communications, 1993, pages 61–63.
A terminally ill child is given the most honorable of send-offs. This is about death with dignity and seeing death as part of life.

359. "Carpe Diem!" Alan Cohen. In *Chicken Soup for the Soul: 101 Stories to Open the Heart and Rekindle the Spirit*. Edited by Jack Canfield and Mark V. Hansen. Deerfield Beach, FL: Health Communications, 1993, pages 46–50.
A simple card can make a great deal of difference—to the sender. This is about personal courage and reaching out—just doing what you really want to do.

360. *The Cay*. Theodore Taylor. New York: Doubleday, 1969. Winner of numerous awards, including the 1970 Jane Addams Book Award, 1970 Lewis Carroll Shelf Award, 1970 Commonwealth Club Award, 1970 Award of the Southern California Council on Literature for Children and Young People, 1970 Woodward School Annual Book Award, and the 1970 Friends of the Library Award, University of California at Irvine.
The entire book is a read-aloud selection. It is definitely too difficult for new readers or entry-level ESL readers to try alone. If you simply read it chapter by chapter to your student or class, you will give them an incredible journey into life, history, human nature, and fine writing. This simply written, fascinating tale provides an objective vehicle for discussion of the parenting that might have cost the boy his only chance at life. Lost at sea in 1942, an eleven-year-old white boy from Virginia and a sixtyish black man of St. Thomas Island are marooned on a raft at sea and then on a tiny island. An accident leaves the boy blind, a disability

that permits him to open his eyes in new ways. Reading this book aloud will encourage discussions of racism and how it had been taught to this young child. Through *The Cay*, parents or would-be parents can discover how bigotry and racism limit the lives of the bigot and racist.

361. "The Gentlest Need." Fred T. Wilhelms. In *Chicken Soup for the Soul: 101 Stories to Open the Heart and Rekindle the Spirit*. Edited by Jack Canfield and Mark V. Hansen. Deerfield Beach, FL: Health Communications, 1993, pages 59–60.

If you have not given your pet enough "purring" lately, it is time. Same goes for your loved ones.

362. "The Good Stuff." In *It Was on Fire When I Lay Down on It*. Robert Fulghum. New York: Ivy Books, 1989, pages 25–29.

Here a father has just a few minutes to redeem himself by rushing back to the office to retrieve a bag of treasures his daughter had packed for him to play with.

363. "How to Encourage Your Child to Read." Erma Bombeck. In *How to Use the Power of the Printed Word*. Edited by Billings S. Fuess, Jr. Preface by Clifton Fadiman. New York: Anchor Press, 1985.

Among the issues covered by Bombeck are "When to Start" and "Picking the Right Book." Children are the focus of Bombeck's contribution, but there are also thirteen essays on the English language, each written by an expert in the field. All are worthwhile reading. Of particular note are "Malcolm Forbes—How to Write a Business Letter"; "George Plimpton—How to Make a Speech"; "Bill Cosby—How to Read Faster"; "Edward T. Thompson—How to Write Clearly"; "James Michener—How to Use a Library"; "Steve Allen—How to Enjoy the Classics"; and "John Irving—How to Spell." Incidentally, Bombeck's newspaper column is nearly always a humor-loaded look at family life and the problems associated with young or teenage children. The columns are short reads, so if you can locate them in your local paper, clip and save them for short bits of time when somebody needs a pick-me-up.

364. *I Want to Tell You: My Response to Your Letters, Your Messages, Your Questions*. O. J. Simpson. Boston: Little, Brown, 1995.

The title describes most of the contents of this easy reader with photographs. Anyone intrigued by the trial, the murders, or the reactions of people of all ages to this public event will find something to read in this book. But there is a pervasive quality concerning the young children of the author and the adult children who also make up his family picture. The complex issues of parenting, divorce, spousal abuse, and how these things influence all parties are presented here in simple text.

365. *The Living Lincoln: The Man, His Mind, His Times, and the War He Fought, Reconstructed from His Own Writings*. Edited by Paul M. Angle and Earl Schenck Miers. New York: Barnes & Noble, 1992.

This is a book of the letters, speeches, and journals documenting the history lived by a literate man. Annotations help create a context for these one-sided communications. The entire book is worth study. And if any part of it was published in booklet form, perhaps with illustrations, it would qualify as a Thin Book or even, for some parts, a First Reader. Lincoln's style was forthright, honest, and to the point. There is no wondering what he meant. On page 619 appears a four-sentence letter to his wife, in which Lincoln mentioned their son's pony and the goats, the death of Mrs. Col. Dimick, and a couple of other items, making the announcement of the death seem quite perfunctory, as if he did not care about people's deaths. Then, starting on page 635 and for several pages after, Lincoln began a series of short letters in which he postponed the execution of one convicted prisoner after another, making it clear that he did, indeed, care. In the personal letters that were kept, he just did not write much about it.

366. "Puppies for Sale." Dan Clark. In *Chicken Soup for the Soul: 101 Stories to Open the Heart and Rekindle the Spirit*. Edited by Jack Canfield and Mark V. Hansen. Deerfield Beach, FL: Health Communications, 1993, pages 65–66.

Here the puppy with a limp is selected by a boy who can relate. This is about diversity and tolerance.

367. *365 TV-Free Activities You Can Do with Your Child*. Steve Bennett and Ruth Bennett. Holbrook, MA: Bob Adams, 1991.

This is a thick Thin Book, with one-page reads and great ideas written in simple, everyday English. Each activity has a cartoon icon to show what the page is about. There is an index to make idea scanning easy. Topics include science, numbers, reading, collecting, environmental issues, and many others. Though the title suggests parents and children do these activities, this is a great source of classroom ideas, too. Adults, whether teachers or learners, will get just as much from the experiences as younger folks.

368. *The Usborne Illustrated Dictionary of Biology*. Corinne Stockley. Designed by Nerissa Davies. Scientific advisers Drs. Margaret Rostron and John Rostron. Illustrated by Kuo Kang Chen. London: Usborne, 1986.

The contents are sectioned into general, plants, animals, humans, and more general. Each section is color coded, so that even the little boxes around information reflect the part of the book you are in. Each page is a storehouse of short passages supported by detailed illustrations with labels and diagrams. Though the scientific terms are incorporated throughout, they are also explained right away. There is a great deal of interesting information parents will want to share with children. Of particular note are two sections on reproduction, plants on pages 30–33 and humans on pages 88–95, which use simple, easy-to-follow language and quality illustrations. Also of value in coming-of-age dialogues may be the topic of genetics and heredity, pages 96–98. Even the complexities of DNA are touched upon, though if many questions come up here, another book will be required.

369. *What Happened to Their Kids? Children of the Rich and Famous*. Malcolm Forbes with Jeff Bloch. New York: Simon & Schuster, 1990.

Paul Revere, the silversmith made famous by a midnight ride in 1775—with the help of the poet Longfellow—had sixteen children, eleven of whom grew to adulthood. Franz Xaver Wolfgang Mozart, son of Wolfgang Amadeus Mozart, was pushed to perform in much the same way his father was. The son of Maria Montessori, the famous early childhood educator, was sent away from his unwed mother at birth, was never recognized as more than an adopted child. Thomas Edison, the genius with only a fourth-grade education, was less celebrated by his children, most of whom disowned him before he died. The children of many other famous parents have their stories told in these two-to-three-page essays. The text is easy to read, vocabulary simple, and topics fascinating, qualifying this as a Thin Book.

Newspaper and Magazine Articles

370. "Bad Vibes Across America over Rock, Rap Lyrics." *USA Today*, June 30–July 2, 1995, page 4-D.

"Opposing forces: C. DeLores Tucker says music lyrics send 'genocidal message'; Dave Marsh calls ratings 'a tyranny.' " So goes the half-page article on lyrics that call for violence against specific groups and the efforts to stop them. One thirty-six-year-old music promoter expresses concern over the impact that reggae music has on youngsters, and a twelve-year-old says she would feel pretty bummed if her listening was censored. After all, she argues, her friends use the "objectionable" language when adults are not around, her parents use it when she and her sister are not around (but they hear it anyway), and even her baby-sitter uses it. This article will not solve the problem, but it will open the door to dialogue about a number of issues.

371. "The Girl Who Wouldn't Give Up." Patricia Hittner. *Woman's World: The Woman's Weekly*, October 13, 1992, pages 6–7.

"I wondered, 'Why Terri? I'd already lived so much of my life—why not me?' I kept wishing I could take Terri's place," said Dorothy Harding, mother of the young girl whose bout with deadly meningitis began with chills and fever a year ago, left her without legs, and caused her left hand to turn black. This short story is both tragic and full of hope. It is also full of information about the fast-moving disease. Like all articles in this grocery store tabloid, it uses language that is simple and straightforward. The stories are action-packed and on topics appropriate to adults.

372. "Helping Kids Who Stutter." *Woman's World: The Woman's Weekly*. October 13, 1992, page 17.

In this quarter-page article, following a brief background on the problem, is some sound advice for parents of young children. First and foremost is the following instruction: "Listen patiently. Don't interrupt, rush or correct your child when he or she speaks." Then, "Don't ask you child to practice hard-to-pronounce words."

373. "The Rose." In "The Kennedy Scandals." *Globe Special*. Edited by Michael J. Irish, 1991, pages 36–41.

The 100-year-old matriarch of the Kennedy clan is celebrated over several pages of historic photographs. She is presented as the saintly figure of her family, always present in times of tragedy and triumph, both of which have accented the Kennedy public lives. Her childhood, education, courtship with Joe Kennedy, seven children in ten years—then humiliation over Joe's womanizing and hurt over his authorizing a frontal lobotomy to control their mildly retarded daughter are contrasted with the image of a socialite busy with charitable and family events. A parenting unit might include her attitude toward physical punishment and appearances. "When they were bad, Rose recalls whacking the children on the hands with a ruler and—like Joan Crawford—spanking the future president and his siblings with a clothes hanger. 'A hanger didn't hurt any more than a ruler, but it is a rather unusual implement . . . and as adults, the children have liked to rag me with how cruel I was to beat them with coat hangers,' she recalls." Even in her position, with money and power, it is interesting to note that her children had not forgiven abuse wielded on them more than half a century earlier. This entire *Globe Special* issue is a series of biographies of one big family. It is written in easy-to-understand prose with a lot of quotes. Grocery store tabloids are one of my favorite sources of high-interest adult reading material.

374. "When Baby Makes Two." Joe Rhodes. *TV Guide*. September 25, 1992, pages 6–10.

The issue of social values is lightly addressed, and concerns about the change of focus from working woman to woman and child are overshadowed by the concern former Vice President Dan Quayle had for the image that Murphy Brown would create when she chose to have a baby without benefit of spouse. There are innuendos on current affairs, not only Quayle's direct hit on the *Murphy Brown* television series plot, but also his highly publicized misspelling of potato as a judge during a spelling bee. This kind of subplot builds background knowledge across topics and shows how background knowledge influences reading comprehension. "Candy Is Dandy, But Don't Mess with Murphy," a mini interview just on the "scandal," is inset on pages 8–9 to help those unaware of the Quayle-Murphy problem. These two pieces, out of an easily accessible publication, provide support for writing about family values, parenting, censorship, child care, economics, politics, or biographies of the real life and fictional characters involved. They also can open a dialogue about broader issues like child care needs for single parents and the changing structure of a family. Not to belabor the point, here is an excellent way of addressing the fact that words only have meaning in context. And context means in the story and in a given historical time. A family of the 1990s is quite different from a family of the 1960s, when communes were popular, and still more different from the family of the 1940s, when the Kennedy clan was taking form.

Other Activities

Following are some activities to support positive parenting skills. There may be ideas in this list that look good, but are not practical for one reason or another. Try finding variations on the themes. If there are subtopics that deal with situations I seem to have overlooked, please let me know how you handled that.

- Book-making books often have ideas for pop-up books that translate easily to greeting cards. Using a book from your local library, select something manageable and make personal greeting cards for your child—just for love—no birthday required.
- Write a letter to your child, telling why the child is important to you.

- Look up recipes for favorite food items as prepared in other countries to share with your child.
- Draw pictures of your children and write poems beneath. No matter that you were not an artist or poet before today.
- Collect family history and keep it for your children.
- Start making a list of things you want your child to know when the child grows up.
- Write the story of how you felt when you first discovered this child was on the way.
- Make up a list of things that you find special about this child. Practice reading it aloud. When the list is perfect, present it at a personal ceremony and read it aloud to the child.
- When there is a problem at home, find a children's book that talks about that kind of problem. Read it to your child. Then discuss it.
- Talk with your child about what the child might become some day. Go to the library to find information on the requirements for the job. Find people who do the kind of work your child is interested in. Introduce them to the child. Together, write follow-up notes.
- Make a little stack of love notes to leave around the house, on the refrigerator door, under your child's pillow, to let the child know you care all the time.
- Look through *365 TV-Free Activities You Can Do with Your Child*, in "Book Chapters and Strong Passages" above, for many creative ideas.

Sickness, Death, and Dying

Unit 7

Few occasions make us more vulnerable than when we are faced with medical problems or the death of a loved one. Even for the accomplished speech maker or letter writer, words can be hard to come by at those times when communication problems can be expensive or deadly. For the parent struggling to ask directions to a clinic or a widow obliged to ask about the cost of a funeral, having a working familiarity with the issues of sickness, death, and dying can make a significant difference to the quality of life. The time of crisis is not the time to acquire the language and background knowledge for emergency dialogues. The readings and suggested activities in this unit will help students get comfortable with speaking and writing about the most difficult of subjects.

The picture books suggested here will facilitate dialogue in the classroom and the home. Parents who have used these picture books to introduce such sensitive topics to their children will not be left groping for words and ways of communicating when communication is key to family survival.

First Readers and Picture Books

375. *All Those Secrets of the World.* Jane Yolen. Illustrated by Leslie Baker. New York: Little, Brown, 1991.

Patriotism, farewells, and a young child's view of the world as her father goes off to war on a big ship are brought together in an emotional story that comes full circle to a happy ending. This child gains both concrete and abstract notions of perspective. The print is large and the well-written text is supported by clear, realistic pictures. It is a good parent-child read aloud, an ESL reader, and a new reader's book about an important topic.

376. *Comic Epitaphs from the Very Best Old Graveyards.* Mount Vernon, NY: Peter Pauper Press, 1957.

One of the joys of epitaphs is their brevity. In just a few words there is the summary of a life, and, in the case of these, the promise of at least one good lesson. Consider one found on page 8:

> Here Lies Pecos Bill
> He Always Lied
> And Always Will:
> He Once Lied Loud
> He Now Lies Still

377. *The Giving Tree.* Written and illustrated by Shel Silverstein. New York: Harper & Row, 1964.

Whether metaphorical or taken at face value, this tree gives everything it has—including, finally, its life. Fine, simple drawings and relentless loving from the tree build to an intellectual crescendo.

378. *Grandad Bill's Song.* Jane Yolen. Illustrated by Melissa Bay Mathis. New York: Philomel, 1994. Picture book.

Jon attempts to sort out his own emotions about a giant loss as he asks adult family members, "What did you do on the day Grandpa died?" Each, in turn, retells the things they remember about the beloved husband, father, friend. Woven amidst a musical running narrative, scrapbook pictures and handwritten captions recall precious moments throughout the life of the man Jon knew as Grandpa.

379. *Heron Street.* Ann Turner. Paintings by Lisa Disimini. New York: Scholastic, 1989.

The pictures alone make an eerie impression on the reader, who is led into a tale of systematic removal of life from a little plot known as Heron Street.

380. *I'll Always Love You.* Hans Wilhelm. New York: Crown, 1985.

Love and saying I love you, death and the grieving process are conveyed in just a handful of simple colored drawings and a few lines of prose. Here less is enough to keep the reader in tears for hours and thinking long, long after.

381. *I'll See You in My Dreams.* Mavis Jukes. Illustrated by Stacey Schuett. New York: Alfred A. Knopf, 1993.

A child starts to deal with signs of old age, sickness, and the impending death of an uncle who is in a nursing home. Brilliantly colored scenery supports her imaginary flight in a fabric and wood biplane. Her thoughts reflect impossible dreams, as the voice of her mother describes the real situation they will encounter when their real jet lands. Easy reader or read aloud. Excellent for a death and dying unit.

382. *Life Doesn't Frighten Me.* Poem by Maya Angelou. Paintings by Jean-Michel Basquiat. New York: Stewart, Tabori & Chang, poem copyright 1978, illustration copyright 1993.

Seeming to be a children's picture book, this collection of illustrations and ideas suddenly shocks the senses with the kinds of things that really frighten us all. Oil pastels, gouache, acrylics, and collage give the illusion of children's art, and the rugged, haphazard-looking type font looks like children's writing, but they combine to convey a level of sophistication that calls for rereading, rereading, rereading. At the end are two-page biographies of the author and the illustrator. They are good reading in themselves and promise insights into the lives of two artists who made a mark beyond the expected. Angelou's call to all to "read everything possible, be it African-American, European, Latin, or other literature— but, especially Shakespeare," makes this even more appropriate for adult new readers. The drug death at an early age of the artist, whose works send the reader on an emotional roller-coaster ride, makes this an even more important book for people concerned about the influence of illegal drugs on our lives. Each of us lost when this young man stopped making art. A read aloud or First Reader for the poem, but this is no solo read—it demands discussion.

383. *Love You Forever.* Robert Munsch. Toronto: Annick Press, 1986.

Here is a life cycle book about a mother and a son who finally trade places. I used to give this to any friend who had a preteen or teenage son. Now I just give it to mothers and sons in general and occasional others, too. But to this day, I am unable to read it aloud. I do not know if anyone can.

384. *Maggie and the Pirate.* Ezra Jack Keats. New York: Scholastic, 1979.

Maggie's family lives in a broken-down school bus. She has friends who hang out with her and try to help her find her pet cricket when the Pirate kidnaps it. In the resulting turmoil, the cricket is killed. Maggie appears quite poor—until you meet the Pirate.

385. *The Middle Passage.* Illustrated by Tom Feelings. New York: Dial Books, 1995.

Feelings describes the evolution of his idea for this text-free book: "[M]uted images flashed across my mind. Pale white sailing ships like huge white birds of prey, plunging forward into mountainous rising white foaming waves of cold water, surrounding and engulfing everything. Our ancestors, hundreds of them locked in the belly of each of these ships, chained together like animals throughout the long voyage from Africa toward unknown destinations, millions dying from the awful conditions in the bowels of the filthy slave galleys." So goes the description of conditions for human beings during the Middle Passage across the Atlantic Ocean—now exposed in a graphic form that is beyond words. Feelings says it took him nearly twenty years to create it. Indeed, it required over 200 years. When I first saw a few of the galleys of this picture book, I was shaken, awestruck, speechless—the close-up faces, the distant views of mystical ships, the cutaways into their holds. Dignity, agony, fear, and wonder rush across the pages. Feelings researched his topic in traditional academic fashion and as ethnographer, going to live in Ghana. It is impossible for me to imagine an educational theme that could not somehow employ this monumental work. It is clearly one of the most important creative works in American history.

386. *My Grandma Lived in Gooligulch.* Graeme Base. New York: Harry N. Abrams, 1990.

Terrific drawings of Australian animals accompany a poetic narrative about Grandma, who could train animals and lived happily in a home overrun by them. A map on the first two-page spread suggests where Gooligulch is located. This is a wonderful poem for anyone who has had a lively grandma who is not around anymore.

387. *Northern Lights: The Soccer Trails.* Michael Arvaarluk Kusugak. Art by Vladyana Krykorka. Toronto-New York: Annick Press, 1993. Ruth Schwartz Award.

Adoration of mother for child and child for mother, a ride on a canoe on a sled pulled by dogs, sickness and the death of a parent, soccer played with a caribou skin ball, and the northern lights are experiences the reader gets through a sensitive tale of one Inuit girl. The beautiful and detailed colored drawings are supplemented by beaded items that reflect the symbolism that is emerging from the text. On the back cover is a summary of the aurora borealis, known on Baffin Island as "Soccer Trails." It is believed that these lights are deceased loved ones playing soccer in the sky.

388. *Sophie*. Mem Fox. Illustrated by Aminah Brenda Lynn Robinson. New York: Harcourt Brace, 1994.

Sophie loves her grandpa, who is always ready to play with her until one day— . The simple funeral illustration shows Grandpa in his casket. Then there is grief. Mem Fox—consistently powerful.

389. *The Spice Alphabet Book: Herbs, Spices, and Other Natural Flavors*. Jerry Pallotta. Illustrated by Leslie Evans. Watertown, MA: Charlesbridge, 1994.

Though only one letter applies specifically to sickness, death, and dying, this is one of the most information-intensive Pallotta books yet. The format appears to offer the traditional young child's ABCs, but this is definitely loaded with adult fare. The Q page gives the historical use of quinine for malaria during the construction of the Panama Canal. There is also an inset map showing the Canal Zone. The last page is solid with other bits of information that the artist found but could not fit into the book proper.

390. *Tough Boris*. Mem Fox. Illustrated by Kathryn Brown. San Diego, CA: Harcourt Brace, 1994.

Almost traditional watercolor illustrations give meaning to the single lines of prose on each two-page spread. There is a thirty-one-word vocabulary for the entire book—though this is not to say the words lack meaning, not to say they are easy words. The story deals with stereotyping, sadness, grief, and death.

391. *The Wall*. Eve Bunting. Illustrated by Ronald Himler. New York: Clarion Books, 1990.

Just a few perfectly chosen words to a page and sensitive, detailed watercolors deliver powerful thoughts about loss and eternity.

392. *Wilfrid Gordon McDonald Partridge*. Mem Fox. Illustrated by Julie Vivas. Brooklyn, NY: Kane/Miller, 1985.

This is an extraordinary example of how text and pictures give meaning together. The lad with the long title name has an active, fun-filled life visiting his next-door neighbors, residents of an old people's home. We are not told he is poor, we just see the markings within the illustrations, just as we see the emotions of the residents of the home. This tale is about memory loss and the importance of having something to think or care about. It is about the contrast between youth and age. It is about valuing human beings. For any age reader, of any culture, this is a powerful book.

Between Picture Books and Thin Books

393. *History's Big Mistakes*. Adam Bowett. Illustrated by Chris Mould. London: Belitha Press, 1994.

The way in which pictures and text support each other makes this book a candidate for a space between Picture Books and Thin Books. A glossary at the end is made even more useful, as all of the words defined there are highlighted in the main text. The witty running stories are interesting and easy to read, with lots

of space devoted to incredibly humorous cartoons. Little bits of additional information are offered in small boxes on nearly every page. Each two-page spread tells
of another historic foible. Strong Passages occur in every section, but one of
particular interest to a unit on death, the 1854 Charge of the Light Brigade, the
most remarkable blunder of the Crimean War.

394. *Jamestown Heritage Readers.* Books A-F. Edited by Lee Mountain, Sharon
Crawley, and Edward Fry. Providence, RI: Jamestown, 1991.
      This series is a beautiful anthology of classic and popular fiction and nonfic-
tion. Stories have the illustrations that came with the reproduced versions of the
tales, many quite remarkable. The books are identified by difficulty level, A being
easiest, F most difficult. But these letters are only guidelines. Some selections in
book D are easier for adult new readers than some in book C, for example. Books
B, C, and D have been most popular among my adult learners. By the time they
get to book F, I suggest they belong in the regular library collection. Though most
of the selections are in their authentic state, some vocabulary has been manipulated. I recommend teachers look at the end of the acknowledgments to see which
stories are still in the original state and just use those. Though some of the changes
may be minimal, the task of figuring out which changes modify the writer's style
is probably too time-consuming. The teacher's guide for this series is quite rich,
giving background information on authors, illustrators, and, occasionally, historical bits. Every page of text of the series is graced by a wide decorative border, an
added delight.

395. *The Pied Piper of Hamelin.* Deborah Hautzig. New York: Random House, 1989.
      This little book is well illustrated and well told. The large print is easy to look
at, and the vocabulary is comprehensible. Though there are many variations on
this tale, this one has worked well for many of my students simply because it is
lightweight and easy to slip into a notebook. Below the same story appears in an
anthology.

396. "The Pied Piper of Hamelin." A European folktale retold by Joseph Jacobs.
In *Jamestown Heritage Reader.* Book C. Providence, RI: Jamestown, 1991, pages
67–75.
      An inexplicable swath of misfortune raced through all of Europe, leaving
death and destroyed lives behind. Rats later proved to be the main culprit. The
Pied Piper tale recounts an actual event in which the children of one small town
were wiped out. I like linking this story, which has been retold in many different
styles, with the companion poems "The Pied Piper of Hamelin" by Robert Browning (detailed in entry 445) and the Shel Silverstein poem "The One Who Stayed,"
in *Where the Sidewalk Ends,* page 153 (entry 443).
      In the two Pied Piper writings, we see how both history and the work of other
artists can affect how we respond to tragedy. There is a scientific link to this story
under "Book Chapters and Strong Passages" in this unit. See *Bugs: Giant Magnified
Images as Seen Through a Microscope* (entry 431).

Thin Books

397. *Abraham Lincoln*. Kathie Billingslea Smith. Illustrated by James Seward. New York: Scholastic, 1987.

A barefoot lad in western Kentucky is introduced. Then his mother dies, his father remarries, and the boy is fortunate enough to have a stepmother who honors his love of books. He is married, a child is born and dies, two more are born, and the man becomes president of the United States. A war over slavery, the Civil War, begins, the Emancipation Proclamation is signed, and another son dies. The war ends, and the reelected president is assassinated. All this in just a few pages of easy-to-read text, with clear drawings on each page.

398. *Body Battles*. Rita Golden Gelman. Illustrated by Elroy Freem. New York: Scholastic, 1992.

This little book starts out sounding quite childish in its presentation of cartoon blood cells and earwax and has the potential for annoying a serious teen or adult. Yet the information is dispensed quickly and easily, making it a good source of basic physiology. Information on how the immune system works is something everyone can use, and here it is accessible. At the end is a pitch against drug abuse, again focusing on preteens.

399. *Bull Run*. Paul Fleischman. Woodcuts by David Frampton. New York: Scholastic, 1993.

Two maps make up the first two pages, one depicting the existing states and their positions in the Session, the other a close-up of the Eastern Theatre of the Civil War, where the Battle of Bull Run took place. At the end, a two-page spread shows two maps of the battle scene, morning on the left, afternoon on the right. One by one, in isolated vignettes, as though reporting to an unseen interviewer, fictional characters tell their stories of hearing about war, getting ready for the battle, heading off and how the battle occurred—the tragic discovery that war is not a game. The momentum of this series of reports builds so subtly that the reader does not realize what has happened until it is done. Each vignette is one or two pages. And each speaker has a personal icon woodcut. The language is quite simple, no long sentences, no big words, and as such, almost chops at the reader's attention, but the overall impact is strong. A pair of passages shows changes in the character of a young boy: Eleven-year-old Toby Boyce, pages 13–14, announces that he is "desperate to kill a Yankee before the supply ran out." In the same passage he bluffs his way into service as a fife player. Then, on page 96, Toby appears on the battlefield and describes the horrors. A badly wounded soldier begs Toby to shoot him. "My stomach emptied. He was a Yank. How I'd longed back home to kill one. Here I finally had my chance. But instead I ran." And on page 94, Dr. William Rye describes the fruits of war in his simple statements of fact about the scene around him.

400. *Buried in Ice: The Mystery of a Lost Arctic Expedition*. Owen Beattie and John Geiger. New York: Scholastic, 1994.

A chronology of the search for the Northwest Passage begins in 1508 and moves through the centuries until an expedition out from 1903 to 1906 completes the passage by boat. A 1984–1986 expedition discovers the remains of the 1848

Franklin Party, theretofore missing. It seems "lead poisoning from food tins played a role in the expedition's disastrous end." Each chapter is supported by historical photos, paintings, illustrations, and artifacts. The text, though high level, is well written. A glossary at the end is most intriguing.

401. *The Curse of King Tut's Tomb: A History Mystery.* Jay Montavon. New York: Avon Books, 1991.

King Tut died mysteriously, while still a child king. A timeline from 4241 B.C. to A.D. 1939, floor plans of the tomb and burial chamber, historical photographs of the ill-fated king's mummy and his equally ill-fated exhumer, and well-written history with speculation about the macabre coincidences—too many of them—combine to make this small book a compelling read. This History Mystery is part of a series of true stories that have kept my adult new readers and ESL students rapt. They also make great read alouds.

402. *The Death of Lincoln.* Leroy Hayman. New York: Scholastic, 1968.

Here is a fascinating history book, complete with historical photographs and on page 20, Lincoln's accounting of a dream in which his death is predicted.

403. *The Fall of Freddie the Leaf: A Story of Life for All Ages.* Leo Buscaglia. Thorofare, NJ: Charles B. Slack, 1982.

This story about the cycle of life is fine read-aloud material. A curious and occasionally fearful Freddie asks questions about the changes he observes as the seasons affect the leaves all around. With Freddie's experience of only one year, there remains much that he cannot foresee. This metaphorical story of one little leaf provides the foundation for discussions about life and death

404. *Florence Nightingale: The Determined English Woman Who Founded Modern Nursing and Reformed Military Medicine.* Pam Brown. Milwaukee, WI: Gareth Stevens, 1989. People Who Have Helped the World series.

In only sixty-eight pages laced with numerous historical photos, paintings, and etchings, the reader is propelled through incredible highs and lows of a young upper-class British woman's desperate struggle to find intellectual stimulation (her parents disapproved of her avid pursuit of math). She faced relentless family problems and mental illness. Despite this, she managed to reach out to find meaning for her life, taking on the wretched conditions in hospitals and on battlefields, where the sick died as much from their care as their wounds. She is famous for saying, "The first requirement of a hospital is that it should do the sick no harm," page 18. Nightingale lived from 1820 to 1915. The book has a useful three-page chronology, a good glossary, a map of war sites where she worked in Europe and Asia, page 26, and several addresses to write to for more information about Nightingale and nursing. There are numerous read-aloud passages, including "Calamity Unparalleled" and "Reform at the Barrack Hospital," pages 34–35, which tell of unconscionable conditions and the inequities that fostered their perpetuation.

405. *The Giver.* Lois Lowry. New York: Houghton Mifflin, 1993. 1994 Newbery Medal.

Death is not even a word in this strange science-fiction tale of a controlled society that has no access to literature and no right to critical thinking. Only one person in the community is permitted knowledge of a time when the weather was not the same and skin colors were different. Genetic engineering and daily doses of drugs prevent nearly everyone in the community from stepping over the line that causes them to be "released." Newborns who fail to measure up to standard are "released," and the old who have passed their usefulness are "released." But no one—except the old Giver and twelve-year-old Jonas—is allowed to discuss the details of where they are released to. This intriguing story, focusing on one young boy, promises hours of leisure reading and thought-provoking dialogues.

406. *The Human Body: Giant Magnified Images As Seen Through a Microscope.* Heather Amery and Jane Songi. New York: Golden Books, 1994.

Incredible magnifications of human skin, hair, eyes, eardrums, sperm, embryos, tissue, blood, and cells are accompanied by easy-to-understand text. In "The Body at War," pages 32–33, highly magnified samples of the HIV virus on a white blood cell, meningitis bacteria, flu bacteria, tuberculosis bacteria, and white cells attacking a cancerous tumor are spectacular. Special information boxes hold bits of scientific trivia that can be useful at parties, on the bus, or in the beauty parlor. One shows microsurgery in process in which the doctor may be using a needle that is only the length of a hyphen (-). This is a fascinating book.

407. *Missing May.* Cynthia Rylant. New York: Dell, 1992. 1993 Newbery Award.

Summer can't remember ever being loved. She was traded from relative to relative after her mother died and finally settled in with Uncle Ob and Aunt May. Now May has died and Ob has sunk into a depression that threatens to orphan Summer once again.

408. *Mummies and Their Mysteries.* Charlotte Wilcox. New York: Scholastic, 1993.

At the start of the book is a metric conversion table. At the back is a helpful glossary. In between, a world tour by mummy find awaits—Egypt, Peru, the Far East. Old mummies and new are discussed, and their photographs are available for close inspection. Some mummies are bundled up, some gift-wrapped, others just lost and then found. All have tales to tell about their times, lives, and deaths.

409. *Red Dirt Jessie.* Anna Myers. New York: Walker, 1992.

"My sister Patsy is dead," opens the first chapter. Jessie, her little brother H.J. and her mother are the survivors on the dirt poor Oklahoma farm. Jessie's father, though officially alive, has dropped into such despair that he seldom looks at anyone and never speaks. The Dust Bowl has left the family with nothing and that is why there wasn't money enough for Patsy's medical treatment. The guilt has robbed Jessie of yet another family member, but she is determined that she is going to get her father back.

410. *The Story of Jonas Salk and the Discovery of the Polio Vaccine.* Jim Hargrove. Cornerstones of Freedom series. Chicago: Childrens Press, 1990.

This booklet opens with a reproduction of a polio poster, and a victim of that terrible epidemic. Paralysis, death, and the virus known as AIDS are all discussed in scientific terms. The reader is led through history and also through the life of a scientist who found a vaccine that stopped another killer from conquering the Earth.

411. *The Titanic.* Deborah Kent. Cornerstones of Freedom series. Chicago: Childrens Press, 1993.

This booklet tells with fast-paced detail the story of one magnificent, doomed ship, lost at sea and found again over seventy years later. Pictures, diagrams, and newspaper articles give a chilling account of people drowned in an icy tomb.

412. "The Trance." Chapter 5. *Dogsong.* Gary Paulsen. New York: Bradbury Press, 1985, pages 66-75. 1986 Newbery Honor Book.

A fourteen-year-old Alaskan attempts to learn something of life from Oogruk, but receives a lesson in death, instead. Death, the old way, with dignity and conscious participation is forced into the book of lessons Russell takes with him as he rides into the wilderness with the old man's dogsled. This brief chapter yields an understanding of death that Paulsen delivers so deftly that it is over in a minute, leaving the reader wanting to say, "But, wait!" Yet, in the struggle to survive, Russell cannot take time to wail with grief, nor can the reader.

Challenging

413. *Anne Frank: Beyond the Diary: A Photographic Remembrance.* Ruud van der Rol and Rian Verhoeven. Translated by Tony Langham and Plym Peters. Introduction by Anna Quindlen. New York: Viking Penguin, 1993.

Just as the title suggests, this book goes beyond the diary of the young girl into the world and the plight of those whose lives were on the brink of terrible change. Photographs, letters, and simple captions make this history book a detailed journey into a time that will mar the history of humankind for all time. This book should be read in conjunction with the diary.

414. "Ben Bolt." A poem by Thomas Dunn English. Illustrated by James Thurber. In *Fables for Our Time and Famous Poems Illustrated.* James Thurber. New York: Harper & Row, 1983, pages 123–28.

Though there are just a few lines per page, this seems to be a Challenging read. This powerful poem brings to the fore the temporary nature of youth and life. Yet Thurber's illustrations reincarnate the literary work.

415. *Creepy Classics: Hair-Raising Horror from the Masters of the Macabre.* Edited by Mary Hill. Illustrated by Dominick R. Domingo. New York: Random House, 1994.

Dramatic charcoal illustrations and a glossary to help the reader through words like sepulcher, which may not be in most 1990s vocabularies, aid the comprehension of timeless tales told, as the title indicates, by masters of the macabre. Further, each selection is prefaced by a brief historical statement, a biography of the author, and an introduction to the circumstances under which the tale first came to light. W. W. Jacobs, Saki, Robert W. Service, Guy de Maupassant, M. R. James, William Shakespeare, Bram Stoker, Edgar Allan Poe, Sir Arthur Conan Doyle, and Mary Shelley are showcased here. This is a fine, brief introduction to many great authors. With any luck, of course, the reader will find one or two that rate further pursuit. Meanwhile, these tales offer short passages that can fill the minutes between this and that—or keep one's mind off everything for hours. Most of the stories give a very close view of sickness, death, or dying;

however two selections are highlighted under "Book Chapters and Strong Passages" (entries 434 and 442).

416. *Death Be Not Proud: A Memoir*. John Gunther. New York: HarperPerennial, 1989.
The book opens with the John Donne poem that inspired the title. Gunther's son, Johnny, was struck down by a cancerous brain tumor when he was only seventeen. This book is his father's memorial to the courage and tragedy of that young man's life and death.

417. *Dr. Elizabeth: The Story of the First Woman Doctor*. Patricia Clapp. New York: Lothrop, Lee & Shepard, 1974.
One hundred and fifty-six fast-moving pages without pictures give insightful details not only on the woman who lived from 1821 to 1910, but also on the gender and social issues of her day that continue to play out in women's struggles. The biography is written in autobiographical form, discussing her life in England and the United States. There is a reference to Florence Nightingale on page 107. The issues of censorship and the right to privacy come up in a letter from her adopted daughter Kitty, pages 125–26. Look for a read aloud under "Book Chapters and Strong Passages," entry 428.

418. *Great Short Works of Joseph Conrad*. Joseph Conrad. New York: Harper & Row, 1967.
Seven Challenging short stories and a biography of Conrad are contained in 405 pages. The power of Conrad's writing comes, in part, from honest storytelling. His descriptions and the emotional reactions and attitudes of his characters convey real people. Even so, the stories in this collection are by no means easy reading. It is the content that drives the reader on. One good way to ruin a Conrad story is to demand a report on it or a reaction paper. One way to work with the text is to let a self-selected group of readers meet to reflect on the passages they find memorable. Though many of the stories focus on death and dying, there is a particularly wonderful read aloud under "Book Chapters and Strong Passages," entry 438.

419. *Into the Mummy's Tomb: The Real-Life Discovery of Tutankhamun's Treasures*. Nicholas Reeves. New York: Scholastic, 1992.
Though the photographs of the art, expeditions, and mummies are exquisite and informing, the graphics are detailed and clear, and the organization of this Thin Book is logical and easy to follow, I have put it under "Challenging" because the language is just that. However, there is a well-done glossary, and the captions on the pictures are relatively easy to follow. This book has history, adventure, science, and even an instruction page on "How Mummies Were Made." It is loaded with facts and makes a great conversation starter.

420. *The Irish Potato Famine*. Don Nardo. Illustrated by Brian McGovern. San Diego, CA: Lucent Books, 1990.
This carefully documented story of Ireland does far more than just talk about the Potato Famine of the mid 1800s. It details the relationships between rich and poor, the impact of external pressures on the island nation, how Britain came to

have power over it, why that seemed righteous, and what exactly happened when a farm family could not pay the rent after a mysterious blight had stricken their food supply. Indeed potatoes were the only source of food millions of Irish peasants had. Though a standard readability scale might suggest this is an easy reader, the many large chunks of solid text and the colorful turns of phrase used make this more difficult reading than a simple score would convey. But it is good reading, presenting historical facts and explaining events in a compelling way. The illustrations and photographs assist with comprehension, a timeline puts the famine in historical perspective, and a simple map makes clear the relationships of Ireland and Great Britain to each other and to France. Quite possibly it was the potato blight and the resulting deaths of thousands of Irish people that established Ireland's status in the modern world. Individual cases and reports are detailed under "Book Chapters and Strong Passages," entry 441.

421.   *Letters from the Promised Land: Swedes in America, 1840–1914.* Edited by H. Arnold Barton. Minneapolis, MN: University of Minnesota Press, for the Swedish Pioneer Historical Society, 1975.

This period of the greatest migration from Sweden to the United States is discussed through immigrants' letters and diaries and travel accounts by Swedish visitors. Religious persecution, language difficulties, economic strife on both sides of the Atlantic, and the most difficult period—the first six months—are detailed in these documents. There are several particularly telling passages: Foul air, cramped quarters below deck, putrid water, moldy and wormy food that was often in short supply, sickness, and death were standard during the eight- to ten-week voyage. This is so much like the slave transport and the experiences of the poor Irish and the Vietnamese and Cambodian boat people, that it bears comparative analysis in the classroom or tutoring situation, particularly for ESL students. No sooner had I proofread those words than I harkened back to the same conditions for many native-born Americans living in the ghetto. This book provides many dialogue opportunities regarding why people get sick and sometimes die younger than expected.

422.   *The Living Lincoln: The Man, His Mind, His Times, and the War He Fought, Reconstructed from His Own Writings.* Edited by Paul M. Angle and Earl Schenck Miers. New York: Barnes & Noble, 1992.

This is a book of the letters, speeches, and journals documenting the history lived by a literate man. Annotations help create a context for these one-sided communications. The entire book is worth study. And, if any part of it was published in booklet form, perhaps with illustrations, it would qualify as a Thin Book or even, for some parts, a First Reader. Lincoln's style was forthright, honest, and to the point. There is no wondering what he meant. On page 619 Lincoln wrote a four-sentence letter to his wife, in which he mentioned their son's pony and the goats, the death of Mrs. Col. Dimick, and a couple other items, making the announcement of the death seem quite perfunctory—as if he did not care about people's deaths. Then, starting on page 635 and for several pages after, Lincoln began a series of short letters in which he postponed the execution of one convicted prisoner after another, making it clear that he did, indeed, care. In the personal letters that were kept, he just did not write much about it.

The following citation is from the series The Story Behind the Scenery, published by KC Publications. In a large magazine format, each book in this series covers the then-to-now story of historical landmarks. They are written by different authors and have a wide range of difficulty levels within any given text, but generally, these books are written on a high level, making the text out of reach for elementary ESL and adult new readers independently researching a topic. However, they have a lot of information in the full-color photographs that grace each page, and that makes the photo captions easy to follow.

423. *Oregon Trail.* Dan Murphy. Photographs by Gary Ladd. Las Vegas, NV: KC Publications, 1993. The Story Behind the Scenery series.

On a simple U.S. map is marked Independence, Missouri, the start of this massive migration westward. Throughout the book, the progression is graphically documented as the dotted line inches toward Oregon City. As has often been the case, hard economic times or crop failures at home made the promise of greener pastures impossible to disbelieve. Quoted on page 3 is Peter Burnett, later governor of California: "Then, with a twinkle in his eye he said, 'Gentlemen, they do say that out in Oregon the pigs are running about under the great acorn trees, round and fat, and already cooked, with knives and forks sticking in them so that you can cut off a slice whenever you are hungry.' . . . Father was the first to sign his name." An equally jubilant quote comes in 1846 from Donner Party member Edwin Bryant, before the terrible blizzard and horrid end to that group of travelers whose name is lent to Donner Pass. Salt Lake City, intended destination for Mormons seeking a safer life and starting point for those harvesting travelers' souls, also documented casualties—some slain for their beliefs and lifestyle, others victims of the heat, cold, and fierce reception by natural elements of Zion. Though the scenery photographs are rich and the close-ups detailed, the large patches of well-written text qualify this book as Challenging reading.

424. *The Raven and Other Poems.* Edgar Allan Poe. New York: Scholastic, 1992.

These are the famous, macabre, and lamenting works of a master storyteller. Any one of these might also have been put under "Book Chapters and Strong Passages," but I figured one might not be enough when the whole book was in your hands.

425. *The Red Pony,* by John Steinbeck. New York: Viking Penquin, 1994.

Set in California is the tale of a boy's turmoil, as he is faced with too much responsibility and fails—a failure that ends in the death of a beloved animal.

426. *The Strange Case of Dr. Jekyll and Mr. Hyde.* Robert Louis Stevenson, unabridged. Mineola, NY: Dover, 1991.

Mystery, suspense, drama, and romance make this timeless tale as good a read now as it was when written in 1885. Here the reader meets a medicine man, one respected for his caring nature, whose alter ego violates all trust. Stevenson's straightforward writing style lets the student of English and the new reader navigate a classic with ease.

427. *Unconditional Surrender: U. S. Grant and the Civil War*. Albert Marrin. New York: Atheneum, 1994.

Two hundred pages of information-heavy text are supported by a generous sprinkling of historical paintings, photos, and etchings, all black-and-white, and a two-page map of the Civil War zone. Here is a storehouse of detail and drama that makes this time come alive. Although the general text is Challenging, the captions alone are a fine read. Insights into battles shed light on national icons. Popular notions about President Abraham Lincoln are deftly laid to rest. And Grant's success in passing the Fifteenth Amendment, assuring blacks, including former slaves, the right to vote, is but one of many successes in the life of this master militia man. There are numerous opportunities for read alouds. This is a moving book that could spur extensive dialogue almost from any page.

Book Chapters and Strong Passages

428. "The Accident." In *Dr. Elizabeth: The Story of the First Woman Doctor*. Patricia Clapp. New York: Lothrop, Lee & Shepard, 1974, pages 73-78.

"The Accident" tells of a bizarre incident in which her own eye was contaminated by fluid from that of a child she was treating, an accident with life-changing implications. This thought-provoking passage is appropriate for high school and older. (More detail is under "Challenging," entry 417.)

429. "Another Way." Terry Dobson. In *Chicken Soup for the Soul: 101 Stories to Open the Heart and Rekindle the Spirit*. Edited by Jack Canfield and Mark V. Hansen. Deerfield Beach, FL: Health Communications, 1993, pages 55–58.

It is so easy to despise what we do not know. Here, in just three pages, is an awakening.

430. "Bopsy." Jack Canfield and Mark V. Hansen. In *Chicken Soup for the Soul: 101 Stories to Open the Heart and Rekindle the Spirit*. Edited by Jack Canfield and Mark V. Hansen. Deerfield Beach, FL: Health Communications, 1993, pages 61–63.

A terminally ill child is given the most honorable of send-offs. This is about death with dignity and seeing the dying process as part of life.

431. *Bugs: Giant Magnified Images as Seen Through a Microscope*. Heather Amery and Jane Songi. New York: Golden Books, 1994.

This elementary science book will capture the interest of any reader, including those who are already familiar with the world of insects. A passage of particular interest to those reading the story of the Pied Piper is an inset on page 27. It is a x450 magnification of a rat flea, the one whose bite killed nearly a quarter of all the people in western Europe during the fourteenth century. The graphic supports comprehension of the caption.

432. *The Cay*. Theodore Taylor. New York: Doubleday, 1969. Winner of six major awards.

The entire book is a read-aloud selection. It is definitely too difficult for new readers or entry-level ESL to read alone. If you simply read it chapter by chapter to your student or class, you will give them an incredible journey into life, history, human nature, and fine writing. I have selected discrete chapters for read alouds just to serve those seeking thematic unit choices. But if you keep the book handy for the learners, eventually, it will all be read by someone. Lost at sea in 1942, an eleven-year-old white boy from Virginia and a sixtyish black man of St. Thomas Island are marooned on a raft and then on a tiny island. An accident leaves the boy blind, a disability that permits him to open his eyes in new ways. Chapter 15, page 106, describes heroism and death in a fresh, almost purging seven pages. Near the end: "I said, 'Timothy,' but he did not answer me. His hand was cold and stiff in mine. Old Timothy, of Charlotte Amalie, was dead. I stayed there beside him for a long time, very tired, thinking that he should have taken me with him wherever he had gone. I did not cry then. There are times when you are beyond tears."

433. *Children of the Dust Bowl: The True Story of the School at Weedpatch Camp*. Jerry Stanley. Illustrated with historical photographs. New York: Crown, 1992.
    "The Dust Bowl killed people who stayed out too long without shelter" (page 8). This was no place to live. But the journey of nearly 2,000 miles to California promised extraordinary suffering, starvation, disease, and death. Chapter 3, "Dead Time," pages 22–33, makes clear the plight of desperate families on the move. The type is easy on the eyes, the margins wide, the historical photographs dramatic, and the prose compelling. This history book will hold the attention of any adult interested in the United States, and it readily lends itself to younger students, if used in a teacher-reads-aloud-and-class-discusses format. The introduction links the Okie experience with John Steinbeck's historical fiction *The Grapes of Wrath*, but the children of the Dust Bowl are absolutely real. The experiences of the Okies can be paralleled with those of the Irish during the Potato Famine a century earlier.

434. "The Dead Girl." Guy de Maupassant. In *Creepy Classics: Hair-Raising Horror from the Masters of the Macabre*. Edited by Mary Hill. Illustrated by Dominick R. Domingo. New York: Random House, 1994.
    "The Dead Girl," pages 33–40, addresses the lies that are told on tombstones and how that insensitive practice, at least once, has to be rectified.

435. "Death and the Legacy." In *Wouldn't Take Nothing for My Journey Now*. Maya Angelou. New York: Random House, 1993, pages 445–49.
    In this brief, Challenging essay, Angelou describes the universal feeling of loss of a loved one and her own way of learning from such love lost.

436. "George Kaufman: Keeping Fit." In *Eccentrics*. Henry Billings and Melissa Billings. Providence, RI: Jamestown, 1987, pages 36–38.
    This story tells of a man who was a successful writer in spite of what might have been a disabling terror of germs. *Eccentrics* is one of a series of books with high-interest short passages for adults. I have used them successfully both with ESL and adult new readers. My only complaint about the series is that often more text space is devoted to tests and skill activities than to the good reads the series authors have proven they can write. This softcover booklet has twenty-one stories about eccentric people.

437. "The Gift." Bennet Cerf. In *Chicken Soup for the Soul: 101 Stories to Open the Heart and Rekindle the Spirit.* Edited by Jack Canfield and Mark V. Hansen. Deerfield Beach, FL: Health Communications, 1993, page 24.

In this one-paragraph story, we learn that the gifts of life are for the living.

438. "Heart of Darkness." In *Great Short Works of Joseph Conrad.* Joseph Conrad. New York: Harper & Row, 1967, pages 210–92.

This Challenging short story is delivered primarily in simple, first-person testimony, in which one man relates details of a journey into the depths of his time. One Strong Passage about discarded slaves, left to die beneath the trees, begins on page 225: "I avoided a vast artificial hole somebody had been digging on the slope." It ends on page 226 with a description of a dying man who seemed to the narrator less than human: "He lapped out of his hand, then sat up in the sunlight, crossing his shins in front of him, and after a time let his wooly head fall on his breast-bone."

439. "Hetty Green: Money Was Everything." In *Eccentrics.* Henry Billings and Melissa Billings. Providence, RI: Jamestown, 1987, pages 74–76.

Hetty Green was notorious for her thrifty habits. Over time, however, her frugality displaced good judgment and humanitarian instincts. Refusing to pay for medical attention to her son's sore knee caused the boy to lose most of his leg.

440. "I, Hungry Hannah Cassandra Glen. . . ." In *Survival!* Norma Fox Mazer. Illustrated by a 1962 Wayne Thiebaud painting, "Salads, Sandwiches and Desserts," and Guiseppe Archimboldo's 1590 oil on wood "Vertumnus (Emperor Rudolf II)," a portrait of a man constructed of fruits and vegetables. Lexington, MA: D. C. Heath, 1995, pages 34–47. Thin Book-level reading.

Two children are confronted by the juxtaposition of the death of the local grocer, who willingly gave credit to his neighbors at the end of the month, and the possibility of getting a feast at the funeral reception. While waiting for the expected feast, the children engage in writing their wills. A one-paragraph biography of the writer on page 47 explains her roots in the same kind of neighborhood she writes about.

441. *The Irish Potato Famine.* Don Nardo. Illustrated by Brian McGovern. San Diego, CA: Lucent Books, 1990.

"Days Without Food," pages 32–34 (one full-page picture), contains firsthand accounts of two men who visited the Emerald Isle during the famine. There is a one full-page picture included. "[A]s we went along, our wonder was not that the people died but that they lived," said one. "In the depth of winter we travelled to Galway, through the very center of that fertile island, and saw sights that will never wholly leave the eyes that beheld them," said another. This passage may lead to discussions of death, poverty, nutrition, health, and politics. Several vignettes related to the Irish Potato Famine give easy-to-understand encapsulations of scientific data. Chapter 2, "A Land Poised on the Brink of Ruin," pages 20–29, the two-thirds of a page vignette "Diseases of the Great Famine," page 44, and "Tens of Thousands Starving," page 39, with a startling illustration, page 38, give meaning to the huge numbers of people who died. For students who have witnessed mind-numbing human suffering, these passages suggest that such tragedy is not limited to one's own group. Other strong passages are identified in Unit 8, entry 536. (A full description is under "Challenging," entry 420.)

442. "The Monkey's Paw." W. W. Jacobs. In *Creepy Classics: Hair-Raising Horror from the Masters of the Macabre*. Edited by Mary Hill. Illustrated by Dominick R. Domingo. New York: Random House, 1994.

"The Monkey's Paw," pages 1–15, could be true. Every horrible event might have been real coincidence. As a magical paw gives people exactly what they wish for, they find that the circumstances of these fortunes are unfortunate indeed. It begins with the need for money, the exact sum of which is delivered as life insurance.

443. "The One Who Stayed." In *Where the Sidewalk Ends*. Poems and drawings by Shel Silverstein. New York: HarperCollins, 1974.

This tells the sad tale of the children stolen by the Pied Piper of Hamelin Town. I have used this incredible collection of poems in many different ways with adults and children. It was quite popular as a community college ESL text and has provided a wealth of material for readers theatre events, too.

444. *The Pearl*. John Steinbeck. New York: Bantam Books, 1947.

The Challenging read-aloud passage starts on page 112: "It was an old and ragged moon, but it threw hard light and hard shadow into the mountain cleft, and now Kino could see the seated figure of the watcher on the little beach beside the pool." The passage continues to build a tense, suspense-filled game between Kino, who owned the Pearl of the World, and the men who would kill anyone to get it. The passage ends on page 115: "And then Kino stood uncertainly. Something was wrong. . . . Tree frogs and cicadas were silent now . . . and he knew the sound—the keening, moaning, rising hysterical cry from the little cave in the side of the stone mountain, the cry of death." Steinbeck's beautifully written descriptions are complemented by his simple, straightforward use of words. Students who would not be expected to understand this level of prose have become avid readers when introduced to *The Pearl*.

445. "The Pied Piper of Hamelin: A Child's Story." Written for and inscribed to W. M. the Younger, by Robert Browning. In *The Complete Works of Robert Browning with Variant Readings & Annotations*, vol. III. General editor Roma A. King, Jr. Athens, Ohio: Ohio University Press, 1971, pages 249–59, editors' notes pages 384–86.

This long poem is written in rhyme and is fun to read aloud. I consider it Challenging simply because it is quite long for a poem and uses many archaic words and phrases that could trip the ESL student or the new reader. But the footnotes at the bottom of each page make finding definitions easy, and it is possible to just skip along reading without looking up anything and get a nice, bouncy, though depressing, story. The editors' notes at the back of the book offer a lot of scholarly information in plain English. For example, there is debate over what Browning's source for this old tale was. It also gives July 22, 1376, as the date of the actual incident. And the notes explain that this poem was written for a sick child who loved to draw, so Browning wrote it and requested the sequestered youngster illustrate it for him.

446. *Pilgrim at Tinker Creek*. Annie Dillard. New York: Harper's Magazine Press, 1974, pages 5–6.

There is a stunning read-aloud passage I discovered through a reference in the *Reading Teacher*. The passage begins by describing the "inelegant" way that frogs take off when scared and settles upon one particular frog that did not move as the author approached and then expired before her eyes in a most unexpected way. If you want to know the details, you have to get the book. This passage is an extraordinary introduction to the topics of death and dying, frogs, bugs, and general biology.

447. "Sick." In *Where the Sidewalk Ends*. Poems and drawings by Shel Silverstein. New York: HarperCollins, 1974, pages 58–59.

This is a great read-aloud poem. It has all kinds of sickly terms needed by the parent writing an excuse for school.

448. *They Led the Way: 14 American Women*. Johanna Johnston. New York: Scholastic, 1973.

Each chapter of this book is about a woman who thought for herself in ways that were inconsistent with the norms of her time. The names are now famous enough that many books have been written at a variety of levels on the women spotlighted. Because it is impossible to get much detail into so few pages, only an overview is provided, but more in-depth reading may occur if a person gets interested in a particular case. Elizabeth Blackwell and Clara Barton chapters are of particular interest to this unit.

Newspaper and Magazine Articles

449. "Fooling the Eye." Suzanne Oliver. *Forbes*, January 16, 1995, page 94.

New technology is helping doctors see—in 3-D images on a big screen—so they can perform intricate eye surgery. The turns of phrase and vocabulary make this one-page article Challenging.

450. "Forget Me Not." In *Life, in Time of War*. March 1991, page 85.

This entire issue of *Life* magazine is dedicated to the story of the Gulf War, or Operation Desert Storm. A message from the editor explains the circumstances of such an edition. Following the overview and the photos of rockets' red glare came the reality. The story of a young man on page 85, shows a photo of him on graduation day, holding his niece's teddy bear; he was the war's first casualty—and MIA. On the last page of this issue a yellow ribbon flickers in the front yard of Lt. Jeffrey Norton Zaum, a prisoner of war.

451. "Neighbors Wary About Plan for Crematory." Cathy Werblin. *The Orange County Register*, May 7, 1995, page Metro-1.

Here are the pros and cons of having a sixth crematory in the county, particularly in a residential area. The residents claim, "Now modern technology is threatening to invade this peaceful—and historic—corner of Garden Grove," where tombstones date back to 1896.

452. "Nursing Home Alternatives: Making the Golden Years Golden." *Forbes*, January 16, 1995, page 98.

This one-page article makes a case for taking care of your body while you are still in charge of your life. Then, during the golden years, there will be increasingly more technology to help you enjoy life. The intermediate ESL student and the new reader who have a grasp of Thin Books will be able to read this.

453. "Possible Weapon Against Alzheimer's Is Found in Blood Protein, Report Says." Stephen D. Moore. *The Wall Street Journal*, May 9, 1995, page B-7.

This article discusses the possibility that a protein can be used to reduce a plaque thought to clog the brain arteries in Alzheimer's victims. Details of the needed experimentation are written in the clear, conversational style typical of *Wall Street Journal* articles.

454. "Sea Change in the Sea Islands: 'Nowhere to Lay Down Weary Head.' " Charles L. Blockson. Photographs by Karen Kasmauski. *National Geographic* 172 no. 6, December 1987, pages 734–63.

Generations of healers, mystics, and medical school graduates now find life on the Sea Islands changing rapidly. Though spirit-protecting rituals continue at deaths, access to slave cemeteries now requires a pass, even for descendents. Development of the islands is encroaching upon tradition. Though far more pictures would be needed to make reading easy, the story adds a dimension to this unit that is worth a read aloud and discussion time.

455. "Some Support for Parents of Kids with Rare Disorders." Diane Rodecker. The Challenger. *The Orange County Register*, May 7, 1995, page Accent-3.

Here is told the story of the Freedman-Harveys, parents of a child with a rare disorder, and the support organization One in a Million Kids, which they started. Also provided are an information phone number and address for the organization and the place to write to The Challenger, a reader advocacy column that helps people find solutions to uncommon and day-to-day problems. All of these contacts promise to enrich a lesson for a parent with a child in need.

456. "Work Week: A Special News Report About Life on the Job—and Trends Taking Shape There." Rochelle Sharpe. *The Wall Street Journal*, May 9, 1995, page A-1.

Subheadings for this front-page column include the following: "Working on Mondays may be hazardous to your health," stating that "Workers suffer more back injuries and heart attacks on the first day of the work-week, new evidence shows." Two information-filled paragraphs offer more detail on this finding. "Smokers can be banned from government jobs in Florida, a court says," devotes two paragraphs to the rights of employers, who are wary of the statistically higher health costs for smokers, and the rights of smokers to be gainfully employed. "Deadly Jobs" tell us that "Cutting timber and fishing were the highest-risk jobs in the country in 1993, the Bureau of Labor Statistics says. Fishermen suffered 155 fatal injuries per 100,000 workers that year, and timber cutters 133, compared with the national average of five fatalities per 100,000." The language used in *The Wall Street Journal* is always clear, and the topics are varied and interesting.

Other Events and Supplements

The issues contained in this unit are best handled before a crisis occurs close to home. Talking about sickness and death allows the person of any age to develop the language that will be hard enough to access in time of grief. The following activities will assist these inevitable processes. I know the list seems long. Just draw from it, don't try to do it all. And in some cases one rests on the foundation of previous items. These kinds of activities need to be addressed in small steps. Always remind callers to keep careful notes when talking on the phone. Be sure to get the correct spelling of the names of the people you talk to. And then, consider sending a thank-you or follow-up note.

- Define grief. Then describe some of the ways in which people address it.
- Look at the same nationally covered event about death and sickness in a variety of newspapers and magazines. Compare the treatment and look for bias among the stories.
- Find copies of old newspapers and look for news of epidemics.
- Read the health and medicine sections of *Time* and *Newsweek*.
- Compare the coverage of health issues in local papers with the coverage in national magazines.
- List the health care providers found in the local Yellow Pages.
- Call them and ask for informational brochures and fee information.
- List the health insurance providers in your area.
- Call them for preventive health pamphlets. Invite one of them to your class.
- Identify the mental health outreach services in your area. There are often volunteer and hot line directories available at the library. Call several to find out what they do: Alzheimer's, drug abuse, addiction rehabilitation, alcoholism, grief counseling, cancer, Heart Association, and so on.
- Create your own hot line and outreach service directory, providing one or two sentences about each provider.
- List the services provided by hospitals and clinics in your area.
- Visit a hospital.
- Interview a hospital or hot line volunteer.
- Write a thank-you letter to the contact person you find helpful.
- Interview a paramedic.
- Interview a mental health professional: counselor, psychologist, psychiatrist, and so on.
- Contact a hospice for information and invite a speaker.

- Contact the activities director of a Veterans Administration hospital near you or far away. Make arrangements to send letters or hand-made greeting cards to veterans who do not usually get mail or have visitors.
- Establish a pen pal program with veterans.
- Contact a funeral home or other bereavement provider in your area. Ask for services provided and costs involved. Compare interment, vault, cremation, burial at sea, donating the body to science, and so on.
- Discuss donating organs in the event of an accident.
- If you are near an old cemetery, visit it and document the life spans indicated on the tombstones.
- Compare life spans of people in current obituaries with those who died fifty years ago.
- Discuss the religious implications for the various ways of addressing a death.
- Compare death by accident, in a hospital, in a hospice, and at home.
- Visit a florist and price get-well and funeral arrangements.
- List the nursing homes in your area.
- Contact local nursing homes regarding resident activities, fees, and volunteer services they use
- Visit the nursing homes that give you the most and the least help over the phone.
- Interview the residents, care providers, and family members you meet there.
- Write a comparative analysis of the homes.
- Interview a geriatric specialist from the community recreation center or city hall.
- Interview an active member of your local American Association of Retired Persons (AARP).
- List recreation facilities with special hours or programs for the elderly.
- Write your own definition of elderly. Collect definitions from people of various ages. Compare them.
- Write your own definition of health.
- Interview friends and neighbors about old family remedies they have seen, used, or heard about.
- Make a collection of folk remedies.
- List all the herbs, spices, and other readily available items that you have heard are useful for medicinal purposes.

- Go to the grocery store and pharmacy to see which of the popular folk remedies are available now.
- Interview your pharmacist about how he or she became interested in the profession.
- Make a list of health care professions and write questions you would like to ask of members of each.
- Write to the professional organizations for information on each category on your list.
- List the health problems associated with different age groups.
- Look for exceptions to your list in the local papers (such as in obituaries).

Racism, Bigotry, and Tolerance

Unit 8

None of us is a bigot. We each believe what we believe to be right thinking. None of us is a racist. At least neither you nor I. We can share and share alike with other mortals on this planet. All of us are tolerant of differences and new ways of living, seeing, believing, knowing, and thinking. So this unit must be for them—those others who have not quite figured out how the world is or how it should be. These readings will allow us to discuss with them the situations that cause war, riots, starvation, inequity, and other forms of human suffering.

Actually, there is such a plethora of intolerance across ethnic, class, religious, economic, and philosophical lines that hardly a humanities collection exists that is free of any mention of bias. Yet many of my students who have experienced intolerance suffer in the belief that they are isolated victims or members of an isolated group. For them, the study of racism, bigotry, and intolerance helps spawn the notions that they are not alone and that they, too, may have participated in at least stereotypical thinking, if not actions that make them the enemy. Through the literature, we can view unthinkable events in an objective or at least disassociated way and perhaps see what we do not want to be. Conversely, we may observe people or actions that help us figure out how to be better human beings. Talking about racism, bigotry, and intolerance may create among the speakers a spirit of higher thinking. The books and stories in this unit may help you help your students to enter a discovery path, a self-discovery path.

Other possible names for thematic units made up from these readings are tolerance, understanding, learning to care, humans and humanity, accommodating differences, diversity discussions.

First Readers and Picture Books

457. *At the Crossroads.* Rachel Isadora. New York: Scholastic, 1991.
The illustrations in this compellingly simple story of poverty and patience show children from tin houses preparing to go out to meet their fathers, who have been gone for ten months, working in the mines. It is a book students can just look at and understand—it is universal.

458. *Babushka Baba Yaga.* Patricia Polacco. New York: Philomel Books, 1993.
Suspicion, intolerance, bigotry, and fear keep the unusual-looking old Baba Yaga from the loving relationships she needs—until she devises a cover-up.

459. "Black Hair." In *A Fire in My Hands: A Book of Poems.* Gary Soto. New York: Scholastic, 1990.
A Mexican boy sits in the bleachers, rooting for the one person on the team who looks like him. As a youth, Soto was no good at sports, and he has written this poem in memory of his good times as a spectator.

460. *The Bracelet*. Yoshiko Uchida and Joanna Yardley. New York: Philomel Books, 1993. Picture book.

"Emi and her family weren't moving because they wanted to. The government was sending them to a prison camp because they were Japanese-Americans. And America was at war with Japan. They hadn't done anything wrong. They were being treated like the enemy just because they looked like the enemy. The FBI had sent Papa to a prisoner-of-war camp in Montana just because he worked for a Japanese company." The year was 1942, and the U.S. government had taken action against some of its own innocent citizens—men, women, and children. Emi had gotten a bracelet from her best friend, a keepsake to remember her by until they met again—if they ever would.

461. "Damon and Pythias, a Greek Legend of Friendship." In *Jamestown Heritage Reader*. Book D. Providence: RI: Jamestown, 1991, pages 149–54.

False imprisonment, discrimination against the foreigner, and disbelief in friendship and honor are some of the themes introduced in these few pages. Like many of the legends and tales retold in the Jamestown Heritage Reader series, this story has been extremely meaningful to my community college ESL students. Students who are literate in their first language may have a background in the myths and legends of their culture, through which they can connect with similar stories, or at least the genre, in the new language. For people who are not familiar with myths and legends, there is still an adult theme, with universal messages that can pass from reader to reader and from parent to child—or the other way around.

462. *Fly Away Home*. Eve Bunting. Illustrated by Ronald Himler. New York: Clarion Books, 1991. Picture book.

This first-person story of a preschool-age boy details activities of a homeless father and son who live in the airport. The child expresses anger and jealousy toward people who are meeting at the airport and then going home together. His only source of hope comes from a little bird that is stranded in the airport for days before finally finding an open door and flying away home. Supported by realistic watercolor drawings, this high-interest text is an easy reader. The contemporary subject provides a backdrop for dialogue and can be used as a prewriting stimulus.

463. *Freedom Child of the Sea*. Richardo Keens-Douglas. Illustrated by Julia Gukova. Toronto-New York: Annick Press, 1995.

Rich, colorful pictures gracing almost every page and big spaces between the lines help the reader navigate text that might be considered too difficult for a First Reader. This is the legend of a young woman discarded from a slave ship just as she is giving birth to the Freedom Child of the Sea.

464. *Here Comes the Cat!* Vladimir Vagin and Frank Asch. New York: Scholastic, 1989.

This collaboration between an American author and a Russian artist is a book of international peace. The simple sentence "Here comes the cat!" appears in English and Russian, foretelling the impending arrival among a community of mice—who seem to be everywhere. The surprise ending leaves such a strong impression that nearly every adult I have shared this book with has had to own a copy.

465. *How Many Days to America?: A Thanksgiving Story*. Eve Bunting. Illustrated by Beth Peck. New York: Clarion Books, 1988.

A family is forced to flee in the night via a small, overcrowded boat, only to be exploited and further denied civil liberties. Though this story is usually listed under Hispanic, I have found its impact equally powerful on Vietnamese and Cambodian immigrants.

466. *If You Lived at the Time of Martin Luther King*. Ellen Levine. Illustrated by Beth Peck. New York: Scholastic, 1990.

Illustrated with brown-line pencil drawings on nearly every page, this book gives insights into the early days of the civil rights struggle as well as the life of Martin Luther King, Jr. The question-answer format addresses segregation, Freedom Riders, violence and nonviolence, voting rights, and King's philosophical conflict with Malcolm X.

467. *If Your Name Was Changed at Ellis Island*. Ellen Levine. Illustrated by Warren Parmenter. New York: Scholastic, 1993.

Here is an eye-opener for many new immigrants. Frequently using the words of the immigrants themselves, this little book unromantically tells about the frustrations and hardships of people struggling to enter and stay in the United States during the years when most newcomers were processed through Ellis Island. It is a good read for citizens and noncitizens alike and an empathetic shoulder for anyone whose family name was altered during the passage from one world to another.

468. *Life Doesn't Frighten Me*. Poem by Maya Angelou. Paintings by Jean-Michel Basquiat. New York: Stewart, Tabori & Chang, poem copyright 1978, illustration copyright 1993.

Seeming to be a children's picture book, this collection of illustrations and ideas suddenly shocks the senses with the kinds of things that really frighten us all. Oil pastels, gouache, acrylics, and collage give the illusion of children's art, and the rugged, haphazard-looking type font looks like children's writing, but they combine to convey a level of sophistication that calls for rereading, rereading, rereading. At the end are two-page biographies of the author and the illustrator. They are good reading in themselves and promise insights into the lives of two artists who made a mark beyond the expected. Angelou's call to everyone to "read everything possible, be it African-American, European, Latin, or other literature— but, especially Shakespeare," makes this even more appropriate for adult new readers. The drug death at an early age of the artist, whose works send the reader on an emotional roller-coaster ride, makes this an even more important book for people concerned about the influence of illegal drugs on our lives; each of us lost when this young man stopped making art. This is a read aloud or First Reader for the poem, but it requires discussion. The biographies of author and illustrator, found at the end of the book, are equivalent to strong chapters in a biographies or celebrities unit. (See Unit 14, "Biographies.")

469. *Maggie and the Pirate*. Ezra Jack Keats. New York: Scholastic, 1979.

Maggie's family lives in a broken-down school bus. She has friends who hang out with her and try to help her find her pet cricket when "the Pirate" kidnaps it. Maggie appears quite poor—until you meet the Pirate.

470. *The Middle Passage.* Illustrated by Tom Feelings. New York: Dial Books, 1995.

In a prepublication brochure, Feelings describes the evolution of his idea for this text-free book: "[M]uted images flashed across my mind. Pale white sailing ships like huge white birds of prey, plunging forward into mountainous raising white foaming waves of cold water, surrounding and engulfing everything. Our ancestors, hundreds of them locked in the belly of each of these ships, chained together like animals throughout the long voyage from Africa toward unknown destinations, millions dying from the awful conditions in the bowels of the filthy slave galleys." So goes the description of conditions for human beings during the Middle Passage across the Atlantic Ocean—now exposed in a graphic form that is beyond words. Feelings says it took him nearly twenty years to create it. Indeed, it required over 200 years. When I first saw a few of the galleys of this picture book, I was shaken, awestruck, speechless—the close-up faces, the distant views of mystical ships, the cutaways into their holds. Dignity, agony, fear, and wonder rush across the pages. Feelings researched his topic both in traditional academic fashion and as ethnographer, going to live in Ghana. It is impossible for me to imagine an educational theme that could not somehow employ this monumental work. It stands above all written works about this period.

471. *The Paper Bag Princess.* Robert Munsch. Toronto: Annick Press, 1980.

Having lost her castle and clothing to a fire-breathing dragon, a princess is left with nothing to wear but a paper bag. The brave and intelligent girl undergoes hardship and danger to save her charming prince. But when she rescues him, he complains about her appearance. Values, self-esteem, male-female relationships, and the importance of thinking things through before judging are imbedded in this well-illustrated, funny, imaginative story.

472. *A Picture Book of Jesse Owens.* David A. Adler. Illustrated by Robert Casilla. New York: Scholastic, 1992.

Important dates are chronicled on the last page, starting with the birth of J. C. Owens on September 12, 1913. Later, a teacher, misunderstanding J. C., wrote Jesse in her roll book and permanently changed the name of the boy who would grow to be a world-class runner. The chronology ends with his death from lung cancer on March 31, 1980. Even as the grandson of a former slave won Olympic victories that honored his country, he was forbidden the right to live where he chose or ride in the front of the bus. Adolf Hitler, too, had shown disdain for the man with black skin and refused to shake hands with him. It was generations later before U.S. President Gerald Ford and then President Jimmy Carter attempted to set right the wrongs cast on this American.

473. *A Picture Book of Simon Bolivar.* David A. Adler. Illustrated by Robert Casilla. New York: Holiday House, 1992.

Simon Bolivar, born in Venezuela in 1783, lived in a time of widespread revolutions. America had just engaged in its freedom fight, Spain was in mortal struggle with France, led by Napoleon Bonaparte, for its right to remain independent, and, likewise, Spanish colonies in South America were aching to be free of Spanish rule. These tumultuous roots fostered a child who eventually came to be known as El Liberator of Venezuela, Colombia, Ecuador, Peru, and Bolivia. Class distinctions and racism marked the environment of Bolivar, son of Creoles who owned copper and silver mines, several plantations, and over a thousand slaves. Tragedy was also a part of Bolivar's youth. By the time he was six, both his parents were dead. Simon was first home schooled, then continued his studies in Spain. Eventually, he began to work for a free life in his homeland. Penniless, in 1830 he died of TB. The book has double-page watercolor illustrations supporting nearly every paragraph of text. Though there is little detail in the text, the easy-to-read book provides some interesting historical information and a list of important dates at the end.

474. *Rechenka's Eggs*. Patricia Polacco. New York: Philomel Books, 1988. A Reading Rainbow selection.

Here is a mystical story of connections between humans, animals, and a universal goodness. It is also about the cycle of life. Old Babushka's main reason for living is winning first place in the painted egg contest each year. She also cares for hungry and wounded animals.

475. *The Rough-Faced Girl*. Rafe Martin and David Shannon. New York: Scholastic, 1992.

This is a retelling of an Algonquin Indian "Cinderella" story, with illustrations that convey all kinds of human qualities—good and evil. The disfigured girl finally gets a chance at happiness. Though there are several solid paragraphs on some pages, the drawings push comprehension along.

476. *Smoky Night*. Eve Bunting. Illustrated by David Diaz. San Diego, CA: Harcourt Brace, 1994. 1995 Caldecott Medal.

The horror of a world gone mad, as riots break out in the street, begins a series of dramatic incidents that cause a young boy, an old woman, and their pets to reach a level of understanding that could not be achieved during a time of peace. Richly textured collages of glass, wrappers, trail mix, and other found objects make this book a visual wonder. The illustrations support the text page by page. The way in which a fearful child expresses his suspicion of a neighbor woman and her cat and then comes to recognize her as a fellow human—and her cat as a creature that purrs just as his does—illustrates that attitudes can change, and that it is okay to rethink and reevaluate our prejudices. In this simple, nonjudgmental book, Bunting demonstrates how personal growth can evolve. This is a fine read aloud, especially for adults. I know, because the author read it to an audience I was in. It is a book all will want to revisit. You may be interested to know that Bunting's powerful story emerged, in part, from her own naive expression of prejudice toward a teacher during World War II. Sometimes personal change takes a long time, indeed.

477. *Sophie*. Mem Fox. Illustrated by Aminah Brenda Lynn Robinson. New York: Harcourt Brace, 1994.

Sophie loves her grandpa, who is always ready to play with her until one day— . The simple funeral illustration shows Grandpa in his casket. Then there is grief. Mem Fox—consistently powerful.

478. *Stellaluna*. Janell Cannon. New York: Scholastic, 1993.

"How can we be so different and feel so much alike?" is the unifying question asked by a little bird whose nest is invaded by the orphan bat Stellaluna.

479. *The Table Where Rich People Sit*. Byrd Baylor. Pictures by Peter Parnall. New York: Macmillan, 1994.

This book was introduced to me by Donald Graves, when he read it aloud to an audience of several hundred at the 40th International Reading Association Conference in Anaheim, California. Need I add that most of the attendees were adults—reading teachers and interested others. After the reading there was silence and tears. Had I known about this incredible book sooner, it might have been the cornerstone for a values unit. In addition, it makes an excellent, gentle discussion-starter on dollar values—on abstract things.

480. *Tar Beach*. Faith Ringgold. New York: Crown, 1991. 1992 Caldecott Honor, 1992 Coretta Scott King Award.

A picture of a quilt and other drawings illustrate this dream come true. Part of the dream is that the little girl's dad will not have to worry about the racism that excludes him from the union and access to work. Part of the dream is that she will wear the bridge with the lights like a diamond necklace. On the last page, Ringgold's biography includes a description of the progression from an actual quilt, which had the story written around the edges, to the design for this book.

481. *Teammates*. Peter Golenbock. Illustrated by Paul Bacon. San Diego, CA: Harcourt Brace Jovanovich, 1990.

This is a simple picture book about baseball, racism, and how one manager, Branch Rickey of the Brooklyn Dodgers, and two players, Jackie Robinson and Pee Wee Reese, started revolutionary change.

482. *Thunder Cake*. Patricia Polacco. New York: Philomel Books, 1990.

Fear and the courage to keep going are the themes for a book with beautiful, detailed color drawings. Grandma helps the young child address her fear of thunder. Though Polacco draws from her family's Russian folk history, this is a universal story.

483. *Tough Boris*. Mem Fox. Illustrated by Kathryn Brown. San Diego, CA: Harcourt Brace, 1994.

Almost traditional watercolor illustrations give meaning to the single lines of prose on each two-page spread. There is a thirty-one-word vocabulary for the entire book—though this is not to say the words lack meaning, not to say they are easy words. The story deals with stereotyping, sadness, grief, and death.

484. *Uncle Jed's Barbershop*. Margaree King Mitchell. Illustrated by James Ransome. New York: Scholastic, 1993. Picture book.

This is a story of hope, a beloved relative, tenacity, a dream deferred and fulfilled, segregation, poverty, and the power of a positive model. This is a simply told story of a man who proved it is never to late to start over and never too late to succeed.

485. *The War Began at Supper: Letters to Miss Loria*. Patricia Reilly Giff. Illustrated by Betsy Lewin. New York: Delacorte Press, 1991.

Miss Loria, a beloved student teacher who has moved away, is the addressee of most of the letters from the students in Mrs. Clark's elementary school class.

The letters about another series of letters, from students to U.S. soldiers in the Gulf War, reveal a change in attitudes regarding gender differences. On January 16, Sara writes a description of Iraq and then tells Miss Loria that Michael M.'s father went to Saudi Arabia. She goes on to say that Karl claims his aunt is going to go to the war. "That Karl. He doesn't know anything" (page 14). On January 28, Alice writes that she got a letter from a soldier. (Writing to soldiers was a class project.) "Guess what? I got a letter from the soldier. I read it in class. The soldier's name is Helen Denning. She's a woman soldier. As soon as Sara heard that, she started to cry. Mrs. Clark kept saying what's the matter? Sara wouldn't tell us though" (pages 28–29). Then on February 1, Alice writes, "She signed her name Helen, so that's what I'm calling her. Mrs. Clark made a copy of the letter for everyone. I think more kids are going to write to soldiers" (page 33). And Private Helen Denning, in a letter, describes the "miserable, hot and sticky" weather, assures her correspondent that they are going to win the war, and complains, "The army dinners taste a little like the food I feed my dog. They look like the food I feed my fish" (page 34). An adjoining illustration shows a young black soldier, seated in the sand, writing a letter, while her fellow soldiers lounge near a tank. On February 5, Karl writes, "My Aunt Ellen is a nurse. She may be going to the war. What would she think if she knew I was afraid?" (page 37). Michael's entire letter, pages 41–42, makes a profound read aloud. See "Book Chapters and Strong Passages" section also.

486. *Wilfrid Gordon McDonald Partridge.* Mem Fox. Illustrated by Julie Vivas. Brooklyn, NY: Kane/Miller, 1985.

This is an extraordinary example of how text and pictures give meaning together. The lad with the long title name has an active, fun-filled life visiting his next-door neighbors, residents of an old people's home. We are not told he is poor, we just see the markings within the illustrations, just as we see the emotions of the residents of the home. Even so, the tale is about memory loss and the importance of having something to think or care about. It is about the contrast between youth and age. It is about valuing human beings. For any age reader, of any culture, this is a powerful book.

Thin Books

487. *Abraham Lincoln.* Kathie Billingslea Smith. Illustrated by James Seward. New York: Scholastic, 1987.

A barefoot lad in western Kentucky is introduced. Then his mother dies, his father remarries, and the boy is fortunate enough to have a stepmother who honors his love of books. He is married, a child is born and dies, two more are born, and the man becomes president of the United States. A war over slavery, the Civil War, begins, the Emancipation Proclamation is signed, and another son dies. The war ends, and the reelected president is assassinated. All this in just a few pages of easy-to-read text, with clear drawings on each page.

488. *Bull Run.* Paul Fleischman. Woodcuts by David Frampton. New York: Scholastic, 1993.

One by one, in isolated vignettes, as though reporting to an unseen interviewer, fictional characters tell their stories of hearing about war, getting ready for battle, heading off, and how the battle occurred—the tragic discovery that war is not a game. The momentum of this series of reports builds so subtly that the reader does not realize what has happened until it is done. Each vignette is one or two pages. And each speaker has a personal icon woodcut. The language is quite simple, no long sentences, no big words, and as such, almost chops at the reader's attention, but the overall impact is strong. The message of each person reflects a different perspective about the war over slavery. Northerner Gideon Adams, page 15, is faced with racism as he tries to volunteer for military service.

489. *Catwings*. Ursula K. Le Guin. Illustrated by S. D. Schindler. New York: Scholastic, 1988.

Imagination and hope are the gifts of this little book, which tells about some most unusual kittens, born with wings. Faced with the condemnation that often meets those who do not match the norm, the kittens are encouraged by their mother to leave the "ghetto" for a better life.

490. *Charlotte's Web*. E. B. White. Illustrated by Garth Williams. New York: Harper & Row, 1980.

Few stories are both suspenseful and heartwarming in the way that the story of Charlotte and her friends is. On the chance that you have neither read nor been told this tale of ingenuity in the face of great peril, I will not go into detail. Suffice it to say that this book tells of friendship and danger and proves that tenacity and the power of positive thinking can change the course of history. This is a wonderful read-aloud book for parent to child, teacher to student, in each case with long time-outs for discussion of what has happened and what might happen next. This teaches that reading is a reflective, thinking process, not a linear one. It also teaches the good reader the strategy of predicting. What is important is not that the readers guess correctly what is coming up. What is important is that they think ahead, predicting the possibilities. This process teaches, among many things, the notion that there may be many solutions to a problem, many good answers to a question. Speaking of thinking beyond, looking at the author as a human who uses literacy in ways other than book writing can foster in learners the idea that they, too, may become literacy users and writers. To that end, I recommend taking a look at a short series of letters between E. B. White and Groucho Marx, found on pages 131–33 in *The Groucho Letters*, published in 1967 by Simon & Schuster (see entry 278).

491. *Children of the Dust Bowl: The True Story of the School at Weedpatch Camp*. Jerry Stanley. Illustrated with historical photographs. New York: Crown, 1992.

This book briefly describes how agricultural jobs in the Dust Bowl states declined by 400,000 between 1930 and 1940, when "nearly 50 percent of Oklahoma's farms changed hands in bankruptcy court sales" and displaced and starving people headed in a mass migration for California. In California, the Okies were believed to be stupid and shiftless, were denied work, food, or housing, and were often told to move on. The type is easy on the eyes, the margins wide, the historical photographs dramatic, and the prose compelling. This history book will hold the attention of any adult interested in the United States, and it readily lends itself to younger students, if used in a teacher reads aloud and class discusses format. The introduction links the Okie experience with John Steinbeck's historical fiction *The Grapes of Wrath*, but the children of the Dust Bowl are absolutely real.

492. *The Crossing*. Gary Paulsen. New York: Dell, 1987.

Red-haired Manny Bustos doesn't know exactly how old he is or who his parents were. He was deserted as an infant, cared for briefly by a church, and then was turned out to join the throngs of other throw-away children on the street. He sleeps in a cardboard box at night, hoping not to get caught again by slave traders. Each day is a struggle for survival as he competes with other street orphans for food and the coins tossed out by tourists into the dry riverbed of the once bountiful Rio Grande. Each day he plans for the time when he will make the crossing to the United States, a place where he expects to find work and escape ever-present hunger. Paulsen's story provides sufficient information to provide rich dialogue concerning the needs of children, the environment, and the impact of war on a young soldier's mind.

493. *Days of Courage: The Little Rock Story*. Richard Kelso. General editor Alex Haley. Illustrated by Mel Williges. New York: Steck-Vaughn, 1993.

The manifestations of racism and bigotry are detailed in historical events stemming from the actions of a small group of people who decided to push the law into reality. An afterword and rich endnotes give more detail about the civil rights efforts of the not-yet-distant past.

494. *The Emancipation Proclamation: Why Lincoln Really Freed the Slaves*. Robert Young. New York: Dillon Press, 1994.

Dramatic photographs, detailed drawings, copies of posters and children's alphabet book pages, vignettes of particular interest, and wide margins all contribute to making this an accessible text. Controversial issues are laid bare in simply stated facts. A timeline starting with the 1600s and ending with 1870, when the Fifteenth Amendment gave blacks the right to vote, gives a meaningful overview of racism in the United States. This is followed by the actual text of the Emancipation Proclamation and a brief list of suggestions for further reading. This book is easy, academic, and informing.

495. *The Freedom Riders*. Deborah Kent. Chicago: Childrens Press, 1993. Cornerstones of Freedom series.

On May 4, 1961, a group of black and white Americans boarded a Greyhound bus and rode through the Deep South in an attempt at nonviolent change. A 1946 U.S. Supreme Court ruling had outlawed segregation on interstate railroads and buses, and in 1960 another ruling outlawed segregated terminals. These laws were openly broken throughout the southern United States. The Freedom Riders agreed to form an integrated group that would peacefully demonstrate for the federal government that civil rights were not being protected as provided by law. Their plan was to ride in unassigned seats and use rest rooms marked for the opposite race, thereby attracting the ire of segregationists and the attention of the FBI. The plan worked, and within a short time, peaceful demonstrations led to bloodshed, false arrests, and killings. It also changed the course of history.

496. *The Freedom Side*. Marcie Miller Stadelhofen. New York: New Readers Press, 1990. Sundown Books series.

This historical fiction is an introduction to the issues of slavery and civil rights in U.S. history. Adult native and nonnative speakers of English get caught up in the intrigue and suspense of historical fiction. I know of no person in the Beaumont (California) Literacy Program who read this book and failed to go looking for its sequel, *Last Chance for Freedom*.

497.   *The Friendship*. Mildred D. Taylor. Pictures by Max Ginsburg. New York: Dial Books for Young Readers, 1987.
    In fifty-three pages, the telling of one incident on a summer afternoon in 1933 gives the reader an up-close view of how racism in Mississippi influenced the behavior of people who would otherwise be friends. The story is told from the perspective of a young girl. The matter of how one person addressed another led to an incident that made social inequities obvious. This language issue is joined by the dialects of the characters. Clear, readable text is only part of this powerful little book. Full-page pencil illustrations give another dimension to the story and support the descriptions with realism and detail. This book is both a social study and an art collection.

498.   *The Hundred Dresses*. Eleanor Estes. Illustrated by Louis Slobodkin. New York: Scholastic, 1973.
    "Wanda Petronski. Most of the children in Room 13 didn't have names like that. . . . Wanda didn't have any friends. . . . She always wore a faded blue dress that didn't hang right. It was clean, but it looked as though it had never been ironed properly." The girls would wait for her and call out, "Wanda, how many dresses do you have hanging in your closet?" and Wanda would reply, "A hundred." Then she would be ridiculed with more questions prying about the colors and the fabrics. The cruelty of children and fear of being at the end of the pecking order are plainly told in this simple little book. Wanda is excruciatingly poor, but Maddie is little better off. Still, she joins in the ridicule, lest the popular Peggy should turn her venom on Maddie. Day in and day out, Wanda is staked out and asked the same tormenting questions. Then, one day, she is not in school. A note from her father to the teacher explains that Wanda, her father, and her brother, Jake, have moved away to escape the misery inflicted by the children. There is one other surprise for Maddie and Peggy, leaving them to wonder at the grief they have brought on a fellow human. This story is simply told and nicely illustrated. Its surprise ending leaves the reader a little off balance. Class distinctions, like many other differences, can create great rifts between people. In this case, there are several ways in which the Petronskis are different.

499.   *Jesse Jackson: A Biography*. Patricia C. McKissack. New York: Scholastic, 1989.
    Documentary photographs support this modern American story of struggle, defeat, and achievement.

500.   *Lafcadio: The Lion Who Shot Back*. Shel Silverstein. New York: Harper & Row, 1963.
    A lion cub is orphaned when hunters kill his mom. Over time he develops fear and then a love for the power of the gun he finds. He goes to the big city and becomes the very thing he abhors. At long last, he tries to return to the tall grassland of his youth. This beautifully written book is a parable for racism and bigotry. It provides so much room for discussion between parent and child or teacher and student or among adults in small discussion groups that I cannot begin

to list the ways in which it has contributed to my work with adults, teens, and young children. It is easy to read, has humorous cartoon illustrations, and messages, messages, messages.

501. *Last Chance for Freedom.* Marcie Miller Stadelhofen. New York: New Readers Press, 1990. Sundown Books series.

This is the sequel to *The Freedom Side.* The books in this series are in a thin, easy-to-carry paperback format with adult pictures on the covers. Although not oversized, the print is clear and legible. All are available with cassette tapes that allow new readers and ESL students to make the sound-symbol connections. The good news is there is a compelling story that provides authentic historical information. The bad news is that the sentences are short. However, many of my students have enjoyed them and claim to have gotten interested in a topic they knew little or nothing about before. One young black mother who had never been introduced to the issues of the civil rights movement became enthralled by this story and, with the help of her tutor, embarked on a voyage to her roots.

502. *Letters from a Slave Girl: The Story of Harriet Jacobs.* Mary E. Lyons. New York: Charles Scribner's Sons, 1992.

Inspired by the autobiographical letters published by the adult Harriet Jacobs, Lyons employs fictional letters by Jacobs to her deceased mother, father, and finally other relatives to convey both the historical events of 1825 to 1842 and the personal imaginings, triumphs, and tragedies of a slave girl who grows up as she strives to gain her freedom. The fictionalized biography is based on true events from the life of Harriet Jacobs. The final section, "Harriet: The Rest of Her Story," takes us from 1842 to 1852 in a narrative of the freedom fighter's life. The black Southern dialect of the slave girl begins to show the influence of white mistresses with whom she has extended contact. Jacobs was taught to read but was left to learn writing on her own initiative. It is presumed that she used discarded account books for writing paper during this period when handmade paper was expensive and slaves forbidden by law to read or write. This book is a powerful telling of one woman's experience as a slave. Gender issues, human rights, civil rights, and, certainly, the Civil War are all addressed through this first-person accounting of suffering, courage, and hope.

503. *Lou Gehrig: One of Baseball's Greatest.* Guernsey Van Riper, Jr. New York: Macmillan, 1986.

This large-print paperback is one of a series of books on the childhoods of famous Americans. The story starts with the dilemma of a young boy who is ridiculed for being fat. It also addresses the pain of ethnic hatred expressed against children with German surnames when President Woodrow Wilson declared war against the German government. This clearly written story is a good, fast read.

504. *My Dad Lives in a Downtown Hotel.* Peggy Mann. Illustrated by Richard Cuffari. New York: Scholastic, 1973.

The impact of a family breakup on school behavior, the sense of isolation a child feels when first confronted with disharmony between his parents, the need to talk about troubles with someone who will not condemn the victim, and fear of the actual breaking up of the household are told in the child's own words: "What's got into you today, Joey?" his teacher asks. "Running around, shoving into everyone! You'd better stay in here til you feel you can behave yourself. And then come out." His teacher closes the closet room door. "I looked around. I felt like knocking over everything in the stupid supply room. Ripping the posters off the walls. Busting my fists through the volleyball nets. Throwing the equipment all over the place. But then I figured, what was the sense. It would only make Miss Clifford trouble. And it wasn't her fault that my dad had walked out on my mom and me last night" (page 1). Then on page 65, he tells about "Our Time," a period during dinner when they have agreed to just talk about "things." "Sometimes these are just regular things, you know—about homework. Or what color to have the bathroom painted because the guy in the apartment above ours let his bathtub overflow and it spoiled all the paint on our bathroom ceiling and walls. And sometimes we talk about—I mean things that are hard to talk about. Like—you know, divorce and all that stuff." Then he talks about isolation and the agony of keeping his terrible secret. "At first I didn't mention anything about it to anyone. I mean, my dad living downtown in that crummy hotel. Him walking out on us and all. I felt—ashamed. Even though the whole thing wasn't my fault, maybe people would think it was." But one day when he and a schoolmate are riding the bus, "for some reason, I found myself spilling the whole works to Pepe," who responds, " 'So what?' Yeah, he didn't bat an eye. 'Lots of kids got no dad living in the house. There's this little kid used to tell everyone his dad got killed in a car crash. But one day when we was playing dominoes on his front stoop, he tells me, "You know, man, maybe my dad got kilt and maybe he didn't. I'll never know, 'cause I never even seen him once. I don't even know who he is!" And then this little kid laughed and laughed. We both did.' " But divorce and broken homes are no laughing matter. Neither are the tensions children are forced to carry around when they have terrible secrets to bear. This is a powerful little book, a quality parent-child read aloud, even if no divorce is in their lives, and a compellingly told story for all ages.

505. *Nelson Mandela: "No Easy Walk to Freedom."* A biography by Barry Denenberg. New York: Scholastic, 1991.
    A chronology starting with the year 1400 and going to February 11, 1990, a bibliography offering more readings, and a detailed index make this a scholarly work. The compelling writing and rich information on racism, political strife, warring tribes, intrigue, and hope make this a fascinating read.

506. *Sarah, Plain and Tall.* Patricia MacLachlan. New York: HarperCollins, 1985. 1986 Newbery Medal.
    This is a touching story about family relationships and humans in general. The simple, direct letters written among the people who were contemplating becoming a family are remarkable exercises in truth. Yet Sarah's self-perception of "plainness" reflects a societal concern with appearances. Tolerance emerges as less superficial values evolve.

507. *The Star Fisher.* Laurence Yep. New York: Scholastic, 1991.
    Set in the spring of 1927, this story of a Chinese American girl spiritedly addresses bigotry and racism with tenacity and courage.

508. *The Story of George Washington Carver*. Eva Moore. New York: Scholastic, 1971.
    This action-packed tale begins with the fear that Moses Carver's slaves, a widow and her two children, would be stolen. The life of George Washington Carver addresses the issues of racism and intellectual freedom. The action continues throughout the life of the man who eventually becomes a world-famous scientist.

509. *The Story of the Women's Movement*. Maureen Ash. Chicago: Childrens Press, 1989. Cornerstones of Freedom series.
    This booklet opens with a photo of two English police officers arresting a woman who is demonstrating for the right to vote in front of the prime minister's house. The story begins in England in 1827 with the case study of Caroline Norton, who, as a married woman, had no right to keep her children or the money she earned from writing. Further, her husband was within his rights when he beat her while she was pregnant and when he separated her from her three sons, one of whom died of blood poisoning in his care. During her lifetime, Norton campaigned for and won some women's rights. Five years after her death, a law was passed allowing married women the same rights as unmarried ones, though not the same rights as men. Numerous other women took up the fight to change laws that were based on their assumed inferiority to men. It was difficult for them to be taken seriously by those who considered them categorically less intelligent and who passed laws denying girls entry into academic schools. "Girls were too weak, it was believed, to learn mathematics—it would make them go mad" (page 9). The story then moves to the United States, whose Constitution at that time totally ignored the rights of women, blacks, and Native Americans. Allowed to serve as emergency substitutes during wars, women in England and America continued to be denied civil rights. During the 1920s they earned the right to vote, but in the 1930s twenty-six states passed laws prohibiting married women from getting jobs, and where they could work they were paid about sixty-five percent of what men earned for the same output. Considerable discussion is given to both sides of the Equal Rights Amendment and to statistics, including the fact that in 1987 women earned seventy cents for every dollar earned by men, and a college-educated woman can expect to earn about the same as a male high school dropout. This dynamic little history book is chock-full of facts and famous names.

510. *The United States Holocaust Memorial Museum: America Keeps the Memory Alive*. Eleanor H. Ayer. New York: Dillon Press, 1994.
    This book leads the reader level by level through the museum and its powerful exhibits, conveying the visitor's experience.

Challenging

511. *Dr. Elizabeth: The Story of the First Woman Doctor*. Patricia Clapp. New York: Lothrop, Lee & Shepard, 1974.
    One hundred and fifty-six fast-moving pages without pictures give insightful details not only on the woman who lived from 1821 to 1910 but also on the gender and social issues of her day that continue to play out in women's struggles. The biography is written in an autobiographical format discussing her life in both England and the United States. There is a reference to Florence Nightingale on

page 107. Issues of censorship and the right to privacy come up in a letter from her adopted daughter, Kitty, pages 125–26. There is a read-aloud passage in "Read Alouds," entry 526.

512. *Ishmael*. Daniel Quinn. New York: Bantam/Turner, 1992. Turner Tomorrow Fellowship winner.

Appropriately printed on recycled paper, this unlikely dialogue between Man and his Teacher evolves into a spiritual investigation of everything we, as civilized beings, accept unquestioningly. This is identified as Challenging not because of its vocabulary or sentence lengths—indeed, the dialogue is in everyday English but because of the abstract thoughts and unusual concepts that will require much more contemplation than a typical Thin Book. Issues of bias and bigotry reflect some of those views held by slave owners in the last century—yet a shocking parallel is presented here. Do not read this if you are unwilling to question your beliefs or your lack of them. In this unusual journey into Western culture, there are many questions that have never been asked or even contemplated by those of us who have always known how to tell right from wrong. This is not a book for those who know what they know without question. Our presumed state of superiority to all other occupants on the Earth is effectively—disturbingly—challenged. Still it offers one being's view of how we, as humans, came to this spot in time and how we may survive our own follies on this planet, as we dominate it. But enough about the content. This is a book of dialogue, all written in wonderful, clear sentences that exhibit how a conversation is expressed. It uses past, present, and future tenses within the confines of the tales, laid bare. It is Challenging reading only because of the concepts and the lack of pictures. With pictures it might become an adolescent's storybook, one that could modify the way we use our time in power on Earth. Any teacher who wants to provide an aide or helper with a meaningful contribution could have the aide read *Ishmael* to the class or to a small group, with frequent discussion breaks.

513. *Malcolm X: By Any Means Necessary*. Walter Dean Myers. New York: Scholastic, 1993.

A dual-column chronology that starts with the birth of Malcolm Little on May 19, 1925, gives Malcolm's important life events on the right and the important events of the world on the left. The chronology ends in 1966, the year Malcolm X was assassinated. There is also a short bibliography. The life of Malcolm X was beset with violence, starting with the death of his father, hit by a streetcar, a perhaps racially motivated event, in 1931. Poverty for the family ensued. At odds with the efforts of some blacks to create change through nonviolence, Malcolm X reflected the hate that he had experienced all of his life.

514. *Oregon Trail*. Dan Murphy. Photographs by Gary Ladd. Las Vegas, NV: KC Publications, 1993.

On a simple U.S. map is marked Independence, Missouri, the start of this massive migration westward. Throughout the book, the progression is graphically documented as the dotted line inches toward Oregon City. As has often been the case, hard economic times or crop failures at home made the promise of greener pastures impossible to disbelieve. Peter Burnett, later governor of California, is quoted on page 3: "Then, with a twinkle in his eye he said, 'Gentlemen, they do say that out in Oregon the pigs are running about under the great acorn trees, round and fat, and already cooked, with knives and forks sticking in them so that you can cut off a slice whenever you are hungry.' . . . Father was the first to sign his name." An equally jubilant quote comes in 1846 from Donner Party member Edwin Bryant, before the terrible blizzard and horrid end to that group of travelers whose name is lent to Donner Pass. Salt Lake City, intended destination for Mormons seeking a safer life and starting point for those harvesting travelers' souls, also documented casualties—some slain for their beliefs and lifestyle, others victims of the heat, cold, and fierce reception by natural elements of Zion. Though the scenery photographs are rich and close-ups detailed, the large patches of well-written text qualify this book as Challenging reading.

515.   *The River with No Bridge.* Sue Sumii. Translated by Susan Wilkinson. Rutland, VT: Charles E. Tuttle, 1990.

Set in the period from 1908 to 1923, this story of the Japanese "untouchables," also known as the *burakumin* and *eta*, exposes a little-discussed form of prejudice the Japanese legally conducted against members of their same gene pool. Distrust and hatred of people whose work involved blood handling, such as the slaughter of animals and midwifery, and the descendants of such persons were passed from parent to child. I became aware of this book through a newspaper book review that I used in my ESL class. Several Japanese students expressed complete surprise at the phenomenon, unaware of the *burakumin* presence in their history. It opened the door to further discussions about prejudice.

Read Alouds

516.   *Always to Remember: The Story of the Vietnam Veterans Memorial.* Brent Ashabranner. Photographs by Jennifer Ashabranner. New York: Scholastic, 1988.

This clear account of the historical and emotional roots of the United States' involvement in the Vietnam War gives many human details about people affected by it. Wounded in action and witness to the deaths or wounding of over half his company, veteran Jan C. Scruggs came home to a legacy of shame for having gone to war. One night, after seeing the movie *The Deer Hunter*, he was driven to make a memorial of substance to the effort and suffering that had transpired. It would have the names of all those men and women lost in the war. This dream became an obsession that led to a nationwide competition, with 1,421 designs submitted and judged without names or identification of any kind. The Wall, entry number 1,026, by twenty-one-year-old Yale student Maya Ying Lin, was selected. The daughter of Chinese immigrants was to make a profound contribution to the art and history of America. Though the entire book is worthwhile reading, the chapter "The Vision of Maya Ying Lin," pages 35–43, is profound read-aloud material and can foster dialogue on many topics. She is quoted as saying, "A memorial shouldn't tell you what to think, but should make you think."

517.   *Anne Frank: Beyond the Diary: A Photographic Remembrance.* Ruud van der Rol and Rian Verhoeven. Translated by Tony Langham and Plym Peters. Introduction by Anna Quindlen. New York: Viking Penguin, 1993.

Just as the title suggests, this book goes beyond the diary of the young girl into the world and the plight of those whose lives were on the brink of terrible change. Photographs, letters, and simple captions make this history book a detailed journey into a time that will mar the history of humankind forever. This book should be read in conjunction with the diary. Possible units are history, tolerance, and war.

518. *The Cay.* Theodore Taylor. New York: Doubleday, 1969. Winner of six major awards.

The entire Thin Book is a read-aloud selection. It is definitely too difficult for new readers or entry-level ESL to read alone. If you simply read it chapter by chapter to your student or class, you will give them an incredible journey into life, history, human nature, and fine writing. I have selected discrete chapters for read alouds just to serve those seeking thematic unit choices. But if you keep the book handy for the learners, eventually, it will all be read by someone. Lost at sea in 1942, an eleven-year-old white boy from Virginia and a sixtyish black man of St. Thomas Island are marooned on a raft and then on a tiny island. An accident leaves the boy blind, a disability that permits him to open his eyes in new ways. Chapter 4, starting on page 39, describes attitudes of racism, bigotry, and stereotypical thinking. Chapter 8, starting on page 61, ends with "I felt good. I knew how to do something that Timothy couldn't do. He couldn't spell. I felt superior to Timothy that day, but I let him play his little game, pretending not to know that he really couldn't spell." Chapter 12, page 88, is the scene of emotional growth through a survival effort. Chapter 13 starts on page 93 and ends with "I asked, 'Timothy, are you still black?' His laughter filled the hut." This entire book is a read aloud.

519. *The Day Pearl Harbor Was Bombed. A Photo History of World War II.* George Sullivan. New York: Scholastic, 1991.

A one-page chronology of important dates from 1933 to 1946 and a bibliography of further reading suggestions supplement this well-organized, action-packed history of World War II. Though there is little text on each page, the vocabulary is by no means easy. Words like strategists, kamikaze, Allies, throngs, victory, stunning, and headquarters pepper the text. Historical references to Okinawa, the Solomon Islands, Berlin, Nazi Germany, the Soviet Union, New Guinea, Guam, Saipan, the Mariana Islands, Leyte Gulf, the Philippines, Manila, Japan, Iwo Jima, the Pacific, the Boeing B-29, and the atomic bomb make this book vocabulary-intensive for the new reader and ESL learner. But the photographs support the text and make just page turning worthwhile for someone seeking an overview of the war. For a read-aloud discussion starter, look at four pages of historical photographs that give a chilling account of the Holocaust, pages 68–71. "Early in April 1945, as a company of British soldiers advanced through Germany toward Berlin, they came upon a barbed-wire-enclosed camp. What they saw sickened them. In trenchlike open graves, piles of naked bodies were stacked like firewood. The soldiers couldn't believe their eyes" (page 69).

520. *The Diary of a Young Girl.* Anne Frank. Translated from the Dutch by B. M. Mooyaart-Doubleday. Introduction by Eleanor Roosevelt. New York: Modern Library, 1952.

The impact of this diary as a historical document must be fostered with each new generation of readers. It is so easy to lose track of war's human impact unless some single story makes the details real. That is what this young girl's diary of the Holocaust does for those who cannot remember. Roosevelt's introduction gives weight to the notion that this is a book that must be read. "Written by a young girl—and the young are not afraid of telling the truth—it is one of the wisest and most moving commentaries on war and its impact on human beings that I have ever read. . . . [H]er diary tells us much about ourselves and about our own children." This edition has a brief passage written in Anne Frank's own pen. This is a history book, a coming-of-age book, a storybook, all under one cover.

521. *Ellis Island*. Wilton S. Tifft. Foreword by Lee Iacocca. Chicago: Contemporary Books, 1990.

This is an oversized picture book with a rich collection of documentary photographs illustrating every chapter. Copies of passports, baggage tags, and architectural drawings also give a sense of reality to this distant time in U.S. history. In chapter four, pages 55–63, "The Rise of Anti-Immigration Sentiment" explains that the announcement by the U.S. Census Bureau that there were no more unclaimed frontier acres led to reluctance to admit more immigrants. The fear of many marginally established laborers that newer immigrants would willingly accept even lesser wages also produced anti-immigrant sentiment. The nativist movement of the 1890s also gave rise to racism. "The fears of nativists were not restricted to the number of immigrants but focused as well on their character and origins" (page 55). The newer immigrants promised unwelcome change. "Many were Catholic. Most spoke unfamiliar languages. Many were unskilled, many uneducated" (page 55). "Anti-immigration factions sought to restrict immigrants of eastern European peasant stock . . . because it was felt they would 'pollute the young nation's bloodline' " (page 57). In 1897, promoting a literacy test as a standard for admission to the United States, Henry Cabot Lodge told the U.S. Senate: "Mr. President, more precious even than forms of government are the mental and moral qualities which make what we call our race." He continued to warn that the nation was in peril of "a single danger, and that is by changing the quality of our race and citizenship through the wholesale infusion of races whose traditions and inheritances, whose thoughts and whose beliefs are wholly alien to ours and with whom we have never assimilated or even been associated in the past, the danger has begun" (page 58). The heated debate over this proposal is detailed. Close-up shots of individuals, masses of people on the deck of a ship in harbor, and remarkable documentation of ethnic dress make this well worth the time of any student of documentary photography.

522. *The Irish Potato Famine*. Don Nardo. Illustrations by Brian McGovern. World Disasters. San Diego, CA: Lucent Books, 1990.

This carefully documented story of Ireland does far more than just talk about the Potato Famine. It details the relationships between rich and poor, the impact of external pressures on the island nation, how Britain came to have power over it, why that seemed righteous, and what exactly happened when a farm family could not pay the rent after a mysterious blight had stricken the only source of food millions of Irish peasants had. Vignettes throughout the book give details about relevant people, incidents, and artifacts. Though a standard readability scale might suggest this is an easy reader, the many large chunks of solid text and the colorful turns of phrase used make this more difficult reading than a simple score would convey. But it is good reading material, presenting historical facts and explaining events in a compelling way. The illustrations and photographs assist with comprehension, a timeline puts the famine in historical perspective, and a simple map makes clear the geographic relationships of Ireland and Great Britain both to each other and to France. NOTE: There are discussion-generating read alouds in the "Book Chapters and Strong Passages" of this unit (entry 536) and also in Unit 7 (entry 441).

523. *Letters from the Promised Land: Swedes in America, 1840–1914.* Edited by H. Arnold Barton. Minneapolis, MN: University of Minnesota Press for the Swedish Pioneer Historical Society, 1975.

This period of the greatest migration from Sweden to the United States is discussed through immigrants' letters and diaries and through travel accounts by Swedish visitors. Religious persecution, language difficulties, economic strife on both sides of the Atlantic, and the most difficult period—the first six months—are all detailed in these documents. There are several particularly telling passages: Foul air, cramped quarters below deck, putrid water, moldy and wormy food that was often in short supply, sickness, and death were standard during the eight- to ten-week voyage. This is so much like the slave transport and the experiences of poor Irish and Vietnamese and Cambodian boat people that it bears comparative analysis in the classroom or tutoring situation, particularly for ESL students. Note the first paragraph on page 14. Poor crops in Sweden from 1867 to 1869 are discussed on page 139. Illiteracy, spelling deficiencies, and the use of mixed Swedish and English in letters are covered in a letter of complaint to the editor of *Hemlandet* from the Swedish postmaster S. M. Korling, who adds that addresses are often so incomplete that letters must be opened to find out who should receive them. Even then, if the letter is unsigned, it must be passed from hand to hand until someone recognizes the handwriting or contents, pages 140–41, Language acquisition is addressed on pages 196–97 in a letter of April 10, 1888, to Sister Lotten. The letter explains what we now call the Silent Period in 1888 terms. The young writer says, "[I]t is hardest the first half year as long as you can't manage with the language, but if you only can happen to find decent folks to work for it goes well and good humor is something wherever you go." About 1902, another letter details how satisfaction with America parallels language acquisition. That is, the immigrant experience begins with overwhelming homesickness that evolves into a love of the new country as English becomes more a part of the immigrant, page 290.

524. *Number the Stars.* Lois Lowry. New York: Dell, 1989. 1990 Newbery Medal.

This beautifully written historical fiction about the Nazi occupation of Denmark is told from the perspective of a young girl. A five-page afterword is profoundly written true history, including a letter excerpt from a young man to his mother on the night before he was executed for his work in the Resistance. Because much of the book is written as everyday dialogue about real events, it is a fine language teacher for the nonnative speaker of English. An emotionally charged read-aloud passage comes in chapter 10, when Annemarie, the heroine, waits with her mother and several friends for an opportunity to smuggle Jews from Denmark to Sweden. It begins on page 83: "Annemarie," Mama whispered to her in the hall, "you may go to bed if you want to. It' very late." Annemarie stays and sees Nazi soldiers enter the house, question the alleged funeral rites taking place in the living room around a coffin, and slap Annemarie's mother across the face. The selection ends on page 87, as a young Resistance soldier reads a Bible passage that names the book: "It is he who heals the broken in spirit and binds up their wounds, he who numbers the stars one by one." This passage gives an immediacy to the tensions present during World War II. An excellent follow-up is Anne Frank's *The Diary of a Young Girl* (see entry 520).

525. "Okie, Go Home!" In *Children of the Dust Bowl: The True Story of the School at Weedpatch Camp*. Jerry Stanley. Illustrated with historical photographs. New York: Crown, 1992, pages 34–39.

This book describes the reaction of established Californians to the impoverished farmworkers from the Dust Bowl who crowded into the counties where Route 66 met Route 99. Because of their poor diet, they were exhausted, and because of their shabby clothing and distinct speech patterns, they stood out. The presence of their unschooled children added to the misconception that the Okies were stupid and shiftless.

526. "The War Years." In *Dr. Elizabeth: The Story of the First Woman Doctor*. Patricia Clapp. New York: Lothrop, Lee & Shepard, 1974, pages 133–46.

This read aloud is an action-packed chapter detailing the implications of April 12, 1861, the day the first shot of the Civil War was fired, and the charge of emotions as both black and white patients feared for their lives should unsympathetic forces find them occupying the same infirmary. There is more detail on the book under "Challenging," entry 511.

527. *Witness to an Era: The Life and Photographs of Alexander Gardner: The Civil War, Lincoln, and the West*. D. Mark Katz. New York: Viking, 1991.

This is an oversized picture book and an extraordinary portrait of an artist's life. Gardner documented the Civil War, made numerous photographs of President Abraham Lincoln, and photographed the conspirators to Lincoln's assassination, as well. Pictures of all of these are in the book. The photograph of young Private William Johnson (June 20, 1864) dangling from a gallows and the accompanying text on page 76 tell of extreme punishment of a black man who attempted to "commit an outrage on a white woman. Considerable importance was given to the affair, in order that the example might be made more effective. Johnson confessed his guilt, and was executed . . . in plain view of the enemy." There are also reproductions of handwritten documents, complete with scratch-outs and in-process editing, of the Civil War era. The running commentary and captions make this part of American history more real than does any other picture book I have seen. And the issues of battlefield agony, racism, slavery, intrigue, crime, and punishment are brought to the fore. This is an excellent book just for page-turning dialogue. It is also well written.

Book Chapters and Strong Passages

528. "Another Way." Terry Dobson. In *Chicken Soup for the Soul: 101 Stories to Open the Heart and Rekindle the Spirit*. Edited by Jack Canfield and Mark V. Hansen. Deerfield Beach, FL: Health Communications, 1993, pages 55–58.

It is so easy to despise what we do not know. Here, in just three pages, is an awakening.

529. "The Bag Lady." Bobbie Probstein. In *Chicken Soup for the Soul: 101 Stories to Open the Heart and Rekindle the Spirit.* Edited by Jack Canfield and Mark V. Hansen. Deerfield Beach, FL: Health Communications, 1993, pages 77–78.
   She knew that some went hungry. And she passed that lesson on.

530. *The Bill of Rights and Landmark Cases.* Edmund Lindop. New York: Franklin Watts, 1989.
   In just 144 pages, this book gives a brief overview of American history and politics as it is documented in our legal system. Chapter 1 describes attitudes about rights and freedoms, including biases that some members of society are more deserving than others. Chapter 2, "The First 10 Amendments," gives the actual wording of those amendments and brief discussions of their meanings. Chapter 3, "The Supreme Court," describes how that group reflects the times in which its members serve and how it influences Americans for generations afterward. Photographs of several historical groups are included. Other chapters discuss civil rights as protected under the Constitution and use specific cases to illustrate how attitudes change as the supreme law of the land is interpreted and reinterpreted. Included are photographs of some of the people behind the historic cases, such as Linda Brown (Brown v. Board of Education, 1954), who, at the age of nine, became the focus of a desegregation suit that was resolved too late to accommodate Brown but opened school doors for her younger siblings and others who followed; and Walter Gobitis and his children (Minersville School District v. Gobitis, 1940), who lost a plea not to salute the U.S. flag in a public school, a case that was reversed only three years later. Also shown are a group of Amish children running from school authorities who wanted to force school attendance on a religious group that feared the influence of education on its members; a 1963 march on Washington against school segregation; Philip Lindsey, general secretary of Rotary International, after the 1987 ruling to allow women membership; Norma McCorvey, aka Jane Roe, of the 1973 abortion case Roe v. Wade; and others. Though many pages are solid print, and the vocabulary is full and descriptive, the news story style makes this interesting history book quite readable. A student might use discrete sections for SSR. And many of the cases described here would serve as read-aloud passages to launch discussion on meaningful adult topics.

531. "Educating a Special Child." In *Hey! Listen to This: Stories to Read Aloud.* Edited by Jim Trelease. New York: Penguin Books, 1992, pages 44–45.
   In this passage we learn of the impact that one person can have on society's attitudes across time. The passage also supports the use of journals. During a trip to America in 1842, when he visited Laura, a blind, deaf, and mute girl, Charles Dickens was surprised to learn that her Boston doctor had taught her to read and write. At the time, such children were societal discards—locked away, hidden, shamefully kept from human interaction. Dickens recorded the discovery of Laura's remarkable learning ability in his journal, which was eventually published. Forty years later, the mother of Helen Keller read about the incident and was inspired to find a teacher for her disabled daughter.

532. "Heart of Darkness." In *Great Short Works of Joseph Conrad.* Joseph Conrad. New York: Harper & Row, 1967, pages 210–92.
   This story is delivered primarily in simple, first-person testimony, in which one man relates details of a journey into the depths of his time. One Strong Passage

about discarded slaves left to die beneath the trees begins on page 225: "I avoided a vast artificial hole somebody had been digging on the slope." It ends on page 226 with a description of a dying man who seemed to the narrator less than human: "He lapped out of his hand, then sat up in the sunlight, crossing his shins in front of him, and after a time let his wooly head fall on his breast-bone." There are seven stories and a biography of Conrad in this collection. The power of Conrad's writing comes, in part, from honest storytelling. His descriptions and the emotional reactions and attitudes of his characters convey real people. Even so, these stories are by no means easy reading. It is the content that drives the reader on. One good way to ruin a Conrad story is to demand a report on it or a reaction paper. On way to work with the text is to let a self-selected group of readers meet to reflect on passages they find memorable.

533. *History's Big Mistakes.* Adam Bowett. Illustrated by Chris Mould. London: Belitha Press, 1994.

The way in which pictures and text support each other makes this book a candidate for a space between Picture Books and Thin Books sections. A glossary at the end is made even more useful, as all of the words defined there are highlighted in the main text. The witty running stories are interesting and easy to read, with lots of space devoted to incredibly humorous cartoons. Little bits of additional information are offered in small boxes on nearly every page. Each two-page spread tells of another historic foible. Strong Passages occur in every section. For example, incredible as it may seem, Johann Sebastian Bach was the victim of a fixed competition for a job as organist of St. James Church in Hamburg, Germany. The winner was a large contributor to the church coffers, pages 24–25.

534. "The Homosexual Hassle." In *The Best of Dear Abby.* Abigail Van Buren. Kansas City, MO: Andrews & McMeel, 1981, pages 67–76.

One of the most emotionally charged social issues of this century is the debate over homosexuality. In letters to Dear Abby, we see many perspectives on the problem of what uninvolved friends and acquaintances are supposed to be told and how important their opinions are to family members grappling with a society in the throes of rapid change. Abby begins this chapter by citing Sigmund Freud's correspondence with a mother who was seeking advice regarding her homosexual son. Interestingly, at the time of this correspondence Freud himself had had to flee the oppression of Adolf Hitler. *The Best of Dear Abby* is a collection of letters to the newspaper lovelorn and life problems specialist.

535. "In Response to Executive Order 9066: All Americans of Japanese Descent Must Report to Relocation Centers." Dwight Okita. In *Survival!* Lexington, MA: D. C. Heath, 1995, pages 70–71.

In a short letter from a fourteen-year-old girl, the U.S. government is told of the reaction a white girl had toward her Japanese American best friend. "You're trying to start a war," she said, "giving secrets away to the enemy. Why can't you keep your big mouth shut?" This fiction takes on a compellingly believable essence as the author explains that his parents were interned in a World War II relocation center set up for 120,000 Japanese Americans.

536. *The Irish Potato Famine*. Don Nardo. Illustrations by Brian McGovern. World Disasters. San Diego, CA: Lucent Books, 1990.

A full description of the book is in this unit under "Read Alouds," entry 522. There are several passages in this book that would lend themselves either to teacher read alouds/discussion starters or to research support for students writing about racism and tolerance. "Prejudice and Hatred," pages 49-50, and "The Irish Endured," pages 50-51, discuss the impact of racism on the Irish in Ireland. A vignette " 'No Irish Need Apply'—Anti-Irish Prejudice," page 51, gives an accounting of anti-Irish sentiments in the United States. Two vignette portraits of British politicians, "Sir Robert Peel," pages 36-37, and "Charles Edward Trevelyan," page 40, explain views of the famine from very different camps. These two portraits also allow one to observe that an attitude toward an entire group of people misses the fact that individuals within a group may not be aligned with one philosophy or another. Though the entire book is filled with interesting detail that sheds strong light on the root causes of intolerance, these passages can stand alone.

Intolerance and bigotry breed hunger. Two startlingly similar passages from different books show the same inhumane reaction to widespread hunger, in spite of the fact that they occurred on different continents in different centuries. In the first paragraph on page 26 of *Children of the Dust Bowl, the True Story of the School at Weedpatch Camp*, by Jerry Stanley, we learn of the destruction of surplus crops to prevent consumption by Okies. The above-referenced vignette, "Charles Edward Trevelyan," tells about rerouting of food-bearing ships away from the docks of famine-stricken Ireland and instructions to dump cargo into the sea, rather than feed the Irish. This pair is a stimulating read aloud. Classroom dialogue or tutor/student discussion, followed by a free writing time would provide a rich two-hour experience.

537. *Letters from a Slave Girl: The Story of Harriet Jacobs*. Mary E. Lyons. New York: Charles Scribner's Sons, 1992.

Special passage concerning literacy: "We know that she had to conceal her literacy from her master. 'One day,' she recalled in *Incidents in the Life of a Slave Girl*, ' he caught me teaching myself to write.' We also know that she received notes and poems from friends. Because writing was forbidden, it is likely that she responded to them in secret" (page 136).

538. "My First Word." From *The Story of My Life*. Helen Keller. In the *Jamestown Heritage Reader*. Book C. Providence, RI: Jamestown, 1991, pages 116–22.

In this Challenging passage, Keller recalls the first time her teacher, Anne Sullivan, arrived at her house and then follows the progression of trials, tantrums, and errors until Keller discovered the meaning of a word. See entry 56 in Unit 1, "The Arts," for more information on the *Jamestown Heritage Readers*.

539. "No Difference." In *Where the Sidewalk Ends*. Poems and drawings by Shel Silverstein. New York: HarperCollins, 1974.

This poem suggests that the only differences between us are the ones on the surface, the ones that disappear when we close our eyes. I have used this incredible collection of poems in many different ways with adults and children. It was popular as a community college ESL text and has provided a wealth of material for readers theatre events, too.

540. "Our Boys." In *Wouldn't Take Nothing for My Journey Now*. Maya Angelou. New York: Random House, 1993, pages 119–25.

This is an incredible essay in which Angelou shows how everyone loses when the insidious disease of intolerance goes unaddressed. This essay should be read aloud. It should be read silently. It should be discussed in homogeneous groups, heterogeneous groups, and families.

541. "Puppies for Sale." Dan Clark. In *Chicken Soup for the Soul: 101 Stories to Open the Heart and Rekindle the Spirit*. Edited by Jack Canfield and Mark V. Hansen. Deerfield Beach, FL: Health Communications, 1993, pages 65–66.

Here the puppy with a limp is selected by a boy who can relate. This is about diversity and tolerance.

542. "The Rabbits Who Caused All the Trouble." In *Fables for Our Time and Famous Poems Illustrated*. James Thurber. New York: Harper & Row, 1983, pages 68–70.

The eating habits and lifestyle of the rabbits give the wolves their excuse for oppressing and then eating the rabbits. And the willingness of all the other animals to stand back, watching in silence, has a chilling parallel to human events—in war, in prisons, and on the streets. A community college ESL discussion of racism, inspired by this fable, led several of my students to write papers on the topic. Thurber's wordplays fall from every paragraph, and the vocabulary is quite sophisticated, too. Even so, my intermediate-level students read it to themselves and enjoyed it. When I read it aloud, however, they enjoyed it even more. I have also used this fable with new readers, with similar student affirmation.

543. "Racism," pages 111–22, and "Footprints in the Sand," pages 127–43. In *I Want to Tell You: My Response to Your Letters, Your Messages, Your Questions*. O. J. Simpson. Boston: Little, Brown, 1995.

Throughout the book there are traces of racism and bigotry, but in these two chapters are letters that illustrate how unaware racists or bigots may be of their own inner conflicts. Some, in the name of Jesus or God, assume remarkably evil postures. The author's responses are also telling. Though there are many passages of interest, I particularly want to call attention to a powerful story on pages 114–15, in which Simpson tells of his awakening to the fact that this is not a simple "black-white thing." While making a movie in South Africa, Simpson discovered a much more complex form of racism. This passage may be of great value as a read aloud and discussion starter. The title describes most of the contents of this easy reader with photographs. Anyone intrigued by the trial, the murders, or the reactions of people of all ages to this public event will find something to read in this book.

544. "Septima Poensette Clark." In *I Dream A World: Portraits of Black Women Who Changed America*. Brian Lanker. Foreword by Maya Angelou. New York: Stewart, Tabori & Chang, 1989, pages 164–65.

This oversized book is 167 pages of American history. On one side of each two-page spread is a full-page, black-and-white, museum quality photographic portrait of a famous African American woman; on the other is a full-page biographical sketch and interview detailing her place in history. The birth date appears just below the name, and a narrow column gives an encapsulated overview of her contributions to society. The daughter of a slave, and a teacher who was forbidden work, Clark discusses her memories of the civil rights movement, her work recruiting teachers to teach blacks, voter registration, Martin Luther King, Jr.'s attitude toward women, and her philosophy of life. This is a passage that lends itself to many discussions about race, bigotry, and tolerance.

Also in the same book see "Rosa Parks" (pages 16–17). Though she talks of job discrimination and the relentless pain of inequity, Rosa Parks is most remembered for her willingness to take a stand by taking a seat on a segregated bus in the deep South, an act that led to her arrest in 1955, an act that "ignited the civil rights movement." This passage details one of the cornerstones of American history.

545. "Service with a Smile." Karl Albrecht and Ron Zenke. In *Chicken Soup for the Soul: 101 Stories to Open the Heart and Rekindle the Spirit*. Edited by Jack Canfield and Mark V. Hansen. Deerfield Beach, FL: Health Communications, 1993, page 224.

Two letters can make us rethink our attitudes about attitudes. Here is a wake-up call.

546. "Slavery—A Profitable Trade." In *Explorers Who Got Lost*. Diane Sansevere Dreher. Illustrated by Ed Renfro. New York: Tom Doherty, 1992.

Describes the progression from initial trade to full country economies dependent on slavery.

547. "The Spanish Inquisition." In *Explorers Who Got Lost*. Diane Sansevere Dreher. Illustrated by Ed Renfro. New York: Tom Doherty, 1992.

Details how God-fearing Christians cruelly punished many of the unfaithful and burned thousands at the stake, permanently damaging that country's position as a world power.

548. "Two Monks." Jack Canfield and Mark V. Hansen. In *Chicken Soup for the Soul: 101 Stories to Open the Heart and Rekindle the Spirit*. Edited by Jack Canfield and Mark V. Hansen. Deerfield Beach, FL: Health Communications, 1993, page 289.

This one-page account allows us to rethink what we think about.

Newspaper and Magazine Articles

549. "Bad Vibes Across America over Rock, Rap Lyrics." *USA Today*, June 30–July 2, 1995, page 4-D.

"Opposing forces: C. DeLores Tucker says music lyrics send 'genocidal message'; Dave Marsh calls ratings 'a tyranny.' " So goes the half-page article on lyrics that call for violence against specific groups and the efforts to stop them. One music promoter expresses concern over the impact reggae music has on youngsters, and a twelve-year-old says she would feel pretty bummed if her listening was censored. After all, she argues, her friends use the "objectionable" language when adults are not around, her parents use it when she and her sister are not around (but they hear it anyway), and even her baby-sitter uses it. This article will not solve the problem, but it will open the door to dialogue about a number of issues.

550. "Court Grows Critical When Race, Law Intersect." *USA Today,* June 30–July 2, 1995, page 8-A.

This is another article showing both sides of the argument over equity. Should desegregation laws be removed from the books? This piece helps to clarify the question.

551. "The New Immigrants: A Changing Nation Now May Close the Door." *USA Today,* June 30–July 2, 1995, pages 1, 2.

This is one of a series of three stories scheduled as a special report. "In a computer analysis of data on the 2.2 million people who became legal immigrants in 1991–1993, *USA Today* illustrates how newcomers have changed the nation, bringing new colors and languages, and a new vibrancy and vigor." Too, the article continues, they bring a variety of skills. But because family ties are the primary criterion for immigration, ethnic groups tend to cluster in already overcrowded areas. If the rules were changed to admit people based primarily on skills, newcomers would be spread more evenly across the United States. This heated issue has been one of major concern in my ESL classes. News articles like this, collected over time, allow me to supply students with research materials for writing meaningful papers—even when their academic skills are just developing.

552. "The New Politics of Race." *Newsweek,* May 6, 1991.

The May 6, 1991, cover story of *Newsweek* attempts to look objectively at affirmative action. Supporting pieces examine other aspects of race. The reader reactions are a treasure trove of attitudes in short passages. Perspectives of blacks, whites, Asians, other members of the population are reflected in "Portrait in Black and White," *Newsweek,* May 27, 1991, page 10.

553. "Racial Districting Biased: Equality Not Served, Says Court." Tony Mauro. *USA Today,* June 30–July 2, 1995, page 1.

In a heated argument about the fairness of changing congressional districts to break up minority voting blocs, it becomes clear that there are two sides. This article brings many issues to the fore in clear, unemotional language.

Other Events and Supplements

It is so difficult to see our own biases and so easy to feel uncovered when we do that on a personal level this topic is best handled in very safe small increments. Notions exposed in a journal are best responded to in the journal. This is a good place for introspection, but only if it is completely confidential. Questions asked in a large forum must not pin down the speaker, even when hypocritical views are exposed. This is where historical references and read alouds can show the same ideas, removed by time or space. When the moderator feels secure about the audience and the outcome, a personal anecdote can be powerful because it connects the condition with a respected human being. Such attempts can have unpredictable positive consequences. But change is an uneven thing and is only lasting when it evolves from within. Rules may raise consciousness, but they don't change minds. Yes, externally we can modify behavior, but the strongest pitch for what we believe is how we live.

- Create a readers theatre dealing with issues of intolerance.
- Visit a Holocaust museum.
- Design an exhibit about a kind of bigotry you have witnessed.
- Write an argument supporting a bigoted or racist act—from the bigot's or racist's perspective.
- Draw a picture of a racist as a young child.
- Discuss ways in which racism and bigotry influence personal freedoms in big cities.
- Write a poem about bigotry.
- Look for articles on bigotry, intolerance, and tolerance in newspapers and magazines.
- Try to remember changes you have experienced in your own attitudes. Write about the event or influence that caused you to start thinking differently.
- Compare local news stories about gender, age, health, or other identified differences with accounts from other regions or countries.
- List as many ways as you can remember of how you were different as a child.
- List commercially promoted ways of arriving at uniformity, e.g, clothing, hair color, scents.
- Monitor an hour of television at the same time each day for three weeks. Document innuendos suggesting superiority, inferiority, or other hierarchial attitudes.

War

Unit 9

Conflict and triumph make war stories a high-interest topic for many adults and teens. Many have been close to war firsthand or through a relative; others via television reporting. But always they have viewed it from some narrow perspective. The chance to follow a struggle from start to finish through the words of a variety of writers gives some students just the right vehicle for learning about historical events, geography, and the related writing styles.

The history of conflict provides a thorough way of studying history and geography. So any person interested in this topic has an incredibly complete line of events that includes the scope of economics, social events, and political shifts—almost everything except the arts, which generally slow or stop during war. And geography can be picked up in the process of following conflict from country to country. At first I thought the biggest stumbling block for designing this unit would be locating picture books and First Readers. Then I remembered *The Prince Who Wrote a Letter*.

First Readers and Picture Books

554. *All Those Secrets of the World*. Jane Yolen. Illustrated by Leslie Baker. New York: Little, Brown, 1991.

Patriotism, farewells, and a young child's view of the world as her father goes off to war on a big ship are brought together in an emotional story that comes full circle to a happy ending. This child gains both concrete and abstract notions of perspective. The print is large and the clearly written text is supported by realistic pictures. It is a good parent-child read aloud, an ESL reader, and a new reader's book about an important topic.

555. *How Many Days to America? A Thanksgiving Story*. Eve Bunting. Illustrated by Beth Peck. New York: Clarion Books, 1988.

A family is forced to flee in the night via a small, overcrowded boat, only to be exploited and denied access to civil liberties. Though this story is usually listed under Hispanic, I have found its impact equally powerful on Vietnamese and Cambodian immigrants.

556. *A Picture Book of Simon Bolivar*. David A. Adler. Illustrated by Robert Casilla. New York: Holiday House, 1992.

Simon Bolivar, born in Venezuela in 1783, lived in a time of widespread revolution. America had just engaged in its freedom fight, Spain was in mortal struggle with France, led by Napoleon Bonaparte, for its right to remain independent, and, likewise, Spanish colonies in South America were aching to be freed of Spanish rule. These tumultuous roots fostered a child who eventually came to be known as El Libertador of Venezuela, Colombia, Ecuador, Peru, and Bolivia. Class distinctions and racism marked the environment of Bolivar, son of Creoles who owned copper and silver mines, several plantations, and over a thousand slaves. Tragedy was also part of Bolivar's youth. By the time he was six, both his parents were dead . Simon was first home schooled and then continued his studies in Spain. Eventually, he began to work for a free life in his homeland. Penniless, in 1830 he died of TB. Double-page watercolor illustrations support nearly every paragraph of text. The easy-to-read book provides some interesting historical information and a list of important dates at the end.

557. *The Prince Who Wrote a Letter*. Ann Love. Illustrated by Toni Goffe. New York: Child's Play International, 1992.
    This is a book about a letter—one that was misunderstood—one that nearly started a war—one that was never written. It is about gossip and the impact it can have.

558. *The Star-Spangled Banner*. Illustrated by Peter Spier. New York: Dell, 1992.
    This is a must have for every American home. Each exquisite two-page illustration demonstrates the meaning of a single line of the national anthem. A brief profile of the nation in the throes of the War of 1812 gives a sense of the people, places, and terrible struggle that framed the poem that would become a famous song. A map of the war zone shows where Francis Scott Key was during his moment of glory and inspiration. A copy of the original handwritten text of Key's poem is opposite the map. There is also a two-page spread of many historical U.S. flags. The lyrics are set to music on one page, for the pianist in our midst. This large paperback looks like a children's book and is a Reading Rainbow selection, but it has value to every adult interested in U.S. history. I have found it useful for both ESL students and adult new readers.

559. *The Wall*. Eve Bunting. Illustrated by Ronald Himler. New York: Clarion Books, 1990.
    Just a few perfectly chosen words about the Vietnam War Memorial and sensitive, detailed watercolors deliver powerful thoughts about loss and eternity. The story is told by a child whose father is searching for his own father's name on the Wall.

560. *The War Began at Supper: Letters to Miss Loria*. Patricia Reilly Giff. Illustrated by Betsy Lewin. New York: Delacorte Press, 1991.
    Miss Loria, a beloved student teacher who has moved away, is the addressee of most of the letters from the students in Mrs. Clark's elementary school class. Concerns about the Persian Gulf War manifest in many ways among the young writers, whose simple prose makes easy reading about difficult subjects. Even the new reader will be able to use this book during SSR. Each letter is short enough to allow completion of a unit during one sitting.

Thin Books

561. *Abraham Lincoln*. Kathie Billingslea Smith. Illustrated by James Seward. New York: Scholastic, 1987.
    A barefoot lad in western Kentucky is introduced. Then his mother dies, father remarries, and the boy is fortunate enough to have a stepmother who honors his love of books. He is married, a child is born and dies, two more are born, and the man becomes president of the United States. A war over slavery, the Civil War, begins, the Emancipation Proclamation is signed, and another son dies. The war ends, and the reelected president is assassinated. All this in just a few pages of easy-to-read text, with clear drawings on each page.

562. *Always to Remember: The Story of the Vietnam Veterans Memorial.* Brent Ashabranner. Photographs by Jennifer Ashabranner. New York: Scholastic, 1988.

This clear accounting of the historical and emotional roots of the United States' involvement in the Vietnam War gives many details about people affected by it. Wounded in action and a witness to the deaths or wounding of over half his company, veteran Jan C. Scruggs came home to a legacy of shame for having gone to war. One night, after seeing the movie *The Deer Hunter,* he was driven to make a memorial of substance to the effort and suffering that had transpired. It would have the names of all those men and women lost in the war. This dream became an obsession that led to a nationwide competition, with 1,421 designs submitted and judged without names or identification of any kind. The Wall, entry number 1,026, by twenty-one-year-old Yale student Maya Ying Lin, was selected. The daughter of Chinese immigrants was to make a profound contribution to the art and history of America.

563. *America at War! Battles That Turned the Tide.* Brian Black. New York: Scholastic, 1992.

From the American Revolution to the Persian Gulf War, America's conflicts from 1763 to 1990 are set in historical and political perspective. This clearly written book gives insights into the emotional and complex issues involving military activities that changed the course of history. An adult new reader and her tutor began trading off passages and came away with far more than literacy. Both sang the praises of this well-written history. It is also appropriate for ESL students who are attempting to learn about America and its past. The range of countries involved in wars with America provides a trek around the map that would illuminate and enliven many a geography unit.

564. *Bull Run.* Paul Fleischman. Woodcuts by David Frampton. New York: Scholastic, 1993.

Two maps make up the first two pages, one depicting the existing states and their positions in the Session, the other a close-up of the Eastern Theatre of the Civil War, where the Battle of Bull Run took place. At the end, a two-page spread shows two maps of the battle scene, morning on the left, afternoon on the right. One by one, in isolated vignettes, as though reporting to an unseen interviewer, fictional characters tell their stories of hearing about war, getting ready for the battle, heading off, and how the battle occurred—the tragic discovery that war is not a game. The momentum of this series of reports builds so subtly that the reader does not realize what has happened until it is done. Each vignette is one or two pages. And each speaker has a personal icon woodcut. The language is quite simple, no long sentences, no big words, and as such, almost chops at the reader's attention, but the overall impact is strong. Four read-aloud passages are listed under "Book Chapters and Strong Passages," entry 587.

565. *The Constitution.* David P. Currie and Joyce L. Stevos. Glenview, IL: Scott, Foresman, 1991.

A clear, simple description of the background of U.S. history and government, starting with our English heritage and the basic laws of the colonies, leads into the Declaration of Independence. The book describes the development of the U.S. Constitution and covers the twenty-six Amendments. Sections of the Constitution and the Amendments are clarified in modern language set in red type. On page 108, an essay details the Civil War Amendments and the problems getting these laws enforced.

566. *D-Day*. R. Conrad Stein. Chicago: Childrens Press, 1993. Cornerstones of Freedom series.
   This book tells of one long day, June 6, 1944, that marked the turn of the tide in the war against Adolf Hitler and all that he represented in human suffering.

567. *The Day Pearl Harbor Was Bombed: A Photo History of World War II*. George Sullivan. New York: Scholastic, 1991.
   A one-page chronology of important dates from 1933 to 1946 and a bibliography of further reading suggestions supplement this well-organized, action-packed history of World War II. Though there is little text on each page, the vocabulary is by no means easy. Words like strategists, kamikaze, Allies, throngs, victory, stunning, and headquarters pepper the text. Historical references to Okinawa, the Solomon Islands, Berlin, Nazis, the Soviet Union, New Guinea, Guam, Saipan, the Mariana Islands, Leyte Gulf, the Philippines, Manila, Japan, Iwo Jima, the Pacific, the Boeing B-29, and the atomic bomb make this book vocabulary intensive for the new reader and ESL learner. But the photographs support the text and make just page turning worthwhile for someone seeking an overview of the war. For a read-aloud discussion starter, see four pages of historical photographs that give a chilling account of the Holocaust, pages 68–71. "Early in April 1945, as a company of British soldiers advanced through Germany toward Berlin, they came upon a barbed-wire-enclosed camp. What they saw sickened them. In trenchlike open graves, piles of naked bodies were stacked like firewood. The soldiers couldn't believe their eyes" (page 69).

568. *Florence Nightingale: The Determined English Woman Who Founded Modern Nursing and Reformed Military Medicine*. Pam Brown. Milwaukee, WI: Gareth Stevens, 1989. People Who Have Helped the World series.
   In only sixty-eight pages laced with numerous historical photos, paintings, and etchings, the reader is propelled through the incredible highs and lows of a young British upper-class woman's desperate struggle to find intellectual stimulation (her parents disapproved of her avid pursuit of math). She faced relentless family problems and mental illness. Despite this, she managed to reach out to find meaning for her life, taking on the wretched conditions in hospitals and on battlefields, where people died as often from their care as their wounds. She is famous for saying, "The first requirement of a hospital is that it should do the sick no harm" (page 18). Nightingale lived from 1820 to 1915. The book has a useful three-page chronology, a good glossary, a map of war sites where she worked in Europe and Asia, page 26, and several addresses to write to for more information about Nightingale and nursing. There are numerous read-aloud passages. Two are referenced under "Book Chapters and Strong Passages," entry 588.

569. *The Freedom Side*. Marcie Miller Stadelhofen. New York: New Readers Press, 1990. Sundown Books series.
   This book is an introduction to the issues of slavery and civil rights in U.S. history. Adult native and nonnative speakers of English get caught up in the

intrigue and suspense of this pre Civil War historical fiction. I know of no one in the Beaumont (California) Literacy Program who read this book and failed to go looking for its sequel, *Last Chance for Freedom*.

570. *George Washington*. Kathie Billingslea Smith. Illustrated by James Seward. New York: Scholastic, 1987.
    This Thin Booklet makes the first president of the United States both human and historical. It also gives a clear picture of how soldiering was done during the time of the American Revolution. The type is large and easy to read, and a large portion of every page is filled with helpful illustrations.

571. *Last Chance for Freedom*. Marcie Miller Stadelhofen. New York: New Readers Press, 1990. Sundown Books series.
    This sequel to *The Freedom Side* is part of a collection written for adult new readers. They are in a thin, easy-to-carry paperback format with adult pictures on the covers. Although not oversized, the print is clear and legible. All are available with cassette tapes that allow new readers and ESL students to make the sound-symbol connections. The good news is there is a compelling story that provides authentic historical information. The bad news is that the sentences are quite short. However, they provide an in-depth view of circumstances that helped lead this country into the Civil War.

572. *Letters from a Slave Girl: The Story of Harriet Jacobs*. Mary E. Lyons. New York: Charles Scribner's Sons, 1992.
    Inspired by the autobiographical letters published by the adult Harriet Jacobs, Lyons employs fictional letters to Jacobs's deceased mother, father, and other relatives to convey the historical events of 1825 to 1842 and the personal imaginings, triumphs, and tragedies of a slave girl who grows up as she strives to gain her freedom. The fictionalized biography is based on true events from the life of Harriet Jacobs. The final section, "Harriet: The Rest of Her Story," takes us from 1842 to 1852 in a narrative of the freedom fighter's life. The black Southern dialect of the slave girl begins to show the influence of white mistresses with whom she has extended contact. Jacobs is taught to read but has to learn writing on her own initiative. It is presumed that she used discarded account books for writing paper, as handmade paper was expensive and slaves were forbidden by law to read or write. This book is a powerful telling of one woman's experience as a slave. Gender issues, human rights, civil rights, and, certainly, the Civil War are addressed through this first-person account of suffering, courage, and hope.

573. *Number the Stars*. Lois Lowry. New York, Dell, 1989. 1990 Newbery Medal.
    This beautifully written historical fiction about the Nazi occupation of Denmark is told from the perspective of a young girl. A five-page afterword is profoundly written true history, including a letter excerpt from a young man to his mother on the night before he was executed for his work in the Resistance. Because much of the book is written as everyday dialogue about real events, it is a fine language teacher for the nonnative speaker of English. An emotionally charged read-aloud passage comes in chapter 10, when Annemarie, the heroine, waits with her mother and several friends for an opportunity to smuggle Jews from Denmark to Sweden. It begins on page 83: "Annemarie," Mama whispered

to her in the hall, "you may go to bed if you want to. It's very late." Annemarie stays and sees Nazi soldiers enter the house, question the alleged funeral rites taking place in the living room around a coffin, and slap Annemarie's mother across the face. The selection ends on page 87, as a young Resistance soldier reads a Bible passage that names the book: "It is he who heals the broken in spirit and binds up their wounds, he who numbers the stars one by one." This passage gives an immediacy to the tensions present during World War II.

574. *The Secret Soldier: The Story of Deborah Sampson.* Ann McGovern. Illustrated by Harold Goodwin. New York: Scholastic, 1975.

In just sixty-four pages of easy reading, McGovern deals with some of our most difficult human rights issues. First we witness the grief of a poverty-stricken widow in eighteenth-century America, as she prepared to give away the five children she could not support, among them Deborah Sampson. The child became a servant for a sickly old woman, then, as part of a minister's household, she was too busy with chores and family activities to do what she loved best—read. A powerful read-aloud passage starts at the top of page 11 and ends at the bottom of page 14. Here we learn that female children were not allowed schooling, even when they were loved, even when they begged for it. Despite this environment, Sampson began to keep a diary that became a historic document of life before the American Revolution. Later, unexpectedly, the poorly educated young woman became a teacher. And then she struck upon an idea for adventure: She disguised herself as a teenage boy and joined the army. This is the secret upon which this true story is built. A compelling read with many surprises, this is an easy reader to talk about.

575. *The Story of the Rough Riders.* Zachary Kent. Chicago: Childrens Press, 1991. Cornerstones of Freedom series.

The first U.S. Volunteer Cavalry Regiment, known as the Rough Riders and led by Colonel Theodore Roosevelt, was a renegade collection of soldiers from wealthy and poor roots who had to tame their own horses before they could use them for training in San Antonio, Texas. This was the beginning of an enormously energetic, very short-lived, gathering of restless young men whose caution-to-the-wind military participation changed the face of the map and blasted one of them into the spotlight of political life. Upon arrival in Cuba in 1898: the Rough Riders liberated Cuba from Spain; transferred control of Puerto Rico from Spain to the United States; and diverted control of the Philippines from Spain to the United States. Their seventeen days of wild, often undisciplined fighting in Cuba was called the Spanish-American War. One hundred and thirty-three days after the Rough Riders were assembled, they disbanded. Roosevelt subsequently became governor of New York, vice president of the United States, and then the twenty-sixth president of the United States.

576. *A Wall of Names: The Story of the Vietnam Veterans Memorial.* Judy Donnelly. Illustrated with photographs. New York: Random House, 1991.

This seemingly simple account of the Vietnam War Memorial moves progressively from the impact of the war on teenage soldiers, inhuman encounters with war in a swamp, the killings of peace protesters in the United States, soldiers coming home, and the memorial design controversy and compromise, to letters and gifts left at The Wall. This American perspective of "The Most Hated War" wrenches the heart while teaching about a piece of history that is too often simplified. Of special interest may be the fact that the winning design for the memorial was done as a school assignment and earned only a grade of "B." The large typeface is easy to read, and the photographs from the United States and Vietnam support this emotionally charged account.

Challenging

577. *Anne Frank: Beyond the Diary: A Photographic Remembrance.* Ruud van der Rol and Rian Verhoeven. Translated by Tony Langham and Plym Peters. Introduction by Anna Quindlen. New York: Viking Penguin, 1993.

Just as the title suggests, this book goes beyond the diary of the young girl, into the world and the plight of those whose lives were on the brink of terrible change. Photographs, letters, and simple captions make this history book a detailed journey into a time that will mar the history of humankind for all time. This book should be read in conjunction with the diary.

578. *Civil War Parks.* Rev. ed. William C. "Jack" Davis. Photography by David Muench. Las Vegas, NV: KC Publications, 1992. The Story Behind the Scenery series.

A centerfold of the Civil War area, historical paintings, a small sample of Lincoln's handwritten Gettysburg Address, and clear, well-composed color photographs serve as support for the challenging yet informing text. It is the kind of book a new speaker of English or new reader might use first as an adult picture book and revisit, gaining vocabulary and historical knowledge over time. The large, thin magazine format makes it easy to carry and allows many sections to have big, easy-on-the-eyes text. This is one of a series of such books on historical American sites designed by different people, all of which are appropriate reading for all levels. I have to rate the books as Challenging because sophisticated language is used. However, these books, by virtue of their layout and visuals, are much easier to read than some others under "Challenging."

579. *The Diary of a Young Girl.* Anne Frank. Translated from the Dutch by B. M. Mooyaart-Doubleday. Introduction by Eleanor Roosevelt. New York: Modern Library, 1952.

The impact of this diary as a historical document must be fostered with each new generation of readers. It is so easy to lose track of war's human impact unless some single story makes the details real. That is what this young girl's diary of the Holocaust does for those who cannot remember. Roosevelt's introductory words give weight to the notion that this is a book that must be read. "Written by a young girl—and the young are not afraid of telling the truth—it is one of the wisest and most moving commentaries on war and its impact on human beings that I have ever read. . . . [H]er diary tells us much about ourselves and about our own children." This edition has a brief passage written in Anne Frank's own pen. This is a history book, a coming-of-age book, a storybook, all under one cover.

580. *Dr. Elizabeth: The Story of the First Woman Doctor.* Patricia Clapp. New York: Lothrop, Lee & Shepard, 1974.

One hundred and fifty-six fast-moving pages without pictures give insightful details not only on the woman who lived from 1821 to 1910, but also on the gender and social issues of her day that continue to play out in women's struggles. The biography is written in an autobiographical format, discussing her life in England and the United States. There is a reference to Florence Nightingale on page 107. A passage on war and bigotry is found under "Book Chapters and Strong Passages," entry 599.

581. *Letters from the Sand: The Letters of Desert Storm and Other Wars.* U.S. Postal Service. Washington, DC: GPO, 1991.

Some reproduced in clear type, some in the original handwriting, letters and postcards document the history of the United States during wartime. Diary entries, children's art, stamps, and historical photographs support the text, which takes the reader on the same emotional roller-coaster rides that the writers themselves experienced. Seldom is the Spanish American War (1898–1899) covered in such detail. "The letters from Vietnam were just too sad to read," said an adult new reader. So much pictorial support is in this high-interest book that it does not really qualify for the Challenging category, yet the vocabulary and writing variety offer a lot of quality input not found elsewhere. There are actual commemorative stamps in the collector editions of this book.

582. *The Living Lincoln: The Man, His Mind, His Times, and the War He Fought,* Reconstructed from His Own Writings. Edited by Paul M. Angle and Earl Schenck Miers. New York: Barnes & Noble, 1992.

This book of letters, speeches, and journals documents the history lived by a literate man. Annotations help create a context for these one-sided communications. The entire book is worth study. And, if any part of it were published in booklet form, perhaps with illustrations, it would qualify as a Thin Book or, for some, a First Reader. Lincoln's style was forthright, honest, and to the point. There is no wondering what he meant. One line letters to field commanders and extensive, thoughtful diary entries show both the public commander in chief and the introspective human during the War Between the States.

583. *Spies of the Revolution.* Katherine Bakeless and John Bakeless. New York: Scholastic, 1962.

Strange messages, codes, and surreptitious goings-on filled the days of the Colonies' revolution against England. Here are the details of the Boston Tea Party and other lesser known events. Consider the simple mapmaker: "As it was Sunday, the two disguised officers dared not leave their lodging. Anyone walking the streets during church services was likely to be arrested. The two men kept out of sight till sunset, the end of the Puritan Sabbath. After that, secure in the early February dusk, they walked freely about the town, seeing what they could see. Then they went out on the hills sketching, and returned safely to their lodging. It was presumably one or the other of these two spies who made the plans for a camp and fortifications on Chandler's Hill, outside Worcester. The plans were found later after the British evacuated Boston" (page 13). This is not easy reading, but the stories offer rich entertainment and call to be read again and again.

584. *Unconditional Surrender: U. S. Grant and the Civil War*. Albert Marrin. New York: Atheneum, 1994.

Two hundred pages of information-heavy text are supported by a generous sprinkling of historical paintings, photos, and etchings, all black-and-white, and a two-page map of the Civil War zone. Here is a storehouse of detail and drama that makes this time come alive. Although the general text is Challenging, the captions alone are a fine read. Insights into battles shed light on national icons. Popular notions about Abraham Lincoln are deftly laid to rest. And Grant's success in passing the Fifteenth Amendment, assuring blacks, including former slaves, the right to vote, is but one of many successes in the life of a master militia man. There are numerous opportunities for read alouds, some of which are under "Book Chapters and Strong Passages" below. This is a moving book that could spur extensive dialogue almost from any page.

585. *Witness to an Era: The Life and Photographs of Alexander Gardner: The Civil War, Lincoln, and the West*. D. Mark Katz. New York: Viking, 1991.

This is an oversized picture book and an extraordinary portrait of an artist's life. Gardner documented the Civil War, made numerous photographs of President Abraham Lincoln, and photographed the conspirators to Lincoln's assassination, as well. Pictures of all of these are in the book. There are also reproductions of letters and other handwritten documents, complete with scratch-outs and in-process editing, of the Civil War era. The running commentary and captions make this part of American history more real than does any other picture book I have seen before. And the issues of battlefield agony, racism, slavery, intrigue, crime, and punishment are brought to the fore. This is an excellent book just for page-turning dialogue. It is also well written.

Book Chapters and Strong Passages

586. *Always to Remember: The Story of the Vietnam Veterans Memorial*. Brent Ashabranner. Photographs by Jennifer Ashabranner. New York: Scholastic, 1988.

Though the entire book is worthwhile reading, the chapter "The Vision of Maya Ying Lin," pages 35–43, is profound read-aloud material and can foster dialogue on many topics. She states: "A memorial shouldn't tell you what to think, but should make you think." Full details under "Thin Books," entry 562.

587. *Bull Run*. Paul Fleischman. Woodcuts by David Frampton. New York: Scholastic, 1993.

One by one, in isolated vignettes, as though reporting to an unseen interviewer, fictional characters tell their stories of hearing about war, getting ready for the battle, heading off, and how the battle occurred—the tragic discovery that war is not a game. There are four strong read-aloud passages: Eleven-year-old Toby Boyce (pages 13–14), announces that he is "desperate to kill a Yankee before the supply ran out." In the same passage he bluffs his way into the service as a fife player. Then, on page 96, Boyce appears on the battlefield, where a badly wounded soldier begs Toby to shoot him. "My stomach emptied. He was a Yank. How I'd longed back home to kill one. Here I finally had my chance. But instead I ran."

Gideon Adams, page 15, is faced with racism as he tries to volunteer for service. And on page 94, Dr. William Rye describes the fruits of war in his simple statements about the scene around him. For further details, see under "Thin Books," entry 564.

588. "The Crimean War." In *Florence Nightingale: The Determined English Woman Who Founded Modern Nursing and Reformed Military Medicine.* Pam Brown. Milwaukee, WI: Gareth Stevens, 1989.

"The Crimean War," pages 23–25, and "The Agony of Victory," pages 25–27, give terrible insights into conditions among the wounded and dying on battlefields during Florence Nightingale's crusades. I cannot begin to give quotes or details. Just read them. There are details under "Thin Books," entry 568.

589. "The Generals." In *Where the Sidewalk Ends.* Poems and drawings of Shel Silverstein. New York: HarperCollins, 1974, pages 150–51.

A poem titled "The Generals" portrays the futility of war, using wonderful vocabulary and punctuation marks. I have used this incredible collection of poems in many different ways with adults and children. It was popular as a community college ESL text. As a readers theatre presentation, this particular poem allowed a pair of Vietnamese generals an outlet for showing classmates how they had come to view their previous life's work.

590. The Gettysburg Address. In *The Living Lincoln: The Man, His Mind, His Times, and the War He Fought, Reconstructed from His Own Writings.* Edited by Paul M. Angle and Earl Schenck Miers. New York: Barnes & Noble, 1992, page 591.

Details on this title are under "Challenging," entry 582.

591. "The Haunted Battle." In *Ghosts, Hauntings and Mysterious Happenings.* Phyllis Raybin Emert. Illustrated by Jael. New York: Tom Doherty, 1990, pages 6–10.

An English tourist witnesses the carnage of battle and scavengers looting clothes and stealing jewelry from the dead and injured in broad daylight. The battle between the British and the Highlanders had taken place on the spot nearly 300 years before.

592. *History's Big Mistakes.* Adam Bowett. Illustrated by Chris Mould. London: Belitha Press, 1994.

"Strong Passages" occur in every section. Three relating to this unit include the following:

- Not one super ship, but two were built in such a way that they got top-heavy with artillery and sank. There are two strong reads in little boxes on pages 6–7.

- The Charge of the Light Brigade in 1854 was the most remarkable blunder of the Crimean War. How it happened is told on pages 22–23.

- "Splitting the Atom," pages 28–29, tells the tale of Albert Einstein, the pacifist whose work created the most terrible of war inventions.

593. "In Response to Executive Order 9066: All Americans of Japanese Descent Must Report to Relocation Centers." Dwight Okita. In *Survival!* Lexington, MA: D. C. Heath, 1995, pages 70–71.

In a short letter from a fourteen-year-old girl, the U.S. government is told of a white girl's reaction toward her Japanese American best friend. "You're trying to start a war," she said, "giving secrets away to the enemy. Why can't you keep your big mouth shut?" The author explains that his parents were interned in a World War II relocation center set up for 120,000 Japanese Americans.

594. "Military & Defense." *The Guinness Book of Records*. 1995 edition. New York: Bantam Books, 1995, pages 446-453.

This section is loaded with interesting extremes of war in very short passages. Under the subtitle War, for example, is *"Most costly*—The material cost of World War II far transcended that of all the rest of history's wars put together and has been estimated at $1.5 trillion" (page 446). And *"Longest march*—The longest march in military history was the famous Long March by the Chinese Communists in 1934-35. In 368 days, of which 268 were days of movement, from October to October, their force of some 100,000 covered 6,000 miles from Rijin, in Jiangxi, to Yan'an, in Shaanxi. They crossed 18 mountain ranges and 24 rivers, and eventually reached Yan'an with only about 8,000 survivors, following continual rearguard actions against nationalist Kuomintang (KMT) forces" (page 448). The war entries are also up-to-date as in *"Chemical warfare*—The greatest number of people killed through chemical warfare were the estimated 4,000 Kurds who died at Halabja, Iraq, in March 1988 when President Saddam Hussein used chemical weapons against Iraq's Kurdish minority in revenge for the support it had given to Iran in the Iran-Iraq war" (page 448).

595. "Pandora's Box." Catherine Gourley. In *Survival!* Lexington, MA: D. C. Heath, 1995, pages 84–101.

This is a one-act play about a nurse, a veteran of the Vietnam War, who visits the memorial in Washington and is forced to remember a war she had been unable to cry about. Though there are six male and four female parts and three narrators, the script can be modified to suit available players. This serious drama would lend itself to variations on themes, with learners recreating their own important events. In a biography on page 101, the author explains her research for this work and personal commitment to commemorating the women overlooked by the Vietnam War Memorial.

596. "The Rabbits Who Caused All the Trouble." In *Fables for Our Time and Famous Poems Illustrated*. James Thurber. New York: Harper & Row, 1983, pages 68–70.

This short spoof on rationalization could have been inspired by headline events leading to almost any war or military skirmish we have known. Using a wolf and rabbits, Thurber employs an Aesop vehicle for mocking the powers that be and their abuse of power, and likewise mocking the players who affirm abuse by their own inaction. When I used this book as an ESL text with a largely Vietnam-era student population, the story took on a life of its own, inspiring discussion and writing well beyond the expected. Thurber's language is by no means simplified; it is laden with culture and content. He also did the illustrations—iconoclastic little ink drawings that mock the weight of his subjects.

597. *Unconditional Surrender: U. S. Grant and the Civil War.* Albert Marrin. New York: Atheneum, 1994.

Following are three Strong Passages from the Challenging book. For details on this title, see "Challenging," entry 584.

- "A House Divided," chapter 2 (pages 25–51), invites the reader to observe the personalities and conflicts that surrounded the professional soldier "who hated war."

- The paragraph on page 42 starting with "Food also" and ending with "death from a frying pan" tells of horrors far worse than enemy fire.

- On the incivility of war, midway down page 130 comes a passage that will give any reader pause. It starts with "Sherman's policy was clearly one of terrorism, that is, using fear as a weapon, largely against civilians and prisoners" and ends as "Thousands of books, some of them centuries old, were tossed from the windows of the State Library."

598. *The War Began at Supper: Letters to Miss Loria.* Patricia Reilly Giff. Illustrated by Betsy Lewin. New York: Delacorte Press, 1991.

Michael's letter of February 5, pages 41–42, makes a profound read aloud.

599. "The War Years." In *Dr. Elizabeth: The Story of the First Woman Doctor.* Patricia Clapp. New York: Lothrop, Lee & Shepard, 1974. pages 133–46.

"The War Years" is an action-packed chapter focusing on April 12, 1861, the day the first shot of the Civil War was fired, and the emotions of patients of both races, who feared for their lives should unsympathetic forces find them occupying the same infirmary. Look under "Challenging," entry 580, for more details.

600. *The World Almanac and Book of Facts 1995.* Edited by Robert Famighetti. Mahwah, NJ: Funk & Wagnalls, 1995.

World War II is remembered on page 37. This book might be viewed as an encyclopedia you can hold in your hand.

Newspaper and Magazine Articles

Books of newspaper stories and front pages are published for nearly every historical time period. Such collections from the Civil War era are certainly among the most collectable. I suggest you go through the local library collection to see what turns up there. History magazines are another source of reading material written in modern English.

601. "After the Storm." Thomas Y. Canby. Photographs by Steve McCurry. *National Geographic* 180, no. 2, August 1991, pages 2–35.

An aerial map of the devastation along the Persian Gulf, with oil fires still blazing in Kuwait, supports the claim of Abdullah Toukan, science adviser to King Hussein of Jordan, "Strategically it was senseless. The only casualty was the environment." Oil-smothered animals and a desert crust that may result in intensified sandstorms are explained in a two-page spread. Also described is an oil slick that has killed shrimp nurseries, pearl oyster beds, turtle and osprey nest sites, waterfowl feeding areas, cormorant and tern breeding areas, coral reefs, and on and on. "Kuwaitis knew their environment was in dire trouble, but they had lost the means to measure the damage. Before the war this wealthy nation had supported one of the premier scientific centers of the Middle East, the Kuwait Institute for Scientific Research. Now KISR was a shell, plundered and partly destroyed. Before fleeing, the Iraqis left their familiar final insult by defecating on the floors" (page 16). Such reporting brings home the fact that governments and individuals took action without apparent understanding of their acts. The cost to our planet is as yet unknown.

602. "Airborne Army." *Fast Times*. Back to School 1995, Volume 12, No. 4, page 20.
    Corporal Angela Petron gives a detailed account of how she trained for a 1,250-foot jump that launched her army career. There is not the tone of foreboding that one might expect from an eighteen-year-old woman who is facing a world where war seems ever-probable. It would be interesting to follow up on her story in a year or two, something that is quite possible through this magazine's Web (Worldwide) connection referenced in "Online from Sarajevo," also in the War Unit. *Fast Times* articles are not written down, but the authors do take care to provide sufficient context for unusual words to be understood without trips to the dictionary. There are also critical thinking assignments and activities.

603. *The Civil War EXTRA: From the Pages of The Charleston Mercury and The New York Times*. Edited by Eugene P. Moehring and Arleen Keylin. New York: Arno Press, 1975.
    Newspaper stories from two perspectives cover the war from 1861 to 1865, giving readers a chance to see how the nation's journalists handled the day-to-day issues of civil war. Most of the pages have been reconstructed from stories throughout the papers, with some sections deleted because the print was illegible. The type is small and the language sometimes amusing, but the war and the salient issues of honor and determination are reflected in both papers. This book is full of read-aloud snippets, though hardly a column is without some impossible-to-decipher words. On April 17, 1861, *The Charleston Mercury* says, "Our readers know that we have repeatedly declared that we did not believe that a war between the North and the South would be the result of a dissolution of the Union by the secession of the Southern States. With the sound of our cannon still ringing in our ears, we are of the same opinion still. That the brutal fanatics who sit in the high places at Washington are ready to plunge the whole country into contest and blood, we have never doubted. It was a thorough conviction of their treacherous and desperate hatred of the South that compelled us to urge, as the only course of safety for the South, a prompt and eternal separation from their power." On the same day, *The New York Times* gave a report on the "Experience of the Times Correspondent as a Prisoner of War" as he reported, "Whenever the haze lifted, I could discover the sacred flag of our country proudly spreading itself to the breeze. Although the shot fell around it thick and fast, yet it seemed to possess an absolute power of intangibility and nothing could disturb it. The scene was solemn in the extreme."

604. *Life, in Time of War*. March 1991.

The entire issue is dedicated to the story of the Persian Gulf War, or Operation Desert Storm. A message from the editor explains the circumstances of the edition. The next page shows a night view of Tel Aviv, as a Patriot missile streaks across the sky. The following pages are a grown-ups' picture book, with two-page spreads and just a few lines of text. Next is an account of the war as American reporters viewed it. Then the photo of a young man on graduation day, holding his niece's teddy bear; he was the first American casualty—a MIA. Following are childhood photos of other soldiers. On the final page, a yellow ribbon flickers in the front yard of a prisoner of war.

605. "Online from Sarajevo." Steve Posner. *Fast Times*. Back to School 1995, vol. 12, no. 4, page 6.

An e-mail message from a high school student in Bosnia gives a historical and firsthand account of how the 1984 Olympic mountains have transformed from a snow-covered paradise to one of the most horrific spots on earth. The article gives the full message and instructions on how to engage in dialogue on the World Wide Web. This piece is up-to-the-minute, engaging, and informing. *Fast Times* is distributed world-wide to high school students who are learning to read English through authentic literature. Send an e-mail message to *StevePo@aol.com* or call (619) 591-9433 to get involved in the *Fast Times* Web connection.

606. "Secret Warriors." Douglas Waller. *Newsweek*, June 17, 1991, pages 20–28.

Here is a special report on a secret commando group that made a significant contribution to the Operation Desert Storm success. Unlike other U.S. military operations in the war, their mission was conducted without fanfare. A private funeral, by word-of-mouth invitation only, was conducted for the three commandos who were killed. This account of what the American people didn't know is one of several good articles on the Gulf War in this issue of *Newsweek*.

607. "Stones' Missal." Fred Goodman. *Entertainment Weekly*, March 8, 1991, page 7.

In just a few paragraphs Goodman summarizes the Rolling Stones' song "High Wire," about Operation Desert Storm, and the controversy it stirred because of its content "in time of war."

Other Events and Supplements

There is hardly a teen or adult alive who doesn't know someone who either served or died in a war somewhere. This topic offers a very personal way of studying geography, politics, economics and sociology. It helps to have both large colored maps on the walls and small, personal copies in everyone's hands. The notion that war is a terrible thing is so commonplace, an interesting shift in perspective might be to begin by listing the advantages of war. Who benefits? How?

- Some groups of history buffs make an annual event of Civil War reenactments. If such a group is active near you, it may be worthwhile going to talk with them and watch the show. If not, you might find a participant who will talk about the association's activities with your class, possibly in Civil War uniform.

- Have your class write letters to veterans in a veteran's hospital nearby or far away.
- Ask a female veteran to share her experiences with your class.
- Arrange a class visit to a veteran's hospital if one is nearby.
- Contact a national veteran's organization for local vets whom students can interview. Tape their stories.
- Have students write to authors for more information or just to say thanks.
- Have students write to historical locations for more information.
- Ask students to look for articles on specific conflicts in current newspapers and magazines. They can draw pictures and write captions about the ones that concern them.
- Collect maps of war zones and use them as discussion starters.
- Pick up the commemorative war stamps from your local post office and research the characters you find interesting.
- Use the Civil War commemorative stamps as a costume clue chart. Who did the actual fighting?
- Read the maps included with WWII stamps. How did that war influence the economy of today?
- Collect newspaper accounts of current military conflicts. How do they differ from wars of the past?

The Planet

Unit 10

Incredible, isn't it? Here we have been, all of our lives, spinning around on this giant sphere, hardly giving it a thought. We have given it so little thought that we have practically worn out the surface—without even working at it. The thought is almost dizzying. Can a handful of books make any difference, when our most obvious subject has been overlooked from countless perspectives? Perhaps not. Some say that we are at the end of our cycle as occupants here, that we have taken so much more than we have given we can never redeem our position. Perhaps that is true. But if we have no hope, we will stop trying, a notion that feels uncomfortable to me. And, I presume, to you, who are looking at this unit. So here are some books that may help us focus on the task at hand, regardless of what perspective we use. In the process, if all we manage to do is foster social responsibility among our fellow travelers, we have spent our time well.

First Readers and Picture Books

608. *The Armadillo from Amarillo.* Lynne Cherry. San Diego, CA: Harcourt Brace Jovanovich, 1994. A Gulliver Breen Book. Printed with environmentally sensitive materials.

Starting with a postcard written in Amarillo, Texas, the armadillo begins a trek that first opens to a breathtaking spread of San Antonio bluebonnets in full bloom. Having lived there and seen them, I can tell you that Cherry has transplanted this sensational gift of nature right inside this book. Postcards run tandem to rhyming text where, for several pages, the armadillo discovers the wonders of endangered species' habitats and the vastly varying landscapes of Texas. In search of a bird's-eye view, the armadillo hitches a ride on the back of an eagle. The two eventually connect with a spacecraft, which gives them and us a perspective on where we are and how we look from outer space. The real and whimsical join to make important statements about our relationships with this planet and the grand scheme of things.

609. *Brother Eagle, Sister Sky.* Paintings by Susan Jeffers. New York: Dial Books, 1991. Picture book. 1992 Abby Award.

The words of Suquamish and Duwamish Chief Seattle, delivered in his native tongue during negotiations with settlers for land rights, are translated here and interpreted with inspirational colored ink illustrations that fill every page. "How can you buy the sky?" he begins, as he slowly recounts the stories of the universe as told to him by his mother, father, and grandfather. If we are all part of a grand system of life, how can one claim ownership of another? When the book is finished, there is a stunning sense that Seattle continues to hope for a more reasonable treaty than the one his broken people had to accept during the time that he lived. There is so much to think about in this giant picture book that it is difficult to assign categories. It is philosophy, logic, wonder, spirituality, honor, memory, respect, dignity—for all, and unity. The best use for this book may just be to let it be—in the learning environment, in the home, on the table, in the chalk trough. Then perhaps the many-layered messages will have time to unfold without shocking the viewer who may not yet be at peace with the Earth.

610. *Dear Children of the Earth, A Letter from Home.* Schim Schimmel. Minocqua, WI: NorthWord Press, 1994.

Surrealistic paintings mix animals of land, sea, and air in brilliant illustrations of each passage of the letter from Mother Earth. It begins, "I am writing this letter to ask for your help. Do you know who I am? I am the planet, earth. But I am much more than just a planet. I am your home." In gentle, powerful language the letter provokes thought about questions. "Tell me, my children where will the animals live when my forests are all gone? Where will the whales and dolphins swim when my oceans are too dirty to live in? And where will the birds fly when my sky is poisoned?" This is an open letter to all the children of the Earth about the fate of our home.

611. *Desert Voices.* Byrd Baylor and Peter Parnall. New York: Macmillan, 1993.

Simple, minimally colored ink drawings and brief, poetic lines of text give the reader a wonderful read, insights into desert creatures' lives, and a fresh look at what a home can be.

612. *The Ever-Living Tree: The Life and Times of a Coast Redwood.* Linda Vieira. Illustrations by Christopher Canyon. New York: Walker, 1994.

This is just the history of the world—all over the world—during the life of a California redwood. The book opens to a two-page spread that tracks a tree across time, from prehistory to 2,500 years of age. A human figure is provided for comparison to the 300-foot tree. All this before you get to the first page. The Greeks, North American Indians, the Chinese, Jesus, George Washington, the American Revolution, space flight, and national park campers pass in and out of time as the tree continues to grow.

613. *The Extinct Alphabet Book.* Jerry Pallotta. Illustrated by Ralph Masiello. Watertown, MA: Charlesbridge, 1993.

If you are harboring the assumption that a Dimetrodon is a dinosaur, this book will correct that thought and tell you how to avoid making such a mistake again. Did you know that "more than ninety-nine percent of all living things that ever lived on Earth are now extinct"? That and a lot of other information critical to our survival rests on some of the most beautiful illustrations we can find. Units on extinct animals, frogs, bats, birds, and general science will benefit from this book.

614. *The Flower Alphabet Book.* Jerry Pallotta. Illustrated by Leslie Evans. Watertown, MA: Charlesbridge, 1988.

This is no ordinary alphabet book. Though each page presents a flower of the letter in sequence, the borders are filled with supplemental illustrations that are discussed by the artist on the last page. Units on flowers, science, geography, history, mythology, superstition, and art would benefit from this book.

615. *The Frog Alphabet Book.* Jerry Pallotta. Illustrated by Ralph Masello. Watertown, MA: Charlesbridge, 1990.

Have this one handy for units on frogs, salamanders, newts, and caecilians. It has photo-like illustrations of frogs from Ecuador, the rain forests of Central America and South America, Europe, Yosemite National Park, and the Cameroons, making it a candidate for a "frogs around the globe" geography unit.

616. *The Giving Tree.* Shel Silverstein. New York: Harper & Row, 1961.

This little picture book shows the metamorphosis of a relationship between a boy and his tree. Or perhaps, a boy and his mother. Yet it could be between humankind and nature. Or humankind and the environment. At each stage of his life, the boy-man returns to the tree to take away more. And the tree is always happy to give. This is an emotion-filled book, one I have never been able to finish reading aloud. It does open many doors. Like many other classics, there are often copies in used bookstores. I always buy them for my students.

617. *The Great Kapok Tree: A Tale of the Amazon Rain Forest.* Lynne Cherry. San Diego, CA: Harcourt Brace Jovanovich, 1990. A Gulliver Breen Book.

Printed on recycled paper, dedicated to the memory of Chico Mendes, "who gave his life in order to preserve a part of the rain forest," and exquisitely illustrated, this book is an irresistible lead-in to a unit on rain forests, the planet, ecology, or geography. The text is well supported with drawings of Amazon animals and loaded with adult-level information. Inside the front and back covers are world maps showing rain forest regions.

618. *Here Is the Tropical Rain Forest.* Madeleine Dunphy. Illustrated by Michael Rothman. New York: Hyperion: New York, 1994.

The interaction of elements and animals in the Central American and South American rain forests is thumped out in a rhythmical pace, as each turn of the page adds another line to the repetitive text. Cool, detailed, full-page illustrations support each addition. On the last page, a collection of the animals introduced and an address to write for more information invite the reader to join the race to save the planet.

619. *How to Hide an Octopus, and Other Sea Creatures.* Ruth Heller. New York: Grossett & Dunlap, 1992.

As with all of Heller's books, the illustrations make this a visual delight. And the rhyming text propels the reader through words like sargassum fish, grotesque, bizarre, creatures, urchins, barnacles, and anemone. Scientific tidbits are served up a few words at a time amid powerful pictures that assist comprehension.

620. *Night Tree.* Eve Bunting. Illustrated by Ted Rand. San Diego, CA: Harcourt Brace Jovanovich, 1991.

Written from the viewpoint of a young boy, this is the story of a family that celebrates Christmas in harmony with the Earth. During a pilgrimage to the tree that has been theirs "forever and ever," they quietly enjoy wild animals of the woods beyond their town. Then they decorate the tree with edibles for the animals who will come after the family has gone home. This sensitive, powerful story has only about six lines of text per two-page spread. And the elaborate pictures support it throughout. A read aloud, First Reader, or picture book.

621. *The Ocean Alphabet Book.* Jerry Pallotta. Illustrated by Frank Mazzola, Jr. Watertown, MA: Charlesbridge, 1986.

This book of random sea creatures is simple and offers some light reading for an oceans, science, or sea creatures unit.

622. *Pigeons*. Bernice Kohn Hunt. Illustrated by Bruce Waldman. Englewood Cliffs, NJ: Prentice-Hall, 1973.

This easy-to-read book, with clear ink drawings and lots of open space, gives scientific information along with everyday anecdotes. It gently leads the reader to the shocking discovery that the passenger pigeon, once the most populous pigeon of all, was thoughtlessly driven to extinction by humans. It is a powerfully simple book. Under "Book Chapters and Strong Passages," entry 661, see "The Passenger Pigeon."

623. *Plants That Never Ever Bloom*. Written and illustrated by Ruth Heller. New York: Grossett & Dunlap, 1984.

Ample time must be given to savor the pictures in this information-rich adventure with few words. Units on science, the sea, frogs, insects, dinosaurs, and fungi would all benefit from this supplement.

624. *The Quicksand Book*. Tomie dePaola. New York: Holiday House, 1977.

A young girl swings into the scene on a vine that breaks, dropping her into quicksand. Fortunately, there is a lad, well informed about quicksand, its causes, which animals avoid its perils and how, and what humans can do to avoid sinking in it. Unfortunately, he opts to lecture the girl about it as she sinks. Fortunately, the story ends well and a wealth of scientific information is assimilated in the space of just sixteen pages. The last page gives instructions on how to make your own quicksand.

625. *Rainforest Secrets*. Written and illustrated by Arthur Dorros. New York: Scholastic, 1990.

"Most of our old-growth temperate rain forests have already been cleared. For every five giant trees that were once in our forests, only one is left. But the old giants are still being cut down," says this simple picture book. "An area of tropical rain forest about the size of four city blocks is being destroyed every minute." Certainly this little paperback has more to tell, but can we wait for a new generation of readers to absorb the meaning of these few words?

626. *The Reason for a Flower*. Written and illustrated by Ruth Heller. New York: Grossett & Dunlap, 1983.

Heller's rhyming text and realistic renderings make this information-filled science book a must have for every classroom. Seed distribution, animals that eat plants, plants that eat animals, and ambitious vocabulary are delivered so well that the reader feels lost when the end arrives. Science, flowers, plants, and insects units would benefit from this easy reader.

627. *A River Ran Wild*. Lynne Cherry. San Diego, CA: Harcourt Brace Jovanovich, 1992. A Gulliver Breen Book.

This exquisitely illustrated, authentic history of a river belongs in every classroom. Most of the two-page spreads have a full-page drawing opposite two or three easy-to-read, large-print paragraphs surrounded by small illustrations. Inside the front and back covers are maps that compare the New England area of the 1500s with the same in the 1900s. It will inspire the artist, the historian, the ecologist, and the humanist in everyone who follows the story of the Nashua River—from teeming with life—to polluted, stinking death—to revitalized life again. It gives a poignant challenge to each of us—and hope. It is a Reading Rainbow selection and fits the following themes: Native Americans, ecology, history, geography, politics, animals, and art.

628.   *The Sign of the Seahorse: A Tale of Greed and High Adventure in Two Acts.* Written and illustrated by Graeme Base. New York: Harry N. Abrams, 1992.

This incredibly beautiful book tells of the value of pollution to those dedicated to greed and ignorant of the eternal impact they can make.

629.   *The Tree of Life: The World of the African Baobab.* Barbara Bash. San Francisco: Little, Brown, 1989.

The legend of this oddly shaped tree, the animals that call it home or friend or food, and the cycle of life that runs from rain to rain are presented with scientific precision and storyteller craft. The detailed watercolors are full of visual information and delights as well.

630.   *The Tree That Would Not Die.* Ellen Levine. Illustrated by Ted Rand. New York: Scholastic, 1995.

It begins with the drop of an acorn hundreds of years ago, followed by the growth of a little oak tree that provided a buffalo calf a place to scratch an itch. Through time the tree saw Comanche, Tejas, Lipan, Tonkawa, Spaniards, and the arrival of a man named Stephen Austin, for which the town was eventually named. There were settlers, soldiers, midnight raids, the Depression, and talk of cutting the tree down to sell the wood or use the land. "Late one night a stranger parked his car across the street. He crept into the park and poured a liquid in a circle by my side. At first it felt cool, and I shuddered. Later it burned." The result was horribly dramatic. The tree began to die. Then the public interest in saving the historic plant yielded letters to "Dear Tree" and coins from children everywhere. The last page of the book tells the history of Treaty Oak and the attempt on its life. It tells of heroic efforts to save the tree that, until then, had towered three stories high. This is a book of emotional highs and lows. It is a definite dialogue generator.

631.   *Welcome to the Green House.* Jane Yolen. Illustrated by Laura Regan. New York: Scholastic, 1993. Picture book.

Yolen plays with words, making a delicious trail across rain forest pictures that would otherwise hold their own alone. The lizards, frogs, birds, and plants are played across the pages like sun-flicked jewels. To read this book aloud is to have fun with text—even if the reader is the only audience around.

Thin Books

632.   *Armies of Ants.* Walter Retan. Illustrated by Jean Cassels. New York: Scholastic, 1994.

Large print, colorful illustrations, and a world of information about ants—found in 9,000 forms and everywhere on Earth, except the Arctic and the Antarctic. How they mate, collect and manage slaves, set up cities, and what they eat are discussed in clear language. A case is also made for appreciation of the ant, which has been around at least since before the dinosaurs. Their value to the planet is manifested in many ways.

633. *Bats: A Nature-Fact Book.* D. J. Arneson. Interior photos by Mervin Tuttle. Chicago: Kidsbooks, 1992.

This Thin Book has an exquisite, close-up photograph of a bat on each left-hand page and informative text on the right. Did you know that the hearing of bats is being studied so that some discoveries may be applied to humans? And bat saliva has properties that thin blood. "Some wild fruit trees depend on bats to spread their seeds." The text includes explanations of why some bats are rare. For example, the Indiana bat was disturbed by humans during hibernation. It is not an easy read, but it is an incredible picture book that is appropriate for any age.

634. *Bugs: Giant Magnified Images As Seen Through a Microscope.* Heather Amery and Jane Songi. New York: Golden Books, 1994.

Did you ever wonder where the Golden Era science horror filmmakers got their ideas? If this book had been around back then, they would have been reading it. The close-up, extra large views of insect parts that allow sight, flight, feeding, and breeding are marvelous indeed. Simple explanations tell how wings evolved from flaps to two to four to two again, and how the bulging surface of the tsetse fly's eye allows a wide range of vision. This elementary science book will capture the interest of any reader, including those who are already familiar with the world of insects.

635. *Children of the Dust Bowl: The True Story of the School at Weedpatch Camp.* Jerry Stanley. Illustrated with historical photographs. New York: Crown, 1992.

Between 1930 and 1940, agricultural jobs in the Dust Bowl states declined by 400,000, "nearly 50 percent of Oklahoma's farms changed hands in bankruptcy court sales," and a mass of displaced and starving people headed for California. On page 5, the Dust Bowl, 1936–1940, is depicted on a map of nine states. A dark, grainy section shows a giant teardrop shape where no rain fell on farmlands for a long time—and then the winds came. A political-topographical map of historic Route 66, "Mother Road," names likely stopover spots, places to find day work, and trouble spots, too—Shamrock, Amarillo, Flagstaff, Kingman, Mojave Desert, Tehachapi Mountains. It has an inset U.S. map with an outline of the Route 66 area, pages 14–15. Another political-topographical map, page 24, shows the intersection of Routes 66 and 99 in California, again with an inset of the whole state. The type is easy on the eyes, the margins wide, the historical photographs dramatic, and the prose compelling. This history book will hold the attention of any adult interested in the United States, and it readily lends itself to younger students, if used in a teacher reads aloud and class discusses format. The introduction links the Okie experience with John Steinbeck's historical fiction *The Grapes of Wrath*, but the children of the Dust Bowl are absolutely real.

636. *Dolphins!* Margaret Davidson. Illustrated by Ian Andrew. New York: Scholastic, text 1964, illustrations 1985.

Colored pencil drawings depict dolphins in their natural habitats, among friends and natural enemies, as well as unnatural ones. Also shown are their lives in captivity, bringing the reader to a new level of awareness about these creatures, and with that, the notion that we have much to learn from them.

637. *Endangered Animals*. Lynn M. Stone. Chicago: Childrens Press, 1984. A New True Book.

Huge type and short sentences are combined with interesting facts. Words like endangered and breathes are carefully nestled into comprehensible text among beautiful photos. There is a useful index at the end of this well-done primer on the title topic. Use it to build background knowledge, provide SSR material, and support research.

638. *Extinct Insects and Those in Danger of Extinction*. Philip Steele. New York: Franklin Watts, 1991.

Loaded with scientific data, clear color drawings and photos of living and fossilized insects, and diagrams of life cycles, this book provides a tour of the world of insects. Though the language includes scientific terms, the format supports comprehension and language acquisition. Small boxes throughout offer fascinating short passages, scientific information in a trivia format. Type is large (20 points). There is a good one-page glossary, places to write for more information, and a timeline showing prehistoric and historic insects in relation to human activity. The last page has a world map naming the places referenced.

639. *The Fascinating World of Bats*. Angels Julivert. New York: Barron's, 1994.

Skillful and detailed drawings of bat wings, ears, tails, tongues, flight habits, nurseries, feeding habits, habitats, and hunting strategies make the scientific terms in the text quite comprehensible.

640. *The Fascinating World of Bees*. Angels Julivert. Illustrated by Carlos de Miguel. New York: Barron's, 1991.

Who's who in the hive—queen, workers, and drones—is quickly covered. Also addressed are wax production, the division of labor, mating and the death of the drone, hive organization, intruders, social problems, dance of the bees, bees' role in pollination, honey production, and bee-keeping. There is also a glossary.

641. *The Fascinating World of Butterflies and Moths*. Angels Julivert. Illustrated by Francisco Arrendondo. New York: Barron's, 1991.

Ever wondered exactly how the silkworm provides silk? Or what happens to the migrating monarchs? How to know if a caterpillar is poisonous? What butterflies and moths eat? Who eats them? These questions and many others are clearly answered and illustrated. A glossary is also provided.

642. *The Fascinating World of Frogs and Toads*. Angels Julivert. New York: Barron's, 1993.

To begin with, page 4 illustrates and explains the differences between frogs and toads. Throughout the book, frog and toad life is laid bare in entertaining text and drawings.

643. *Four Against the Odds: The Struggle to Save Our Environment*. Stephen Krensky. New York: Scholastic, 1992.

This is a series of four biographies, each telling of heroic efforts made by ordinary people. John Muir, Rachel Carson, Lois Gibbs, and Chico Mendes each provide inspiration and consciousness-raising about our planet. The easy-to-read style provides history, geography, and social science commentary.

644. *A Living Desert*. Guy Spencer. Photography by Tim Fuller. Mahwah, NJ: Troll, 1988.

It is as the title suggests and the photos attest—a desert full of living cactuses, coyotes, frogs, mountain lions, flowers, bats, butterflies, javelinas, birds, deer, bighorn sheep, venomous Gila monsters and diamondback rattlesnakes, tarantulas, scorpions, desert tortoises, kangaroo rats, bears, lakes, streams, and much more.

645. *The Man Who Planted Trees*. Jean Giono. Wood engravings by Michael McCurdy. Afterword by Norma Goodrich. Chelsea, VT: Chelsea Green, 1985.

Here is a story of hope with a message that one person can make an incredible difference to our planet. A widower in his forties seeks a solitary life in a barren and deserted expanse of land. By methodically planting trees that are suited to the natural elements, over time he manages to restore life and even a change in atmosphere for miles and miles. It is not his land, nor does he know who owns it. He is just doing what he feels is right and is rewarded by making a difference. First published as a short story in *Vogue* in 1954, under another title, this first-person narrative sounds absolutely believable. The language is simple and the story compelling. The afterword gives an overview of Giono's productive storyteller's life, with summaries of several intriguing tales, and may cause the reader to think, "I could do that." The address and phone number of environmental group Global ReLeaf are provided at the end of the book.

646. *Marvelously Meaningful Maps: Let's Investigate*. Madelyn Wood Carlisle. New York: Barron's, 1992.

This is not a book about the planet, except in technical and global (pardon the pun) terms. But it may help with the study of whatever issues are at hand. The index gives a quick insight into the many items presented in this well-illustrated, well-written little book. Words like cartographer, computers, constellations, legends, parallels, pipelines, satellites, topographic, and treasure are linked with places such as Africa, California, Detroit, Guatemala, Hawaii, international date line, equator, Lake Huron, Middle East, Mount Vernon, North Pole, Old Faithful, Pacific Ocean, and Yellowstone National Park. Instructions on making maps, the use of a weather balloon, and the use of a compass are linked with maps of all sorts from all over the world. If you never thought maps could entertain, you will be pleasantly surprised. This book could facilitate many family projects, travel fun, and the calming of any phobias a learner might have about maps.

647. *1000 Facts About the Earth*. Moira Butterfield. New York: Scholastic, 1992.

The contents include the Earth in Space, the Earth's Surface, Volcanoes and Geysers, Earthquakes, Weather, Wild Weather, Rain Forests, Deserts, Polar Regions, Saving the Earth, Earth Facts and Lists, and more. Graphics, maps, illustrations, and easy-to-understand text make this a useful book in short passages. For example, on page 40, "The U. S. uses 29 percent of the world's gasoline and 33 percent of all the world's electricity," is followed by "Some Chinese farmers use flocks of ducks to kill harmful insects," then "The industrial complex of Cubatao in Brazil is known as the Valley of Death because its pollution has destroyed the trees and rivers nearby." Also on that page is a forest alert: "It is estimated that 1 sq. mile of rain forest is destroyed every 6 minutes. If this continues, the rain forests will disappear by the year 2050. The destruction of the rain forests is caused by: People clearing vast areas to graze their cattle herds. Flooding caused by hydroelectric dams being build across rivers. Chopping down hardwood trees to make products such as mahogany furniture." Caution: If your students cannot tolerate information suggesting that the destruction of the Earth is humanly stoppable and that stopping the destruction is absolutely necessary, this book will not provide a pleasant reading experience.

648. *Our World of Mysteries: Fascinating Facts About the Planet Earth.* Suzanne Lord. New York: Scholastic, 1991.

This small paperback is loaded with things the ESL or adult literacy teachers want—many short passages, high-interest adult subject matter, easy-to-read type, and topics that move around the globe. Though it does not discuss ecology per se, each chapter unveils magical secrets about the way things used to be and how such concepts may help us understand how the world may be in the future. Want to know about life in a cave, deep in the ocean, out in the desert? How about fish in the desert, lions in Alaska, flies in amber, or 40,000-year-old fossils in Los Angeles? They are here. The mysteries of vanishing peoples of Thailand, the Marajoara, or the Anasazi? How about cities underwater, Troy, or Camelot? Again, this is the place. Mysteries of Easter Island, Angkor Wat, Nazca, Peru, and more are discussed in easy-to-understand English. Even so, it is not without its vocabulary development advantages. Words like Druids, Stonehenge, worshipers, explorer, graffiti, mummies, suggested, chemically, preventing, handsome, and fantastically are used in the compelling contexts of mysteries about the planet Earth.

649. *Sam the Sea Cow.* Francine Jacobs. Illustrated by Laura Kelly. New York: Walker, 1979.

The birth of Sam the Sea Cow takes the reader into the Florida habitat and introduces a scientific wonder, a mammal beneath the water. Factual information about the manatee and its endangered lifestyle are presented in an easy-to-read format supported by clear illustrations. The artist's perspective shows the world above and below the water, a world that is affected by nature and civilization. We see the relationship of the sea cow to fish, humans, other life forms, and motorboats. An afterword gives a brief scientific history of the gentle mammal. This is good support reading for a research paper on the manatee, marine life, or issues concerning the planet. On the last page is the address of the Save the Manatee Club.

650. *Snakes.* Seymour Simon. New York: HarperCollins, 1992.

"There are about twenty-five hundred different kinds of snakes in the world," and they live everywhere except the Arctic, the Antarctic, Iceland, Ireland, New Zealand, and a few small islands. The text of this book is plainly written with lots of scientific data that can easily be understood. The photographs are anything but plain. Snakes eating and protecting their eggs, eggs hatching, and even a cobra about to strike make this a wondrous look through.

651. *Trees and Forests.* New York: Scholastic, 1995.

This is a science book you can play with. Every page unfolds new surprises. There are foldouts, flaps, transparent films, cutouts, and even a collection of stickers. On page 3 is a mini booklet showing the progression of the landscape as it may have been before trees about 400 million years ago, to 100 million years ago when mammals enjoyed pines and oaks. Tiny black and white insets show samples of fossils that give clues to the time covered. How trees grow and get food is followed by a tactile page of bark from six trees with the silhouette of each tree on the reverse of its bark. Forests worldwide are identified by trees of different styles in postcard-type photos with tiny world maps identifying where the respective forests occur. A foldout spread reveals the lush colors of the rain forest with wildlife strewn throughout the levels. Creatures, critters, fungi and plants are illustrated in clear, beautiful colored illustrations. Sacred groves of Africa, topics of fairy tales, people of the forests—Pygmies of Africa and Native Americans—industrial uses for trees, medicinal uses, and ways to save the forests are touched upon. There are addresses of places you can visit, a short list of other books about trees, a series of one paragraph biographies of people famous for their connections with trees, legendary characters, a glossary or terms, and an index. Though there are plenty of pages that will, over time, get bent or damaged, the laminated cardstock used for nearly every page guarantee many hours of enjoyment, regardless of the age of the readers using this. The print is easy to see and the language understandable. This might qualify as a first reader, but because there are technical terms throughout, it seemed wiser to put it in the "Thin Books" section.

652. *Will We Miss Them? Endangered Species.* Alexandra Wright. Illustrated by Marshall Peck III. Watertown, MA: Charlesbridge, 1992.
     Endangered species from all over the planet are featured in two-page spreads that show the animals in their habitats. The text gives a few facts about the animal and the reasons why it is endangered. Bald eagles, blue whales, elephants, pandas, Galapagos tortoises, mountain lions, whooping cranes, grizzly bears, manatees, muriquis, rhinoceroses, gorillas, and crocodiles are presented in an easy-to-understand format. At the end, a world map depicts each animal on location, bringing home the notion that endangered animals are a global issue. Though an informative book on its own, it can also provide a strong foundation for the study of the planet or a research paper on any of the animals featured.

Challenging

653. *Ishi, Last of His Tribe.* Theodora Kroeber. Text illustrations by Ruth Robbins. New York: Bantam Books, 1964.
     Lost while searching for his homeland and driven by spirits into the land of white men, Ishi, the last of the Yahi of the Yana tribe, offered a final glimpse into a spiritual and physical way of life now extinguished. Small ink drawings enhance this incredible tale. A map of Ishi's journey gives us an idea of the lengths to which this man went to protect the spirits of his ancestors. Though written in the third person and in simple language, the book uses enough Yahi, Ishi's language, to build atmosphere. There is a glossary of Yahi terms at the end. I used this book in an individualized program for a Native American student who, three months earlier, had been preliterate. He recommended that I continue to use it. It would not have been effective to give him this in the beginning, but after he built background knowledge through a variety of readings, he could enjoy and learn from "real" books. The point is, the materials selected must fit the individual reader.

654. *Ishmael*. Daniel Quinn. New York: Bantam/Turner, 1992. Turner Tomorrow Fellowship winner.

Appropriately printed on recycled paper, this unlikely dialogue between Man and his Teacher is a spiritual investigation of everything we, as civilized beings, accept unquestioningly. It is labeled Challenging not because of vocabulary or sentence lengths (indeed, the dialogue is in everyday English), but because of the abstract thoughts and unusual concepts that require much more contemplation than does the average Thin Book. The way we are using our planet is viewed in a unique way. Do not read this if you are unwilling to question your beliefs or lack of them. It is not a read for people who believe they are divinely entitled to plunder and rule the Earth with no respect for the rights of other life forms. The challenge to this mighty position is sure to disturb and anger. But it does offer one being's view of how we, as humans, came to this spot in time and how we may survive our own follies on this planet, survive our own domination of it. But enough of the content. This is a book of dialogue, written in wonderful, clear sentences. With pictures it might become an adolescent's storybook, one that could modify the way we use our time in power on Earth. Any teacher wanting to build a planet-friendly unit, using a long-term read aloud, could rely on *Ishmael*. Any teacher who wants to provide an aide or helper with a meaningful contribution could assign *Ishmael* to the class or small group, with frequent discussion breaks. The book might comprise the critical thinking component required of many teachers. At the end is an invitation to write to the author.

655. *Island of the Blue Dolphins*. Scott O'Dell. New York: Dell, 1960. 1961 Newbery Medal, 1972 Hans Christian Andersen Medal.

This historical fiction is based on a true story of a young Indian girl who lived alone, with her dog, on a South Pacific Island for eighteen years during the early 1800s.

656. *The Rainforest Book*. Scott Lewis. Preface by Robert Redford. Los Angeles: Living Planet Press, 1990.

The book offers a combination of running text and short informational passages in little boxes—unusual bits of scientific information, historical insights, and political summaries. It is an excellent book for the teacher to read to the student at the end of a lesson, so the student can go home with something to talk about.

657. *The Ultimate Dinosaur, Past-Present-Future*. Edited by Byron Preiss and Robert Silverberg. New York: Bantam Books, 1992.

This book offers a mix of science and fiction through scientific essays and enthralling science-fiction short stories. The clear type is set in a magazine format that supports the reader. Though the text might not look Challenging at first blush, the scientific names of plants, animals, and periods serve to slow the reader, but never to a full stop. It is illustrated with a mix of pen and ink drawings and full-color paintings that document the history of the dinosaur through time—past, present, and future. It is informative, entertaining, and a wonderful picture-book adventure. An appendix supports the scientific reader who wants a clear timeline with land and animal distributions during the days of the dinosaurs.

Book Chapters and Strong Passages

658. *The Groucho Letters: Letters from and to Groucho Marx.* New York: Simon & Schuster, 1967, pages 170–71.

To the president of the Chrysler Corporation, on December 1, 1954, comedian Groucho Marx wrote a serious letter in which he said:

> Each year the motor manufacturers hammer home the idea of more horsepower. I realize a reasonable amount of power is necessary, but I think it would be much smarter if emphasis were placed on safety rather than on additional speed. Perhaps the ads next year should read, "prettier, faster and safe." I also think that if a device could be installed on the carburetor (I understand there are such things) that would eliminate the belching of carbon monoxide through the city streets. . . .

> . . . The average car driver in a modern automobile is a sitting duck. There is nothing to protect him. The records show he would be far safer on a battlefield.

> Your new cars look good, but the fact of the matter is that all the new cars look good, and I firmly believe that the first automobile company that starts stressing safety instead of speed will win far more than its share of the business.

Isn't it interesting that this was written before the issue of automobile pollution was taken seriously by automobile manufacturers, perhaps twenty years before seat belts were mandatory, and thirty years before air bags began to appear? Even now there is little said about safety except for the most expensive cars, and looks continue to be the main ploy advertisers use to pull in customers.

659. *The Irish Potato Famine.* Don Nardo. Illustrations by Brian McGovern. San Diego, CA: Lucent Books.

Three passages deal with the issue of population control: "A Hoe to Turn the Earth," pages 22–27; "The Poor Married Young," page 27; and all of chapter 5, "World Hunger—Famine Still Plagues Humanity," pages 52–59, particularly the passage "Overpopulation a Key Factor," pages 54–55. These would serve well as discussion starters or research support.

660. *Mojave.* Diane Seibert. Paintings by Wendell Minor. New York: Thomas Y. Crowell, 1988.

Written in the first person, person being the Mojave Desert, this poem gives an inside perspective of the desert's interactions with rivers, windstorms, time, lakes, tumbleweeds, lizards, birds, rats, hedgehogs, cactuses, mustangs, miners, ghost towns, burros, seasons, butterflies, coyotes, and bighorn sheep. There is a tremendous amount of vocabulary in this seemingly brief poem, but the rhyming couplets and complete sentences facilitate comprehension and assist prediction. As with most rhymes, this is an easy way to introduce the concepts of phonics—in process. Scientific information is also dispensed casually, for example:

> Here, silvery mirages dance
> Among the prickly cactus plants
> Whose spines and bristles help them thrive
> Where weaker plants could not survive.

Can you see how the pronunciations of "dance" and "plants" compel the reader into a phonetic awareness that a phonic rule would be hard-pressed to convey? At the same time, the reader learns that the "spines and bristles" serve a scientific purpose. Large-print, easy-to-follow text on the left is supported by realistic, full-page illustrations on the right.

661. "The Passenger Pigeon." In *I Am Phoenix: Poems for Two Voices*. Paul Fleischman. Illustrated by Ken Nutt. New York: Harper & Row, 1985, pages 17–19.

This poem for two voices tells in rhythmic verse of the unbelievable destruction of the passenger pigeon. Haunting, authentic, eerie. Under "First Readers and Picture Books," see *Pigeons*, entry 661.

662. "Splitting the Atom." In *History's Big Mistakes*. Adam Bowett. Illustrated by Chris Mould. London: Belitha Press, 1994.

"Splitting the Atom," pages 28–29, tells the tale of Albert Einstein, the pacifist whose work created the most terrible of war inventions.

Newspaper and Magazine Articles

663. "Habitats of Threatened Wildlife Win High Court Protection." *USA Today*, June 30–July 2, 1995, page 1.

The photo of a spotted owl, victorious as the U.S. Supreme Court rules that government can force private landowners to protect habitats for imperiled wildlife.

664. "Mars: Bringing a Dead World to Life." Brad Darrach and Steve Petranek. *Life*, May 1991, pages 24–35.

Photographs of the Red Planet as it exists and graphic illustrations of how it might look if we attempted to cultivate it to provide Earth with a new food source.

665. "Our Endangered Species." Illustrated by Bill Pitzer. Research by David W. Wooddell, based on a September 1994 list. *National Geographic* 187, no. 3, pages 16–21.

Following an extensive story of animals covered by the Endangered Species Act, this foldout section identifies 632 species and subspecies of endangered plants and animals in the United States and their most likely causes of extinction. It is a simple, thought-provoking graphic.

666. "Parklands' Growing Pains." *National Geographic* 180, no. 2, August 1991, pages 58–59.

Here a two-page spread of a U.S. map shows the 357 sites where the National Park System works to protect the unique features of our natural environment. But the great popularity of these locations is threatening them. Only three paragraphs of prose makes this an easy reader. The possibilities as a history, geography, environmental studies, or economics unit foundation make this an item worth having in the library.

Other Events and Supplements

The range of planet issues addressed in the books mentioned here are so vast that almost everyone, even the most cynical, can identify a reason to hope and a way to make a difference. For adults, identifying a problem and then taking positive steps is rewarding, but sometimes just making a statement is enough. The following activities address both perspectives.

- Collect household product packaging that is wastefill bound. List ways the product or the container might be used to lessen the impact on the environment. For example, a lipstick box that is three times the size of the item may benefit the merchant concerned about theft, but perhaps there's another way. Write a letter of suggestion.

- Collect all dry household discards for a week and heap them on a table. Photograph the pile and write a poem about it.

- Contact the local environmental agency to find out how to recycle plastic items. Document whether the suggestions are practical or not.

- Identify sources of possible industrial pollution. Make inquiry calls and document who you spoke to and what the explanations for the conditions are.

- Contact all fast food providers in your area. List the ones who are using recycled packaging. Write them letters of recognition—just an appreciative consumer.

- Collect your neighbors' discarded plastic bags for a week. Donate them to a library or used bookstore for recycling. Write about the encounters along the way.

- Photograph construction sites in your area. Are there signs of environmental waste?

- If you are near a lake, stream, or ocean, take a walk along the shoreline and photograph what you see. Think like a detective. Where did it come from? How long has it been there? What is the impact on the environment? On your personal quality of life? On the lives of creatures in and around the water? Write a short essay about that.

- Visit a wildlife sanctuary. Learn all you can about one interesting creature you find there. Become its advocate.

- In a class setting, establish endangered animal support groups. Identify what the animals need for survival and things students can do to help.

- Every day and night for a week list everything you smell in your environment: foods, perfumes, paint, chemicals, plants, etc. Make a bar graph of the scents and odors that occur most frequently. How might this graph compare to one of the same area ten years ago? To one from another region?

- Look for environmental issues in the newspaper. Follow up by phone and mail to learn the outcomes.

- Compare environmental concerns in the local area with those in a distant country. Identify the reasons. Economic? Culture? Politics?

- Post a world map and mark each place you have identified an environmental issue.

Numbers, Math, and Money

Unit 11

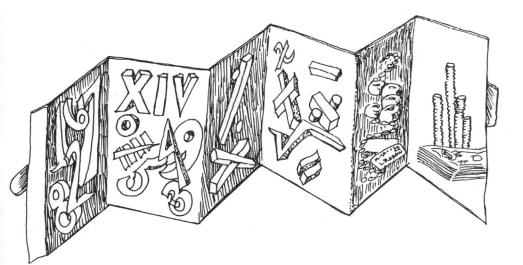

Numbers talk can be a major source of frustration to adults who are learning to read and write and those who are just learning English. What is written or said is either right or wrong. And although it is often unforgiving, it is also absent from many natural language practice scenes. Too, the language of numbers, math, and money is sometimes quite different from the language spoken in daily family life. Children evolve into this slowly acquired set of words and terms over time, with little stress over the outcomes. Not so for adults. When the adult is unfamiliar with a situation and the language related to it, the potential for making expensive mistakes or withdrawing from a beneficial encounter, such as buying a home, is increased.

The knowledge of this specialized language evolves, just as do other language proficiencies. What is important for students to realize is that nobody is born knowing the words, but that anyone who can talk can certainly become proficient at it. Reading easy materials is one way to develop background knowledge in the world of numbers. Another way is collecting data and interpreting them, as suggested at the end of this unit.

First Readers and Picture Books

667. *Alexander, Who Used to Be Rich Last Sunday.* Judith Viorst. New York: Aladdin, 1987.

In this episode, young Alexander is having a difficult time hanging onto his money. This story allows people to talk about the problems surrounding finances for kids and adults.

668. *The Ever-Living Tree: The Life and Times of a Coast Redwood.* Linda Vieira. Illustrated by Christopher Canyon. New York: Walker, 1994.

This is just the history of the world—all over the world—during the life of a California redwood. The book opens to a two-page spread that tracks a tree across time, from prehistory to 2,500 years of age. A human figure is provided for contrast with a 300-foot tree. And that is before you get to the first page. The Greeks, North American Indians, the Chinese, Jesus, George Washington, the American Revolution, space flight, and national park campers pass in and out of time as the tree continues to grow.

669. *A Giraffe and a Half.* Written and illustrated by Shel Silverstein. New York: Harper & Row, 1964.

Here are basic fractions in animal format with a funny set of illustrations that build comprehension and make the whole book one a person could go home and read aloud.

670. *How Much Is a Million?* David Schwartz. Illustrated by Steven Kellogg. New York: Scholastic, 1985.

If you had a goldfish bowl big enough to hold a million goldfish, it would also be big enough to hold a whale! Schwartz uses comparative measurements, time required to do things, distance, and other practical applications to answer the title question. Meanwhile, the learner, adult or child, is acquiring the language of numbers from the meaning-filled context of fantastic Kellogg illustrations. This book will give you a tour inside the mind of a man who loves numbers, and it could make you a numbers lover, too, even if you are numbers-shy. I have used this in individual tutoring with adults and children, and several Beaumont (California) Literacy Volunteers report the book has been successful not only in vocabulary building but also in supporting early reading. A good follow-up to this book is Schwartz's *If You Made a Million* (entry 671).

671. *If You Made a Million.* David Schwartz. Illustrated by Steven Kellogg. New York: Scholastic, 1989.

Now hop into the pipe dream with Schwartz and Kellogg to see what making a million dollars would be like. This is definitely grown-up talk, with adult reference materials included, but kids love it and learn from it, too. I keep forgetting that Schwartz thinks he wrote it for kids in the first place (Also see *How Much Is a Million?*, entry 670.)

672. *The King's Chessboard.* David Birch. Pictures by Devis Grebu. New York: Puffin Books, 1988. Picture book.

Like *The Rajah's Rice* (see entry 677), this is a story about grains of rice and a chessboard. In this telling, the hero is an old wise man who, when forced by his king to ask for a reward, obliges by requesting a grain of rice, doubled each day, until the king is without resources. The parade of rice bags and dramatic gestures in beautifully illustrated caricatures make the issue of doubling numbers day by day an enjoyable problem to see unfold.

673. *Maps of the U.S.A.* Jo Ellen Moore and Leslie Tryon. Monterey, CA: Evan Moor, 1989.

Included are a map of each of the fifty states, a blank U.S. map and one with the state names written in, a map showing time zones, a map of the original thirteen Colonies, an oceans and rivers map, one with major mountain ranges and deserts, and a world map. All are in black and white, and permission is granted to duplicate for classroom use. The area of each state in square miles is next to that state's map, and that is the primary use for this unit, as I see it. But, of course, there are numbers involved, even when they are not printed, so I am open to input on this one.

674. *Merry-Go-Round: A Book About Nouns.* Ruth Heller. New York: Grossett & Dunlap, 1990.

There is only one two-page spread about numbers in this book, but Heller's introduction of collective nouns allows the integration of language and math concepts. "A tumble of feathers, a clamor of birds and a riot of colors abound. Nouns are all around." Numbers are, too. They are out of this world, as she illustrates a countdown and ratio during a rocket blast. She also covers, oh so gently, how to create plurals and what a determiner is.

675. *More Stories to Solve: Fifteen Folktales from Around the World.* Told by George Shannon. Illustrated by Peter Sis. New York: Beech Tree, 1991.

This is the sequel to *Stories to Solve . . .* and is presented in the same format, except some stories are longer. The first part has the story riddle. The second has the solution. The third has an illustration of the solution. These are fun, fast reads often with mathematical and scientific solutions.

676. *One Was Johnny: A Counting Book.* Written and illustrated by Maurice Sendak. New York: HarperCollins, 1962.
Here is an illustrated counting and addition book that hits midpoint and becomes a counting backward and subtraction book. In the process, your basic, everyday visitors—rat, cat, dog, monkey, robber, and so on—pass through Johnny's living room. The clear illustrations support comprehension for new readers and ESL beginners.

677. *The Rajah's Rice: A Mathematical Folktale from India.* Adapted by David Barry. Illustrated by Donna Perrone. New York: W. H. Freeman, 1994. Picture book.
This tale has been retold in a variety of forms. Here, a young girl, bather of the king's elephants, uses her love of numbers to learn and her love of elephants to open the door to change for her impoverished village people. By using a numbers trick, she gets all of the rajah's rice from him. At the end of the book, a chessboard is used to graphically illustrate the power of two. Compare this to *The King's Chessboard* (entry 672).

678. *Six Sleepy Sheep.* Jeffie Ross Gordon. Illustrated by John O'Brien. New York: Puffin Books, 1991.
As will be well understood by readers from any large family, these sleepy sheep cannot sleep simultaneously in the same bed. Six start out trying, and the plot leads to basic subtraction.

679. *Stories to Solve: Folktales from Around the World.* Told by George Shannon. Illustrated by Peter Sis. New York: Beech Tree, 1985.
Fourteen tales of wit and mystery are presented in a three-page format. The first page has the story riddle. The second has the solution. The third has an illustration of the solution. These are fun, fast reads.

680. *The Table Where Rich People Sit.* Byrd Baylor. Pictures by Peter Parnall. New York: Macmillan, 1994.
This book was introduced to me by Donald Graves when he read it aloud to an audience of several hundred at the 40th International Reading Association Conference in Anaheim, California. Most of the attendees were adults—reading teachers and interested others. After the reading there was silence and tears. Had I known about this incredible table sooner, it might have been the cornerstone for a values unit. However, it makes an excellent, gentle discussion starter of dollar values on abstract things.

681. *Thunder Cake.* Patricia Polacco. New York: Philomel Books, 1990.
Fear and the courage to keep going are the themes for a book with beautiful, detailed colored drawings. Grandma helps the young child address her fear of thunder by counting the time between claps of thunder as they race to collect the ingredients for their cake. Though Polacco draws from her family's Russian folk history, this is a universal story.

Thin Books

682. *Amazing Anthony Ant.* Lorna Philpot and Graham Philpot. New York: Random House, 1993.

This is a pull-up-the-flaps-on-every-page-and-sing-to-the-tune-of "Johnny-Comes-Marching-Home" book. Anthony Ant has an endless number of ways of not staying in line with his fellows. The easy-to-follow text makes reading it fun, and the illustrations provide thought-provoking designs on the real ant community. The underground tunnels show what an ant farm might reveal, and on each page above ground new perils lurk—anteater, lizard, frog, and hen. Music, science, math, and humor are four units this book would supplement.

683. *Coins.* Eva Knox Evans. Illustrated by Raymond Burns. Photography by Aldo Vinai. New York: Golden Press, n.d.

This book is designed to foster an interest in coin collecting. In the process, however, the reader will discover a world of animals, geography, history, and politics. No matter what your unit, you might be able to squeeze something about coins into it. "You could have a coin with a salmon on it from Ireland, one with a cod fish from Danzig, and a turtle from the Fiji Islands. And there is a little bee smelling flowers on a ten centesimi piece from Italy" (page 47). Photos of paper money and historical details are also fascinating. For example, take the currency designed for the state of Arizona in 1865. "Many of the early settlers couldn't read, and so pictures of animals were used to show how much each piece was worth. A pig was 12 1/2 cents; a calf equaled a quarter; a rooster, fifty cents and a picture of a horse, a dollar" (page 67). On page 68 are the names of presidents who appear on today's currency, as well as translations of Latin phrases used. Ample instructions are provided on how to detect counterfeit currency, and a "Coin Collector's Dictionary" is included. Numismatics is the official term for the "science of coins and money" and a numismatist is the person who studies coins and money. These are terms that may come in handy when you begin to help students find more reading material on the topic. Though it is wise to check the current values of money worldwide against the daily newspaper, there is a "World Currency Guide" that gives the names of currencies for individual countries. The pages are largely text, but it is well written and there are enough pictures to qualify this as a Thin Book. It might even serve as a leisure reading book for some.

684. *The Go-Around Dollar.* Barbara Johnston Adams. Illustrated by Joyce Audy Zarins. New York: Maxwell Macmillan International, 1992.

This is almost a picture book. It has huge, clear illustrations on every page. This easy reader takes you on a whirlwind tour through a lot of little-known data about money. Presented almost as trivia snippets, legal and practical information and related vocabulary are conveyed easily. This is a great supplement to a money lesson.

685. *The Guinness Book of Records.* 1995 ed. Edited by Peter Matthews. New York: Bantam Books, 1995.

The cover reads "The unmatched, authoritative collection of world-class facts, figures, and feats from around the globe, completely revised with all-new photos and features." Consider the math applications of a short passage on sneezing: "The longest sneezing fit ever recorded is that of Donna Griffiths (b. 1969) of Pershore, Great Britain. She started sneezing on 13 Jan 1981 and sneezed an estimated one million times in the first 365 days. She achieved her first sneeze-free day on 16 September 1983—the 978th day. The fastest speed at which particles expelled by sneezing have ever been measured to travel is 306.6 mph" (page 32). Other topics for science and math units can be found on page 31, where you will find the details on the longest hospital stay (103 years and six months), the heaviest internal organ (a 3.3-pound liver), and more. Details on organ transplants include double heart, animal to human, heart-lung-liver, artificial (1982 was the first), first synthetic heart implant (way back in 1969), kidney (1950), longest surviving (kidney, 1960 and still going), first lung (1963 and the patient died eleven days later), pages 37–39. The potential for talking statistics is infinite, isn't it? This is a thick book classified as a Thin Book because nobody can handle more than a few pages of this intensive info at a time.

Consider building graphs showing these data or comparing these sneezing records with those of people you know. Discussions about time and distance are also natural outcomes of reading these passages. The 788-page book is full of them. They are adult reading material, no doubt about it. And they are loaded with useful, everyday numbers and vocabulary in clear, modern English. This is a SSR dream come true, a high-interest attention getter. If you have five Guinness books available for free voluntary reading (FVR) in your classroom, they will all be used every day. I guarantee it.

686. *The I Hate Mathematics! Book.* Marilyn Burns. Illustrated by Martha Weston. Boston: Little, Brown, 1975.

"If you can peel an orange and keep the skin in 1 piece you have solved a topological problem," assures the author (page 22). That achievement, along with the new vocabulary, will propel the reader into a series of incredible experiments that have cartoon-style illustrations and simple directions. Even the math-sensitive tutor or teacher (there is a reason why folks go into the humanities, you know) is likely to acquire some math right along with the language.

687. *More Magic Science Tricks.* Dinah Moche. Illustrated by Richard Rosenblum. New York: Scholastic, 1980.

There is almost a 1:1 ratio of text to picture space, making this a comprehensible science text. The use of graphs, charts, and tape measures makes it a good numbers introduction, too. Page 30 shows how to take fingerprints and set up a fingerprint file. On page 32, learn to lift fingerprints.

688. *More Sideways Arithmetic from Wayside School: More Than 50 Brainteasing Math Puzzles.* Louis Sachar. New York: Scholastic, 1994.

There is a lot of reading in these brainteasers. And there are clues and hints on different pages for the brave soul trying to figure out mathematically "Why boys and girls are silly" and such as that. These problems can entertain a single student or serve as a small group activity—with a lot of dialogue in the process.

689. *1001 Fascinating Baseball Facts: Facts, Records, Anecdotes, Quotes, Lore, and More.* David Nemec and Pete Palmer. Lincolnwood, IL: Publications International, 1994.

You want numbers? Here are isolated, amazing numbers: "On June 9, 1914, Honus Wagner became the first player in history to collect 3,000 hits" (page 81). Here are fractions, decimals, statistics, and scores. Oh, yes, and everything you always needed to know about baseball, but thought you already knew. A brief history of the game is followed by myriad small chunks of information in well-written, sometimes spell-binding prose, supported by historical and current photographs, documentary statistics, and lists. This is a wonderful SSR library item and can be used to bring sports fans of all ages into the world of reading.

690. *Science Research Experiments for Young People.* George Barr. Illustrated by John Teppich. New York: Dover, 1989.

There are simple, easy-to-follow line drawings and really interesting experiments. The language is by no means simplified. Words like magnification, telescope, and binoculars appeared in the first sentence I randomly turned to. The use of measuring devices, graphs, charts, and other means of documentation make this a great numbers book, too. Answer questions like "How much does a lens magnify?" "How strong is your electromagnet?" "How many miles on a gallon of gasoline?" "Who has the largest lung capacity?" (Teacher or student?) "What is your body temperature during the day?" "How accurate is the weather bureau?" "Can a cricket chirp give us the temperature?" "How much salt is there in sea water?" page 78. "Can you read by firefly light?" page 83. "How much water is in an apple?" "Can you split seconds accurately?" "Where are the ants going?" page 87.

691. *Who Dunnit? How to be a Detective in Ten Easy Lessons.* Marvin Miller. New York: Scholastic, 1991.

There is a new unit every two pages, making this a good SSR choice. Page 8 shows how to set up a ruler code. And pages 42–43 show how to set up codes using the push buttons on the phone pad. On page 44, learn how to convert a watch into a compass. The skills needed for solving crimes range from using rulers to solving puzzles to analyzing handwriting.

692. *The World Almanac and Book of Facts 1995.* Edited by Robert Famighetti. Mahwah, NJ: Funk & Wagnalls, 1995.

Statistics of many sorts are displayed in narrative and column format. Do you want to know who is spending money on the arts and how much? Arts and the Media starts on page 300 and continues for thirteen information-intensive pages. U.S. history is chronicled in a variety of formats, and world maps are in color. So are the flags. Sports, international politics, and commerce—with all kinds of demographic and statistical data—are all available.

693. *You Be the Jury: Courtroom IV.* Marvin Miller. New York: Scholastic, 1991.

Reading this book requires problem-solving skills, as readers decide which clues to accept, which pages to turn to next, and then turn the book upside down to get answers. Fingerprint analysis, water flow study, counterfeit versus genuine dollar bill recognition, map study, and invoice reconciliation are just a few of the skills needed to get to the bottom of the crime. There are good illustrations throughout, but this is not a simple read. Some of my students love the challenge, and others think it is a frustrating puzzle.

Challenging

694. *Mathematical Brain-Teasers*. J. A. H. Hunter. New York: Dover, 1976.

There are a lot of numbers in this book, and there are a lot of short reading problems, too. It is the word problems that will be of most interest, I think. Challenging has been assigned to these short passages, not because of the vocabulary but because the concepts are frequently complex and compact, with no supportive pictures or other opportunity for the reader to develop background knowledge. The puzzles, however, if carefully selected, can provide a lot of high-interest activity in tutoring, cooperative learning groups, or even large classes.

695. *Multicultural Math: Hands-On Math Activities from Around the World*. Claudia Zaslavsky. New York: Scholastic, 1994.

Although the primary content of this teacher guide is a collection of activities that involve math as it applies to world cultures, the wealth of cultural information may be its most valuable offering. Any geography or culture class might benefit from information found here. It is an excellent multicultural reference book.

696. *Real Estate Licensing SuperCourse*. 2d ed. Julie Garton-Good. New York: DREI, Arco, Macmillan, 1994.

This book has a wealth of everyday survival information as well as the essentials for passing the professional exam of the real estate salesperson. On page 233, a brief passage, "The Money Supply," introduces the longer unit on the Federal Reserve system and how it works. Copies of an actual mortgage contract, a loan application, a contract of sale/purchase, and parts of a title insurance policy are accompanied by plain language that explains how these documents are used. And lesson 19, "Real Estate Math," gives a brief overview of many kinds of math needed for the profession. There is a twenty-four-page glossary with full-sentence definitions and references to the chapters in which the words are used.

Book Chapters and Strong Passages

697. "The Googies Are Coming." In *Where the Sidewalk Ends*. Poems and drawings of Shel Silverstein. New York: HarperCollins, 1974.

"The Googies Are Coming," pages 50–51, discusses the prices offered by the Googies for all manner of children. ("They never buy the bad ones.") I have used this incredible collection of poems in many different ways with adults and children. It was popular as a community college ESL text and has provided a wealth of material for readers theatre events, too.

698. "Hetty Green: Money Was Everything." In *Eccentrics*. Henry Billings and Melissa Billings. Providence, RI: Jamestown, 1987, pages 74–76.

Hetty Green was notorious for her thrifty habits. Over time, her frugality displaced good judgment and humanitarian instincts. Refusing to pay for medical attention to her son's sore knee caused the boy to lose most of his leg. This softcover booklet has twenty-one stories about eccentric people.

699. *How to Reach Your Favorite Sports Star.* Larry Strauss. Chicago: Contemporary Books, 1994.

Birthdays, vital statistics, sports stats, and brief biographies and photos of forty-six men and women athletes are available in a fast, easy-to-follow format. As each two-page spread is a separate feature, this is catalogued under "Book Chapters and Strong Passages."

700. *The Living Lincoln: The Man, His Mind, His Times, and The War He Fought, Reconstructed from His Own Writings.* Edited by Paul M. Angle and Earl Schenck Miers. New York: Barnes & Noble, 1992.

Three short letters to his stepbrother, on behalf of his loving stepmother, deserve note in this section. They are identified as Shelbyville, November 4, 1851; Shelbyville, November 9, 1851; and Springfield, November 25, 1851, and show the concern Lincoln felt when his stepbrother proposed to take advantage of their widowed mother's land, selling it so that she would receive little income, pages 146–48. In the letters Lincoln spelled out the problems with the interest their mother would receive, and the ways his brother might make profitable use of his time—by getting a job. On March 16, 1860, he wrote to Mark W. Delahay about the propriety of money in the political process, pages 321–22. On page 467 is a draft for $5, naming his son Tad payee, upon his restored health. This check was designed to encourage the sickly lad to recover.

701. "Oranges." In *A Fire in My Hands: A Book of Poems.* Gary Soto. New York: Scholastic, 1990, pages 23–24.

Easy, honest telling lets the reader relate to the twelve-year-old boy who comes up short on money for the ten-cent candy selected by his "date." The resolution to this conflict in just a handful of words leaves everybody celebrating. Before each poem in this book, Soto tells the circumstances of its coming to life.

Also in this book, "Finding a Lucky Number," pages 52–53. The boy's age and the old man's teeth create a numerical coincidence.

702. "Smart." Shel Silverstein. In *Jamestown Heritage Reader.* Book G. Providence, RI: Jamestown, 1995, page 210.

You will also find "Smart" in Silverstein's book of poems *Where the Sidewalk Ends,* page 35. I have found it quite meaningful to adults who are just figuring out our strange system of money. It tells of a young man who trades up from a little dime to much bigger change.

703. *365 TV-Free Activities You Can Do with Your Child.* Steve Bennett and Ruth Bennett. Holbrook, MA: Bob Adams, 1991.

This is a thick Thin Book with one-page reads and great ideas in simple, everyday English. Each activity has a cartoon icon to help you see what the page is about. There is an index at the end to make idea scanning easy. Topics include science, numbers, reading, collecting, environmental issues, and many others. Though the title suggests parents and children do these activities, this is a great source of classroom ideas, too. Adults, whether teachers or learners, will get just as much from the experiences as younger folks.

Newspaper and Magazine Articles

704. "Collectors: Tables with Dragonfly Legs." Christie Brown. *Forbes*, January 16, 1995, pages 101–104.

Numbers need not be the subject of the article. Take, for example, the prices suggested here: Though much of the article reads like a decorator's promotion, there is solid content here for the adult who is interested in antiques or investments. "Collectors will not find many bargains. Over the last decade, prices have risen about 30 percent. A famous *dragonfly* table by Galle now brings $25,000 to $30,000, up from about $20,000 in 1984." It would be interesting to track this kind of information across time and other magazines, such as *Architectural Digest*, if a reader is interested in this topic. The reading, though not simple, may prove compelling to the right person.

705. "A Dismal Report Card." Barbara Kantrowitz and Pat Wingert. *Newsweek*, June 17, 1991, pages 64–67.

"The best students watched the least TV; the worst admit to six hours a day" (page 67). This report is on national math scores, not reading. Examples of the kinds of math problems are reproduced in the article and may help readers understand that math of the 1990s is quite different from the old workbook page chock-full of numbers.

706. "Travel" section. *The Los Angeles Times*. Sunday edition.

The travel section of *The Los Angeles Times* (Sunday edition), always gives the current exchange rates for money around the world—country by country. Temperatures are also listed. These features offer an opportunity to do long-term comparative studies and support geography awareness at the same time.

707. "The Triangle Cycle." Clifford A. Pickover. *Discover*, March 1995, page 96, puzzle answer on page 95.

Here is a graphic puzzle calling for a triangle that has numbered corners with multiples of one and seven. The directions for creating the triangle within a triangle within a triangle are simple—at first. Then the instructions get Challenging, not because of the language but because of the math needed to check the selections. This is strictly for the numbers-oriented reader.

708. *The Wall Street Journal*.

The Wall Street Journal gives standard stock prices every weekday and has related news stories. Here reading and number study are well integrated. *Journal* articles are consistently well written and are usually short enough to be read in one sitting.

Other Events and Supplements

Just about anything you can count can be put into a graphic form. This may not sound particularly tantalizing until the data in the graph pertains specifically to you and your loved ones or your interests. Consider graph gifts as a very personal way of saying happy birthday and getting the necessary practice time in to boot. It is possible to enjoy numbers. It may never be possible to enjoy being tested on them, but that's an entirely different matter, isn't it?

- Collect statistics on the same topic from a variety of sources or from different time periods. Put collected data into graphic or chart forms, write a narrative report on the findings, or create word problems from the data.

- Look for articles using current statistical information in newspapers and magazines.

- Compare test score information given in newspapers with the same information given in government publications.

- Collect posters of graphs and charts. Discuss which make the information salient and which make a dramatic impact.

- Design a poster on which literacy data (for example, the availability of books or the hours libraries are open) show a possible cause and effect. For example, the number of high school dropouts is an indication of illiteracy. Is there a correlation between dropouts and access to books? Library hours? Money spent on school library books?

- Collect local maps from a variety of historical periods. Compare the numerical information contained in them.

- Collect newspaper ads on homes or cars for sale. Then collect promotional materials from the agencies selling homes or cars. Compare the language used in each of those situations with that found in consumer magazines.

- Go into a bank and collect interest rate information on homes, cars, and credit cards. Collect the same kinds of information over the phone.

- Compare information on old and new baseball or football trading cards.

- Check prices on old magazines at the library and compare the prices with newer ones. Also check the number of pages and the amount of space devoted to advertising. Make a graph of the findings.

Science

Unit 12

This is a smorgasbord of scientific readings, assembled to provide a strong language base for many science disciplines. Perusal of the selections in the First Readers section has caused several science teachers to hunker down for a new look at the topics they present and the support materials they provide. It is possible to grasp high-level concepts when they are grounded in meaningful support activities and materials. The pictures in many of these books provide a wealth of information to both the proficient and the not-so-proficient reader.

A few of the books here specifically target youths or children. According to users in both my community college classes and my university teacher ed classes, these books offer enough material to fill a year of lesson plans. I hasten to warn, however, that not all books fit all learners. Take, for example, the Magic School Bus series. It is written in a comic book format that can be difficult to follow for some who are not comics enthusiasts. Still, they do offer a lot of high-interest material for many students.

As you design your lessons and get input from your students, you will no doubt discover issues I have not addressed. As always, I invite your feedback.

First Readers and Picture Books

709.   *Animalia*. Graeme Base. New York: Harry N. Abrams, 1986.
   Animalia is my all-time favorite alphabet book. Each letter is illustrated with an exquisite one- or two-page spread filled with objects beginning with that letter. This is the ultimate lesson in phonics, alliteration, and imagination. It is definitely suitable for adults. I know, having given it to many of my friends for birthdays and anniversaries. Some of the pages offer delights for specific thematic units. Myths and legends units will benefit from the "Diabolical Dragons Daintily Devouring Delicious Delicacies" on the same page as you find dice, dropping things, a dictionary, a diamond, a doll, and a decanter. Ingenious Iguanas and Wicked Warrior Wasps will likely do well in a natural science unit but may belong with critters and creatures, too. The Vulture Ventriloquist might also be well advised to stay in the creature collection. No matter what unit it ends up in, however, if you leave this book around, it will be studied for its content and loved for its wonderful illustrations.

710.   *Coral Reefs: Facts, Stories, Activities*. Jenny Wood. New York: Scholastic, 1991.
   Graphics, maps, and high-quality close-up photographs make the unique qualities of coral reefs and the creatures that live in them come alive. The print is quite large. The scientific information is worthwhile.

711.   *Desert Voices*. Byrd Baylor and Peter Parnall. New York: Macmillan, 1993.
   Simple, minimally colored ink drawings and brief, poetic lines of text give the reader a wonderful read, insights into desert creatures' lives, and a fresh look at what a home can be.

712. *The Ever-Living Tree: The Life and Times of a Coast Redwood*. Linda Vieira. Illustrations by Christopher Canyon. New York: Walker, 1994.

This is just the history of the world—all over the world—during the life of a California redwood. The book opens to a two-page spread that tracks a tree across time, from prehistory to 2,500 years of age. A human figure is provided for comparison to a 300-foot tree. And that is before you get to the first page. The Greeks, North American Indians, the Chinese, Jesus, George Washington, the American Revolution, space flight, and national park campers pass in and out of time as the tree continues to grow.

713. *The Extinct Alphabet Book*. Jerry Pallotta. Illustrated by Ralph Masiello. Watertown, MA: Charlesbridge, 1993.

If you are harboring the assumption that a Dimetrodon is a dinosaur, this book will correct that thought and tell you how to avoid making such a mistake again. Did you know that "more than ninety-nine percent of all living things that ever lived on Earth are now extinct"? That and lot of other information critical to our survival rests on some of the most beautiful illustrations we have seen. Units on extinct animals, frogs, bats, birds, and general science will benefit from this book.

714. *The Flower Alphabet Book*. Jerry Pallotta. Illustrated by Leslie Evans. Watertown, MA: Charlesbridge, 1988.

This is no ordinary alphabet book. Though each page presents a flower beginning with the letter in ABC sequence, the borders are filled with supplemental illustrations that are discussed by the artist on the last page.

715. *The Frog Alphabet Book*. Jerry Pallotta. Illustrated by Ralph Masiello. Watertown, MA: Charlesbridge, 1990.

Have this one handy for units on frogs, salamanders, newts, and caecilians. It has photo-like illustrations of frogs from Ecuador, the rain forests of Central America and South America, Europe, Yosemite National Park, and the Cameroons, making it a candidate for a "frogs around the globe" geography unit.

716. *The Great Kapok Tree: A Tale of the Amazon Rain Forest*. Lynne Cherry. San Diego, CA: Harcourt Brace Jovanovich, 1990.

This is a beautiful introduction to the environmental issues of the rain forest and deforestation. The high-level text is supported by exquisite illustrations of authentic flora and fauna, some of which come down the great tree to explain to a sleeping man why he should not destroy their tree home. Inside the front and back covers are world maps that color code the rain forest regions around the equator. A border filled with illustrations of more rain forest animals surrounds each map. The book is printed on recycled paper and is dedicated to the memory of Chico Mendes, who was slain while trying to stop the destruction of the Amazon rain forests. Though a new reader or ESL student could struggle through this compelling story, I have found that *The Great Kapok Tree* is a great read-aloud book.

717. *Here Is the Tropical Rain Forest*. Madeleine Dunphy. Illustrated by Michael Rothman. New York: Hyperion, 1994.

The interaction of elements and animals in the Central American and South American rain forests is thumped out in a rhythmical pace as each turn of the page adds another line to the repetitive text. Cool, detailed, full-page illustrations support each addition. On the last page, an address is provided for writing for more information, inviting the reader to join the race to save the planet.

718. *How to Hide a Crocodile, and Other Reptiles*. Ruth Heller. New York: Grossett & Dunlap, 1994.

Heller's poetic style and beautiful, realistic drawings join with a thorough understanding of her subject to give the reader a lot of scientific information almost incidentally. Meet a crocodile, matamata, green tree snake, python, iguana, chameleon, and gecko. Now you see them, now you don't.

719. *How to Hide a Polar Bear, and Other Mammals*. Ruth Heller. New York: Grossett & Dunlap, 1994.

Words like camouflaged, snowshoe hare, patches, dappled, deer, disappear, zebra, silhouette, leopard, sunshine, lion, mane, sloth, algae, thrive, hostile, detection, and predators come up naturally in Heller's compelling rhymes. The colored drawings give strong meaning to words that can hardly be forgotten, once the book has been read aloud.

720. *How to Hide an Octopus, and Other Sea Creatures*. Ruth Heller. New York: Grossett & Dunlap, 1992.

As with all of Heller's books, the illustrations make this a visual delight. And the rhyming text propels the reader through words like sargassum fish, grotesque, bizarre, creatures, urchins, barnacles, and anemone. Scientific tidbits are served up a few words at a time amid powerful pictures that assist comprehension.

721. *The Magic School Bus: Inside the Earth*. Joanna Cole. Illustrated by Bruce Degen. New York: Scholastic, 1987. A Reading Rainbow selection.

Ms. Frizzel, a teacher whose name seems to emerge from either her unkempt hair or the unorthodox brain beneath it, leads her students on hands-on, bodies-in scientific field trips of all sorts. A comic book format, augmented with documentary notes written by the students, supplies a wealth of information on fossils, time, shale, limestone, stalagmites, stalactites, marble formation, volcano formation, and other issues concerning the inner Earth. This is palatable science made fun.

722. *The Magic School Bus: Lost in the Solar System*. Joanna Cole. Illustrated by Bruce Degen. New York: Scholastic, 1990. A Reading Rainbow selection.

Astronomy under the direction of Ms. Frizzle is out of this world. She drives a busload of children into the realm of weightlessness, without benefit of orbit. A quick stop at the moon is followed by a pass over the sun, with Frizzle advising the children that they should never look directly at the huge ball of fire under them. Every couple of pages there is a map showing where the bus has gone so far. The presence of deadly sulfuric acid vapor explains the color of Venus. Vocabulary like Centigrade, canyon, channels, dust storm, autopilot, asteroid, and malfunctioning are eased into the cartoon format. The data collected on the voyage are neatly organized on "Our Planet Chart," which is exhibited in the classroom where a mobile of the entire solar system hangs. A warning on the last page gives three major reasons why students should not attempt this journey on their own school bus.

723. *Northern Lights: The Soccer Trails.* Michael Arvaarluk Kusugak. Art by Vladyana Krykorka. Toronto-New York: Annick Press, 1993. Ruth Schwartz Award.

Adoration of mother for child and child for mother, a ride on a canoe on a sled pulled by dogs, sickness and the death of a parent, soccer played with a caribou skin ball, and the northern lights are experiences the reader gets through a sensitive tale of one Inuit girl. The beautiful and detailed colored drawings are supplemented by beaded items that reflect the symbolism emerging from the text. On the back cover is a summary of the aurora borealis, known on Baffin Island as "Soccer Trails." It is believed that these lights are deceased loved ones playing soccer in the sky.

724. *The Ocean Alphabet Book.* Jerry Pallotta. Illustrated by Frank Mazzola, Jr. Watertown, MA: Charlesbridge, 1986.

This book of random sea creatures is simple and offers light reading for ocean enthusiasts.

725. *Pigeons.* Bernice Kohn Hunt. Illustrated by Bruce Waldman. Englewood Cliffs, NJ: Prentice-Hall, 1973.

This easy-to-read book with clear ink drawings and lots of open space simply describes pigeons, giving scientific information along with everyday anecdotes. It gently leads the reader to the shocking discovery that the passenger pigeon, once most populous pigeon of all, was thoughtlessly driven to extinction by humans. It is a powerfully simple book. Under "Book Chapters and Strong Passages," see "The Passenger Pigeon," entry 795.

726. *Plants That Never Ever Bloom.* Ruth Heller. New York: Grossett & Dunlap, 1984.

Ample time must be given to just savor the pictures in this information-rich adventure with few words.

727. *The Quicksand Book.* Tomie dePaola. New York: Holiday House, 1977.

A young girl swings into the scene on a vine that breaks, dropping her into quicksand. Fortunately, there is a lad, well informed about quicksand, its causes, which animals avoid its perils and how, and what humans can do to avoid sinking in it. Unfortunately, he opts to lecture the girl about it as she sinks. Fortunately, the story ends well and a wealth of scientific information is assimilated in just sixteen pages. The last page gives instructions on how to make your own quicksand.

728. *Radical Robots—Can You Be Replaced?* George Harrar. New York: Scholastic, 1990.

This little book is loaded with interesting robot info. Try reading the first paragraph on page 29, the one about "Tricky Words," aloud to the group. It describes how hard it is for a robot to understand what it hears.

729. *The Reason for a Flower.* Ruth Heller. New York: Grossett & Dunlap, 1983.

Heller's trademark rhymes with authentic renderings make this information-filled science book a must have for every classroom. Seed distribution, animals that eat plants, plants that eat animals, and ambitious vocabulary are delivered so well that the reader feels lost when the end arrives.

730.   *Snake*. Mary Hoffman. New York: Scholastic, 1986. Animals in the Wild series.

Extraordinary, detailed photographs—that would allow this to be a picture book without words—support the limited text. Each page gives common and little-known facts. With your nose almost touching its, you meet a snake hatching from its egg. As though you are on a rock nearby, you see both ends of a rattler about to strike. From a safe distance, you view the marks of a viper in the sand—and their maker. The swollen neck of a snake that has just had a whole egg for lunch makes your own throat ache. The acts of shedding, sleeping, and dying are all presented in this simple and informative text. It is appropriate for the nonreader, the new reader, and the graduate student.

731.   *The Spice Alphabet Book: Herbs, Spices, and Other Natural Flavors*. Jerry Pallotta. Illustrated by Leslie Evans. Watertown, MA: Charlesbridge, 1994.

This is one of the most information-intensive Pallotta books yet. Though the format appears to offer the traditional young child's ABCs, this is definitely loaded with adult fare. Almost incidentally paper-clipped to the G page is an index card with Grandma's Molasses Spice Crisps recipe. The Q page gives the historical use of quinine for malaria during the construction of the Panama Canal. There is also an inset map showing the Canal Zone. The last page is solid tiny print, filled with bits of information that the artist found but could not fit into the book proper.

732.   *Spotted Owlets*. Victoria Miles. Illustrated by Elizabeth Gatt. Victoria, BC, Canada: Orca, 1993.

Here is a small-format booklet with realistic illustrations and just a few lines of text per page. Those pages convey the struggle for survival of brother and sister owlets, the physical limitations of the young creatures, their family life, and habitat.

733.   *Storms*. Seymour Simon. New York: Scholastic, 1989.

Graphic photos of tornadoes, lightning, hurricanes, and hail support interestingly written scientific facts about what storms are and why they happen.

734.   *Thunder Cake*. Patricia Polacco. New York: Philomel Books, 1990.

Fear and the courage to keep going are the themes for this book with beautiful, detailed colored drawings. Grandma helps the young child address her fear of thunder. The predictable nature of this natural phenomenon is woven into the story through Grandma's counting out the interval between the lightning flash and each clap of thunder. Though Polacco draws from her family's Russian folk history, this is a universal story. The recipe for Grandma's Thunder Cake is on the last page—a practical, grown-up way of reviewing the words of the ingredients covered in the book. For those who must be pragmatists, the recipe is a way of learning about written instructions.

735.   *The Tree of Life: The World of the African Baobab*. Barbara Bash. San Francisco: Little, Brown, 1989.

The legend of this oddly shaped tree, the animals that call it home or friend or food, and the cycle of life that runs from rain to rain are presented with scientific detail and storyteller craft. The detailed watercolors are full of visual information and delights as well.

Thin Books

736. *Action*. Written and photographed by Kim Taylor. Illustrated by Guy Smith. New York: John Wiley, 1992.

Have you have ever wondered how insects sit on top of the water, how a snake manages to move through the grass, or why a rider flies forward when her pony stops short? This book features stop-action photographs of these puzzles and provides easy experiments to demonstrate the scientific concepts involved. The thirty-two-page paperback offers a world of insights into action, clear illustrations and photographs, and easy-to-follow text. Instructions for the scientific experiments are lucid, and there are enough experiments to support a mini science fair.

737. *Amazing Lizards*. Jayne Pettit. New York: Scholastic, 1990.

A geological timeline on the first page sets the stage for thinking about lizards across eons. The glossary will attract many students, even if they do not really need to go there for meaning. The index is extensive, considering the few pages in the book. Having said all that housekeeping stuff, let me add that this book is chock-full of scientific information, offered in an easy-to-read style augmented by a chunk of full-color photos at the center that drive home visually that all lizards are not created equal. "There are as many as 3,751 different species and they inhabit every continent but Antarctica," states the chapter that also tells of Charles Darwin's study of the iguana. He found both live specimens and ancient fossils on the Galapagos Islands. You may consider teaching world geography by lizard. Page after page offers interesting and unexpected features of these adaptable creatures. And social issues concerning some species are made clear. The green iguana, known as the "tree chicken," for example, is being hunted into rarity because of its delicate flavor, and the destruction of the rain forests is removing its habitat. Others are exploited by humans because their bodies yield medicine and their skins are attractive as clothing. This tiny book offers so much rich information, it could easily be used as a class text for several weeks.

738. *Armies of Ants*. Walter Retan. Illustrated by Jean Cassels. New York: Scholastic, 1994.

Large print, clear, colorful illustrations, and a world of information about ants, which are found in 9,000 forms and everywhere except the Arctic and the Antarctic. How they mate, collect and manage slaves, set up cities, and what they eat are discussed. The case is also made for appreciation of the ant, which has been around at least since before the dinosaurs. Their value to the planet is manifested in many ways.

739. *Bats: A Nature-Fact Book*. D. J. Arneson. Interior photos by Mervin Tuttle. Chicago: Kidsbooks, 1992.

This Thin Book has an exquisite, close-up photograph of a bat on each left-hand page and a page of informative text on the right. Did you know that the hearing of bats is being studied so that some discoveries may be applied to humans? And bat saliva has properties that thin blood. "Some wild fruit trees depend on bats to spread their seeds." It includes explanations of why some bats are rare; for example, the Indiana bat was disturbed by humans during hibernation. Not an easy read, but it is an incredible picture book that is appropriate for any age.

740. *Body Battles.* Rita Golden Gelman. Illustrated by Elroy Freem. New York: Scholastic, 1992.

This little book starts out sounding quite childish in its presentation of cartoon blood cells and earwax. It has the potential for annoying a serious teen or adult. Yet the information is dispensed quickly and easily, making it a good source of basic physiology. Knowledge of how the immune system works is useful to everyone, and here it is accessible. At the end is a pitch against drug use, again focusing on preteens.

741. *Bugs: Giant Magnified Images As Seen Through a Microscope.* Heather Amery and Jane Songi. New York: Golden Books, 1994.

Did you ever wonder where the Golden Era science horror filmmakers got their ideas? If this book had been around back then, they would have been reading it. Marvelous indeed are the close-up, extra large views of parts that allow sight, flight, feeding, and breeding. Simple explanations tell how wings evolved from flaps to two to four to two again, and how the bulging surface of the tsetse fly's eye allows a wide range of vision. This elementary science book will capture the interest of any reader, including those already familiar with the scientific world of insects. There is an excellent link to the Pied Piper story in a small inset on page 27. It is a 450X magnification of a rat flea, the one whose bite killed nearly a quarter of the people in western Europe in the fourteenth century.

742. *Children of the Dust Bowl: The True Story of the School at Weedpatch Camp.* Jerry Stanley. Illustrated with historical photographs. New York: Crown, 1992.

This book briefly describes how agricultural jobs in the Dust Bowl states declined by 400,000 between 1930 and 1940, when "nearly 50 percent of Oklahoma's farms changed hands in bankruptcy court sales." A mass of displaced and starving people headed for California. On page 5, the Dust Bowl, 1936–1940, is depicted on a map of nine states. A dark, grainy section shows a giant teardrop shape where no rain fell on farmlands for a long time—and then the winds came. The type is easy on the eyes, the margins wide, the historical photographs dramatic, and the prose compelling. This history book will hold the attention of any adult interested in the United States and readily lends itself to younger students, if used in a teacher reads aloud and class discusses format.

743. *Dolphins!* Margaret Davidson. Illustrated by Ian Andrew. New York: Scholastic, text 1964, illustrations 1985.

Colored pencil drawings depict dolphins in their natural habitats, among friends and natural enemies as well as unnatural ones. Also shown are their lives in captivity, bringing the reader to a new level of social consciousness about these creatures, and with that, the notion that we have much to learn from them.

744. *Endangered Animals.* Lynn M. Stone. Chicago: Childrens Press, 1984.

Huge type and short sentences are combined with interesting facts. Words like endangered and breathes are carefully nestled into comprehensible text among beautiful photos. There is a useful index also. Use this well-done primer to build background knowledge, provide SSR material, and support research.

745. *Explorers Who Got Lost.* Diane Sansevere Dreher. Illustrated by Ed Renfro. New York: Tom Doherty, 1992.

"During the fifteenth century just about every explorer who sailed beyond the horizon to find new lands thought he knew where he was going. But in fact most got terribly lost and stumbled on places no one had ever heard of before. That is why the fifteenth century began what is known as the 'Age of Discovery'" (page 1). The book measures about twelve by nine inches but is gigantic in terms of information and entertainment that teach history even to the most reluctant. There are a variety of formats within the book. The running text is straightforward and readable. Little boxes with special focus information occur as random treats, as do humorous cartoons. A chronology starts with the establishment of the first school of navigation in Sagres, Portugal, in 1419, earning fame for Prince Henry the Navigator. In 1441, he began the kidnapping of African natives to be sold as slaves in Europe, establishing a profitable trade, and for Prince Henry, a place in infamy. In 1520, "Magellan discovers a strait passing through the tip of South America, now called the Strait of Magellan." In 1536, "Cartier returns to Saint Malo with Donnacona, an Indian chieftain kidnapped from Stadacona." The final entry for 1610: "In June, Hudson's crew mutinies and sets him adrift in a rowboat, along with eight other men. Hudson and his companions are never seen again." On page 11, "The Caravels" passage describes this new, swifter ship, what its sails were like, and how its design changed with time.

746. *Extinct Insects and Those in Danger of Extinction.* Philip Steele. New York: Franklin Watts, 1991.

Loaded with scientific data, clear color drawings and photos of living and fossilized insects, and diagrams of life cycles, this book is a world guide to insects. Though the language includes scientific terms, the format supports comprehension and language acquisition. Small boxes throughout offer fascinating short passages, scientific information in a trivia format. There is a good one-page glossary, places to write for more information, and a time chart showing prehistoric and historic insects in relation to human activity. The print is large. The last page has a world map naming the places referenced.

747. *The Fall of Freddie the Leaf: A Story of Life for All Ages.* Leo Buscaglia. Thorofare, NJ: Charles B. Slack, 1982.

A curious and occasionally fearful Freddie asks questions about the changes he observes as the seasons affect the leaves all around. With Freddie's experience of only one year, there remains much that he cannot foresee. This metaphorical story of one little leaf provides the foundation for discussions about life and death. This is also a fine read-aloud book.

748. *The Fascinating World of Bats.* Angels Julivert. New York: Barron's, 1994.

Skillful and detailed drawings of bat wings, ears, tails, tongues, flight habits, nurseries, feeding habits, habitats, and hunting strategies make the meanings in the scientific term-laden text quite comprehensible.

749. *The Fascinating World of Bees.* Angels Julivert. Illustrated by Carlos de Miguel. New York: Barron's, 1991.

Who's who—queen, workers, and drones—is quickly covered. Then wax production, division of labor, mating and the death of the drone, hive organization, intruders, social problems, dance of the bees, bees' role in pollination, honey production, and bee-keeping are addressed. There is also a glossary.

750. *The Fascinating World of Butterflies and Moths.* Angels Julivert. Illustrated by Francisco Arrendondo. New York: Barron's, 1991.

Ever wonder exactly how the silkworm provides silk? What happens to the migrating monarchs? How to know if a caterpillar is poisonous? What butterflies and moths eat? Who eats them? These questions are clearly answered and illustrated. A glossary is also provided.

751. *The Fascinating World of Frogs and Toads.* Angels Julivert. New York: Barron's, 1993.

To begin with, page 4 illustrates and explains the differences between frogs and toads. Throughout the book, frog and toad life is laid bare in text and drawings.

752. *The First Dog.* Written and illustrated by Jan Brett. Orlando, FL: Voyager Books, 1988.

Here is a beautifully illustrated story of a prehistoric boy and his dog. The few lines of text per page are imbedded in incredibly informative drawings of cave art and ancient animals.

753. *Fish.* Jane P. Resnick. Chicago: Kidsbooks, 1993.

Here is a book of fascinating short passages with wonderful photographs. The parts of a fish and the reasons why a seahorse is a fish and starfish and crayfish are not fish are quickly detailed. Migration, disguises, defenses, and habitats are discussed in detail. Did you know the frog-faced mudskipper takes water into its gills and then goes out for a walk—on land? And the archer fish can blow water up to twelve inches to knock a bug off a leaf and onto the lunch menu? This is a wonderful little book that would be a big help to students collecting ideas or information for research papers.

754. *History's Big Mistakes.* Adam Bowett. Illustrated by Chris Mould. London: Belitha Press, 1994.

These witty running stories are easy to read, with lots of space devoted to incredibly humorous cartoons. Bits of additional information are offered in boxes on nearly every page. Each two-page spread tells of another historic foible. Strong Passages occur in every section. See the two-page read aloud under "Book Chapters and Strong Passages," entry 799. Top-heavy gun boats, poor engineering, and agricultural practices leading to the Dust Bowl are but a few of the fantastic foibles found in this book.

755. *The Human Body: Giant Magnified Images As Seen Through a Microscope.* Heather Amery and Jane Songi. New York: Golden Books, 1994.

Incredible magnifications of human skin, hair, eyes, eardrums, sperm, embryos, tissue, blood, and cells are accompanied by easy-to-understand text. In "The Body at War," pages 32–33, are highly magnified, spectacular samples of HIV virus on a white blood cell, meningitis bacteria, flu bacteria, tuberculosis bacteria, and white cells attacking a cancerous tumor. Special information boxes hold scientific trivia that can be useful at parties, on the bus, or in the beauty parlor. One shows microsurgery in process in which the doctor may be using a needle the length of a hyphen (-). This is a fascinating book.

756. *A Living Desert*. Guy Spencer. Photography by Tim Fuller. Mahwah, NJ: Troll, 1988.

It is as the title suggests and the photos attest—a desert full of living cactuses, coyotes, frogs, mountain lions, flowers, bats, butterflies, javelinas, birds, deer, bighorn sheep, venomous Gila monsters and diamondback rattlesnakes, tarantulas, scorpions, desert tortoises, kangaroo rats, bears, lakes, streams, and much more.

757. *Machines: Make It Work!* David Glover. New York: Scholastic, 1994.

This well-illustrated science book explains a mechanical concept in two pages. First comes the description of a phenomenon. Then come easy experiments to demonstrate how the phenomenon works. Make some clocks, design a popcorn screw, create ball bearings from a plate and some marbles, or gears with corrugated cardboard. On pages 40–41 are instructions for simulating a steamboat race. I have not begun to tell all. This is a fine science book for home or school. It has tremendous recreational promise. And even beginning level students can handle this text.

758. *The Man Who Planted Trees*. Jean Giono. Wood engravings by Michael McCurdy. Afterword by Norma Goodrich. Chelsea, VT: Chelsea Green, 1985.

Here is a story of hope with a message that one person can make an incredible difference to our planet. A widower in his forties seeks a solitary life in a barren and deserted expanse of land. By methodically planting trees that are suited to the natural elements, over time he manages to restore life and even a change in atmosphere for miles and miles. It is not his land, nor does he know who owns it. He is just doing what he feels is right and is rewarded by making a difference. First published as a short story in *Vogue* in 1954, under another title, this first-person narrative sounds absolutely believable. The language is simple and the story compelling. The afterword gives an overview of Giono's productive storyteller's life, with summaries of several intriguing tales, and may cause the reader to think, "I could do that." The address and phone number of environmental group Global ReLeaf appear at the end of the book.

759. *Marvelously Meaningful Maps: Let's Investigate*. Madelyn Wood Carlisle. New York: Barron's, 1992.

The index gives a quick insight into the many items taught in this well-illustrated, well-written little book. Words like cartographer, computers, constellations, legends, parallels, pipelines, satellites, topographic, and treasure are linked with places such as Africa, California, Detroit, Guatemala, Hawaii, international date line, equator, Lake Huron, Middle East, Mount Vernon, North Pole,

Old Faithful, Pacific Ocean, and Yellowstone National Park. Instructions on making maps, the use of a weather balloon, and the use of a compass are linked with maps of all sorts from all over the world. If you never thought maps could entertain, you will be pleasantly surprised. This book could facilitate many family projects, travel fun, and the calming of any phobias a learner might have about maps.

760. *Motorcycles: How It Goes*. Kate Scarborough. New York: Barron's, 1993.
    "Follow Mr. Fixit as he introduces the moving parts of the motorcycle and explains how they work," says the book cover. This is the perfect book for the layperson who wants to learn the basic language of motors or motorcycles. The glossary and cartoon illustrations make comprehension quite likely. Want to understand how a spring does what it has to do? Page 25 is the place to start. Gears, camshaft, throttle, suspension, transmission system, fuel system, firing, and brakes are other items available for study here. This is a good how-to for anyone who wants to understand mechanics better.

761. *Mummies and Their Mysteries*. Charlotte Wilcox. New York: Scholastic, 1993.
    At the start of the book is a metric conversion table. At the back is a helpful glossary. In between, a world tour by mummy finds awaits—Egypt, Peru, the Far East. Old mummies and new are discussed and their photographs shown for close inspection. Some mummies are bundled up, some gift-wrapped, others just lost and then found. All have tales to tell about their times, lives, and deaths.

762. *Mysteries of Animal Intelligence*. Sherry Hansen Steiger and Brad Steiger. New York: Tom Doherty Associates, 1995.
    This little paperback is chock-full of short passages that will serve well during SSR. For those who are convinced that they have an outstanding pet, there is an animal IQ test at the back of the book.

763. *1000 Facts About the Earth*. Moira Butterfield. New York: Scholastic, 1992.
    The contents include the Earth in space, the Earth's surface, volcanoes and geysers, earthquakes, weather, wild weather, rain forests, deserts, polar regions, saving the Earth, Earth facts and lists, and more. Graphics, maps, illustrations, and easy-to-understand text make this a useful book. It is loaded with—well—1,000 facts in short passages. "The U.S. uses 29 percent of the world's gasoline and 33 percent of all the world's electricity" is followed by "Some Chinese farmers use flocks of ducks to kill harmful insects," then "The industrial complex of Cubatao in Brazil is known as the Valley of Death because its pollution has destroyed the trees and rivers nearby" (page 40). Also on that page is a forest alert: "It is estimated that 1 sq. mile of rain forest is destroyed every 6 minutes. If this continues, the rain forests will disappear by the year 2050. The destruction of the rain forests is caused by: People clearing vast areas to graze their cattle herds. Flooding caused by hydroelectric dams being built across rivers. Chopping down hardwood trees to make products such as mahogany furniture." Caution: If your students cannot tolerate information suggesting that the destruction of the Earth is humanly stoppable and that stopping the destruction is absolutely necessary, this book will not provide a pleasant reading experience.

764. *Our United States Geography: Our Regions and People*. Beverly Vaillancourt. Maywood, NJ: Peoples Publishing Group, 1994.

The United States is broken into nine regions, clusters of states that give a logical sense to the areas where Americans live, work, and play. A regional map shows the group of states, and detailed information is provided on each state within the region. A state history, local customs, industries, and items of interest are conveyed in easy-to-read text. Local color is provided through details like the recipe for sourdough pancakes popular in Arkansas. This is an excellent way to introduce the nation to someone who has not had an opportunity to study it. It also provides good background for an adult planning a trip. "The Emigrants of the 1800s," page 157, has a continental U.S. map and identifies the National Road, the Oregon Trail, the Bozeman Trail, the California Trail, the Mormon Trail, the Santa Fe Trail, and the Gila Trail. "The Climate of the United States," page 124, has a weather map and a brief description of weather across the land.

765. *Our World of Mysteries: Fascinating Facts About the Planet Earth*. Suzanne Lord. New York: Scholastic, 1991.

This small paperback is loaded with things the ESL or adult literacy teacher wants—many short passages, high-interest adult subject matter, easy-to-read type face, and topics that move around the globe. Want to know about life in a cave, deep in the ocean, out in the desert? How about fish in the desert, lions in Alaska, flies in amber, or 40,000-year-old fossils in Los Angeles? They are all here. The mysteries of vanishing peoples of Thailand, the Marajoara, or the Anasazi? This is the book. How about cities underwater, or Troy, or Camelot? Again, this is the place. Mysteries of Easter Island, Angkor Wat, Nazca, Peru, and more are discussed in easy-to-understand English. Even so, it does offer vocabulary development. Druids, Stonehenge, worshipers, explorer, graffiti, mummies, suggested, chemically, preventing, handsome, and fantastically are among the words used in the compelling context of mysteries about the planet Earth.

766. *Sam the Sea Cow*. Francine Jacobs. Illustrations by Laura Kelly. New York: Walker, 1979.

The birth of Sam the Sea Cow takes the reader into the Florida habitat and introduces a scientific wonder, a mammal beneath the water. Factual information about the manatee and its endangered lifestyle are presented in an easy-to-read format that is supported by clear illustrations. The artist's perspective shows the world above and below the water, a world that is affected by both nature and civilization. We see the relationship of the sea cow to fish, humans, other life forms, and motorboats. An afterword gives a brief scientific history of the gentle mammal. This is good support reading for a research paper on the manatee, marine life, or issues concerning the planet. On the last page is the address of the Save the Manatee Club.

767. *Science Experiments You Can Eat*. Vicki Cobb. Illustrated by Peter Lippman. New York: Scholastic, 1972.

Each experiment has an explanation, a recipe for the product, and a discussion of the scientific observations the person can make in the process. There are occasional illustrations.

768. *Snakes*. Seymour Simon. New York: HarperCollins, 1992.

"There are about twenty-five hundred different kinds of snakes in the world," and they live everywhere except the Arctic, the Antarctic, Iceland, Ireland, New Zealand, and a few small islands. The text of this book is plainly written with lots of scientific data that can easily be understood. The photographs are anything but plain. Snakes eating, protecting their eggs, eggs hatching, and even a cobra about to strike make this a wondrous look through.

769. *The Story of George Washington Carver*. Eva Moore. New York: Scholastic, 1971.

This action-packed tale begins with the fear that Moses Carver's slaves, a widow and her two children, would be stolen. The life of George Washington Carver addresses the issues of racism and intellectual freedom. The action continues throughout the life of the man who eventually becomes a world-famous scientist.

770. *The Story of Jonas Salk and the Discovery of the Polio Vaccine*. Jim Hargrove. Chicago: Childrens Press, 1990. Cornerstones of Freedom series.

The booklet opens with a reproduction of a polio poster and a victim of that terrible epidemic. Paralysis, death, and polio are discussed in scientific terms. This booklet leads the reader through history and through the life of the scientist who found the vaccine that stopped a killer from conquering the Earth.

771. *They Led the Way: 14 American Women*. Johanna Johnston. New York: Scholastic, 1973.

Each chapter is about a woman who thought for herself in ways inconsistent with the norms of her time. The rights to preach, tend the sick, get an education, practice medicine, break sports records, run for mayor, run for president, and vote were all demanded by the women of this book in times when only men were considered able. Chapters about the medical women, Elizabeth Blackwell and Clara Barton, will contribute nicely to the science unit.

772. *Trees and Forests*. New York: Scholastic, 1995.

This is a science book you can play with. Every page unfolds new surprises. There are foldouts, flaps, transparent films, cutouts, and even a collection of stickers. On page 3 is a mini booklet showing the progression of the landscape as it may have been before trees about 400 million years ago, to 100 million years ago when mammals enjoyed pines and oaks. Tiny black and white insets show samples of fossils that give clues to the time covered. How trees grow and get food is followed by a tactile page of bark from six trees with the silhouette of each tree on the reverse of its bark. Forests worldwide are identified by trees of different styles in postcard-type photos with tiny world maps identifying where the respective forests occur. A foldout spread reveals the lush colors of the rain forest with wildlife strewn throughout the levels. Creatures, critters, fungi and plants are illustrated in clear, beautiful colored illustrations. Sacred groves of Africa, topics of fairy tales, people of the forests—Pygmies of Africa and Native Americans—industrial uses for trees, medicinal uses, and ways to save the forests are touched upon. There are addresses of places you can visit, a short list of other books about trees, a series of one paragraph biographies of people famous for their connections with trees, legendary characters, a glossary or terms, and an index. Though there are plenty of pages that will, over time, get bent or damaged, the laminated cardstock used for nearly every page guarantees many hours of enjoyment, regardless of the age of the readers using this. The print is easy to see and the language understandable. This might qualify as a First Reader, but because there are technical terms throughout, it seemed wiser to put it in the "Thin Books" section.

773. *The Usborne Illustrated Dictionary of Biology.* Corinne Stockley. Designed by Nerissa Davies. Illustrated by Kuo Kang Chen. London: Usborne, 1986.

The contents is sectioned into general, plants, animals, humans, and more general. Each section is color coded, so that even the little boxes around information reflect the section they are in. Each page is a storehouse of short passages supported by detailed illustrations with labels and diagrams. Though many sections will appeal to the science enthusiast, of special interest may be the animals section on animal feeding, most particularly arthropod (insect) mouth parts, explained on pages 42–43, and the diagram of a bird's intestines showing the gizzard on page 43. In the plant section is a detailed set of illustrations comparing old and new plant growth from central tissue to tree rings. Scientific terms are incorporated throughout and explained right away. There is much solid information for adults and children here.

774. *Volcanoes.* Seymour Simon. New York: Mulberry, 1995.

This oversized, thin paperback has large photos of volcanoes—active, dormant, and covered with snow. A shot of the currently quiet Mt. St. Helens conveys the eerie quality of life snuffed out. The large type carries strong chunks of technical information, but there is so much support in the photographs that this is easy, high-interest reading.

775. *Who Dunnit? How to Be a Detective in Ten Easy Lessons.* Marvin Miller. New York: Scholastic, 1991.

There is a new unit every two pages, making this a good SSR choice. On page 8 are instructions for setting up a ruler code. And pages 42–43 show how to set up codes using the push buttons on the phone pad. On page 44 are directions for converting a watch into a compass. The skills needed for solving crimes range from using rulers, to solving puzzles, to analyzing handwriting.

776. *Who Really Discovered America?* Stephen Krensky. Illustrated by Steve Sullivan. New York: Scholastic, 1987.

This thought-provoking book does not attempt to answer the title question. Instead, it casts questions on conventional givens and modern reinterpretations by starting out with unwitting settlers riding out great continental drifts.

777. *Why Doesn't the Earth Fall Up? and Other Not Such Dumb Questions About Motion.* Vicki Cobb. Illustrated by Ted Enick. New York: Scholastic, 1988.

Each of the quiz questions in this book could lead to a great scientific discussion.

778. *Why Is a Frog Not a Toad? Discovering the Differences Between Animal Look-Alikes.* Q. L. Pearce. Illustrated by Ron Mazellan. Chicago: Contemporary Books, 1992.

This little book of differences is not just about frogs and toads. There are bees and wasps, alligators and crocodiles, coyotes and wolves, ducks and geese, jaguars and leopards, antelope and deer, turtles and tortoises, rabbits and hares, apes and monkeys, and butterflies and moths. By the way, a toad's skin is rough, bumpy, and usually dry; the frog's is smooth and may be brightly colored.

779. *Will We Miss Them? Endangered Species*. Alexandra Wright. Illustrated by Marshall Peck III. Watertown, MA: Charlesbridge, 1992.
Endangered species from all over the planet are featured in two-page spreads that show the animals in their habitats. The text gives a few facts about the animal and the reasons why it is endangered. Bald eagles, blue whales, elephants, pandas, Galapagos tortoises, mountain lions, whooping cranes, grizzly bears, manatees, muriquis, rhinoceroses, gorillas, and crocodiles are presented in an easy-to-understand format. At the end, a world map depicts each animal on location, bringing home the notion that endangered animals are a global issue. Though an informative book on its own, it can also provide a strong foundation for the study of the planet or a research paper on any of the animals featured. Easy reading, great illustrations.

780. *You Be the Jury: Courtroom IV*. Marvin Miller. New York: Scholastic, 1991.
This book requires problem-solving skills as the reader decides which clues to accept, which pages to turn to next, and then turns the book upside down to get answers. Fingerprint analysis, water flow study, counterfeit versus genuine dollar bill recognition, map study, and invoice reconciliation are just a few of the skills needed to get to the bottom of the crime. There are good illustrations throughout, but this is not a simple read. Some of my students love the challenge and others think it is a frustrating puzzle.

Challenging

781. *Buried in Ice: The Mystery of a Lost Arctic Expedition*. Owen Beattie and John Geiger. New York: Scholastic, 1994.
A chronology of the search for the Northwest Passage begins in 1508 and moves through the centuries until an expedition out from 1903 to 1906 completes the passage by boat. A 1984–1986 expedition discovers the remains of the 1848 Franklin Party, theretofore missing. It seems "lead poisoning from food tins played a role in the expedition's disastrous end." Each chapter is supported by historical photos, paintings, illustrations, and artifacts. The text, though high level, is well written. A glossary at the end is most intriguing.

782. *The Dragon in the Cliff: A Novel Based on the Life of Mary Anning*. Sheila Cole. Illustrated by T. C. Farrow. New York: Lothrop, Lee & Shepard, 1991.
So little is known about the personal life of Mary Anning, born in May 1799, that Cole decided to reconstruct the pieces she could find and set them in the coastal area where this unsung scientist, at the age of thirteen, discovered the first complete fossil skeleton of an entire marine dinosaurlike creature. The reader not only finds a wealth of scientific information but also learns of the social system that prevented this woman from being recognized for her work. "Mary Anning

lived at a time when women were excluded from scientific activity even if they came from well-to-do families. The fact that Mary Anning was not only female, but that she came from a poor family in a small town and still managed to contribute to the scientific work of her time is what makes her achievements so remarkable. It was in trying to imagine what it must have been like for her to have made such a discovery and how it affected her life that I came to write this book" (pages ix–x). Facing page 1 is a map of England with an inset detailing the town, road, and cliffs where Anning unearthed many superb fossils. A two-page spread on pages 116–17 shows the ichthyosaur against a seventeen-foot scale and details of a paddle, skull, and vertebrae. On 159 are illustrations of a dapedium and several fossilized teeth and scales. A fossilized brittle starfish, belemnites, and a sea lily are detailed on page 179. This is fascinating reading for an adult or child. Most pages are solid text, qualifying it for the Challenging category, though the vocabulary is by no means overwhelming.

783. *Into the Mummy's Tomb: The Real-Life Discovery of Tutankhamun's Treasures.* Nicholas Reeves. New York: Scholastic, 1992.

Though the photographs of the art, expeditions, and mummies are exquisite and informative, the graphics are detailed and clear, and the organization of this Thin Book is logical and easy to follow, I have put it under "Challenging" because the language is just that. However, there is a well-done glossary and the picture captions are relatively easy to follow. This book has history, adventure, science, and even an instruction page on how mummies were made. It is loaded with facts and makes a great conversation starter.

784. *Jurassic Park.* Michael Crichton. New York: Ballantine Books, 1993.

This is science fiction, well-researched science fiction, with loads of thought-provoking insights into old questions about dinosaurs and modern ones about DNA. It would be a great read aloud for any language arts setting.

785. *Letters from the Promised Land: Swedes in America, 1840–1914.* Edited by H. Arnold Barton. Minneapolis, MN: University of Minnesota Press for the Swedish Pioneer Historical Society, 1975.

This period of greatest migration from Sweden to the United States is discussed by the immigrants through their letters and diaries and travel accounts by Swedish visitors. Religious tolerance and persecution, language difficulties, economic strife on both sides of the Atlantic, and the most difficult period—the first six months—are all detailed in these authentic documents. The connections between impoverished lives and poor health began to appear universal when used as points of comparison. There are several particularly telling passages in the book: Foul air, cramped quarters below deck, putrid water, moldy and wormy food that was often in short supply, sickness, and death were standard during the eight- to ten-week voyage. This is so much like the slave transport, the experiences of the poor Irish, and the Vietnamese and Cambodian boat people, that it bears comparative analysis in the classroom or tutoring situation, particularly for ESL students. Note the first paragraph on page 14. Poor crops in Sweden from 1867 to 1869 are discussed on page 139.

786. *My Side of the Mountain*. Jean Craighead George. New York: Puffin Books: 1988. 1960 Newbery Honor Book.

This is the story of a runaway boy who manages to survive in the wilderness. He chronicles his adventures in his journal and does little drawings of some of the natural elements he discovers. This is an intriguing story of survival and discovery. The first-person, simple language of the boy makes this a rich storehouse of comprehensible language.

787. *Romance of the Sea*. J. H. Parry. Washington, DC: National Geographic Society, 1981.

This oversized book is coffee-table fare that is typically found in libraries. It has large, easy-to-look-at print and a well-written section on the *Titanic*. But that is not its main feature. Once students are familiar with the *Titanic* story, they can use this book as an excellent guide into maritime history, including a float made of and still shaped like the hide of a water buffalo. Canoes and dugouts quickly lead to Viking ships and Chinese junks and then to more elaborate vessels. Close-up shots of decorations and details help the viewer understand the lifestyles of the occupants of these vessels, including the *Queen Mary*, which enjoys a large, two-sided foldout drawing with the interior on one side and the exterior on the reverse.

788. *The Ultimate Dinosaur: Past-Present-Future*. Edited by Byron Preiss and Robert Silverberg. New York: Bantam Books, 1992.

This book offers a mix of scientific essays and enthralling science-fiction short stories. The clear type is set in a magazine format that supports the reader. Though the text might not look Challenging at first blush, the scientific names of plants, animals, and periods serve to slow the reader down—but never to a full stop. It is illustrated with a mix of pen and ink drawings and full-color paintings that document the history of the dinosaur through time—past, present, and future. It is informative, entertaining, and a wonderful picture-book adventure. An appendix supports the scientific reader who wants to get a clear timeline with land and animal distributions during the days of the dinosaurs.

Book Chapters and Strong Passages

789. *Ghosts, Hauntings and Mysterious Happenings*. Phyllis Raybin Emert. Illustrated by Jael. New York: Tom Doherty, 1990.

There are twenty-seven spellbinding stories of the unexplained in this easy-to-carry little book. ESP, dousing, premonitions, and ghostly sightings, all reportedly true, offer a full story in five to fifteen minutes. The vocabulary is not simple, but the writing is direct and easy to follow.

790. *The Guinness Book of Records*. 1995 ed. Edited by Peter Matthews. New York: Bantam Books, 1995.

The cover reads, "The unmatched, authoritative collection of world-class facts, figures, and feats from around the globe, completely revised with all-new photos and features." This is a thick book, but it is classified as a Thin Book, because nobody can handle more than a few pages of this intensive info at a time.

791. "The Killer Bees Are Coming!" In *Phenomena*. Henry Billings and Melissa Billings. Providence, RI: Jamestown, 1984, pages 24–26.

Here is a phenomenon that has been increasingly on our minds for several years now.

792. *Mojave*. Diane Seibert. Paintings by Wendell Minor. New York: Thomas Y. Crowell, 1988.

Written in the first person, person being the Mojave Desert, this poem gives an inside perspective of the desert's interactions with rivers, windstorms, time, lakes, tumbleweeds, lizards, birds, rats, hedgehogs, cactuses, mustangs, miners, ghost towns, burros, seasons, butterflies, coyotes, and bighorn sheep. There is a tremendous amount of vocabulary in this seemingly brief poem, but the rhyming couplets and complete sentences facilitate comprehension and assist prediction. This is, as is the case with most rhymes, an easy way to provide the concepts of phonics—in process. Scientific information is also dispensed casually, for example:

> Here, silvery mirages dance
> Among the prickly cactus plants
> Whose spines and bristles help them thrive
> Where weaker plants could not survive.

Can you see how the pronunciations of "dance" and "plants" compel the reader into a phonetic awareness that a phonic rule would be hard-pressed to convey? At the same time, the reader learns that the "spines and bristles" serve a scientific purpose. Large-print, easy-to-follow text on the left is supported by clear, realistic, full-page illustrations on the right.

793. *More Magic Science Tricks*. Dinah Moche. Illustrated by Richard Rosenblum. New York: Scholastic, 1980.

There is almost a 1:1 ratio of text to picture space, making this a quite comprehensible science text. The use of graphs, charts, and tape measures make a good numbers introduction, too. On page 30, readers find out how to take fingerprints and set up a fingerprint file. On page 32, they learn to lift fingerprints. Lots of short readings.

794. *Nine True Dolphin Stories*. Margaret Davidson. Illustrated by Pamela Johnson. New York: Scholastic, 1990.

These fascinating short stories are great for the intermediate and advanced student. The text is well written, and the occasional illustrations offer timely visual relief.

795. "The Passenger Pigeon." In *I Am Phoenix: Poems for Two Voices*. Paul Fleischman. Illustrated by Ken Nutt. New York: Harper & Row, 1985, pages 17–19.

This poem tells in rhythmic verse of the unbelievable destruction of the passenger pigeon. Haunting, authentic, eerie. Under "Picture Books," see *Pigeons*, entry 725.

796. *Ripley's Believe It or Not! Weird Inventions and Discoveries.* New York: Tom Doherty, 1990.

Believe it or not, this little paperback has one to three inventions per page! Did you know the first passenger elevator was lowered and raised by hand? The first picture of a bicycle appeared with an angel riding it in a stained-glass window—200 years before the invention of the bicycle? Living in Taiwan is a 6,000-year-old cypress tree? The idea of the safety pin was sold for only $400? Well, there are even more surprises in this great trivia collection. The print is quite large for most, not all, and there are illustrations for everything.

797. *Science Research Experiments for Young People.* George Barr. Illustrations by John Teppich. New York: Dover, 1989.

Each unit in this book is a separate reading item. There are simple, easy-to-follow line drawings and compelling experiments. The language is by no means simplified. Magnification, telescope, and binoculars appeared in the first sentence I randomly turned to. But the book is intriguing and the contents will support a number of science classes. The use of measuring devices, graphs, charts, and other means of documentation make this a great numbers book, too. Lots of short readings with answers to questions such as the following: How much does a lens magnify? How strong is your electromagnet? How many miles on a gallon of gasoline? Who has the largest lung capacity? What is your body temperature during the day? How accurate is the weather bureau? Can a cricket chirp give us the temperature? How much salt is there in sea water? Can you read by firefly light? How much water is in an apple? Can you split seconds accurately? Where are the ants going?

798. *Simple Science Says: Take One Balloon.* Melvin Berger. Illustrated by G. Brian Karas. New York: Scholastic, 1988.

This book has brought great fun, language acquisition ideas, and, yes, even scientific information to my community college ESL students, my adult literacy tutors, my USC graduate students, and my son. It is written to a youth audience, but that seems to bother no one. The experiments are doable and informative. Lots of short readings.

799. "Splitting the Atom." In *History's Big Mistakes.* Adam Bowett. Illustrated by Chris Mould. London: Belitha Press, 1994.

"Splitting the Atom," pages 28–29, tells the tale of Albert Einstein, the pacifist whose work created the most terrible of war inventions. Details are under "Thin Books," entry 754.

800. *Stranger Than Fiction: Weird Stories and Ghostly Happenings.* Martin Walsh. New York: Scholastic, 1979.

Bigfoot, the Loch Ness monster, and Lincoln's dreams become reality in these eight- to ten-page tales. This is great read-aloud fare.

801. *365 TV-Free Activities You Can Do With Your Child.* Steve Bennett and Ruth Bennett. Holbrook, MA: Bob Adams, 1991.

This is a thick book with one-page reads and great ideas written in simple, everyday English. Each activity has a cartoon icon to help you see what the page is about. There is an index at the end to make idea scanning easy. Topics include science, numbers, reading, collecting, environmental issues, and many others. Though the title suggests parents and children do these activities, this is a great source of classroom ideas, too. Adults, whether teachers or learners, will get just as much from the experiences as younger folks.

802. "The Triangle of Fear." In *Phenomena*. Henry Billings and Melissa Billings. Providence, RI: Jamestown, 1984, pages 48–50.

Mysterious disappearances and crashes in the sea just southwest of the tip of Florida have baffled scientists for many years. A map of the infamous Bermuda Triangle is on page 48.

803. "Voodoo Magic." In *Phenomena*. Henry Billings and Melissa Billings. Providence, RI: Jamestown, 1984, pages 30–32.

For the people who believe in voodoo, there are psychological explanations of how mind over matter can be hazardous to your health. Yet this short story goes beyond the scientifically explainable.

804. *The World Almanac and Book of Facts 1995*. Edited by Robert Famighetti. Mahwah, NJ: Funk & Wagnalls, 1995.

Statistics of many sorts are offered in narrative and column format. Anthropology, paleontology, medicine, earth science, astronomy, biology, physics, and technology sections include fast summary information of 1994 accomplishments on page 168. This book might be viewed as an encyclopedia you can hold in your hand.

805. "The Year Without a Summer." In *Phenomena*. Henry Billings and Melissa Billings. Providence, RI: Jamestown, 1984, pages 10–11.

Extraordinary weather conditions like those experienced in 1816 have not been documented before or since. *Phenomena* is one of a series of books with high-interest short passages for adults. I have used them successfully with ESL and adult new readers. My only complaint about the series is that often more text space is devoted to tests and skill activities than to the good reads the series authors have proven they can write. This softcover booklet has twenty-one stories about incredible phenomena.

Newspaper and Magazine Articles

806. "After the Storm." Thomas Y. Canby. Photographs by Steve McCurry. *National Geographic* 180, no. 2, August 1991, pages 2–35.

An aerial map of the devastation along the Persian Gulf, with oil fires still blazing in Kuwait, supports the claim of Abdullah Toukan, science adviser to King Hussein of Jordan, "Strategically it was senseless. The only casualty was the environment." Oil-smothered animals and a desert crust that may result in intensified sandstorms are explained in a two-page spread. Also described is an oil slick that has killed shrimp nurseries, pearl oyster beds, turtle and osprey nest sites, waterfowl feeding areas, cormorant and tern breeding areas, coral reefs, and on and on. "Kuwaitis knew their environment was in dire trouble, but they had lost the means to measure the damage. Before the war this wealthy nation had supported one of the premier scientific centers of the Middle East, the Kuwait Institute for Scientific Research. Now KISR was a shell, plundered and partly destroyed. Before fleeing, the Iraqis left their familiar final insult by defecating on the floors" (page 16). Such reporting brings to our attention the fact that individuals and governments took action without understanding their acts. This is a story that belongs in the consciousness of everyone. The cost to our planet is as yet unknown.

807. "Fooling the Eye." Suzanne Oliver. *Forbes*, January 16, 1995, page 94.
New technology is helping doctors see in 3-D images on a big screen—so they can perform intricate eye surgery. The turns of phrase and vocabulary make this one-page article Challenging.

808. "Gray Matters." Sharon Begley. *Newsweek*, March 27, 1995, pages 48–54.
"Science: New technologies that catch the mind in the very act of thinking show how men and women use their brains differently." Challenging text is supported by numerous photographs and insets with related information. The implications regarding the differences between men's and women's thinking processes are sure to foster good dialogue in cooperative learning groups. A second article, "It's Time to Rethink Nature and Nurture," by Geoffrey Cowley, pages 52–53, builds on the same vocabulary and through the eyes of three psychologists takes a different scientific look at how the brain responds. For high intermediate and advanced classes and for a tutor to read to a learner in a one-on-one situation, these two texts may offer an opportunity to enter more in-depth reading material.

809. "Making Magic." *Omni*, July 1993, pages 64–67 and 86–93.
This firsthand account of Peruvian rituals involving rain forest creatures and plants is written in a strong storytelling style. But the content is scientific and may be too detailed for the new reader to stay with. This makes it a good candidate for a read-aloud piece.

810. "Mars: Bringing a Dead World to Life." Brad Darrach and Steve Petranek. *Life*, May 1991, pages 24–35.
Photographs of the Red Planet as it exists and graphic illustrations of how it might look if we attempted to cultivate it to provide Earth with a new food source.

811. "Our Endangered Species." Illustrated by Bill Pitzer. Research by David W. Wooddell, based on a September 1994 list. *National Geographic* 187, no. 3, pages 16–21.
Following an extensive story of animals covered by the Endangered Species Act, this foldout section identifies 632 species and subspecies of endangered plants and animals in the United States and their most likely causes of extinction. It is a simple, thought-provoking graphic.

812. "Parklands' Growing Pains." *National Geographic* 180, no. 2, August 1991, pages 58–59.
Here a two-page-spread map of the United States shows the 357 sites of the National Park System, which works to protect the unique features of our natural

environment. But the popularity of these locations is threatening them. Only three paragraphs of prose make this an easy reader. The possibilities as a history, geography, environmental studies, or economics unit foundation make this an item worth having in the library.

813. "Playing God at the Zoo." Jared Diamond. Photographs by Russell Kaye. *Discover*, March 1995, pages 78–85.

This well-researched article on the care, feeding, and control of zoo animals raises ethical questions about what animals should be housed in zoos, what birth control methods are required when funding and space are short, and whether or not wild animals have the right to expect live game at mealtime. Answers to these and other troubling questions are neither simple nor apparent. Issues concerning the safekeeping of endangered animals are also brought up. The dialogue this Challenging reading will generate may result in more reading and extensive writing activities.

814. "The Secret Lives of Rocks." *Discover*, March 1995, page 24.

This Walt Disney Company publication has a wide range of scientific topics and story lengths. This article is only one column long, including a quarter-column photograph showing a huge rock in Death Valley that has moved on its own, leaving a swath of disturbed ground that suggests no human or animal has been near the site. This mysterious movement occurs with rocks up to 700 pounds. Along with a possible explanation for the phenomenon, the article promises a lot of science-related dialogue and consideration of geography, too. This is a moderately easy read because of the picture and brevity of the passage.

815. "The Triangle Cycle." Clifford A. Pickover. *Discover*, March 1995, page 96, puzzle answer on page 95.

Here is a graphic puzzle calling for a triangle that has numbered corners with multiples of one and seven. The directions for creating the triangle within a triangle within a triangle are simple—at first. Then the instructions get Challenging, not because of the language, but because of the math needed to check the selections. This is strictly for the numbers-oriented reader (and teacher)!

Other Events and Supplements

Actual hands-on experiments can be fun for people of any age. The language arts link is made to science through writing about an experience. In the process of writing, we sometimes discover there is still more we want to read about. Writing helps you clarify your thoughts, but it also points up the empty spots in your information—particularly when you're writing about something of interest to you. Keep pulling the science experiences together with reading and writing. That will foster the in-depth study that just trivia chasers miss.

- Readers theatre is an excellent way of reinforcing both content and language skills in a low-stress format. For details, see the introduction.

- Make a list of questions that a particularly interesting book didn't answer for you. Include them in a letter to the author. (Authors can often be reached by mail through their publishers.)

- Have someone take a series of photographs of you as you perform an experiment. Write captions to the photos.

- Track down local specialists in fields that interest you. That might mean an astronomers club, observatories, geological society, rock hounds, friends of the zoo, or others who share common interests. Attend a meeting or just connect by phone. Write a follow-up note.

- Create an exhibit of posters of extinct, endangered or local animals.

- Make a slide show or multimedia program using photos of local flowers. Include members of garden clubs, nursery owners, competition winners.

- Collect leaves, seed pods and other natural found objects. Document where they were found, how much they weighed, what time of year it was.

- Visit natural history museums and collect brochures and posters for exhibit purposes and research support.

- Try the experiments in the book *Action* found in this unit.

Reference

Although reading is the primary source of vocabulary, spelling, and complex grammatical structures, there are rules that are either too elusive or too seldom used to be remembered. Even so, it can be helpful to know the rules exist and where to find them when you really need them. Some of the books in this unit should be perused for just that purpose. Dictionaries, the thesaurus, and other sources of words come in handy during the writing process but can be confusing to those who are not oriented. The moment you need a word is not the time you want to explore the possibilities of a thesaurus. Again, familiarity with how the resource works—and that it exists at all—is all that is needed until writing time.

Formal word and rule books are not the only ones adult learners will want to have available as they write school papers, reports for work, speeches for their kid's schools, or letters for personal business. So I have gathered together the kinds of materials I keep handy for student use. Though encyclopedias and topic-specific resources should be used in time, collections of information that can be carried about, kept, and referenced are most useful to adults who are just starting to write papers. Let's face it, you are much more likely to double-check a fact if you have the source at your elbow than if you have to enter an unfamiliar labyrinth at the library.

Part of the language learning process is discovering the differences among reference materials. For example, a small dictionary that is easy to carry may serve a person quite well for finding definitions in beginner reading materials. But the person who has moved into advanced readings or who is struggling to write sophisticated papers will need to face the fact that the bigger books have more words and longer definitions. So that students can evolve into this discovery, it is a good idea to have several different items lined up, perhaps with the same word marked in all.

Whenever possible, I introduce students to published authors so they can discuss the writing process with someone who has no motivation to get them to do anything—no hidden agenda. Another way of exposing them to how "real" writers think is to read to them what published authors have written about their craft. To that end, some such publications are at the end of this unit.

My own process of teaching involves ongoing student self-evaluations and their evaluation of the materials I use. That is accomplished via questionnaire and informal communications. Sometimes I completely eliminate a practice or a book, based on student feedback. Sometimes I increase time spent on a particularly popular activity. As for books, reference and otherwise, I haunt used bookstores in search of multiple copies of items my students praise. (And Scholastic has marvelous sales on reference materials throughout the year. At year's end, the Scholastic Book Fairs also dump a lot of stock on hand at incredible savings. When I can, I buy sale items to have on hand.)

I am not in favor of direct teaching of most grammatical forms, but the parts of speech do allow us to talk about the language in meaningful ways. So for that purpose, I issue handouts with definitions of the parts of speech. Sooner or later, some students want more on the parts of speech and related terms. Enter Ruth Heller. Below you see only part of her series on the parts of speech. The collection is still growing. On my desk I keep copies of all that I can find for students to use. They often fall in love with them. As a result, I have given away quite literally hundreds of the little Heller *Kites Sail High*. In these books, the forms are gently and expertly presented.

The reference books discussed here are some that both ESL learners and adult new readers have found useful in my classes. Roughly speaking, within the subcategories, they are in a progressively more-difficult-to-navigate order.

Elementary Answers

816. *A Basic Dictionary: A Student's Reference.* Compiled by E. W. Hobson. Baltimore, MD: Ottenheimer, 1994.

There are appendixes on the parts of speech, capital letters, common abbreviations, calendar, and Roman numerals, fleshing out this small, easy-to-handle paperback. Bold type makes each word stand apart from its definition. The definitions are brief and clear, though they do accommodate multiple meanings. For example: "inflation n. 1. the act of blowing up. 2. a drop in the value of money." Dark lines separate the columns of each page and there is plenty of white space. Certainly this does not contain as many words as bigger dictionaries, but it does provide quick access to entry-level vocabulary and will facilitate learning to use a dictionary or other alphabetical reference books.

817. *A Cache of Jewels, and Other Collective Nouns.* Ruth Heller. New York: Grossett & Dunlap, 1987.

A royal crown, strings of pearls, rubies, diamonds, and a lush assortment of other gems illustrate a cache of jewels. Throughout the book, collective nouns are in bold type. You will find a lock of hair and an army of ants accompanied by much more surprising and incredibly illustrated collective nouns.

818. *Choose Your Words: A School Thesaurus.* C. Windridge. Baltimore, MD: Ottenheimer, 1994.

At the end are tips on "Forming Opposites," "Prefixes and Suffixes," "Archaic Words," and a list of common and not-so-common foreign words and phrases. And at the beginning are instructions for using a thesaurus. The main body comprises the target word in bold, a white space, the part of speech abbreviated, and a string of synonyms. Each page has a clean, easy-to-navigate feeling. About twenty-five two-column pages make up the "opposites" supplement. Like the dictionary mentioned above, this is a lightweight, user-friendly introduction to the world of reference materials.

819. *George Washington's Breakfast.* Jean Fritz. Pictures by Paul Galdone. New York: Coward-McCann, 1969.

George W. Allen was named for the Father of Our Country, George Washington, and he had the same birthday. That inspired him to want to know all he could about his benefactor. Though he knew a great deal, he didn't know what Washington ate for breakfast, so he set out on a research project that would model good practice even in the best of academic circles. I suggest this little book for the reference unit for just that reason. It makes the hunt for authentic information child's play.

820. *Kites Sail High: A Book About Verbs.* Ruth Heller. New York: Grossett & Dunlap, 1988.

With rarely more than a dozen words per page, Heller's exquisite illustrations demonstrate the meanings of individual verbs and then ease the reader into an understanding of tense forms. It is an ideal introduction to verbs for adults and also one they can take back to their children to enjoy and teach. Any teacher or tutor who is rusty on the parts of speech will appreciate this and the companion books in Heller's well-done series.

821. *Longman Dictionary of American English: A Dictionary for Learners of English.* White Plains, NY: Longman, 1983.

Written for use by English as a Second Language (ESL) and English as a foreign language learners, this clearly written book also works well for the adult new reader. It includes definitions and provides full sentences or illustrative phrases using the words. Fifteen full-page illustrations of common places like the bathroom and the airport have each item identified. Over five pages are dedicated to identifying and illustrating uses for word beginnings and endings. For example, "dis" is explained as "1. the opposite of: **discontented** not happy; not contented / **disagree** to have a different opinion; not agree 2. to reverse; remove: **disconnect** to remove a connection of (something, esp. something electrical)." Several pages walk you through the use of the dictionary, providing details on some abbreviations. For example, [I] is used for an intransitive verb and [T] for a transitive. That may leave quite a few students and teachers clueless about the significance of [I] or [T] until they read that one cannot be followed by a direct object. Then it gives sentences in which the same meaning is conveyed, one using a direct and one using an indirect object. Little boxes in the lower left-hand corner of many pages give spelling notes. And there is more. Whether teaching a large class or an individual student, a native speaker or someone learning English as a second, third, or fourth language, an adult or a youngster, this is a wonderful support document. Many sections can be used as the starting points for lessons. It is possible to walk through it over and over without discovering all of the resources it contains. Though not oversized, the type is clearly readable. It is small enough for the student to carry around yet has enough words to get you through most texts that ESL and new readers would tackle. I have used it at all levels of ESL and basic literacy in the community, the community college, and the workplace. Students always give it high marks.

822. *Many Luscious Lollipops: A Book About Adjectives*. Ruth Heller. New York: Grossett & Dunlap, 1989.

Not only are adjectives exquisitely illustrated, but readers also see what makes a predicated adjective, a demonstrative, and possessives. Believe it or not, Heller even makes "a, an, and the" beautiful. Capitalization of proper nouns is deftly done, and then those suffixes ible, able, ous, and ive are joined by many others. Comparatives, superlatives, and exceptions are taught easily, but reinforcement comes on a summary page at the end. I cannot begin to explain the parts of speech better than Heller does. So I keep a set of her wonderful books in my office, another in my car, and two or more on my classroom desk. Whenever I present at conferences, I welcome the chance to show off the parts of speech as Heller sees them.

823. *Merry-Go-Round: A Book About Nouns*. Ruth Heller. New York: Grossett & Dunlap, 1990.

"Nouns name a person, place, or thing . . . a damsel, a forest, a dragon," then the reader must turn from this lavish two-page spread of a fairy-tale damsel riding the head of a ferocious dragon through the woods, to find "a king" awaiting the reader's arrival in Camelot. The parts of speech have never been more romantic than they are in Heller land. They are out of this world as she illustrates a countdown to a rocket blast. She covers, oh so gently, how to create plurals and what a determiner is.

824. *Up, Up and Away: A Book About Adverbs*. Ruth Heller. New York: Grossett & Dunlap, 1991.

Not only does this book explain what an adverb is, it addresses syntax: "Before an ADVERB answers 'When?' it always answers 'Where?' " Consistent with Heller's rhyming information delivery system, this little book delivers all kinds of information—gently, rhythmically, and with incredible illustrations. One two-page spread has a map of Africa, Asia, and the Indian Ocean. Why? So you can find the answer to "WHERE in the world is Timbuktu?" My students have praised every book they have seen from this series—which is still in process.

Understanding the Unpredictable

825. *Barron's Handbook of Commonly Used American Idioms*. Adam Makkai, Maxine T. Boatner, and John E. Gates. Hauppauge, NY: Barron's Educational Series, 1984.

We take a lot for granted when we grow up using a language, particularly if we are readers. But English is fraught with special meanings that cannot be found by looking up isolated words in a dictionary. And even when you have looked up a whole phrase, if you do not instinctively know how to handle it, it may turn up a confusing jumble. This handy guide gives idioms in sentences to make meaning more apparent. The simple verb "to call" is called into action through the terms call it a day, call it quits, call names, call in question, calling down, and call a halt. This is a no-frills, easy-to-hold-in-the-hand little book of good information. I like using idioms for introducing some grammar in process. Students who feel the need to memorize something at least are memorizing things they may be able to use later. Of course, the ones who do not memorize the idioms will also be able to use them later because they will acquire them over time.

826. *The Complete Rhyming Dictionary*. Edited by Clement Wood. Revised by Ronald Bogus. New York: Dell, 1991.

Here the poet will find quick comfort in the search for logical rhymes. Page upon page of lists cover like sounds such as replay, résumé, resurvey, ricochet, risqué, roadway, Roget, sachet, screenplay, sleigh, slay, sley, slipway, soiree, and so on. But a goodly chunk of the front of the book will serve the one who seeks rules of rhyme. There are techniques for rhythm and rhyme, divisions of poetry from the epic to the song lyric to the sonnet, and techniques for translation. Although it will not foster a love of reading, this dictionary does offer great support to native and nonnative speaker alike, in terms of searching for sounds.

827. *A Dictionary of American Idioms*. 2d ed. Adam Makkai. New York: Barron's, 1987. Barron's Educational Series

Idiomatic phrases are listed alphabetically. First a similar phrase is given, then a full sentence using the idiom is shown in italics. If there is more than one meaning to the term, it is demonstrated in several ways. This is an excellent way for students to get well-constructed sentences.

Grammar Galore—At a Safe Distance

828. *Anguished English: An Anthology of Accidental Assaults upon Our Language*. Richard Lederer. Illustrations by Bill Thompson. Charleston, SC: Wyrick, 1987.

A help wanted ad reads "Wanted: Widower with school-age children requires person to assume general housekeeping duties. Must be capable of contributing to growth of family"; a shop sign proclaims "Ears Pierced While You Wait"; and a social column reports, "The bride was showered with pieces of her chosen china." If your students have understood and enjoyed the humor of Amelia Bedelia, *Teach Me, Amelia Bedelia*, they may soon be ready for *Anguished English*. This is a great introduction to grammar through the foibles of others.

For Mighty Mechanics and Fabulous Form

829. *Beginning Writers Manual*. Edward Fry and Elizabeth Sakiey. Laguna Beach, CA: Laguna Beach Educational Books, 1993.

Anyone who has trouble spelling will appreciate the spelling check in this little reference book. It is broken up alphabetically and then by first sounds. For example, "ads (advertisement)" is followed by "adds (combines)" and then "adz (ax-like tool)." "Allowed" and "aloud" and "billed" and "build" are also neatly set out with brief definitions for the confused to study. Spelling rules, suffix rules, prefix rules, capitalization rules, punctuation rules, abbreviations, some basic grammar rules, and proofreading marks are all presented in large, easy-access type.

830. *The Elements of Style*. 3d ed. William Strunk, Jr. and E. B. White. New York: Macmillan, 1979.

In this tiny reference book is a world of wisdom about how to make a research paper presentable. Punctuation, possessives, word choices, topic delineation, and much more are presented in clear language. It can be carried in a purse or hip pocket. Because it is standard fare for many school classes, I often find copies at used bookstores for little money. Always leaving the used book prices in place, I make the finds available on my desk at school for students to use when they are ready to think about such things. Part of my teaching is to show students where to find reasonably priced reference and reading materials. Never have I ended the semester still owning the Strunk and Whites I have brought in, because the students who actually use them want them.

831. "How to Punctuate." Russell Baker. In *How to Use the Power of the Printed Word*. Edited by Billings S. Fuess, Jr. Preface by Clifton Fadiman. New York: Anchor Press, 1985, pages 100–107.

"Punctuation puts body language on the printed page. Show bewilderment with a question mark, a whisper with parentheses, emphasis with an exclamation point," advises the Pulitzer prize-winning essayist and author. His essay also gives a variety of punctuation rules, but he suggests that the dictionary be consulted for further instructions. Even so, he asserts that the writer is in charge of the punctuation. To see if punctuation is working, have another person read your work aloud to you.

832. "How to Spell." John Irving. In *How to Use the Power of the Printed Word*. Edited by Billings S. Fuess, Jr. Preface by Clifton Fadiman. New York: Anchor Press, 1985, pages 85–90.

When I read novelist John Irving's tips on looking up words, I felt he had been looking into my dictionary. First, he suggests you find a dictionary you like and guard it like a diary. "You wouldn't lend a diary, would you?" he asks. (I have had one precious dictionary for thirty years. It has some words they do not even use anymore.) Make a mark beside every word when you look it up. (My words are underlined.) Keep track of words you look up. "I have looked up 'strictly' fourteen times since 1964. I prefer to spell it with a k—as in 'stricktly.' " (I have a running list in the front of the dictionary, some words there several times.) And for the really terrible speller who cannot even get close enough to the spelling to look it up, he suggests looking up a synonym that may have the word you need in the definition. (I keep a thesaurus next to my dictionary for this purpose on days when library is closed. When the library is open, I call the reference department. Those folks can spell almost any word I give them.) Irving also gives a few spelling rules that seem consistent. He admits that he cannot remember the rules but offers them for your entertainment. The entire piece is written with great humor and common sense about this nonsensical topic—English spelling. What moved this essay close to my heart, however, was his closing paragraph. "And remember what's really important about good writing is not good spelling. If you spell badly but write well, you should hold your head up. As the poet T. S. Eliot recommended, 'Write for as large and miscellaneous an audience as possible'— and don't be overly concerned if you can't spell 'miscellaneous.' Also remember that you can spell correctly and write well and still be misunderstood." There are several humorous follow-ups here that I will let you discover when you read the essay by the author of *The World According to Garp*. There is more on this book under Malcolm Forbes's essay "How to Write a Business Letter," entry 833.

833. "How to Write a Business Letter." Malcolm Forbes. In *How to Use the Power of the Printed Word*. Edited by Billings S. Fuess, Jr. Preface by Clifton Fadiman. New York: Anchor Press, 1985.

Among the issues covered by Forbes are knowing what you want, editing, and ending a letter. Editing is the special area of the founder of *Forbes* financial magazine. Each of these thirteen essays on the English language is written by an expert in the field. All are worthwhile reading. Of particular note are "Bill Cosby—How to Read Faster"; "Edward T. Thompson—How to Write Clearly"; "James Michener—How to Use a Library"; "Steve Allen—How to Enjoy the Classics"; "John Irving—How to Spell"; "Erma Bombeck—How to Encourage Your Child to Read"; and "George Plimpton—How to Make a Speech."

834. *A Writer's Guide to Transitional Words and Expressions*. Victor C. Pellegrino. Maui, HI: Maui Arthoughts, 1991.

This tiny paper booklet is so chock-full of great words that I use it when I am writing, too. Invariably, when students start using it, they want to send for their own copies. It is simply lists of words. The transitional words are grouped by purpose. For example, "To indicate time order: in the past, in retrospect, before, heretofore, previously, preceding, formerly." In addition, there are two solid pages of columns of words to use instead of "said." For example: "abided, accepted, accused, acquiesced, ad-libbed, admonished, hollered, howled, submitted, summoned, supposed." In just a few pages, there are hundreds of good ideas on how to enliven your writing. Still, it looks high priced when compared with other reference materials on an ounce-by-ounce basis. There have been semesters when I have put this on the list of books required for a class. But not everyone is ready for this one at the same time. I now think it is better to let students decide that they value it and then let them order it independently. (Order from the author, P.O. Box 967, Wailuku, Maui, HI 96793-0967.)

For Quality Content

835. *Baja California*. Automobile Club of Southern California, 1993.

Page 17 has an excellent guide to metric conversion, useful travel and driving terms appear throughout the book, and clearly designed maps assist dialogue regarding directions. Pictures of cathedrals, mountains, and other items provide language support. There are lots of hotel 800 numbers, so a homework assignment to get information would be practical.

836. *The Guinness Book of Records*. 1995 ed. Edited by Peter Matthews. New York: Bantam Books, 1995.

The cover reads, "The unmatched, authoritative collection of world-class facts, figures, and feats from around the globe, completely revised with all-new photos and features." Consider short passages on sports or wills.

837. *How to Reach Your Favorite Sports Star*. Larry Strauss. Chicago: Contemporary Books, 1994.

Birthdays, vital statistics, sports stats, and brief biographies and photos of forty-six men and women athletes are available in a fast, easy-to-follow format. Each two-page spread is a separate feature.

838. *Mathematical Brain-Teasers.* J. A. H. Hunter. New York: Dover, 1976.

There are a lot of numbers in this book and a lot of short reading problems, too. The word problems will be of most interest to people using the book, I think. These short passages are classified as Challenging not because of the vocabulary but because the concepts are frequently complex and compact, with no supportive pictures or other opportunities for the reader to develop background knowledge. The puzzles, however, if carefully selected, can provide a lot of high-interest activity in tutoring, cooperative learning groups, or even large classes.

839. *Multicultural Math: Hands-On Math Activities from Around the World.* Claudia Zaslavsky. New York: Scholastic, 1994.

Although the primary content of this teacher guidebook is a collection of activities that involve math as it applies to world cultures, the wealth of cultural information may be its most valuable offering. Any geography or culture class might benefit from information found here. It is an excellent multicultural reference book.

840. *1001 Fascinating Baseball Facts: Facts, Records, Anecdotes, Quotes, Lore, and More.* David Nemec and Pete Palmer. Lincolnwood, IL: Publications International, 1994.

Here is everything you always needed to know about baseball but thought you should already know. A brief history of the game is followed by myriad small chunks of information in well-written, sometimes spell-binding prose, supported by historical and current photographs, documentary statistics, and lists. This is a wonderful SSR library item and can be used to bring sports fans of all ages into the world of reading. It will also support writing about the great American pastime.

841. *Real Estate Licensing SuperCourse.* 2d ed. Julie Garton-Good. New York: DREI, Arco, Macmillan, 1994.

This book has a wealth of everyday survival information, as well as the essentials for passing the professional exam of the real estate salesperson. On page 233, a brief passage, "The Money Supply," introduces the longer unit on the Federal Reserve system and how it works. Copies of an actual mortgage contract, a loan application, a contract of sale-purchase, and parts of a title insurance policy are accompanied by plain language that explains how these documents are used. And lesson 19, "Real Estate Math," gives a brief overview of many kinds of math needed for the profession. There is a twenty-four-page glossary with full-sentence definitions and references to the chapters in which the words are used.

842. *The Star-Spangled Banner.* Illustrated by Peter Spier. New York: Dell, 1992.

This is a must have for every American home. Each exquisite two-page illustration demonstrates the meaning of a single line of the national anthem. A brief description of the state' of the nation in the throes of the War of 1812 gives readers a sense of the people, places, and terrible struggle that framed the poem that would become a famous song. A map of the war zone gives a clear idea of where the author, Francis Scott Key, was during his moment of glory and inspiration. A copy of the original handwritten text is opposite the map. There is also a two-page spread of many historical U.S. flags. The lyrics are set to music on one page, for the pianist in our midst. This large paperback looks like a children's book, and is, indeed, a Reading Rainbow selection, but it has value to every adult interested in U.S. history or those needing to write about U.S. history or government.

843. *The Usborne Illustrated Dictionary of Biology.* Corinne Stockley. Designed by Nerissa Davies. Illustrated by Kuo Kang Chen. London: Usborne, 1986.

The contents is sectioned into general, plants, animals, humans, and more general, and each section is color coded, so that even the little boxes around information reflect the part of the book you are in. Each page is a storehouse of short passages supported by detailed illustrations with labels and diagrams. Though scientific terms are incorporated throughout, they are also explained right away. There is a great deal of information for adults and children. Here is scientific language, ready to apply to that science project tag or to use in the term paper.

844. *The World Almanac and Book of Facts 1995.* Edited by Robert Famighetti. Mahwah, NJ: Funk & Wagnalls, 1995.

The table of contents is an idea prompt for thematic units: agriculture, economics, defense, anniversaries, flags and maps, taxes, disasters, language, elections, sports, obituaries, and much more. More detail is offered in the general index. Assassinations, for example, is broken down into attempts, international, U.S. presidents, and United States. Under each of those is a list of names of people involved. Vice President Al Gore has written an essay on the meaning of the information superhighway, pages 35–36. World War II is remembered on page 37. The attack on figure skater Nancy Kerrigan and the current status of the Menendez brothers' trial are detailed. Statistics of many sorts are presented in narrative and column formats. Do you want to know who is spending money on the arts and how much? "Arts and the Media" starts on page 300 and continues for thirteen information-intensive pages. U.S. history is chronicled in several formats, and world maps are in color. So are the flags. Sports, international politics, and commerce are available in surprising detail. This book might be viewed as an encyclopedia you can hold in your hand.

For Sparkling Speeches

845. *Comic Epitaphs from the Very Best Old Graveyards.* Mount Vernon, NY: Peter Pauper Press, 1957.

One of the joys of epitaphs is their brevity. In just a few words there is the summary of a life and, in the case of these, the promise of at least one good lesson. Consider one first found in Grand Forks and now found on page 8:

> Here Lies Pecos Bill
> He Always Lied
> And Always Will:
> He Once Lied Loud
> He Now Lies Still

846. "How to Make a Speech." George Plimpton. In *How to Use the Power of the Printed Word*. Edited by Billings S. Fuess, Jr. Preface by Clifton Fadiman. New York: Anchor Press, 1985, pages 70–76.

Among points covered by Plimpton are how to pick a topic and how to sound spontaneous. This book includes thirteen essays on the English language, each written by an expert in the field. More is under Malcolm Forbes's article "How to Write a Business Letter," entry 833.

847. *I Wish I'd Said That! The Greatest One-Liners, Comebacks, Put-Downs, Epitaphs, Quips, Show Stoppers, & Wise Cracks of All Time*. Nick Harris. Illustrated by Heath. Secaucus, NJ: Castle, 1984.

Though the title suggests that the quotes are for speaking and writing, they may also be used to foster great dialogues in the ESL class. They can evoke meaningful language experience stories from adult and teen learners. The Duke of Windsor (former king of England) who gave up his throne to marry a divorced commoner, is quoted, "The thing that impresses me most about America is the way parents obey their children" (page 16). And Robert Frost gives a definition: "Home is the place where, when you have to go there, they have to take you in" (page 93). A carefully selected quote may prove the perfect opener—or closer—for a speech.

848. *The Mother Tongue: English and How It Got That Way*. Bill Bryson. New York: Avon Books, 1990.

This is a well-documented, humorously written analysis of English dialects, language patterns, and grammar matters. It pokes fun at how we speak and discusses what we do when friends are near and how our speech changes with our company. It is the kind of book you can pick up and open anywhere for an entertaining time. You will find yourself quoting from it again and again. It is great for the ten-minute reading session but might keep readers intrigued for hours.

849. *3,500 Good Quotes for Speakers*. Gerald F. Lieberman. New York: Doubleday, 1983.

I almost did not buy this book because the extensive list of subjects failed to contain "reading." But when I checked for "writing" and "writers," I found several pages of great quotes and decided those entries made the book worth adding to my collection. Actually, most such books are of value if they have enough modern language to give students ideas on how to say things well in a few words. For adult new readers and ESL students, books of quotes are good for reference and for brief moments of reading time and SSR.

Capturing the Writer's Craft

850. "The Hardest-Working Woman in Trash Fiction." Margy Rochlin. *The Los Angeles Times Magazine*, December 2, 1990, pages 12–22 and 52–54.

In 1949, Judith Krantz supervised fashion shoots for hat designers in Paris. Eventually she wrote articles for several women's magazines and then spent nine years at *Cosmopolitan*. When Krantz was forty-eight, she decided to drag her Smith-Corona portable into the guest bedroom to take her first crack at fiction writing. *Scruples* sold for $50,000 and in four months was a best-seller. The paperback rights for *Princess Daisy* earned her a record-breaking $3,208,875. Such are the fruits of six hours a day, five days a week. Sometimes she is asked why she keeps writing—she does not need the money. It is not about money, she argues, it is about getting something out of herself. Still, others fail to take her lurid modern fairy tales seriously. She claims that people do not understand how much work it takes to write. Indeed, her manuscripts are reportedly so well done that they are published almost as they are turned in. This inside look at a successful writer's life may prove inspirational to the mature student who is contemplating whether literacy can be worthwhile during the second fifty years of life.

851.   "How to Use a Library." James Michener. In *How to Use the Power of the Printed Word*. Edited by Billings S. Fuess, Jr. Preface by Clifton Fadiman. New York: Anchor Press, 1985, pages 40–48.

"My first suggestion for making the most of your library is to do what I did: Read and read and read. For pleasure—and for understanding. . . . If you like what you read, you can follow up with other satisfying books by the same authors," advises the Pulitzer prize-winning author. He tells about using the open stacks in the library not just to find what you want, but also to find what you are not looking for. Getting to know the reference librarian is another bit of advice—he even married one.

852.   "MM Interview: Sue Grafton and Tony Hillerman." Susan Goodman. *Modern Maturity*, July–August 1995, pages 74–82.

Here is an easy how-to lesson in writing. Mystery writer Sue Grafton flew from her home in Santa Barbara, California, to Albuquerque, New Mexico, where Tony Hillerman opened his home for the dual interview. This compare-contrast story of mystery writers tells of a country boy and a city girl, both of whom live by the pen. Both writers share techniques; neither is able to follow a plot outline. They write, and the twists present themselves in process. Grafton admits, "When I was writing *'E' Is for Evidence,* I was on chapter 23 of 24 and didn't have the faintest idea how the book was going to end. I thought, I sure hope this book ends with a bang and not a whimper. And a little voice said, 'Put a bomb in it, Grafton.' So the book ends with a bombing. People who outline don't have nearly the fun we do." Hillerman, struggling to invent an excuse for a policeman to be out in a desolate area, himself went out onto a nearby reservation. There, a vandalized windmill gave him a subplot for *The Dark Wind* that proved more exciting than the main plot. "A writer is like a bag lady going through life with a sack and pointed stick collecting stuff," he explains. Then he goes on, "You're writing all the time. I'm writing when I'm eating breakfast, when my wife is telling me something, when I'm driving—I'm running red lights and people are honking at me. I developed a great reputation in committee meetings—the guy who always took great notes." Grafton has a regular routine, getting up at 5:37 A.M., running three miles, and then reading the newspaper, mostly to check on the latest homicides. She may not have thought about it, but that is comprehensible input! She is using her reading to get stimulation and new information for her writing. It is useful to read what writers have to say about the writing craft, because they are not trying to sell you on anything you must do. They just tell what works for them, and you can be the judge.

853. "Pure Gore." Barbara Grizzuti Harrison. *The Los Angeles Times Magazine,* January 28, 1990, pages 8–16 and 38–39.

"What is the joy of writing a novel? Finishing it," says Gore Vidal. Complete with full-page photographs, references to the rich and famous—Jacqueline Kennedy, John Kennedy, the Duke and Duchess of Windsor, Eleanor Roosevelt—with whom he had close ties, his favorite authors and those he knows and despises, and a lengthy excerpt from his Hollywood exposé novel *The Perils of Caroline,* this is the biography of an author of our time. It is in straightforward, first-person style, making it ideal for the ESL student. And Harrison has written a piece that could stand alone as biography, making it fine reading for the native speaker as well.

Other Events and Supplements

I want to draw to your attention Jean Fritz's little book *George Washington's Breakfast.* It demonstrates that research can be child's play. Young George, namesake of the first president, wanted to have a meal just like the one George Washington had, but first he had to find out what that might have been. Books did not provide the answer straightaway, so the lad was left to do field investigation. Ferreting out information about something you really want to know makes primary research a normal, natural part of living. Interviews, observations, and little leaps of the imagination can help any detective. However, books, newspapers, and other print media can save a lot of time on occasion. The purpose of the following activities is to get familiar with how to locate and store data on the topic of choice.

- Collect articles from the current papers and discarded magazines on a topic of general interest. Make sure to write the full source information on each clipping—newspaper or magazine name, day, date, page number. Cooperative groups can identify a topic and develop classroom reference volumes. Either way, there is the foundation for a significant amount of high-interest reading that will build the background knowledge needed for informed writing.

- Collect artifacts related to a given topic, such as sewing. Make identification tags for each item, giving as much information as possible. Small things like thimbles, pins and needles are best stored in plastic sandwich bags so their identification tags show. These collections can be the foundation for written and oral reports as well as exhibitions. Other generic collections are: seeds, buttons, hand tools, hair and cosmetic supplies, gloves, earrings, advertising and campaign buttons.

- Collect campaign mail over several months before an election. A tandem collection of news clippings will allow interesting compare/contrast analysis.

- Bring to class all the work you can find by a single author such as Shakespeare or Aesop. Perusing a lot of single author work can present ideas for reading and writing that wouldn't otherwise occur, such as noting how the works may have changed over time. Before disbanding the collection, have the students make bibliographical lists, documenting title, author, publisher, city and state, date, and any other features of interest that might help them remember one from another.

- Collect books, magazine articles, newspaper clippings, and leaflets on a topic of general interest and just spend time looking over them. Pursue areas of interest, researching, specific issues.

- I like bringing all the Ruth Heller parts of speech books (referenced in this unit) and Jerry Pallotta's alphabet books (some of each are referenced in Science, Unit 12, entries 713, 714, 715, 724, and 731) in and just letting people read them or have me read them aloud. Both authors show what can happen when research is taken as seriously as art and vice versa. These collections combine quality content and beautiful illustrations so that learning occurs.

Biographies

Unit 14

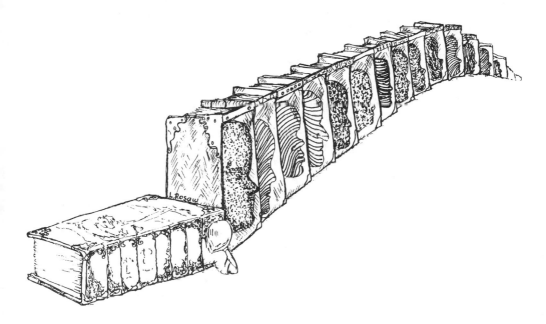

The stories of people's lives, whether simply told or in eloquent prose, make consistently popular adult fare. That is not to say that every adult likes biographies or autobiographies, but enough do to make it worthwhile assembling reading materials around that theme. We are fortunate that now there are stories about all sorts of notable people written for all kinds of reading audiences. Frequently, the high-level literacy and language students in my classes select readings that are traditionally under the jurisdiction of the children's librarian because the factual information is laid out neatly and the type is large, no small matter when the student is under pressure to find information fast. So I keep a healthy supply of all levels available, regardless of the level of the students.

First Readers and Picture Books

854. *The Death of Lincoln.* A picture history of the assassination. Leroy Hayman. New York: Scholastic, 1968.

Here is a fascinating history book, complete with historical photographs and on page 20, Lincoln's accounting of a dream in which his death is predicted.

855. *Explorers Who Got Lost.* Diane Sansevere Dreher. Illustrated by Ed Renfro. New York: Tom Doherty, 1992.

"During the fifteenth century just about every explorer who sailed beyond the horizon to find new lands thought he knew where he was going. But in fact most got terribly lost and stumbled on places no one had ever heard of before. That is why the fifteenth century began what is known as the 'Age of Discovery' " (page 1). The book is about twelve by nine inches but is gigantic in terms of information and entertainment that promise to teach history even to the most reluctant. There are a variety of formats. The running text is straightforward and readable. Little boxes with special focus information occur as random treats, as do humorous cartoons. A chronology starts with the establishment of the first school of navigation in Sagres, Portugal, in 1419, earning fame for Prince Henry the Navigator. In 1441, he started the kidnapping of African natives to be sold as slaves in Europe, establishing a profitable trade and, for Prince Henry, a place in infamy. Many historic events show the movement of civilization on and off the sea. In 1520, "Magellan discovers a strait passing through the tip of South America, now called the Strait of Magellan." In 1536, "Cartier returns to Saint Malo with Donnacona, an Indian chieftain kidnapped from Stadacona." The final entry for 1610: "In June, Hudson's crew mutinies and sets him adrift in a rowboat, along with eight other men. Hudson and his companions are never seen again."

856. *Flight: The Journey of Charles Lindbergh.* Robert Burleigh. Illustrated by Mike Wimmer. Introduction by Jean Fritz. New York: Philomel Books, 1991.

Fritz's firsthand account of hearing about Lindbergh's triumphal flight across the Atlantic connects much of this story with the lives of adults who are struggling against difficult odds. Fritz was a child in Shanghai, China, listening to her mother read of the twenty-five-year-old's lonely flight—an adventure of worldwide importance. Wimmer's graphic paintings make a wondrous journey in themselves as they show the story from multiple perspectives—Lindbergh's feet on the ground, the farewell scene, in the cockpit, under the plane at sea, in a dense fog, and from the cockpit looking down at the Eiffel Tower at night, just to name a few. The story is written in the present tense—you are there; it is 1927. "In the airfield's hangar, he tells the story of his flight to the other pilots: The cramped cockpit, the aloneness, the long, long night. Meanwhile, unknown to Lindbergh, newspaper headlines all over the world are beginning to blazon the news: AMERICAN HERO SAFE IN PARIS!"

857. *"Wanted Dead or Alive": The True Story of Harriet Tubman*. Ann McGovern. New York: Scholastic, 1965.

This story of a courageous slave who helped over 300 others to freedom begins when seven-year-old Harriet was rented out as a servant. Beatings with a whip left lifelong scars on a human being who would live to read of the Emancipation Proclamation and to nurse the sick throughout the Civil War. Large print and poetic language assist the reader through a pivotal period in U.S. history.

858. *Westward with Columbus: Set Sail on the Voyage That Changed the World*. John Dyson. Photographs by Peter Christopher. New York: Scholastic, 1991.

You could almost be there. This book reads like a novel. Details like the discovery of gold in riverbeds and edible iguanas help bring to life the triumphs and ordeals of this most important sea adventure. A two-page illustration of the sinking *Santa Maria* makes it clear that this was no child's play. There is a glossary full of fascinating facts. A map on page 42 shows the Atlantic Ocean, all land points on both sides that played a role in the Columbus adventures, probable routes taken by the explorer, and the ocean currents that clearly played a part in history.

Thin Books

859. *Abraham Lincoln*. Kathie Billingslea Smith. Illustrated by James Seward. New York: Scholastic, 1987.

A barefoot lad in western Kentucky is introduced. Then his mother dies, father remarries, and the boy is fortunate enough to have a stepmother who honors his love of books. He is married, a child is born and dies, two more are born, and the man becomes president of the United States. A war over slavery, the Civil War, begins, the Emancipation Proclamation is signed, and another son dies. The war ends, and the reelected president is assassinated. All this in just a few pages of easy-to-read text, with clear drawings on each of them.

860. *Ask Dale Murphy*. Dale Murphy with Curtis Patton. Introduction by Furman Bisher. Chapel Hill, NC: Algonquin, 1987.

Every coach and parent should have a chance to read this tender, thoughtful, insightful, and inspirational book. It began as a newspaper column by the same name. The format is questions from young fans, in bold type, answered in half-page essays on the topic, making it great SSR reading. The question "Do you have trouble unwinding after a game? Sometimes I can't sleep and I'm just in Little League—Billy Taylor, 11" is answered in several paragraphs that end with the following: "My main advice to Little Leaguers is to enjoy the game and have fun.

It's good to be excited and have butterflies in your stomach. But if you haven't had a good time, it's not worth it" (pages 85–86).

861. *Elvis Presley: The King*. Katherine E. Krohn. Minneapolis, MN: Lerner, 1994.
You will not find an index, and the table of contents is not particularly informative, but the little book on Elvis the Pelvis, born in Tupelo, Mississippi, in 1935, tells the great American success story in a unique way. Humble beginnings, disappointments, a teenage romance, hopes of big-time recordings, broken promises and a broken marriage, drug addiction, and death at the peak of his career, all combine to make this the start of a legend that has not ended. "On the day Elvis Presley died, every florist in Memphis ran out of flowers" (page 55).

862. *George Washington*. Kathie Billingslea Smith. Illustrated by James Seward. New York: Scholastic, 1987.
This Thin Booklet makes the first president both human and historical. It also gives a clear picture of how soldiering was done during the American Revolution. The type is large and easy to read, and a large portion of every page is filled with helpful illustrations.

863. *I Was a Teenage Professional Wrestler*. Ted Lewin. New York: Scholastic, 1993.
A glossary of wrestling lingo and wrestling holds fills the last three pages of the book. Many may want to start there. Though the book has an ample supply of photographs of known, unknown, and colorful wrestlers from the 1950s and 1960s, there are also drawings and paintings by the author, who used wrestling to pay the rent while he attended the Pratt Institute. This split life allowed him a unique place among artists and wrestlers. In this autobiography, Lewin begins recounting the fun times he and his brothers had as children when their father took them to the fights. It was a father-son occasion that set the course for Ted. He also recounts stories about the wrestlers who lived in his house and how they spent their time outside the ring—none, that he could recall, ever read. This is a good read, whether you are a sports fan, an art enthusiast, or neither.

864. *Lost Star: The Story of Amelia Earhart*. Patricia Lauber. New York: Scholastic, 1988.
This is the incredible story of a woman who always seemed to have a philosophical response to what others might view as adversity. A read-aloud passage begins on page 16, as Amelia, or "Meely," headed for a school poetry reciting contest. Along the way, she stopped to visit a horse she sometimes rode and discovered it unfed and without water. Disregarding her dress and school schedule, she took time to feed and water the horse. "But, she told her favorite teacher later, she didn't mind. She was glad to know the poem and had fun learning it. That was what counted, not the prize" (page 17). This notion of learning for learning's sake may prove an inspiration to those who are discouraged by test scores and other extrinsic rewards. Eventually, Earhart became an enthusiastic pilot, determined to do what had never been done before. In the process, she vanished from the face of the Earth. Historical photographs accompany this well-told tale. Pages 100–102 offer an interesting mythological passage, telling of the naming of the plane and the odd coincidence that the star known as Amelia

was lost, just as the namesake was. It was a toss-up for me whether to go Thin Books or Challenging on this one.

865. *Nelson Mandela: "No Easy Walk to Freedom."* Barry Denenberg. New York: Scholastic, 1991.

A chronology starting with A.D. 1400 and going to February 11, 1990, a bibliography offering more readings, and a detailed index make this a scholarly work. The compelling writing and rich information on racism, intolerance, political strife, warring tribes, intrigue, and hope make this a fascinating read.

866. *The Picture Life of Corazon Aquino.* Margaret M. Scariano. New York: Franklin Watts, 1987.

This easy-to-read, sixty-two-page, whirlwind tour of the Philippines ranges from the Spanish-American War in 1898 to the present. It reveals the political, religious, and personal struggles of Corazon Aquino, who became her country's first woman president. The news-report-style text is supported by lots of photos and maps showing the Philippines up close and as related to China and Australia.

867. *What Happened to Their Kids? Children of the Rich and Famous.* Malcolm Forbes with Jeff Bloch. New York: Simon & Schuster, 1990.

Paul Revere, the silversmith made famous by a midnight ride in 1775 (with the help of the poet Longfellow), had a total of sixteen children, eleven of whom grew to adulthood. Franz Xaver Wolfgang Mozart, son of Wolfgang Amadeus Mozart, was pushed to perform in much the same way his father had been. The son of Maria Montessori, the early childhood educator, sent away from his unwed mother at birth, was never recognized as more than an adopted child. Thomas Edison, the genius with only a fourth-grade education, was less celebrated by his children, most of whom disowned him before he died. The children of many other famous parents have their stories told in these two-to-three-page essays. The text is easy to read, vocabulary simple, and topics fascinating, qualifying this as a Thin Book.

868. *Who Shot the President? The Death of John F. Kennedy.* Judy Donnelly. New York: Random House, 1988.

When I first took this book into my entry-level ESL class, I did not think the cover would attract enough attention to get it picked up. It was borrowed, read, reborrowed, passed around the class, and finally was completely falling apart, carried in and out in a plastic bag. This true mystery story, delivered in simple language and printed in a large typeface, has proven one of my all-time most popular books for all levels of ESL and literacy.

869. *Will You Sign Here, John Hancock?* Jean Fritz. Pictures by Trina Schart Hyman. New York: Scholastic, 1976.

There is a chronology with page references on the last page of this entertaining booklet. Though there are lots of pictures, the text is solid in full- or half-page chunks, making this book seem more intimidating than it needs to be. Even so, sentences start and finish on the same page and complete passages are carefully tucked into spaces that limit confusion. Were the print larger, it would qualify as a First Reader. The story of this colorful signer of the Declaration of Independence, frightful military leader, and wonderful host is good read-aloud fare. Here is a man who is accustomed to all the creature comforts of the moneyed class. Suffering, in his way of seeing it, will bring smiles to readers of today. Take, for example, the problems discussed on page 31: "But there were times when the war came so close that Congress had to move out of Philadelphia and John had to give up some of his comforts. Occasionally he had to eat without a tablecloth. Once he was so cold that he had to borrow two blankets. Once he was without a candle snuffer and complained that he had to use common scissors to put out his candle. Once he was forced to dip out his gravy with a pewter teaspoon until someone took pity and lent him a large silver spoon. Once he ate turkey that was so tough that he broke a tooth. 'I wish I could do better,' he wrote after some of these hardships, 'but we must Ruff [sic] it.' " Another page shows four John Hancock signatures as he practiced increasingly more ostentatious flourishes, the grandest of which is on the Declaration of Independence.

870. *The Wizard of Sound: A Story About Thomas Edison*. Barbara Mitchell. Illustrated by Hetty Mitchell. New York: Scholastic, 1991.
  Chapter 4, "The Machine Must Talk" pages 42 to 49 is a great read-aloud passage about the scientist's 1877 invention, the phonograph. This book has large print, but only occasional pictures.

Challenging

871. *The Dragon in the Cliff: A Novel Based on the Life of Mary Anning*. Sheila Cole. Illustrated by T. C. Farrow. New York: Lothrop, Lee & Shepard, 1991.
  So little is known about the personal life of Mary Anning, born in May 1799, that Cole decided to reconstruct the pieces she could find and set them in the coastal area where this unsung scientist, at the age of thirteen, discovered the first complete fossil skeleton of a marine dinosaurlike creature. A wealth of scientific information is blended with descriptions of a social system that prevented Anning from being recognized for her work. "Mary Anning lived at a time when women were excluded from scientific activity even if they came from well-to-do families. The fact that Mary Anning was not only female, but that she came from a poor family in a small town and still managed to contribute to the scientific work of her time is what makes her achievements so remarkable. It was in trying to imagine what it must have been like for her to have made such a discovery and how it affected her life that I came to write this book" (pages ix–x). Facing page 1 is a map of England with an inset detailing the town, road, and cliffs where many superb fossils were unearthed by Anning. A two-page spread on pages 116–17 shows the ichthyosaur against a seventeen-foot scale and details of a paddle, skull, and vertebrae. On page 159 are illustrations of a dapedium and several fossilized teeth and scales. A fossilized brittle starfish, belemnites, and a sea lily are detailed on page 179. This is a captivating read for an adult or child. Most pages are solid text, qualifying it for the Challenging category, though the vocabulary is by no means overwhelming.

872. *I Dream a World: Portraits of Black Women Who Changed America*. Brian Lanker. Foreword by Maya Angelou. New York: Stewart, Tabori & Chang, 1989.

This oversized book has 167 pages of American history. On one side of each two-page spread is a full-page, black-and-white, museum-quality photographic portrait of a famous African American woman, on the other is a full-page biographical sketch-interview, detailing her place in history. The birth date appears just below the name, and a narrow column gives an encapsulated overview of her contributions to society. There are several politicians, literary figures, and artists whose stories belong in a variety of units.

873. *The Life of Sir Arthur Conan Doyle*. John Dickson Carr. New York: Carroll & Graf, 1976.

This story is as entertaining as the life reported by Dr. Watson as he described the activities of Sherlock Holmes. A devout spiritualist, Sir Arthur Conan Doyle believed that one might communicate with the dead.

874. *The Living Lincoln: The Man, His Mind, His Times, and the War He Fought, Reconstructed from His Own Writings*. Edited by Paul M. Angle and Earl Schenck Miers. New York: Barnes & Noble, 1992.

This book of letters, speeches, and journals documents the history lived by a literate man. Annotations help create a context for these one-sided communications. The entire book is worth study. If any part of it was published in booklet form, perhaps with illustrations, it would qualify as a Thin Book or even, for some parts, a First Reader. Lincoln's style was forthright, honest, and to the point. There is no wondering what he meant.

875. *Wouldn't Take Nothing for My Journey Now*. Maya Angelou. New York: Random House, 1993.

This is a collection of philosophical essays, most only a page and a half long, all thought-provoking. It makes a good read aloud or a good SSR collection. The complexity of thought, not the sentence structure or vocabulary, makes the text Challenging. If each essay was illustrated—somehow, I do not know how—it could be a Picture Book.

Book Chapters and Strong Passages

876. "Death and the Legacy." In *Wouldn't Take Nothing for My Journey Now*. Maya Angelou. New York: Random House, 1993, pages 445–49.

In this brief essay, Angelou describes the universal feeling of loss of a loved one and her own way of learning from such love lost. Here is poetry. For details on this book, see under "Challenging," entry 275.

877. "George Kaufman: Keeping Fit." In *Eccentrics*. Henry Billings and Melissa Billings. Providence, RI: Jamestown, 1987, pages 36–38.

This story tells of a man who was a successful writer in spite of what might have appeared to be a disabling terror of germs. *Eccentrics*, one of a series of books with high-interest short passages for adults, has twenty-one stories about eccentric people.

878. *The Groucho Letters: Letters from and to Groucho Marx.* New York: Simon & Schuster, 1967.

Tongue-in-cheek, teasing, and sometimes even serious, Marx responds to television shows of his friends (and it seems not friends?), opponents, news articles, and actual mail. I always thought of Marx as that funny talk show host from the early days of television. He was one funny writer, too. He discusses the possibilities of being unemployed and the impossibilities of accepting invitations to tea 3,000 miles away. He makes it his business to set things straight; for example, he assures that one Miss Bankhead is, in real life, a shy and retiring type who leads a sedentary existence, pining away for a little farm where she might have peace and quiet. In addition to his exchanges about famous folks, there are exchanges with them. In an exchange of letters with author E. B. White, the two discuss the unlikelihood of their ever meeting face to face. In most cases the exchanges are in understandable language, some of it bordering on strong—in yesteryear's terms—and the topics are generally human—in Marx humor terms. Still, there are references that current readers may not recognize, and some letters employ atypical forms. F. Allen, for example, uses no capital letters. I hope that many teachers will find little chunks of this book appropriate for linking with "Thin Books" and even "First Readers." This is a biography of the man through his own correspondence.

879. "Hetty Green: Money Was Everything." In *Eccentrics*. Henry Billings and Melissa Billings. Providence, RI: Jamestown, 1987, pages 74–76.

Hetty Green was notorious for her thrifty habits. Over time, however, her frugality displaced good judgment and humanitarian instincts. Refusing to pay for medical attention to her son's sore knee caused the boy to lose most of his leg. See "Jay Johnstone" entry 880 for details on this series.

880. "Jay Johnstone." In *Eccentrics*. Henry Billings and Melissa Billings. Providence, RI: Jamestown, 1987, pages 24–26.

"From 1966 to 1984, Jay Johnstone played major league baseball for eight different teams." My only complaint about *Eccentrics* is that often more text space is devoted to tests and skill activities than to the good reads the series authors have proven they can write. This softcover booklet has twenty-one stories about eccentric people.

881. *Life Doesn't Frighten Me.* Poem by Maya Angelou. Paintings by Jean-Michel Basquiat. New York: Stewart, Tabori & Chang, poem copyright 1978, illustrations copyright 1993.

Seeming to be a children's picture book, this collection of illustrations and ideas shocks the senses with the kinds of things that really frighten us all. Oil pastels, gouache, acrylics, and collage give the illusion of children's art, and the rugged, haphazard-looking typeface looks like children's writing, but they combine to convey a level of sophistication that calls for rereading, rereading, rereading. At the end are two-page biographies of the author and the illustrator. They are good reading in themselves and promise insights into the lives of two artists who made a mark beyond the expected. Angelou's call to everyone to "read everything possible, be it African American, European, Latin, or other literature— but, especially Shakespeare," makes this even more appropriate for adult new readers. The drug death at an early age of the artist, whose works have just sent the reader on an emotional roller-coaster ride, makes this an even more important book for people concerned about the influence of illegal drugs on our lives; each of us lost when this young man stopped making art. Read aloud or First Reader for the poem, but it requires discussion. The biographies are equivalent to chapters in a biographies or celebrities unit.

882. "Lincoln's Ghost." In *The World's Most Famous Ghosts*. Daniel Cohen. New York: Minstrel Books, 1989, pages 1–15.
   The ghost of President Lincoln is not the only one haunting the halls of the White House. This story get stranger with each page.

883. *Lives of the Musicians: Good Times, Bad Times (and What the Neighbors Thought)*. Kathleen Krull. Illustrated by Kathryn Hewitt. San Diego, CA: Harcourt Brace, 1993.
   Each featured musician's story is a Strong Passage and a good read aloud. Antonio Vivaldi, Johann Sebastian Bach, William Gilbert and Arthur Sullivan, Erik Satie, Scott Joplin, Wolfgang Amadeus Mozart, Johannes Brahms, Clara Schumann, Ludwig van Beethoven, Charles Ives, Frederic Chopin, Igor Stravinsky, Stephen Foster, Peter Ilich Tchaikovsky, Giuseppe Verdi, Woody Guthrie, George Gershwin, Nadia Boulanger, and Sergei Prokofiev are each introduced via a full-page, full-color, documentary-style cartoon that tells a great deal about the musician, even before the name is known. Birth and death information and a three-line summary of the artist's life let the reader gather more research data than several minutes searching through an encyclopedia might net. Two and a half pages of spirited text tell the inside information about the person and use quotes. "Musical Notes," with details that must not have fit into the story, end each presentation. For those who want more information, there is more at the back of the book in "Musical Terms," "Index of Composers" (some lives crossed paths), and "For Further Reading . . . And Listening."

884. *Lives of the Writers: Comedies, Tragedies (and What the Neighbors Thought)*. Kathleen Krull. Illustrated by Kathryn Hewitt. San Diego, CA: Harcourt Brace, 1994.
   Each featured writer's story is a Strong Passage and a good read aloud. Murasaki Shikibu, Miguel de Cervantes, William Shakespeare, Jane Austen, Hans Christian Andersen, Edgar Allan Poe, Charles Dickens, Charlotte Bronte, Emily Bronte, Emily Dickinson, Louisa May Alcott, Mark Twain, Frances Hodgson Burnett, Robert Louis Stevenson, Jack London, Carl Sandburg, E. B. White, Zora Neale Hurston, Langston Hughes, and Isaac Bashevis Singer are summarized first in a Hewitt cartoon and then demographically described by Krull. After that, a fun-filled or tragedy-torn tale of survival as a creative being is told in two and a half or so pages. This is excellent SSR fare for the new reader who has entered the Thin Books level. "Bookmarks" gives further details that Krull thinks you might enjoy. Students might read one each day for SSR and learn everything they ever wanted to know about these folks. But Krull takes no chances. After a page of literary terms and an index of writers, the last page offers "For Further Reading . . . And Writing."

885. "My First Word." From *The Story of My Life*. Helen Keller. Providence: Jamestown Publishers, 1991. Jamestown Heritage Readers series.

In this passage, Keller recalls the first time her teacher, Anne Sullivan, arrived at her house and then follows the progression of trials, tantrums, and errors until she discovered the meaning of a word.

886. "Our Boys." In *Wouldn't Take Nothing for My Journey Now*. Maya Angelou. New York: Random House, 1993, pages 119–25.

This is an incredible essay on tolerance. In it Angelou shows how everyone loses when the insidious disease of bigotry goes unaddressed. Angelou's autobiographical reports are all captivating. This passage has even more. I would sell its power short to call it a critical thinking passage. This essay should be read aloud. It should be read silently. It should be discussed in homogeneous groups, heterogeneous groups, and families.

887. "The Wild Boy of Aveyron." In *Phenomena*. Henry Billings and Melissa Billings. Providence, RI: Jamestown, 1984, pages 18–20.

"He was found digging for vegetables in the garden of a tanner who lived near Aveyron, in southern France." *Phenomena* includes twenty-one stories about incredible phenomena.

Newspaper and Magazine Articles

888. "The Andalusian Dog." L. S. Klepp. *Entertainment Weekly*, March 8, 1991, pages 50–51.

This is a book review of volume 1 (1881–1906) of John Richardson's projected four-volume *A Life of Picasso*. New York: Random House, 1995. "Richardson sensibly sees the sign of emerging genius not in the precocious, workmanlike early sketches and paintings but in the fledgling artist's stunning capacity for concentration and hard work—from the beginning, Picasso was possessed." Klepp also observes that the "brilliantly illustrated book" is in "a geographical and cultural landscape" (page 50).

889. "Bette Midler: In the Hot Seat." Patricia Nolan. *Woman's World: The Woman's Weekly* 41 October 13, 1992, pages 38 and 39.

In this question-and-answer interview, Midler tells about her little girl and how the baby changed her lifestyle, insecurities, and hopes. The sentences are pretty short and the language easy to follow.

890. "Dunaway's Big Production." Daniel Cerone. *TV Times*. *Los Angeles Times*, November 25–December 1, 1990, page 3.

After hair, makeup, and wardrobe preparations that made her four hours late for her interview, Faye Dunaway became the epitome of poise and charm. Now entering the field of movie production, she says she wants to "destroy the belief that women become less attractive, and less marketable, with age." This one-page story gives almost the entire career history of the glamour queen and her effort to design an image as a thinking human. *TV Times* and other weekly television publications that are included in the Sunday newspapers are wonderful sources of short biographies about popular people.

891. "The Hardest-Working Woman in Trash Fiction." Margy Rochlin. *The Los Angeles Times Magazine*, December 2, 1990, pages 12–22 and 52–54.

In 1949, Judith Krantz supervised fashion shoots for hat designers in Paris. Eventually she wrote articles for several women's magazines and then spent nine years at *Cosmopolitan*. When Krantz was forty-eight, she decided to drag her Smith-Corona portable into the guest bedroom to take her first crack at fiction writing. *Scruples* sold for $50,000 and in four months was a best-seller. The paperback rights for *Princess Daisy* sold for a record-breaking $3,208,875. Such are the fruits of six hours a day, five days a week. Sometimes she is asked why she keeps writing—she does not need the money. It is not about money, she argues, it is about getting something out of herself. Still, others fail to take her lurid modern fairy tales seriously. She claims that people do not understand how much work it takes to write. Indeed, her manuscripts are reportedly so well done that they are published almost as they are turned in. This inside look at a successful writer's life may prove inspirational to the mature student who is contemplating whether literacy can be worthwhile during the second fifty years of life.

892. "MM Interview: Sue Grafton and Tony Hillerman." Susan Goodman. *Modern Maturity*, July–August, 1995, pages 74–82.

Here is an easy how-to lesson on writing. Mystery writer Sue Grafton flew from her home in Santa Barbara, California, to Albuquerque, New Mexico, where Tony Hillerman opened his home for the dual interview. This compare-and-contrast story of mystery writers tells of a country boy and a city girl, both of whom live by the pen. The writers share techniques; neither is able to follow a plot outline. They write and the twists present themselves in process. Grafton admits, "When I was writing 'E' Is for Evidence I was on chapter 23 of 24 and didn't have the faintest idea how the book was going to end. I thought, I sure hope this book ends with a bang and not a whimper. And a little voice said, 'Put a bomb in it, Grafton.' So the book ends with a bombing. People who outline don't have nearly the fun we do." Hillerman was struggling to find an excuse for his policeman character to be out in a desolate area and decided to go out onto a nearby reservation. There, a vandalized windmill gave him a subplot for *The Dark Wind* that proved more exciting than the main plot. "A writer is like a bag lady going through life with a sack and pointed stick collecting stuff," he explains. Then he goes on, "You're writing all the time. I'm writing when I'm eating breakfast, when my wife is telling me something, when I'm driving   I'm running red lights and people are honking at me. I developed a great reputation in committee meetings— the guy who always took great notes." Grafton has a regular routine, getting up at 5:37 A.M., running three miles, then reading the newspaper, mostly to check on the latest homicides. She may not have thought about it, but that is comprehensible input! She is using her reading to get stimulation and new information for her writing. It is useful to read what writers have to say about the writing craft, because they are not trying to sell you on anything you must do. They just tell what works for them, and you can be the judge.

893. "Princess Stephanie Opens Her Heart in Love Song to Grace." *National Enquirer*, July 16, 1991, page 39.

The child of an American movie star and the Prince of Monaco has written a song for her late mother. "The feelings have been there since 1982 when my mother died, and they wanted to come out," explained the real-life princess, who has found a receptive audience for her singing. This half-page article is mostly simple interview quotes and the song lyrics. There is a photograph of the princess, with an inset of her mother. In just a few lines, a person can complete a full article from this tabloid, available in grocery stores across the nation. I have found the *National Enquirer* excellent sustained silent reading fare and a great starter newspaper for adults and teens. The high-interest topics build on background knowledge most Americans gain from television and help build it for newcomers who need to learn who is who.

894. "Pure Gore." Barbara Grizzuti Harrison. *The Los Angeles Times Magazine*, January 28, 1990, pages 8–16 and 38–39.

"What is the joy of writing a novel? Finishing it," says Gore Vidal, author. Complete with full-page photographs, references to the rich and famous— Jacqueline Kennedy, John Kennedy, the Duke and Duchess of Windsor, Eleanor Roosevelt—with whom he had close ties, his favorite authors and those he knows and despises, and a lengthy excerpt from his Hollywood exposé novel *The Perils of Caroline*, this is the biography of an author of our time. It is in straightforward, first-person style, making it ideal for the ESL student. Harrison has written a piece that can stand alone as a biography, making it fine reading for the native speaker as well.

895. "The Rose." In " The Kennedy Scandals." *Globe Special*. Edited by Michael J. Irish, 1991, pages 36–41.

The 100-year-old matriarch of the Kennedy clan is celebrated over several pages of historical photographs. She is presented as the saint of her family, always present in times of tragedy and triumph, both of which have accented the Kennedys' public lives. Her childhood, education, courtship with Joe Kennedy, seven children in ten years, humiliation over Joe's womanizing, and hurt over his authorizing a frontal lobotomy for their mildly retarded daughter are contrasted with the image of a busy socialite. This entire *Globe Special* issue is a series of biographies of one big family. It is written in easy-to-understand prose with a lot of quotes.

896. "When Baby Makes Two." Joe Rhodes. *TV Guide*, September 25, 1992, pages 6–10.

The issue of social values is lightly addressed, and concerns about the change of focus from working woman to woman and child are overshadowed by concern former Vice President Dan Quayle had for the image that Murphy Brown would create when she chose to have a baby without benefit of spouse. There is innuendo on current affairs, not only Quayle's direct hit on the *Murphy Brown* television series plot, but also his highly publicized misspelling of potato as a judge in a spelling bee. This kind of subplot helps build background knowledge across topics and shows how background knowledge influences comprehension. "Candy Is Dandy, But Don't Mess with Murphy," a mini interview just on the "scandal," is inset on pages 8 and 9 to help those who are not aware of the Dan Quayle-Murphy Brown problem. These two pieces, out of an easily accessible publication, provide support for writing about biographies of the real life and fictional characters involved.

Other Events and Supplements

There seems to be no lukewarm attitude about biographies. Early exposure either makes readers love 'em or leave 'em completely alone. The following activities are set up to help foster an interest in biographies by showing that the old encyclopedia-type person description is not what living breathing human beings are about. Almost anyone could be a source for an action-packed adventure. It's the writing that makes the tale.

- Interview senior citizens in your community and write their stories.

- Write a series of autobiographical incidents.

- Collect baseball and basketball cards. Compare the biographies of current sports stars with those of the past.

- Study the biographies of movie stars, identifying how getting into the industry now compares with how it was for movie greats of yesterday.

- Select a celebrity and collect news stories about that person. Compare the news stories with authorized and unauthorized biographies.

- Compare stories from small newspapers with those found in *People* magazine.

- Study the writing style of a profile in *Forbes*. Write a *Forbes*-type profile of a financier you know.

Preparing for the GED and Other Standardized Tests

Unit 15

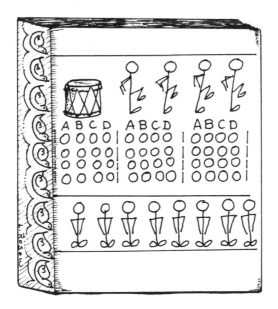

Dear Test Taker to Be,

Use of aptitude and proficiency tests is on the rise. Although they may be presented as unbiased, means based, valid, and reliable, there is one thing students worldwide have figured out: How you prepare for the specific test you have to take can make a significant impact on your scores. And one thing publishers have figured out is that students will use any book that seems to give them an edge during exam time. The books that I am previewing here are only a small portion of those published annually. There may be some helpful ones that are not on the list. So, if you find one that is helpful to you, use it—and when you pass the test, drop me a note so I can add it to the next edition of this book.

Before launching into the test preparation books themselves, I want to offer a few helpful hints:

- The more you read for pleasure, the bigger your vocabulary will get. And language—how many words you know and how you use them—will temper your reading and writing skills.

- The more you understand about history, politics, science, the arts, and social sciences, the easier it will be when you encounter a short passage that refers to a minuscule area. So read as much as you can about current and past events.

- If you read things that are easy for you to understand, you will read more, more quickly. Try using one of the thematic units in this book. Work your way from the easy reading to the challenging. The more you know about a specific topic, the more complex the material you will be able to understand.

- The more you have experienced in the arts and classical literature, the easier it will be for you to relate to references to classical figures and situations at test time. Consider, for example, all of the meaning chucked into the simple term Trojan horse. If you are not familiar with classical literature, ease into the more contemporary works first, go to plays, attend slide shows, and see old movies. Everything works together. Everything builds your background knowledge. And that helps you understand more, more quickly, when you are under pressure.

This kind of study takes time, like almost anything worthwhile. It is not intended to just get you through an exam. It will help you have a more interesting life.

Sincerely,

La Vergne Rosow

Dear Tutor and Teacher,

Note that test preparation guidebooks are updated from time to time to stay current with the tests. Libraries generally have older editions available for checkout and newer ones in the reference department. An older guidebook is fine for getting started with a student, but you want to scan the most recent edition when the student is ready to take the test. Some new test features and exam procedures may influence the student's success.

Note that most standardized tests are designed to allow for bulk processing. They are also administered in as short a period of time as possible. That means that readings are limited to short passages, and writing samples, if taken at all, are administered in a short time that allows little prewriting, thinking, editing, or development. In other words, reading and writing for a standardized test are not like the literacy-for-thinking processes we espouse in our teaching. The examples in the test books show the kinds of tasks a student will encounter during an actual exam.

Just being able to underline, attach a sticky note, or use a pencil to mark the right section can make a person feel secure. So, once students have previewed the various preparation books in the library, they may want to purchase the ones that seem most helpful.

All best,

La Vergne Rosow

Standardized Tests

General Education Development (GED)

California High School Proficiency Examination (CHSPE)

Secondary School Admission Test (SSAT)

Independent School Entrance Examination (ISEE)

Scholastic Testing Service High School Placement Test (STS)

Cooperative Entrance Exam (COOP)

U.S. Citizenship Test

Test of English as a Foreign Language (TOEFL)

Real Estate Licensing (California)

897. *Arco High School Entrance Exams.* 4th ed. Jacqueline Robinson, Dennis M. Robinson, and Eve P. Steinberg. New York: Prentice Hall Press, 1991.

Part I gives facts about the Secondary School Admission Test (SSAT), the Independent School Entrance Examination (ISEE), the Scholastic Testing Service High School Placement Test (STS), and the Cooperative Entrance Exam (COOP). Part II has a diagnostic test for synonyms, verbal analogies, sentence completions, reading comprehension, mathematics, an answer key for all of these, and a brief evaluation section that explains why one answer is more correct than another. Reading through this section can help the student understand the thinking of test designers. Note that this preparation for students wanting to enter America's best private high schools acknowledges the impact of reading on standardized test scores. "Students in the lower grades are not expected to have read as widely, are not expected to have developed as extensive a vocabulary, nor to have developed as mature an understanding of relationships as students in the upper grades" (page 53). This quote makes it clear that children of families that can afford private schools will be children who do a significant amount of reading each year, because it presumes that for those children the knowledge base of things learned from books will increase each year. So, even within the scope of the test prep book, there is the assumption that the successful test takers will be widely read.

898. *Barron's Eighth Edition GED: How to Prepare for the High School Equivalency Examination.* Murray Rockowitz, Samuel C. Brownstein, and Max Peters. New York: Barron's, 1990.

The five areas of the GED test are writing skills, social studies, science, interpreting literature and the arts, and mathematics. It is interesting to note that the reading passages for all five, including the math area, deal with real issues that are accessible through a broad base of pleasure reading. If, for example, a passage refers to the American Revolution, test takers will be able to move through the reading passage much more quickly, with greater comprehension, if they have already read about that period of U.S. history. The book gives insights into the content of the questions and the kinds of conditions under which they will be asked. For example, sixty-five minutes are allowed for the forty-five questions on interpreting literature and the arts. Of those questions, fifty percent are on popular literature, twenty-five percent on classical literature, and twenty-five percent on commentary about literature and the arts. This guide has a diagnostic exam, review tests, practice exams, study plans, and test strategies. The adult learners in my program give it a thumbs-up.

899. *Barron's Fourth Edition: How to Prepare for the CHSPE, California High School Proficiency Examination.* Sharon Weiner Green and Michael Siemon. New York: Barron's, 1993.

A diagnostic section; writing, reading, and math study guides; and two model tests with answers explained make up this book. It would be of value to look through as many editions as possible to see the kinds of reading passages that can come up and the tasks attached to them.

900. "A Dismal Report Card." Barbara Kantrowitz and Pat Wingert. *Newsweek,* June 17, 1991, pages 64–67.

This article looks at some of the issues surrounding standardized tests. "Most mainstream educators already agree that American math instruction needs a drastic overhaul, with more emphasis on group problem-solving and creative thinking rather than repetitive drills. But local schools continue to resist these prescriptions" (page 64). And the problem is nationwide, with only fourteen percent of eighth-graders scoring at or above the seventh-grade level. Money was reportedly not the only issue, as one of the best-funded school programs was near the bottom of the score chart. "The best students watched the least TV; the worst admit to six hours a day" (page 67). This report is on national math scores, not reading. Examples of various kinds of math problems, accompanied by visuals, are reproduced in the article and may help readers understand that math of the 1990s is quite different from the old workbook page chock-full of numbers. In addition, these students all had calculators to use during the test.

901. *How to Prepare for the U.S. Citizenship Test.* Gladys Alesi. New York: Barron's, 1992.

The book contains a pretest, with answers in the back of the book, a lot of government and civics information in textbook-like form, a sample citizenship test, and many collections of American trivia, such as a chronological list of the presidents with details about each. An elaborate graph giving highlights of American history from A.D. 1,000 to 1992 is certainly no way to try learning history. But it does provide an excellent vehicle for review. The person who has read short books or stories on the various topics in the citizenship test will be much better prepared than one who has tried to memorize lists of meaningless facts. This book also provides a great deal of information about how the government works—or does not work—and what to do when you are in trouble or confused.

902. *Immigration the Easy Way: The First Comprehensive Guide to U.S. Immigration Explains Sweeping Changes Under the New Immigration and Nationality Act.* Howard David Deutsch. New York: Barron's, 1992.

The introduction gives instructions on how to use this book and explains the role of the immigration lawyer. Having had many students go through the citizenship process and having seen some of them suffer extreme hardship after selecting the wrong counsel, I believe this section is well worth the time it takes to read it *before giving money to anyone*. Negotiating and understanding fees is essential, and this section uses plain talk about this sometimes embarrassing issue. Entering the country, visas, rules, green cards, the test, dual citizenship, and much more are covered in clear, easy-to-understand language. There are also fee scales and copies of forms, addresses of Immigration and Naturalization Service regional service centers in the United States, and addresses of U.S. embassies and consulates abroad.

903.   *The Princeton Review: Cracking the GED (General Education Development)*. 1994 ed. Geoff Martz. Diagnostic exams by Laurice Pearson. New York: Villard Books, 1993.

This guide takes a simple "this is the problem, how to crack it" approach to each section of the exam. Step by step, the reader is led through problems and shown how to avoid pitfalls. Actual essays and grades given by reviewers are included. There is a lot of quality lesson material in this book.

904.   *The Princeton Review: Cracking the TOEFL (Test of English as a Foreign Language)*. 1994 ed. Laurice Pearson and Liz Buffa. New York: Villard Books, 1994.

Perhaps the most valuable part of this 269-page guide comes on pages viii and ix, where there is an overview of the general academic degrees available in higher education in the United States. My students frequently ask about this puzzling maze, and I have written a number of class- or learner-specific essays on it. But the four-part answer given here is quite clear. Not so the cassette tape that is ostensibly set up to help the learner prepare for listening comprehension. It amounts to an annoying series of "stems," with a woman and man taking turns saying, "Da-da-da-da-da-DA-Da." I hope students find copies in their libraries so they do not spend precious leisure reading material dollars on it. I have found no one so far who claims this tape is even comprehensible, let alone helpful. In all fairness, I have to admit that the section "Evaluating Your Performance," which starts on page 209, offers some good ideas on that topic. It also suggests that the student should be the primary evaluator of communication success.

905.   *Real Estate Licensing SuperCourse*. 2d ed. Julie Garton-Good. New York: DREI, Arco, Macmillan, 1994.

This book has a wealth of everyday survival information, as well as the essentials for passing the professional exam of the real estate salesperson. On page 233, a brief passage, "The Money Supply," introduces the longer unit on the Federal Reserve system and how it works. Copies of an actual mortgage contract, a loan application, a contract of sale and purchase, and parts of a title insurance policy are accompanied by plain language that explains how these documents are used. There is a twenty-four-page glossary with full-sentence definitions and references to the chapters in which the words are used.

U.S.
Citizenship

Unit 16

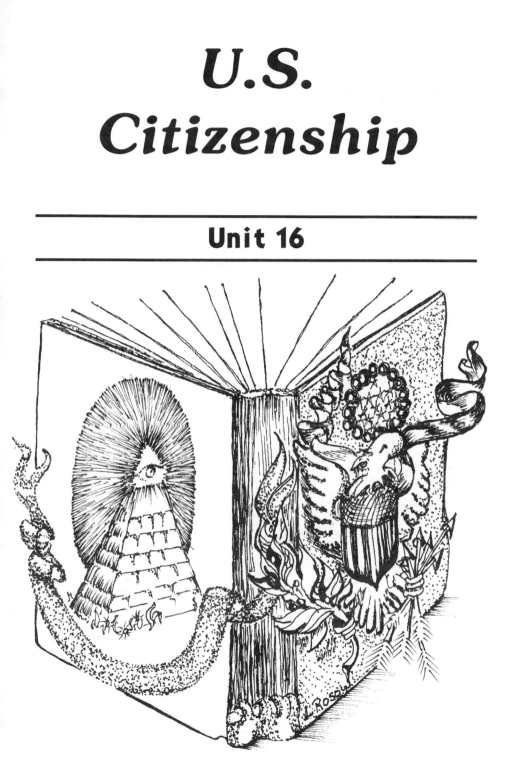

Many resident aliens are perfectly content with their status as temporary members of our society. We need to remember that as we encounter citizens of other countries. They may have a great interest in learning about Americans and how we do things, but they continue to be, first and forever, citizens of their homelands. Nonetheless, thousands of people from other lands do seek citizenship in what appears to be the promise land. For them the contents of this unit will offer progressively more informative readings, while teaching them the fundamentals of what makes Americans who they are.

An interest in this unit will come from adult students who

> want to become citizens,
>
> have family members who want to become U.S. citizens,
>
> want to learn history while developing English language skills,
>
> want to learn history while becoming better readers and writers,
>
> are already naturalized citizens but want to have informed dialogues with friends and acquaintances,
>
> want to understand present attitudes by studying past events,
>
> want to learn more about American culture, or
>
> want to learn English through history and government.

In addition to using this unit to help them establish a range of readings and related vocabulary, you may also want to encourage them to read selections from the units on U.S. history, the arts, science, and the planet. A few selections from those units are already in this unit but by no means all.

If students have a nonreading background or little education, they may not understand the power of reading easy, interesting texts. The more they read, the easier it will be to read faster and with better comprehension. Starting out with easy books is best, even if the student is in a great hurry to earn citizenship. Easy reading will provide the foundation—the background knowledge—essential to comprehend more complex material on the same subject. Consider, too, that books with a lot of relevant, supportive pictures will give students tremendous amounts of information at a glance. It is not cheating to try to learn as much as you can in as many different ways as you can at the same time. That is the intelligent approach to conscious learning.

At one time I taught amnesty classes and had to acquire a range of materials to fit the citizenship test. With that experience in mind, I put little emphasis on some parts of our history that you may believe are of value, and I offer multiple opportunities to read about others. This is because getting the same information from a variety of contexts will help the student prepare for the citizenship test without trekking through a mass of material unrelated to the test. Even picture books have been selected with a thought to providing the content of that test.

First Readers and Picture Books

906. *By the Dawn's Early Light: The Story of the Star-Spangled Banner.* Steven Kroll. Illustrated by Dan Adreasen. New York: Scholastic, 1994.

The illustrations alone make this book worth opening. On the last page is an index that ranges from Africa to Woodrow Wilson. A one-page bibliography is provided, and there is an 1814 map of Washington, D.C., and a map of the Battle of Baltimore area, September 12–14, 1814. There is a well-written description of the sea battle and how the British attempted to land during a rain. An author's note provides further information on that historic incident, noting the years it took for Key's poem to become popular and the fact that it was not until 1931 that it became the official national anthem. A photograph of Key's original manuscript is across from the author's note.

907. *The Go-Around Dollar.* Barbara Johnston Adams. Illustrated by Joyce Audy Zarins. New York: Maxwell Macmillan International, 1992.

This is almost a picture book, with huge, clear illustrations on every page. This easy reader takes you on a whirlwind tour through a lot of little-known data about money. Presented almost as trivia snippets, legal and practical information and related vocabulary are conveyed easily. This is a great supplement to a money lesson.

908. *How Many Days to America? A Thanksgiving Story.* Eve Bunting. Illustrated by Beth Peck. New York: Clarion, 1988.

A family is forced to flee in the night via a small, overcrowded boat, only to be exploited and further denied civil liberties. Though this story is usually listed under Hispanic reading, I have found its impact equally powerful on Vietnamese and Cambodian immigrants.

909. *If You Grew Up with Abraham Lincoln.* Ann McGovern. Illustrated by George Ulrich. New York: Scholastic, 1992.

This book gives historical insights on day-to-day living—what people ate, how they built houses, what they did for fun, what school was like, what a typical lesson was like, the dangers people faced, and how they traveled. McGovern's style is consistently light, her research is consistently professional. These qualities seem typical of all books in this series.

910. *If You Lived at the Time of Martin Luther King.* Ellen Levine. Illustrated by Beth Peck. New York: Scholastic, 1990.

Illustrated with brown-line pencil drawings on nearly every page, this book gives insights into the early days of the civil rights struggle as well as the life of Martin Luther King, Jr. In a question-and-answer format, segregation, Freedom Riders, violence, nonviolence, voting rights, and the conflict with Malcolm X are addressed.

911. *If You Lived in Colonial Times.* Ann McGovern. Illustrated by June Otani. New York: Scholastic, 1992.

The book opens to a timeline that places Colonial times in American history. This clearly illustrated document of life from the early 1600s to 1730 is set up in a short question and long answer format. For example, what happened to people who broke laws? This is answered in one full page of illustrated text that details the kind of punishment a woman who committed a crime might have experienced. The next full page does the same for men. Although the book is clearly designed for children, I found it informative, and many of my adult students have enjoyed the informal introduction to that period, too.

912. *If You Traveled on the Underground Railroad.* Ellen Levine. Illustrated by Larry Johnson. New York: Scholastic, 1988.

From 1830 to 1865, the Underground Railroad offered the prospect of liberty to slaves who used the secret network. This book is handled in a question-and-answer format that addresses the who, what, when, where, and why of the role that the Underground Railroad played. The heavy, large print holds its own, even on those pages with overpowering illustrations. This sixty-four-page book is an excellent introduction to units on slavery, U.S. history, human rights, racism and tolerance, the Constitution, and the Civil War.

913. *If You Were There When They Signed the Constitution.* Elizabeth Levy. Illustrated by Joan Holub. New York: Scholastic, 1992.

Large print, clear illustrations, and easy-to-follow text give a wealth of information about the social and political climate that prevailed in America in 1787. A question-and-answer format gives both historical information and short biographies of the key players involved in designing the Constitution. The high-interest story bounces between close-up shots of daily life and general statements about the period. It is an excellent reader for anyone wanting a fast report on a complex time.

914. *A More Perfect Union: The Story of Our Constitution.* Betsy Maestro and Giulio Maestro. New York: Lothrop, Lee & Shepard, 1987.

Ten years after the signing of the Declaration of Independence, the colonies were in need of a more secure alliance. The story of how that alliance was written unfolds quickly in the first forty-two pages. A map of the colonies of 1787 sets the stage, and simple colored drawings show up on every page. Then, on page 44, the Preamble and summaries of Articles I–VII appear. On page 45 the names of the signers and the colonies from which they came appear. Then a table of dates from 1774 to 1791 gives the historical high points, followed by notes on the Connecticut Compromise, a list of facts about the delegates, and a chronological list of colonies that ratified the Constitution. On the last page are brief summaries of the Amendments to the Constitution, numbers I–XXVI. It looks like a children's book. It informs like a history and government text.

915. *Paul Revere's Ride.* Henry Wadsworth Longfellow. Illustrated by Ted Rand. New York: Dutton Children's Books, 1990.

The Old North Church, Boston, the Charles River with HMS *Somerset*, Charlestown, Bunker Hill, Arlington, Lexington, and many other historical names on maps inside the front and back covers give a visual reference to the full trek suggested by Longfellow's famous poem. The rhythm and flow of Longfellow's language provide a fine opportunity for the teacher to demonstrate how to deliver text in an entertaining way. Dramatically powerful yet detailed watercolors support the large print. On the last page, a brief historical note gives background on the war that this spark ignited.

916.   *The President's Cabinet and How It Grew.* Nancy Winslow Parker. New York: HarperCollins, 1992.

This clearly illustrated book traces the development of the president's cabinet from 1789, when George Washington began with a cabinet of four. It has an easy reference chart that shows which additions or subtractions occurred under which presidents, and it gives brief job descriptions for each post. There is also a colorful graph detailing the millions of dollars spent by various departments in 1991. The top spender, for example, was Defense at $317,662 million; number eight was education at $23,711 million; and last was Commerce at $2,771 million. All of this information is presented in a salient form that fosters dialogue about contemporary issues.

917.   *The Star-Spangled Banner.* Illustrated by Peter Spier. New York: Dell, 1992.

This is a must have for every American home. Each exquisite two-page illustration demonstrates the meaning of a single line of the national anthem. A brief profile of the state of the nation in the throes of the War of 1812 gives a sense of the people, places, and terrible struggle that framed the poem that would become a famous song. A map of the war zone gives a clear idea of where the author, Francis Scott Key, was during his moment of glory and inspiration. A copy of the original handwritten text is opposite the map. There is also a two-page spread of historical U.S. flags. The lyrics are set to music on one page, for the pianist in our midst. This large paperback looks like a children's book, and is, indeed, a Reading Rainbow selection, but it has value to every adult interested in American history. I have found it useful for ESL students and adult new readers. For a person who wants to understand the language of the national anthem, this is the book.

918.   *The Wall.* Eve Bunting. Illustrated by Ronald Himler. New York: Clarion Books, 1990.

Just a few perfectly chosen words to a page and sensitive, detailed watercolors deliver powerful thoughts about loss and eternity. A young boy describes the visitors to the Vietnam War memorial as his father searches for his father's name. As they leave, the child acknowledges the honor of having your name on the wall, but he'd rather have his grandpa. This book puts the Vietnam War into an understandable timeframe for people born since 1965.

919.   *"Wanted Dead or Alive": The True Story of Harriet Tubman.* Ann McGovern. New York: Scholastic, 1965.

This story of a courageous slave who helped over 300 others to freedom begins when seven-year-old Harriet was rented out as a servant. Beatings with a whip left lifelong scars on a woman who lived to read of the Emancipation Proclamation and to nurse the sick throughout the Civil War. Large print and poetic language assist the reader through a pivotal period in history.

Between Picture Books and Thin Books

920. *The Declaration of Independence.* Dennis Fradin. Chicago: Childrens Press, 1988. New True Books series.

This book starts with a Fourth of July celebration and leads the reader through an extremely complex part of American history in just a few pages. The impact of Thomas Paine's book *Common Sense*, in which Paine expounds the reasons why colonists should want independence, is made obvious. And the pragmatics of how the document was written are spelled out in easy-to-understand language.

921. *True Stories About Abraham Lincoln.* Ruth Belov Gross. Illustrated by Charles Turzak. New York: Scholastic, 1973.

Each story is one page long and is written in simple past tense. There is a straightforward progression from Lincoln's birth to his death, with the salient historical features of his life simply laid out. Though the style is less than compelling, there is good, everyday language throughout, and the short format allows the reader to complete a story at one sitting. Meanwhile, the format provides a linear history lesson that will be valuable to adults just learning about U.S. history and the concepts of the Lincoln era. The book is illustrated by Charles Turzak in strong black-and-white woodcuts. The text is in easy-to-read type that is well leaded. Words are never broken at the end of lines, a positive feature for a new reader or one unfamiliar with the language. The naturalized citizen is expected to know about Abraham Lincoln.

Thin Books

922. *Abraham Lincoln.* Kathie Billingslea Smith. Illustrated by James Seward. New York: Scholastic, 1987.

A barefoot lad in western Kentucky is introduced. Then his mother dies, father remarries, and the boy is fortunate enough to have a stepmother who honors his love of books. He is married, a child is born and dies, two more are born, and the man becomes president of the United States. A war over slavery, the Civil War, begins, the Emancipation Proclamation is signed, and another son dies. The war ends, and the reelected president is assassinated. All this in just a few pages of easy-to-read text, with clear drawings on each of them.

923. *Always to Remember: The Story of the Vietnam Veterans Memorial.* Brent Ashabranner. Photographs by Jennifer Ashabranner. New York: Scholastic, 1988.

This clear account of the historical and emotional roots of the U.S. involvement in the Vietnam War gives many human details about people affected by it. Wounded in action and witness to the deaths or wounding of over half his company, veteran Jan C. Scruggs came home to a legacy of shame for having gone to war. One night after seeing the movie *The Deer Hunter*, he was driven to make a memorial of substance to the effort and suffering that had transpired. It would have the names of all those men and women lost in the Vietnam War. This dream became an obsession that led to a nationwide competition, with 1,421 designs submitted and judged without names or identification of any kind. The Wall, entry number 1,026, by twenty-one-year-old Yale student Maya Ying Lin, was selected.

The daughter of Chinese immigrants was to make a profound contribution to the art and history of America.

924.   *America at War! Battles That Turned the Tide*. Brian Black. New York: Scholastic, 1992.

From the American Revolution to the Persian Gulf War, battles are set in historical and political perspectives. This clearly written book gives insights into the emotional and complex issues surrounding military activities that changed the course of history. An adult new reader and her tutor began trading off passages of this book and came away with far more than literacy. Both sang the praises of this well-written history. It is also appropriate for ESL students who are attempting to learn about America and its past. This book provides an introduction to world geography.

925.   *The Bill of Rights*. E. B. Fincher. New York: Franklin Watts, 1978.

In just sixty-six pages, historical details, discussion of each amendment, and controversies over wording are supported by occasional etchings and photographs. A two-page glossary explains simply terms like double jeopardy, ex post facto, and petit jury. The first ten Amendments are at the end of the book.

926.   *The Constitution*. David P. Currie and Joyce L. Stevos. Glenview, IL: Scott, Foresman, 1991.

A clear, simple description of the background of American history, starting with our English heritage and the basic laws of the colonies, leads into the Declaration of Independence. The book discusses the development of the Constitution and covers the twenty-six Amendments. Sections of the Constitution and the Amendments are clarified in modern language set in red. On page 108, an essay details the Civil War Amendments and the problems getting these laws enforced.

927.   *D-Day*. R. Conrad Stein. Chicago: Childrens Press, 1993.

This Cornerstones of Freedom series book tells of one long day, June 6, 1944, that marked the turn of the tide in the war against Adolf Hitler and all that he represented in human suffering.

928.   *The Day Pearl Harbor Was Bombed: A Photo History of World War II*. George Sullivan. New York: Scholastic, 1991.

A one-page chronology of important dates from 1933 to 1946 and a bibliography of further reading suggestions supplement this well-organized, action-packed history of World War II. Though there is little text on each page, the vocabulary is by no means easy. Words like strategists, kamikaze, Allies, throngs, victory, stunning, and headquarters pepper the text. Historical references to Okinawa, the Solomon Islands, Berlin, Nazis, the Soviet Union, New Guinea, Guam, Saipan, the Mariana Islands, Leyte Gulf, the Philippines, Manila, Japan, Iwo Jima, the Pacific, the Boeing B-29, and the atomic bomb make this vocabulary intensive for the new reader and ESL learner. But the photographs support the text and make just page turning a worthwhile activity for someone seeking an overview of the war.

929. *Days of Courage: The Little Rock Story*. Richard Kelso. General editor Alex Haley. Illustrated by Mel Williges. New York: Steck-Vaughn, 1993.

The manifestations of racism and bigotry are detailed in historical events stemming from the actions of a small group of people who decided to push the Constitution into reality. An afterword and rich endnotes give more detail about the civil rights efforts of the not-yet-distant past.

930. *The Emancipation Proclamation: Why Lincoln Really Freed the Slaves*. Robert Young. New York: Dillon Press, 1994.

Dramatic photographs, detailed drawings, copies of posters and children's alphabet book pages, vignettes of particular interest, and wide margins all contribute to making this an accessible text. Controversial issues are laid bare in simply stated facts. A timeline starting with the 1600s and ending with the 1870 Fifteenth Amendment, which gave blacks the right to vote, gives a meaningful overview of racism in the United States. That is followed by the actual text of the Emancipation Proclamation and a brief list of suggestions for further reading. This book is easy, academic, and informative.

931. *George Washington*. Kathie Billingslea Smith. Illustrated by James Seward. New York: Scholastic, 1987.

This thin booklet makes the first president both human and historical. It also gives a clear picture of how soldiering was done during the American Revolution. The type is large and easy to read, and a large portion of every page is filled with helpful illustrations.

932. *How the White House Really Works*. George Sullivan. New York: Scholastic, 1989.

Exactly what goes on in that giant house that belongs to all Americans is the subject of this book. The reader is taken on a whirlwind tour and introduced to a few of the famous residents, the fourth-floor correspondence office, the games people who live there play, and the guards who protect them. This book humanizes one part of the president's life.

933. *The John F. Kennedy Assassination*. R. Conrad Stein. Chicago: Childrens Press, 1992. Cornerstones of Freedom series.

This book details the day of November 22, 1963, and the mood of the nation, politically, spiritually, and socially, during that time. The radio announcement, the words of the assassin, and the swearing in of Vice President Lyndon Johnson give an immediacy to the moment that was followed by an incredible funeral, the spotlight on a first lady and two little children turned widow and orphans, and the bizarre assassination of the assassin. Questions that continue to haunt those who remember the day are raised anew for the readers of this book.

934. *Lou Gehrig: One of Baseball's Greatest*. Guernsey Van Riper, Jr. New York: Macmillan, 1986.

This large-print paperback is one of a series of books called Childhood of Famous Americans. The story starts with the dilemma of a young boy ridiculed for being fat. It also addresses the pain of ethnic hatred expressed against children with German surnames when President Wilson declared war against the German government. This clearly written story is a good, fast read.

935. *Our Constitution*. Linda Carlson Johnson. Brookfield, CT: Millbrook Press, 1992. I Know America series.

Historical paintings and drawings support an easy-to-read text that focuses on numerous conflicts during the design of the Constitution and the changes made both in the process and through Amendments. For example, on page 25, a vignette discusses the problem of how to count slaves. Slaves were not counted as full people: ". . . they decided that a state's population would be the total of all 'free Persons' plus 'three-fifths of all other Persons.' In other words, a slave would count as only three fifths of a person. It wasn't until after the bloody Civil War that black people would be counted as full citizens in the United States." On page 37, a rally for the Equal Rights Amendment is shown with a brief caption stating it failed to be ratified, and on page 43, the ERA and the Nineteenth Amendment are mentioned. Page 46 has a chronology from A.D. 1215 to 1993, and a bibliography of further readings is provided. So is an extensive index. This book has been prepared for study with textbook attention, but it is much more palatable and certainly easier to carry around.

936. *Our United States Geography: Our Regions and People*. Beverly Vaillancourt. Maywood, NJ: Peoples Publishing Group, 1994.

This book is chock-full of coherent, informative short passages, ideal for sustained silent reading or for lunch breaks. The United States is broken into nine regions, clusters of states that give a logical sense to the areas where Americans live, work, and play. A regional map shows the group of states; detailed information is provided on each state within the region. A state history, local customs, industries, and items of interest are conveyed in easy-to-read text. Local color is provided through details like the recipe for sourdough pancakes popular in Arkansas. This is an excellent way of introducing the entire nation to someone who has not had an opportunity to study about America. It would also provide good background information for an adult planning a trip.

937. *Shh! We're Writing the Constitution*. Jean Fritz. Pictures by Tomie dePaola. New York: G. P. Putnam's Sons, 1987.

The humorous dePaola illustrations poke fun at all the pomp and circumstance surrounding the company of men. (Indeed, the only woman in the book is shown with her face half hidden, and the only girl is in her important father's pipe dream.) And Jean Fritz's equally irreverent style of addressing the problems of logistics and personalities makes this a lively adventure back in time. The text is quite readable without seeming simplified, and a section of notes gives this an academic flavor. After that comes the actual Constitution of the United States. This is a fine teaching text. I have used it many times with ESL students and others who were preparing for U.S. citizenship.

938. *The Story of Henry Ford and the Automobile*. Zachary Kent. Chicago: Childrens Press, 1990. Cornerstones of Freedom series.

The book opens with a pictorial history of the evolution of the automobile. The fast-moving story bounces into action with an 1896 episode in which the impulsive engineer breaks down a wall to remove the vehicle he has built too large for the doorway. The story progresses through the development of affordable transportation for most Americans and ends with the demise of Ford's honor and control over his company, and finally the 1947 death of the man who was a legend in his own time.

939. *The Story of Mississippi Steamboats.* R. Conrad Stein. Illustrated by Tom Dunnington. Chicago: Childrens Press, 1987. Cornerstones of Freedom series.

This book covers about 100 years on the Mississippi River, from 1850 to 1950, and tells the tale of capitalism and luxury and a lifestyle that is part of Americana. This approach to both history and geography will help the would-be citizen get a handle on a large section of the United States.

940. *The Story of Presidential Elections.* Jim Hargrove. Chicago: Childrens Press, 1988. Cornerstones of Freedom series.

This book opens to a 1789 inaugural painting of George Washington and then quickly jumps to the ballot box and the formal procedure related to it. The tumultuous evolution of this process is neatly spelled out. Also covered are various Amendments to the Constitution, the Electoral College, the emerging power of PACs, national conventions, and more. Suffice it to say, it is not just a how-to-vote booklet, though it does make a sound statement about why so many people consider the right to vote so important. Many ESL students have given this book a thumbs-up, even after they passed the test. They suggest that the book explains the process that being a citizen is all about.

941. *The Story of the Boston Tea Party.* R. Conrad Stein. Illustrated by Keith Neely. Chicago: Childrens Press, 1984. Cornerstones of Freedom series.

Details of the Boston Massacre and historic names like Samuel Adams, John Adams, John Hancock, Paul Revere, and Joseph Warren make this little history book come alive with information about how the colonies broke loose from British rule. Notions of taxation without representation and a tax on tea that might have changed Americans' beverage of choice from tea to coffee are all spelled out in thirty-two action-packed pages.

942. *The Story of the Nineteenth Amendment.* R. Conrad Stein. Illustrated by Keith Neely. Chicago: Childrens Press, 1983. Cornerstones of Freedom series.

Large print, occasionally obstructed by illustration washes, tells of women's efforts to get the right to vote. A century of struggle over this human rights issue is covered in just thirty-one pages of easy-to-understand language. Drawings of the various players in this U.S. drama give the names human characteristics. This book offers newsreel reporting with fireside anecdotes. It is a good introductory reader for a small group or an individual who is ready to discuss or write about suffrage.

943. *The Story of the Rough Riders.* Zachary Kent. Chicago: Childrens Press, 1991. Cornerstones of Freedom series.

The First U.S. Volunteer Cavalry Regiment, known as the Rough Riders and led by Colonel Theodore Roosevelt, was a renegade collection of soldiers from wealthy and poor roots who had to tame their own horses before they could use them for training in San Antonio, Texas. Upon arrival in Cuba, they diminished Spain's holdings three times: Cuba was freed; the United States gained control of Puerto Rico; and the United States also gained 48 years of control over the

Philippines. The seventeen days of wild, often undisciplined fighting in Cuba in 1898 was called the Spanish-American War. One hundred and thirty-three days after the Rough Riders assembled, they disbanded. Roosevelt subsequently became governor of New York, vice president of the United States, and then the twenty-sixth president.

944. *The Story of the Teapot Dome Scandal.* Jim Hargrove. Chicago: Childrens Press, 1989. Cornerstones of Freedom series.

This is, in fact, a story of the Roaring Twenties, also known as the Jazz Age, when women's skirts for the first time rose above the knee, the number of Americans who owned automobiles tripled, and the Eighteenth Amendment to the Constitution was passed (January 16, 1920) prohibiting the manufacture, sale, and transport of alcohol, and then repealed in 1933. President Warren G. Harding, one of the most popular presidents ever, was known for extramarital affairs, heavy drinking, and associations with scoundrels of all sorts, many of whom ended up as presidential appointees. The scandal was not about tea but government-owned oil reserves in Wyoming and other areas that were exploited in bizarre and creative ways. When Harding died amid extraordinary controversy, Vice President Calvin Coolidge became president, did little to bring about reforms, and won reelection with no trouble. " 'The nation wanted nothing done,' humorist Will Rogers joked about Coolidge, 'and he done it.' "

945. *The Story of the Women's Movement.* Maureen Ash. Chicago: Childrens Press, 1989. Cornerstones of Freedom series.

This booklet opens with a photo of two English police officers arresting a woman who was demonstrating for the right to vote in front of the prime minister's house. The story begins in England in 1827 with the case study of Caroline Norton, who, as a married woman, had no right to keep her children or the money she earned from writing. Further, her husband was within his rights when he beat her while she was pregnant and when he separated her from her three sons, one of whom died of blood poisoning in his care. During her lifetime, Norton campaigned for and won some women's rights. Five years after her death, a law was passed allowing married women the same rights as unmarried ones, though not the same rights as men. Numerous other women took up the fight to change laws that were based on their assumed inferiority to men. It was difficult for them to be taken seriously by those who considered them categorically less intelligent and who passed laws denying girls entry into academic schools. "Girls were too weak, it was believed, to learn mathematics—it would make them go mad" (page 9). The story then moves to the United States, whose Constitution at that time totally ignored the rights of women, blacks, and Native Americans. Allowed to serve as emergency substitutes during wars, women in England and America continued to be denied civil rights. During the 1920s they earned the right to vote, but in the 1930s, twenty-six states passed laws prohibiting married women from getting jobs, and where they could work they were paid about sixty-five percent of what men earned for the same output. Considerable discussion is given to both sides of the Equal Rights Amendment and to statistics, including that fact that in 1987 women earned seventy cents for every dollar earned by men, and a college-educated woman can expect to earn about the same as a male high school dropout. This dynamic little history book is chock-full of facts and famous names.

946. *Thunder at Gettysburg*. Patricia Lee Gauch. Illustrated by Stephen Gammell. New York: Bantam Books, 1975.

Through the experience of fourteen-year-old Tillie Pierce, the reader discovers the terrible reality of one dreadful day in 1863. Based on an actual account, this simply told, tear-wrenching adventure gives a strong sense of how it was as North fought South. The large print and wide margins offer a quick read. A simple map at the front assists comprehension of text that tells how war moved from an entertaining idea to grim reality.

947. *The United States Holocaust Memorial Museum: America Keeps the Memory Alive*. Eleanor H. Ayer. New York: Dillon Press, 1994.

This book introduces the contents of the museum by leading the reader level by level through the powerful exhibits and impressions the visitor experiences there.

948. *A Wall of Names: The Story of the Vietnam Veterans Memorial*. Judy Donnelly. Illustrated with photographs. New York: Random House, 1991.

This seemingly simple account of the Vietnam War Memorial moves progressively through the impact of the war on teenage soldiers, inhuman encounters with the elements of war in a swamp, the killings of U.S. peace protesters, veterans' return home, the memorial design controversy and compromise, and letters and gifts left at the Wall. Documented with photographs taken in the United States and Vietnam, this American perspective of "The Most Hated War" wrenches the heart while teaching details about a piece of history that is too often simplified. Of special interest may be the fact that the winning design for the Wall was done as a school assignment and earned only a grade of "B." The large text is easy to read, and the photographs support this emotionally charged account.

949. *Westward with Columbus: Set Sail on the Voyage That Changed the World*. John Dyson. Photographs by Peter Christopher. New York: Scholastic, 1991.

You could almost be there. This book reads like a novel. Details like the discovery of gold in the riverbeds and edible iguanas help bring to life the triumphs and ordeals of this most important sea adventure. A two-page illustration of the sinking *Santa Maria* makes it clear that this was no child's play. A glossary at the end of the book is full of fascinating facts. A map on page 42 shows the Atlantic Ocean, all the land points on both sides that played a role in the Columbus adventures, probable routes taken by the explorer, and the ocean currents that clearly played a part in history.

Challenging

950. *Children of the Dust Bowl: The True Story of the School at Weedpatch Camp*. Jerry Stanley. Illustrated with historical photographs. New York: Crown, 1992.

This book briefly describes how agricultural jobs in the Dust Bowl states declined by 400,000 between 1930 and 1940, when "nearly 50 percent of Oklahoma's farms changed hands in bankruptcy court sales" and a mass of displaced and starving people headed for California. On page 5, the Dust Bowl, 1936–1940, is depicted on a map of nine states. A dark, grainy section shows a giant teardrop shape where no rain fell on farmlands for a long time—and then the winds came.

A political-topographical map of historic Route 66, "Mother Road," names the likely stopover spots, places to find day work, and trouble spots, too—Shamrock, Amarillo, Flagstaff, Kingman, Mojave Desert, Tehachapi Mountains. It has an inset U.S. map with an outline of the Route 66 area, pages 14–15. Another political-topographical map, page 24, shows the intersection of Routes 66 and 99 in California, again with an inset of the whole state. Kern County, Tulare County, Kings County, Visalia, Delano, Bakersfield, and Weedpatch are shown. In California, the Okies were believed to be stupid and shiftless and were often told to move on. The type is easy on the eyes, the margins wide, the historical photographs dramatic, and the prose compelling. This history book will hold the attention of any adult interested in the United States, and it readily lends itself to younger students, if used in a teacher reads aloud and class discusses format. The introduction links the Okie experience with John Steinbeck's historical fiction *The Grapes of Wrath*, but the children of the Dust Bowl are absolutely real. This is another part of our history that will not be on the citizenship test, but it has a lot to do with the survival of newcomers.

951. *The Civil War EXTRA: From the Pages of The Charleston Mercury and The New York Times*. Edited by Eugene P. Moehring and Arleen Keylin. New York: Arno Press, 1975.

Newspaper stories from two perspectives cover the war from 1861 to 1865, giving the reader a chance to see how the nation's journalists handled the day-to-day issues of civil war. Most of the pages have been reconstructed from stories throughout the papers, with some sections deleted simply because the print was illegible. The typeface is small, and the language is sometimes amusing, but the story of the war and the salient issues of honor and determination are reflected in both papers. This book is full of interesting read-aloud snippets, though hardly a column is without some impossible-to-decipher words. On April 17, 1861, *The Charleston Mercury* says, "Our readers know that we have repeatedly declared that we did not believe that a war between the North and the South would be the result of a dissolution of the Union by the secession of the Southern States. With the sound of our cannon still ringing in our ears, we are of the same opinion still. That the brutal fanatics who sit in the high places at Washington are ready to plunge the whole country into contest and blood, we have never doubted. It was a thorough conviction of their treacherous and desperate hatred of the South that compelled us to urge, as the only course of safety for the South, a prompt and eternal separation from their power." On the same day, *The New York Times* gave a report on the "Experience of the Times Correspondent as a Prisoner of War," as he reported, "Whenever the haze lifted, I could discover the sacred flag of our country proudly spreading itself to the breeze. Although the shot fell around it thick and fast, yet it seemed to possess an absolute power of intangibility and nothing could disturb it. The scene was solemn in the extreme."

952. *Civil War Parks*. Rev. ed. William C. "Jack" Davis. Photography by David Muench. Las Vegas, NV: KC Publications, 1992. The Story Behind the Scenery series.

A centerfold of the Civil War area, historical paintings, a small sample of Lincoln's handwritten Gettysburg Address, and well-composed color photographs all serve as support for Challenging yet entertaining text. It is the kind of book a new speaker of English or a new reader might use first as an adult picture book and revisit, gaining vocabulary and historical knowledge over time. The large magazine format makes the book easy to carry and allows considerable amounts of text to be large and easy on the eyes. This is one of a series of such books—designed by different people—all of which are loaded with rich data. I have to rate the books as Challenging because sophisticated language is used. However, these books, by virtue of their layout and visuals, are much easier to read than some other works under the Challenging heading. This and the rest of the books in the series will foster an understanding of American geography and history.

953. *Ellis Island.* Wilton S. Tifft. Foreword by Lee Iacocca. Chicago: Contemporary Books, 1990.
   This is an oversized picture book with a rich collection of documentary photographs illustrating every chapter. Copies of passports, baggage tags, and architectural drawings also give a sense of reality to this distant time in U.S. history. On pages 55–63, "The Rise of Anti-Immigration Sentiment" explains that the U.S. Census Bureau's announcement that there were no more unclaimed frontier acres led to reluctance to admit more immigrants. And the fears of many marginally established laborers that newer immigrants would take even lesser wages produced anti-immigrant sentiment. The nativist movement of the 1890s also gave rise to racism. "The fears of nativists were not restricted to the number of immigrants but focused as well on their character and origins" (page 55). The newer immigrants promised unwelcome change. "Many were Catholic. Most spoke unfamiliar languages. Many were unskilled, many uneducated" (page 55). "Anti-immigration factions sought to restrict immigrants of eastern European peasant stock . . . because it was felt they would 'pollute the young nation's bloodline' " (page 57). In 1897, promoting a literacy test as a standard for admission, Henry Cabot Lodge spoke to the U.S. Senate: "Mr. President, more precious even than forms of government are the mental and moral qualities which make what we call our race." He continued to warn that the nation was in peril of "a single danger, and that is by changing the quality of our race and citizenship through the wholesale infusion of races whose traditions and inheritances, whose thoughts and whose beliefs are wholly alien to ours and with whom we have never assimilated or even been associated in the past, the danger has begun" (page 58). The heated debate over this proposal is detailed. Close-up shots of individuals, photos of crowds of people on the deck of a ship in harbor, and remarkable documentation of ethnic dress make this well worth the time of any student of documentary photography. Today, most Americans enter the United States via other channels. This book will help them see how immigration occurred during an earlier part of our history.

954. *Letters from the Promised Land: Swedes in America, 1840–1914.* Edited by H. Arnold Barton. Minneapolis, MN: University of Minnesota Press for the Swedish Pioneer Historical Society, 1975.
   This period of greatest migration from Sweden to the United States is discussed through immigrants' letters and diaries and through travel accounts by Swedish visitors. Religious persecution, language difficulties, economic strife on both sides of the Atlantic, and the most difficult period—the first six months—are

all detailed in these documents. There are several particularly telling passages: Foul air, cramped quarters below deck, putrid water, moldy and wormy food that was often in short supply, sickness, and death were standard during the eight- to ten-week voyage. This is so much like the slave transport, the experiences of the poor Irish, and the Vietnamese and Cambodian boat people, that it bears comparative analysis in the classroom or tutoring situation, particularly for ESL students. Note the first paragraph on page 14. Poor crops in Sweden from 1867 to 1869 are discussed on page 139. Illiteracy, spelling deficiencies, and the use of mixed Swedish and English in letters are covered in a letter of complaint to the editor of *Hemlandet* from the Swedish postmaster S. M. Korling, who also complains that addresses are often so incomplete that letters must be opened to find out who should receive them. Even then, if the letter is unsigned, it must be passed from hand to hand until someone recognizes the handwriting or contents, pages 140–41. Language acquisition is addressed on pages 196–97 in a letter of April 10, 1888, to Sister Lotten. The letter explains what we now call the Silent Period in 1888 terms. The young writer says, "[I]t is hardest the first half year as long as you can't manage with the language, but if you only can happen to find decent folks to work for it goes well and good humor is something wherever you go." About 1902 another letter details how satisfaction with America parallels language acquisition. That is, the immigrant experience begins with overwhelming homesickness that evolves into a love of the new country as English becomes more a part of the immigrant, page 290. These letters will not help anyone pass the U.S. citizenship test, but I have included them because they tell a universal tale, one that may have emotional value for the person who discovers America and what it really is not.

955. *Oregon Trail.* Dan Murphy. Photography by Gary Ladd. Las Vegas, NV: KC Publications, 1993. The Story Behind the Scenery series.

On a simple U.S. map is marked Independence, Missouri, the start of this massive migration westward. Throughout the book, the progression is graphically documented as the dotted line inches toward Oregon City. As often has been the case, hard economic times or crop failures at home made the promise of greener pastures impossible to disbelieve. Quoted on page 3 is Peter Burnett, future governor of California: "Then, with a twinkle in his eye he said, 'Gentlemen, they do say that out in Oregon the pigs are running about under the great acorn trees, round and fat, and already cooked, with knives and forks sticking in them so that you can cut off a slice whenever you are hungry.' . . . Father was the first to sign his name." An equally jubilant quote comes in 1846 from Donner Party member Edwin Bryant, before the terrible blizzard and horrid end to that group of travelers whose name is lent to Donner Pass. Salt Lake City, intended destination for Mormons seeking a safer life and starting point for those harvesting travelers' souls, also documented casualties—some killed for their beliefs and lifestyle, others victims of the heat, cold, and fierce reception by natural elements of Zion. Though the scenery photographs are rich and close-ups detailed, the large patches of well-written text qualify this book as Challenging reading. With this magazine-format book, the adult will become informed about a large geographic area of the United States and a significant chunk of history.

956. *A Pocket History of the United States.* 8th rev. ed. Allan Nevins and Henry Steele Commager with Jeffrey Morris. New York: Washington Square Press, 1986.

This is a chronology of the United States from colonization through the 1984 presidential election. It may be regarded as a primer for an adult who wants to learn about the United States in one difficult read. However, the units are set up so that topics are covered within just a few pages. For example, "Church and State in the Colonies," pages 19–23, offers a fast history of the issue, the emotional and practical pros and cons, and a summary statement: "As the decades passed, most colonists became convinced that it was just and prudent to let men worship as they pleased." Now, the sexist language may reflect the times in which this unit is cast, so I will hold comment on that, though the issue of gender-laden language is a major topic in all my language and literacy classes. This little book offers an opportunity to get in a complete read during ten minutes of SSR or a lunch break. A well-organized bibliography offers further readings grouped by period and topic, and there are several meaningful maps supporting the text.

957. *USKids History: Book of the American Revolution.* Howard Egger-Bovet and Marlene Smith Baranzini. Illustrated by Bill Sanchez. New York: Little, Brown, 1994.

Most of this book is written either from a child's perspective or about a child of the period. And some of the text seems to have been written down to make the words and sentences shorter, netting less comprehension. Even so, there is a lot of interesting information, and it is worth having this available for the would-be citizen.

Book Chapters and Strong Passages

958. "Cesar Chavez: Uniting Farm Workers." In *Heroes: 21 True Stories of Courage and Honor.* Providence, RI: Jamestown, 1985, pages 36–38.

Having emerged from poverty, Chavez risked all of his hard-earned worldly goods to enter the fight for the rights of other farm workers. This is a grand introduction to units on biographies and U.S. history of the 1960s.

959. *The Constitution.* David P. Currie and Joyce L. Stevos. Glenview, IL: Scott, Foresman, 1991.

On page 108, an essay details the Civil War Amendments and the problems getting these laws enforced. (For complete annotation, see under "Thin Books," entry 926.)

960. "The Vision of Maya Ying Lin." In *Always to Remember: The Story of the Vietnam Veterans Memorial.* Brent Ashabranner. Photographs by Jennifer Ashabranner. New York: Scholastic, 1988, pages 35–43.

Though the entire book is worthwhile reading, this chapter is profound read-aloud material and can foster dialogue on many topics. She is quoted as saying, "A memorial shouldn't tell you what to think, but should make you think." These empowering words can be a spiritual contribution to the newcomer. (Full details are under "Thin Books," entry 923.)

Newspaper and Magazine Articles

961. "George Washington's Patowmack Canal: Waterway That Led to the Constitution." Wilbur E. Garrett. Photographs by Kenneth Garrett. *National Geographic* 171, no. 6, June 1987, pages 716–53.

Rich photographs, skilled drawings, and foldout maps squire the reader on a voyage through time on a historical waterway. Not simple reading, this article still affords background information on early America in an intriguing way. A petroglyph, antique and modern industry and architecture, and up-to-the minute fishing reports give an understanding of the canal that would be difficult to acquire from many history books. This is an excellent supplement to units on Colonial history, geography, government, and the Constitution.

962. *Time, Newsweek, Forbes,* and *Fortune* magazines.

Time, Newsweek, Forbes, and *Fortune* magazines, as well as *The New York Times* and *The Los Angeles Times,* all have regular news stories and features that support the study of national issues. Likewise, regional and local papers give readers the fundamentals of local politics. Of special note are the editorial pages and the follow-up letters to the editors.

Study Books—Challenging

This is not an endorsement attempt. There are many study guides available, and most have unique features that, taken with other resources, will help the reader reach the citizenship goal. However, the points discussed below may alert the book buyer about what kinds of features to check for. Not all study guides are created equal.

963. *How to Prepare for the U.S. Citizenship Test.* Gladys Alesi. New York: Barron's, 1992.

The book contains pretests, with answers in the back of the book, a lot of government and civics information in textbook-like form, a sample citizenship test, and many collections of American trivia, such as a chronological list of the presidents with details about each. An elaborate graph giving highlights of American history from A.D. 1,000 to 1992 is certainly no way to try learning history. But it does provide an excellent vehicle for review. The person who has read short books or stories on the various topics in the citizenship test will be much better prepared than one who has tried to memorize lists of meaningless facts. This book also provides a great deal of information about how the government works—or does not work—and what to do when you are in trouble or confused. Of exceptional value is the "Appendix for Ready Reference." In it are complete texts of the Declaration of Independence and the Constitution. Other items include "A Look at American History," "Immigration Update," a sample completed Form N-400, and a word list (a minidictionary of words used in the citizenship process).

964. *Immigration the Easy Way: The First Comprehensive Guide to U.S. Immigration Explains Sweeping Changes Under the New Immigration and Nationality Act.* Howard David Deutsch. New York: Barron's, 1992.

The introduction gives instructions on how to use this book and explains the role of the immigration lawyer. Having had many students go through the citizenship process and having seen some of them suffer extreme hardship after selecting the wrong counsel, I believe this section is well worth the time it takes to read it *before giving money to anyone.* Negotiating and understanding fees is essential, and this section uses plain talk about this sometimes embarrassing issue. Entering the country, visas, rules, green cards, the test, dual citizenship, and much more are covered in clear, easy-to-understand language. There are also fee scales and copies of forms, addresses of Immigration and Naturalization Service regional service centers in the United States, and addresses of U.S. embassies and consulates abroad.

965. *It's Easy to Become a Citizen! The Complete, Simple Guide to American Citizenship.* Carolyn Bain. New York: Hawthorn Books, 1968.

This old book holds many easy-to-comprehend items that are of value to the person preparing for the citizenship exam and for students of American social studies. As I checked around, I discovered a number of public and school libraries in California have it. The "how-to" sections are out of date, but there is much more to this book than just instructions. Near the start of each chapter is a glossary of "New words you will meet." One valuable read-aloud passage regards the naming of America: "Amerigo Vespucci (1451–1512), an Italian, was one of many explorers who wrote about the discoveries in the New World. When a German map maker read what Vespucci had written about one of his own voyages, he was so impressed that he named the new land 'America,' in honor of Amerigo Vespucci." Chapter 13, "Our Flag," gives many salient details about the history of and regulations of early U.S. flags, the Grand Union flag of the Continental Army (1776), and the reasons for the various symbols of the modern flag. This kind of information may well show up as part of the naturalization process. And there are also flag regulations. Did you know that the flag should never be used for advertising purposes? The book also has a copy of the Pledge of Allegiance.

Other Events and Supplements

When an individual tutor, such as a literacy volunteer, and a student are working together, they can devise field trips that will facilitate study and help calm the natural concerns about this awesome process of obtaining citizenship. In large classes, as ESL classes tend to be, there is also much that can be done to prepare students and reduce stress. Consider the following or variations on these themes:

- A trip to a bookstore to look for how-to books on the naturalization process will help the adult understand that there is more than one source and that each source may have valuable information.

The teacher or tutor also can have students do any of the following:

- Write to historical locations for more information.
- Look for articles on the subject of citizenship in newspapers and magazines.
- Write a letter to the editor of a local paper.
- Write to special interest groups regarding areas of concern or special interest.
- Attend a citizenship ceremony and write about it.
- Hold discussions in small groups or pairs about the changes the American flag has gone through and the historical reasons for those changes.
- Make lists of concerns and questions about the citizenship process.
- Interview a new citizen about the process.
- Design a poster with the Pledge of Allegiance.
- Make a paper model of the flag.
- Collect magazine pictures of flags and create a collage.

America: Who, Where, and When

American or U.S. history and government selections may be used to support the work of students who

> want to become citizens,
>
> want to learn history while developing English language skills,
>
> want to learn history while becoming better readers and writers,
>
> want to expand the information that they began to acquire in the K-12 system,
>
> want to have informed dialogues with friends and acquaintances,
>
> want to learn how to write about history or current events or both,
>
> want to understand present attitudes by studying past events,
>
> want to learn about American culture,
>
> need to pass standardized tests on U.S. history,
>
> have an interest in the various groups that make up this nation,
>
> enjoy reading nonfiction and historical fiction,
>
> want to find good books to share with their children or grand-children, or
>
> want to gather data and ideas for writing children's books.

The introduction of U.S. history through literature can be powerful. Because comprehension relies so much on the reader's background knowledge, a good way to start students on a new subject area is by reading aloud to them and exposing them to books with a lot of pictures to support the text. Even though modern history of the United States is relatively brief, so many different groups of people have affected its social, political, and governmental profile that many themes emerge. Some books give an overview of the United States through a single perspective, such as war, and single topic books focus on one group, person, place, or time. I am not suggesting that any of these ways of studying history is better than another. Indeed, a mix and match approach could be exactly what interests a reader who is curious about one area and then another. After all, thinking is not a linear activity.

For the teacher of a large class, it is beneficial to have as many reading selections as possible for a show and tell. Perhaps the teacher can read one or two short passages or strong chapters to demonstrate the depth and diversity of content within this unit. I happen to be a strong believer in teacher reading as a regular part of a class. This goes for all ages of students, ESL, basic literacy, large classes, and individual tutoring. When the teacher reads something well, the students hear how written text sounds. That is powerful in itself. The read-aloud passages can also serve as discussion starters. Talking about reading is an excellent way of reinforcing critical thinking processes.

Note that some fiction has been included here, either because of its own historical value or because it makes clear the particular topic.

At first, I tried grouping these selections chronologically within the subheadings, but there is far too much overlap for that to happen without cutting out readings that could be of extreme interest to some students. And part of the process is to encourage readers to make their own choices. However, just in case you are sorting according to chronology, when the selection focuses on a specific period, I have indicated that.

Though a student may be able to read the Challenging selections, that student may find the Thin Books or picture books informative or just enjoyable. So, movement back and forth among selections is simply a natural process—in a print-rich environment.

Many more books similar to these can be found in libraries and bookstores. Even as I prepare to print this final copy, I think of others that might be included. I particularly like searching in youth, young adult, junior, and picture-book sections. In my own collection there are many titles I have not included, simply because of redundancy and space. If you find something that seems likely to work, try it. If the learner says, "It was good," it was good.

First Readers and Picture Books

966. *Brother Eagle, Sister Sky: A Message from Chief Seattle.* Paintings by Susan Jeffers. New York: Dial Books, 1991.
A conflict in philosophies occurred when the European notion of land ownership and the Native American notion of the world met face to face. The words of Suquamish and Duwamish Chief Seattle, delivered in his native tongue during negotiations with settlers for land rights, are translated here and interpreted with inspirational colored ink illustrations that fill every page. "How can you buy the sky?" he begins, as he slowly recounts the stories of the universe as told to him by his mother, father, and grandfather. If we are all part of a grand system of life, how can one claim ownership of another? When the book is finished, there is a stunning sense that Seattle continues to hope for a more reasonable treaty than the one his broken people had to accept during the time that he lived. There is so much to think about in this giant picture book that it is difficult to assign categories. It is philosophy, logic, wonder, spirituality, honor, memory, respect, dignity—for all, and unity. The best use for this book may just be to let it be—in the learning environment, in the home, on the table, in the chalk trough. Then perhaps the many-layered messages will have time to unfold without shocking the viewer who may not yet be at peace with the Earth.

967. *Flight: The Journey of Charles Lindbergh.* Robert Burleigh. Illustrated by Mike Wimmer. Introduction by Jean Fritz. New York: Philomel Books, 1991.
Jean Fritz's firsthand account of hearing about Lindbergh's triumphal flight across the Atlantic connects this story with the lives of adults who are struggling against difficult odds. Fritz was a child in Shanghai, China, listening to her mother read of the twenty-five-year-old's lonely flight—an adventure of worldwide

importance. Wimmer's graphic paintings make a wondrous journey in themselves as they show the story from multiple perspectives—Lindbergh's feet on the ground, the farewell scene, in the cockpit, under the plane at sea, in a dense fog, and from the cockpit looking down at the Eiffel Tower at night, just to name a few. The story is written in the present tense—you are there; it is 1927. "In the airfield's hangar, he tells the story of his flight to the other pilots: The cramped cockpit, the aloneness, the long, long night. Meanwhile, unknown to Lindbergh, newspaper headlines all over the world are beginning to blazon the news: AMERICAN HERO SAFE IN PARIS!"

968. *George Washington's Breakfast.* Jean Fritz. Pictures by Paul Galdone. New York: Coward-McCann, 1969.

George W. Allen was named for the Father of Our Country, George Washington, and he had the same birthday. That inspired him to want to know all he could about his benefactor.

969. *If You Lived at the Time of the Great San Francisco Earthquake.* Ellen Levine. Illustrated by Richard Williams. New York: Scholastic, 1987. Focus: April 18, 1906.

Crushed homes, fire, food and water shortages, animals' reactions, people helping people, sacrifice, and even humor are covered in these well-illustrated, easy-to-read pages. Employing the question-and-answer format, this book makes the famous earthquake quite contemporary. The devastation is by no means understated, but this historical account ends on a positive note. On the wall of a new building were the words: FIRST TO SHAKE, FIRST TO BURN, FIRST TO TAKE ANOTHER NEW TURN! Here is a little book about an important historical event. It can lead to further reading on the San Francisco quake, California, disasters, survival, emergency preparedness, or individual heroism.

970. *If You Lived in Colonial Times.* Ann McGovern. Illustrated by June Otani. New York: Scholastic, 1992. Focus: 1600s–1730.

The book begins with a timeline that places Colonial times in U.S. history. This clearly illustrated document of life from the early 1600s to 1730 is then set up in a short question and long answer format. For example, what happened to people who broke laws? This is answered in one full page of illustrated text that details the kind of punishment a woman who committed a crime might have experienced; the next full page does the same for men. Although it is clearly designed for children, I found the book informative, and many of my adult students have enjoyed the informal introduction to the time period, too.

971. *If You Traveled on the Underground Railroad.* Ellen Levine. Illustrated by Larry Johnson. New York: Scholastic, 1988.

From 1830 to 1865, the Underground Railroad offered the prospect of liberty to slaves who used this secret network. This book is handled in a question-and-answer format that addresses the who, what, when, where, and why of the role that the Underground Railroad played. The heavy, large-size print holds its own, even on those pages with overpowering illustrations. This sixty-four-page book is an excellent introduction to units on slavery, U.S. history, human rights, racism and tolerance, the Constitution, and the Civil War.

972. *If You Were There When They Signed the Constitution*. Elizabeth Levy. Illustrated by Joan Holub. New York: Scholastic, 1992.

Large print, clear illustrations, and easy-to-follow text give the reader a wealth of information about the social and political climate that prevailed in America in 1787. A question-and-answer format gives both historical information and short biographies of the key players involved in designing the Constitution. The high-interest story bounces between close-up shots of daily life and general statements about the period. It is an excellent reader for anyone wanting a fast report on a complex time.

973. *If Your Name Was Changed at Ellis Island*. Ellen Levine. Illustrated by Warren Parmenter. New York: Scholastic, 1993.

Here is an eye-opener for many new immigrants. Often using the words of the immigrants themselves, this little book unromantically tells about the frustrations and hardships of people struggling to enter and stay in the United States during the years when most newcomers were processed through Ellis Island. It is a good read for citizens and noncitizens alike and an empathetic shoulder for anyone whose family name was altered during the passage from one world to another.

974. *Just a Few Words, Mr. Lincoln: The Story of the Gettysburg Address*. Jean Fritz. Illustrated by Charles Robinson. New York: Grossett & Dunlap, 1993.

One might imagine that in forty-eight pages there would be little room for detail, but, in this case, one would be wrong. Not only is there a lot of historical trivia, such as a bed that broke down when three women tried to sleep in it at once, but the typical Jean Fritz humor is equaled this time by illustrations that show delightful imagination. Had Mr. Lincoln had the help of this pair, the Gettysburg Address might now be fare for the midnight comedy hour. Even as it stands, the address is noteworthy and this book is informative.

975. *The Middle Passage*. Illustrated by Tom Feelings. New York: Dial Books, 1995.

In a prepublication brochure, Feelings describes the evolution of his idea for this text-free book: "[M]uted images flashed across my mind. Pale white sailing ships like huge white birds of prey, plunging forward into mountainous rising white foaming waves of cold water, surrounding and engulfing everything. Our ancestors, hundreds of them locked in the belly of each of these ships, chained together like animals throughout the long voyage from Africa toward unknown destinations, millions dying from the awful conditions in the bowels of the filthy slave galleys." So goes the description of conditions for human beings during the Middle Passage across the Atlantic Ocean—now exposed in a graphic form that is beyond words. Feelings says it took him nearly twenty years to create it. Indeed, it required over 200 years. When I first saw a few of the galleys of this picture book, I was shaken, awestruck, speechless—the close-up faces, the distant views of mystical ships, the cutaways into their holds. Dignity, agony, fear, and wonder rush across the pages. Feelings researched his topic in traditional academic fashion and as ethnographer, going to live in Ghana. As soon as my copy of this book arrived I shared it with a workplace ESL class, allowing it to pass from one student to the next. A Vietnamese man who can barely see and who rarely speaks in class became enthralled, first with the pictures and then with the introductory texts by

Feelings and John Heinrick Clarke (who wrote the introduction). Because of his vision, he needed more time and had to take the book home with him. The following session he entered a transformed person. "It's so sad, so sad," he told us. Then he paralleled the enslavement of the African nationals—and especially the treatment of the women—to the Vietnamese nationals sold into slavery in China, Korea, and Japan. *The Middle Passage* had made a human connection and awakened language that had been dormant. This is an adult picture book. It is impossible for me to imagine an educational theme that could not somehow employ this monumental work. It is clearly one of the most important creative works in American history.

976. *A More Perfect Union: The Story of Our Constitution*. Betsy Maestro and Giulio Maestro. New York: Lothrop, Lee & Shepard, 1987.

Ten years after the signing of the Declaration of Independence, the colonies needed a more secure alliance. The story of how that alliance was written unfolds quickly in the first forty-two pages of this book. A map of the colonies of 1787 sets the stage, and simple colored drawings show up on every page. On page 44, the Preamble and summaries of Articles I–VII appear. On page 45 the names of the signers and the colonies from which they came appear. Then a table of dates from 1774–1791 gives the historic high points, followed by notes on the Connecticut Compromise, a list of facts about some of the delegates, and a chronological list of colonies that ratified the Constitution. On the last page are brief summaries of the Amendments to the Constitution, numbers I–XXVI. It looks like a children's book. It informs like a history and government text.

977. *Paul Revere's Ride*. Henry Wadsworth Longfellow. Illustrated by Ted Rand. New York: Dutton Children's Books, 1990.

The Old North Church, Boston, the Charles River with HMS *Somerset*, Charlestown, Bunker Hill, Arlington, Lexington, and many other historical names on maps inside the front and back covers give a visual reference to the full trek suggested by this famous poem. The rhythm and flow of Longfellow's language provide a fine opportunity for the teacher to demonstrate how to deliver text in an entertaining way. Dramatically powerful, detailed watercolors support the large print as, page by page, they illustrate the start of the American Revolution. On the last page, a brief historical note gives background for the war that this spark ignited. This is an enchanting introduction to a unit on U.S. or Colonial history. It is a good supplement for a geography unit, and it would also make a stimulating addition to an art and illustration discussion. This story lends itself to dramatic interpretation in a play or readers theatre form.

978. *A Picture Book of Jesse Owens*. David A. Adler. Illustrated by Robert Casilla. New York: Scholastic, 1992.

Important dates are chronicled on the last page, starting with the birth of J. C. Owens on September 12, 1913. (Later, a teacher, misunderstanding J. C., wrote Jesse in her roll book and permanently changed the name of the boy who would grow to be a world-class runner.) The chronology ends with his death from lung cancer on March 31, 1980. Even as the grandson of a former slave won Olympic victories that honored his country, he was forbidden the right to live where he chose or ride in the front of the bus. Adolf Hitler, too, showed disdain for the man with black skin and refused to shake hands with him. It was generations later before President Gerald Ford and then President Jimmy Carter attempted to set right the wrongs cast on this American.

979. *Pink and Say*. Patricia Polacco. New York: Philomel Books, 1994.

Two very young teenagers get caught up in the treachery of the Civil War, Pink with a black unit, Say with a white. Their stories join as the black boy takes time to save the life of his fellow soldier, dragging him home to be doctored. Say is overcome with awe when he discovers Pink can teach him to read, a skill forbidden slaves and obviously not the birthright of the poor white. Pink's mother is as caring of her son's friend as she is of her own child and pays dearly for it. This is an American history book, a parenting book, a literacy issues book, a social science cornerstone, and much much more. Warning: This book cannot be read aloud without drawing many tears from all present.

980. *The President's Cabinet and How it Grew*. Nancy Winslow Parker. New York: HarperCollins, 1992.

This clearly illustrated book traces the development of the president's cabinet from 1789, when George Washington began with a cabinet of four. It has an easy reference chart that shows which additions or subtractions occurred under which presidents, and it gives brief job descriptions for each post. There is also a colorful graph detailing the millions of dollars spent by the various departments in 1991. The top spender, for example, was Defense at $317,662 million; number eight was education at $23,711 million; and last was Commerce at $2,771 million. All of this information is presented in a salient form that fosters dialogue about authentic, contemporary issues.

981. *A River Ran Wild*. Lynne Cherry. San Diego, CA: Harcourt Brace Jovanovich, 1992. A Gulliver Breen Book.

This exquisitely illustrated, authentic history of a river belongs in every classroom. Most of the two-page spreads have a full-page drawing opposite two or three easy-to-read, large-print paragraphs surrounded by small illustrations. Inside the front and back covers are maps that contrast the New England area of the 1500s with the same in the 1900s. It will inspire the artist, the historian, the ecologist, and the humanist in everyone who follows the story of the Nashua River—from teeming with life—to polluted, stinking death—to revitalized life again. It gives a poignant challenge to each of us—and hope. It is a Reading Rainbow selection and fits the following themes: Native Americans, ecology, U.S. history, geography, politics, animals, and art.

982. *The Story of the White House*. Kate Waters. New York: Scholastic, 1991.

A map of Washington, D.C., photographs of paper money in large sheets, the Capitol building, a painting commemorating the burning of Washington by the British in 1812, photos of visitors and the gardens in summer, spring, fall, and winter, all combine to make this picture book an incredible source of information. Add to that two pages of trivia about the White House and three pages of White House portraits, and you have consistent support for comprehension of the text that is scattered sparsely throughout this book.

983. *True Stories About Abraham Lincoln*. Ruth Belov Gross. Illustrated by Charles Turzak. New York: Scholastic, 1973.

Each story is one page long and written in simple past tense. There is a straightforward progression from Lincoln's birth to his death, with the salient historical features of his life laid out. Though the style is less than compelling, everyday language is used throughout, and the short passage format allows the reader to complete a "story" in one break period. Meanwhile, the format provides a linear history lesson that will be valuable to adults just learning about U.S. history and the concepts of the Lincoln era. The book is illustrated by Charles Turzak in strong black-and-white woodcuts. The text is in easy-to-read type that is well leaded. Words are never broken at the end of lines, a positive feature for a new reader or one unfamiliar with the language.

984. *"Wanted Dead or Alive": The True Story of Harriet Tubman*. Ann McGovern. New York: Scholastic, 1965.

This story of a courageous slave who helped over 300 others to freedom begins when seven-year-old Harriet was rented out as a servant. Beatings with a whip left lifelong scars on a woman who lived to read of the Emancipation Proclamation and to nurse the sick throughout the Civil War. Large print and poetic language assist the reader through a pivotal period in U.S. history.

985. *What's the Big Idea, Ben Franklin?* Jean Fritz. Illustrated by Margot Tomes. New York: Scholastic, 1976.

This is more than just a big idea; it is the entire story of Ben Franklin's life, complete with ideas for inventions, experiments and politics. The fast-paced text bounces through one of the most productive lifetimes America has ever produced. The last page is a collection of field notes containing tid-bits that wouldn't fit into the regular text.

Between Picture Books and Thin Books

986. *The Apache*. Patricia McKissack. Chicago: Childrens Press, 1984. A New True Book series.

This title gives the history of a tribe of hunters, fighters, and raiders that called itself the Tinde. The tribe moved into the southwestern United States in the 1400s, disrupting the farming lifestyles of more peaceful tribes. The Apache nation included the Navajo, who later moved on to become a separate nation, Chiricahua, Lipan, Western Apache, Mescalero, and Jicarilla. They were nomads who followed the herds and took other necessities from their neighbors. The Apaches' war dance was a menacing sign for their enemies.

987. *The Cayuga*. Jill Duvall. Chicago: Childrens Press, 1991. A New True Book series.

This title tells of the Gueugwehono, "People of the Mucky Land," that area around Lake Cayuga where annual rains created just that—mucky land. A member of the league of Iroquois nations (Mohawk, Oneida, Onondaga, Cayuga, and Seneca), they lived in what is now New York. The book gives an overview of their present-day political struggles to regain the land where their ancestors are buried as well as details of life, such as the peach pit game, before the arrival of Europeans.

988. *The Cheyenne*. Dennis Fradin. Chicago: Childrens Press, 1992. A New True Book series.

This is the story of a once-nomadic tribe, known as the Tsistsistas (and by the Sioux as the Shahiyena—people of strange speech), that moved freely all over the continent. They were influenced greatly by the introduction of horses from Spain in the 1500s and the abundance of buffalo, but the famous battle in 1876 with General Custer at the Little Big Horn marked a dramatic change in the Cheyenne lifestyle. They were subsequently restricted to reservations in Montana and Oklahoma. But modern Cheyenne continue to follow traditional ceremonies and many ancient customs.

989. *The Chippewa*. Alice Osinski. Chicago: Childrens Press, 1992. A New True Book series.

This book tells of several bands of Indians from Canada who migrated toward the Great Lakes of the United States and began to merge with bigger tribes around 1840. They survived on the land by trading furs and guns.

990. *The Chumash*. Jill D. Duvall. Chicago: Childrens Press, 1994. A New True Book series.

This title tells how scholars are reconstructing the history of the Chumash, who lived in and around what is now Santa Barbara, California. They were linked only by a common language, Hokan, and a lifestyle that required little work in the naturally abundant mountains from Malibu to San Luis Obispo and the islands now known as Santa Cruz, Santa Rosa, Anacapa, and San Miguel. A small map of California identifies the Chumash area. The history of this group, now numbering 3,000, is based mainly on the notes of early 1900s scholar John P. Harrington and diaries of the Franciscans who came from Mexico to convert the Chumash to Christianity.

991. *The Declaration of Independence*. Dennis Fradin. Chicago: Childrens Press, 1988. A New True Book series.

Starting with a Fourth of July celebration, this little book leads the reader through an extremely complex part of American history in just a few pages. The impact of Thomas Paine's book *Common Sense*, in which Paine expounded the reasons why colonists should want independence, is made obvious. And the pragmatics of how the document was written are spelled out in easy-to-understand language.

992. *The Hopi*. Ann Heinrichs Tomchek. Chicago: Childrens Press, 1992. A New True Book series.

The Hopi live high on three mesas in Arizona and, though called descendants of the Anasazi, have unknown roots. Their language is quite different from any other on record. Legends of the Anasazi, documented in cave drawings, continue to be told in Hopi pueblos today. A student of religion or spirituality will be intrigued by the description and photograph of the sipapu, a raised hole in the Grand Canyon that is said to be the hole through which the human race was born. For the Hopi, this is the holiest spot on Earth. Hopi dances, silver work, and customs are well described.

993. *The Mohawk.* Jill Duvall. Chicago: Childrens Press, 1991. A New True Book series.
   This people now based in New York once traveled freely from the St. Lawrence River to Tennessee and west to the Mississippi. Arts, games, and lifestyles are discussed. The significance of wampum and how it was traded is of particular interest to a reader who has heard this term with no notion of its roots. The traditional longhouse and modern living are compared.

994. *The Oneida.* Jill Duvall. Chicago: Childrens Press, 1991. A New True Book series.
   A member of the Iroquois Confederacy, or People of the Longhouse, the Oneida were written about in 1634 by a Dutchman, Harmen Meyndertsz, who described them as peaceful, friendly people who had plenty of food and gentle manners. Greatly affected by Christianity and immigrants, the Oneida have only recently begun to reassemble their land.

995. *The Seneca.* Jill Duvall. Chicago: Childrens Press, 1991. A New True Book series.
   The Great Hill People had an ownership policy that allowed men to possess their own weapons and personal items, but the longhouses and farm tools belonged to the women.

996. *The Star-Spangled Banner.* Illustrated by Peter Spier. New York: Dell, 1992.
   This is a must have for every American home. This is a picture book in the true sense of the word. Each exquisite two-page illustration demonstrates the meaning of a single line of the national anthem. A brief account of the state of the nation in the throes of the War of 1812 gives readers a sense of the people, places, and terrible struggle that framed the poem that would become a famous song. A map of the war zone shows where the author, Francis Scott Key, was during his moment of glory and inspiration. A copy of the original handwritten text is opposite the map. There is also a two-page spread of many historical U.S. flags. The lyrics are set to music on one page, for the pianist in our midst. This large paperback looks like a children's book, and is, indeed, a Reading Rainbow selection, but it has value to every adult interested in American history. I have found it useful for both ESL students and adult new readers.

997. *The War Began at Supper: Letters to Miss Loria.* Patricia Reilly Giff. Illustrated by Betsy Lewin. New York: Delacorte Press, 1991.
   Miss Loria, a beloved student teacher who has moved away, is the addressee of most of the letters from the students in Mrs. Clark's elementary school class. Concerns about the Persian Gulf War manifest in many ways among the young writers, whose simple prose makes for easy reading about difficult subjects. Also under "Book Chapters and Strong Passages," entry 1080.

Thin Books

998. *Always to Remember: The Story of the Vietnam Veterans Memorial.* Brent Ashabranner. Photographs by Jennifer Ashabranner. New York: Scholastic, 1988.
   This clear account of the historical and emotional roots of the U.S. involvement in the Vietnam War gives many human details about people affected by it. Wounded in action and witness to the deaths or wounding of over half his company, veteran Jan C. Scruggs came home to a legacy of shame for having gone

to war. One night, after seeing the movie *The Deer Hunter*, he was driven to make a memorial of substance to the effort and suffering that had transpired. It would have the names of all those men and women lost in the Vietnam War. This dream became an obsession that led to a nationwide competition, with 1,421 designs submitted and judged without names or identification of any kind. The Wall, entry number 1,026, by twenty-one-year-old Yale student Maya Ying Lin, was selected. The daughter of Chinese immigrants was to make a profound contribution to the art and history of America.

999. *America at War! Battles That Turned the Tide*. Brian Black. New York: Scholastic, 1992.

Battles from the American Revolution to the Persian Gulf War are set in their historic political perspectives, covering America's conflicts from 1763 to 1990. This is a clearly written book, giving insights into the emotional and complex issues around military activities that changed the course of history. An adult new reader and her tutor began trading off passages of this book and came away with far more than literacy. Both sang the praises of this well-written history. It is also appropriate for ESL students who are attempting to learn about America and its past. The range of countries involved in wars with the United States provides a trek around the map that would illuminate and enliven many a geography unit.

1000. *And Then What Happened, Paul Revere?* Jean Fritz. Illustrated by Margaret Tomes. New York: Scholastic, 1973.

This book is chock full of history delivered in a humorous tone. Note page 23, "Sometimes on his missions things went just right. He got past the sentries, got through the snow, kept his horse on the road, and kept himself on his horse."

1001. *Annie Oakley: The Shooting Star*. Charles P. Graves. Illustrated by Cary. New York: Chelsea House, 1991.

This is a fast-paced, easy reader about the turn-of-the-century life of an unschooled orphan who found fame through her natural ability to shoot a gun. Other famous names in the book include Sitting Bull, Buffalo Bill Cody, and Mark Twain. Oakley died in 1926. Almost every other page in this seventy-eight-page book is a full-page illustration. The pictures and large print combine to make it comfortable for the new reader.

1002. *The Bill of Rights*. E. B. Fincher. New York: Franklin Watts, 1978.

In just sixty-six pages, historical details, discussion of each Amendment, and controversy over words are supported by occasional etchings and photographs. A two-page glossary simplifies terms like double jeopardy, ex post facto, and petit jury. The first ten Amendments are at the end of the book.

1003. *Bull Run*. Paul Fleischman. Woodcuts by David Frampton. New York: Scholastic, 1993. Focus: 1861.

Here is a fictional account of a real battle. Two maps make up the first two pages, one depicting the existing states and their positions in the Session, the other giving a close-up of the Eastern Theatre, where the Battle of Bull Run took place. At the end, a two-page spread shows two maps of the battle scene, morning on the left, afternoon on the right. One by one, in isolated vignettes, as though reporting to an unseen interviewer, fictional characters tell their stories of hearing about war, getting ready for the battle, heading off, and how the battle occurred— the tragic discovery that war is not a game. The momentum of this series of reports builds so subtly that the reader does not realize what has happened until it is done. Each vignette is one or two pages. And each speaker has a personal icon woodcut. The language is quite simple, no long sentences, no big words, and as such, almost chops at the reader's attention, but the overall impact is strong.

1004. *The Constitution.* David P. Currie and Joyce L. Stevos. Glenview, IL: Scott, Foresman, 1991.

A clear, simple description of the background of U.S. government, starting with our English heritage and the basic laws of the colonies, leads into the Declaration of Independence. The book covers the development of the Constitution and the twenty-six Amendments. Sections of the Constitution and the Amendments are clarified in modern language set in red. On page 108, an essay details the Civil War Amendments and the problems getting these laws enforced.

1005. *D-Day.* R. Conrad Stein. Chicago: Childrens Press, 1993. Cornerstones of Freedom series.

This is the story of one long day, June 6, 1944, that marked the turn of the tide in the war against Adolf Hitler and all that he represented in human suffering.

1006. *The Day Pearl Harbor Was Bombed: A Photo History of World War II.* George Sullivan. New York: Scholastic, 1991.

A one-page chronology of important dates from 1933 to 1946 and a bibliography of further reading supplement this well-organized, action-packed history of World War II. Though there is little text on each page, the vocabulary is by no means easy. Words like strategists, kamikaze, Allies, throngs, victory, stunning, and headquarters pepper the text. Historical references to Okinawa, the Solomon Islands, Berlin, Nazis, the Soviet Union, New Guinea, Guam, Saipan, the Mariana Islands, Leyte Gulf, the Philippines, Manila, Japan, Iwo Jima, the Pacific, the Boeing B-29, and the atomic bomb make it vocabulary intensive for the new reader and ESL learner. But the photographs support the text and make just page turning a worthwhile activity for someone seeking an overview of the war. Also see the read-aloud passage under "Book Chapters and Strong Passages," entry 1072.

1007. *Days of Courage: The Little Rock Story.* Richard Kelso. General editor Alex Haley. Illustrations by Mel Williges. New York: Steck-Vaughn, 1993. Focus: 1957– 1986.

The manifestations of racism and bigotry are detailed in historical events stemming from the actions of a small group of people who decided to push the Constitution into reality. An afterword and rich endnotes give more detail about the civil rights efforts of the not-yet-distant past.

1008. *The Death of Lincoln.* A picture history of the assassination. Leroy Hayman. New York: Scholastic, 1968.

Here is a fascinating history book, complete with historical photographs and on page 20, Lincoln's accounting of a dream in which his death is predicted.

1009. *The Defenders.* Ann McGovern. New York: Scholastic, 1970.

Osceola, Swamp Fighter, Tecumseh, Wise Leader, Cochise, Man of Honor are honored by the informative, readable McGovern style. At the front of the book is a guide, "How to say these Indian names."

1010. *Eleanor Roosevelt: First Lady of the World.* Doris Faber. Illustrated by Donna Ruff. New York: Viking, 1985.

This engaging, easy-to-read history book has a running series of pencil drawings that support the text and give a sense of the times in which Eleanor Roosevelt lived. A sad child whose adoring father was taken away to be treated for alcoholism and whose mother died the following year, Eleanor was sent to live with her maternal grandmother. Thereafter she was not allowed contact with her father. Occasional salient quotes bring the personalities to life. When hearing that her father had died, young Eleanor said, "I did want to see him again" (page 8). This book is quality material for new readers of any age and for ESL students who have an interest in U.S. history from a personal perspective. It is also a portrait of courage, a view of a woman who developed beyond the expectations for women of her class and time.

1011. *The Emancipation Proclamation: Why Lincoln Really Freed the Slaves.* Robert Young. New York: Dillon Press, 1994. Focus: 1863–1870.

Dramatic photographs, detailed drawings, copies of posters and children's alphabet book pages, vignettes of particular interest, and wide margins all contribute to making this an accessible text. Controversial issues are laid bare in simply stated facts. A timeline starting with the 1600s and ending with the 1870 Fifteenth Amendment, giving blacks the right to vote, gives a meaningful overview of racism in the United States. That is followed by the actual text of the Emancipation Proclamation, then a brief list of suggestions for further reading. This book is easy, academic, and informative.

1012. *Five Brave Explorers: Great Black Heroes.* Wade Hudson. Illustrated by Ron Garnett. Scholastic: New York, 1995.

Born free, explorer Esteban Dorantes (1500–1539) was captured and sold as a slave in Spain to explorer Andres Dorantes, to accompany him on expeditions to Mexico and the lands north. At the end of Andres Dorantes's career, he sold Esteban to the governor of Mexico City. From there, Esteban managed to be sent on one last expedition but was killed during the trip. A diagram of Mexico City of the 1500s accompanies his story. Jean Baptiste Pointe DuSable, a black Frenchman (1745–1818), married a Native American woman and founded what is now Chicago. James Pierce Beckworth (1798–1866) was known as a trailblazer among whites and Native Americans. Matthew A. Henson (1866–1955) was a North Pole explorer, part of the Peary expedition. This chapter is a nice companion to Zachary Kent's *The Story of Admiral Peary at the North Pole,* entry 1036. Mae C. Jemison, space explorer, (1956–) was a member of the 1991 Endeavor mission.

1013. *The Freedom Riders.* Deborah Kent. Chicago: Childrens Press, 1993. Cornerstones of Freedom series. Focus: 1946–1965.

On May 4, 1961, a group of black and white Americans boarded a Greyhound bus and rode through the Deep South in an attempt at nonviolent change. In 1955, in Montgomery, Alabama, a black seamstress had refused to give up her seat on a bus to a white person, thereby violating a law that later proved unconstitutional. A 1946 U.S. Supreme Court ruling had outlawed segregation on interstate rail-roads and buses, and in 1960 another ruling outlawed segregated terminals. These laws were openly broken throughout the southern United States. The Freedom Riders simply agreed to form an integrated group that would peacefully demon-strate for the federal government that civil rights were not being protected as provided by law. Their plan was to ride in unassigned seats and use rest rooms marked for the opposite race, thereby attracting the ire of segregationists and the attention of the FBI. The plan worked, and within a short time, peaceful demon-strations led to bloodshed, false arrests, and killings. It also changed the course of history.

1014. *The Great American Gold Rush*. Rhoda Blumberg. New York: Scholastic, 1989. History focus: 1848–1852.

Modern and historical illustrations abound in this exciting tale of the many people who made the trip to California under the magical spell of gold for the taking. By boat, wagon, horse, and sometimes foot, the hardy and sick, hopeful and disillusioned, thronged toward the promised land of the 1840s, California. With them came fortune, fame, greed, crime, violence, hatred, disappointment, joy, wonder, and the promise of life as it had never been known before. Not only is this a good read, it is well researched and serves as a model for those wanting to see how useful a good bibliography and index can be. The footnotes make an interesting skip through the literature themselves.

1015. *I, Columbus: My Journal, 1442–1443*. Edited by Peter Roop and Connie Roop. Illustrated by Peter E. Hanson. New York: Avon Books, 1991.

A prologue gives a historical setting and some background on Columbus, how he came to be a seaman, his pitch to Queen Isabella and King Ferdinand on how profits from the trip that incidentally led to America would support their efforts to acquire Jerusalem, and his gratitude as he set sail on August 3, 1492, on an adventure beyond his own imaginings. Then his own prologue references India, the prince known as Great Khan, and Columbus's pledge to keep a log of his experience on the seas. The log itself is a translation made from Columbus's copy of the log he ultimately presented to Queen Isabella. Inside the front cover is a map of Columbus's voyage to the New World (though he never knew it as such), and inside the back cover is a map of his trek home. This is easy reading, filled with adventure and history. Columbus also spells out the day of the week and the month, just as my students do in their own journals, though Columbus places the number of the date before the name of the month, in the European style. This practice helps students learn to spell and write with ease the days and months in a meaningful process.

1016. *If You Lived at the Time of the Civil War*. Kay Moore. Illustrated by Anni Matsick. New York: Scholastic, 1994.

1017. *If You Lived with the Sioux Indians*. Ann McGovern. Illustrated by Jean Syverud Drew. New York: Scholastic, 1974, illustrations 1992.

1018. *If You Traveled on the Underground Railroad*. Ellen Levine. Illustrated by Larry Johnson. New York: Scholastic, 1988, illustrations 1992.

1019. *If You Traveled West in a Covered Wagon*. Ellen Levine. Illustrated by Elroy Freem. New York: Scholastic, text 1986, illustrations 1992.

1020. *Jesse Jackson: A Biography*. Patricia C. McKissack. New York: Scholastic, 1989.
Documentary photographs support this modern American story of struggle, defeat, and achievement.

1021. *The John F. Kennedy Assassination*. R. Conrad Stein. Chicago. Childrens Press, 1992. Cornerstones of Freedom series. Focus: 1963–1979.
This book details November 22, 1963, and the mood of the nation, politically, spiritually, and socially, during that time. The radio announcement, the words of the assassin, and the swearing in of Vice President Lyndon Johnson give an immediacy to the moment that was followed by an incredible funeral, the spotlight on a first lady and two little children turned widow and orphans, and the bizarre assassination of the assassin. Questions that continue to haunt the memories of those who remember the day are raised anew for the readers of this book.

1022. *Last Chance for Freedom*. Marcie Miller Stadelhofen. New York: New Readers Press, 1990. Sundown Books series.
This sequel to *The Freedom Side* is part of a collection written for adult new readers. They are in thin, easy-to-carry paperback format with adult pictures on the covers. Although not oversized, the print is clear and legible. All are available with cassette tapes that allow new readers and ESL students to make the sound-symbol connections. The good news is there is a compelling story that provides authentic historical information. The bad news is that the sentences are short. However, many of my students have enjoyed them and claim to have gotten interested in a topic they knew little or nothing about before.

1023. *Letters from a Slave Girl: The Story of Harriet Jacobs*. Mary E. Lyons. New York: Charles Scribner's Sons, 1992.
Inspired by the autobiographical letters published by the adult Harriet Jacobs, Lyons employs fictional letters to Jacobs's deceased mother, father, and other relatives to convey the historical events from 1825 to 1842 and the personal imaginings, triumphs, and tragedies of a slave girl who grows up as she strives to gain her freedom. The fictionalized biography is based on true events from the life of Harriet Jacobs. The final section, "Harriet: The Rest of Her Story," takes us from 1842 to 1852 in a narrative of the freedom fighter's life. The black Southern dialect of the slave girl begins to show the influence of white mistresses with whom she has extended contact. Jacobs is taught to read but left to learn writing on her own initiative. It is presumed that she used discarded account books for writing paper during this period when handmade paper was expensive and slaves were forbidden by law to read or write. This book is a powerful telling of one woman's experience as a slave. Gender issues, human rights, civil rights, and, certainly, the Civil War are all addressed through this first-person account of human suffering, courage, and hope.

1024. *Like Father, Like Son: Baseball's Major League Families.* Sarah Gardiner White. New York: Scholastic, 1993.

Not just fathers and sons but many familial relationships emerge in this entertaining assortment of high-profile sports names. It is a well-written book with a few nice black-and-white photos.

1025. *Lost Star: The Story of Amelia Earhart.* Patricia Lauber. New York: Scholastic, 1988.

This is the incredible story of a woman who always seemed to have a philosophical response to what others might view as adversity. A read-aloud passage begins on page 16, as Amelia, "Meely," headed for a school poetry reciting contest. Along the way, she stopped to visit a horse she sometimes rode and discovered it unfed and without water. Disregarding her dress and school schedule, she missed the contest to take time to feed and water the horse. "But, she told her favorite teacher later, she didn't mind. She was glad to know the poem and had fun learning it. That was what counted, not the prize" (page 17). This notion of learning for learning's sake may prove an inspiration to those who are discouraged by test scores and other extrinsic rewards. Eventually, Earhart became an enthusiastic pilot, determined to do what had never been done before. In the process, she vanished from the face of the Earth. Historical photographs accompany this well-told tale. Pages 100–102 offer an interesting mythological passage, telling of the naming of the plane and an odd coincidence that the star known as Amelia was lost, just as the namesake was. It was a toss-up for me whether to go Thin Books or Challenging on this one.

1026. *Lou Gehrig: One of Baseball's Greatest.* Guernsey Van Riper, Jr. New York: Macmillan, 1986.

This large-print paperback is one of a series on childhoods of famous Americans. The story starts with the dilemma of a young boy who is ridiculed for being fat. It also addresses the pain of ethnic hatred expressed against children with German surnames when President Woodrow Wilson declared war against the German government. This clearly written story is a good, fast read.

1027. *Our Constitution.* Linda Carlson Johnson. Brookfield, CT: Millbrook Press, 1992. I Know America series.

Historical paintings and drawings support an easy-to-read text that focuses on numerous conflicts during the design of the Constitution. This book has been prepared for study with textbook attention, but it is much more palatable and certainly easier to carry around.

1028. *Our United States Geography: Our Regions and People.* Beverly Vaillancourt. Maywood, NJ: Peoples Publishing Group, 1994.

The United States is broken into nine regions, clusters of states that give a logical sense to the areas where Americans live, work, and play. A regional map shows the group of states and provides detailed information on each state. A state history, local customs, industries, and items of interest are conveyed in easy-to-read text. Local color is provided through details like the recipe for sourdough pancakes popular in Arkansas. This is an excellent way of introducing the entire nation to someone who has not had an opportunity to study about America. It would also provide good background information for an adult planning a trip.

"The Emigrants of the 1800s," page 157, has a continental U.S. map and identifies the National Road, the Oregon Trail, the Bozeman Trail, the California Trail, the Mormon Trail, the Santa Fe Trail, and the Gila Trail. "The Climate of the United States," page 124, has a weather map and a brief description of weather across the land.

1029. *Ready, Aim, Fire! The Real Adventures of Annie Oakley.* Ellen Levine. New York: Scholastic, 1989.

There is a lot of dialogue, providing quality English in action, and a dramatic story of an orphan girl turned legend. Occasional historical photographs provide visual treats.

1030. *The Secret Soldier: The Story of Deborah Sampson.* Ann McGovern. Illustrated by Harold Goodwin. New York: Scholastic, 1975. Focus: 1765–1827.

In just sixty-four pages of easy reading, McGovern deals with some of our most difficult human rights issues. First we witness a poverty-stricken widow's grief as she prepared to give away the five children she could not support, among them Deborah Sampson. The child became a servant for a sickly old woman. Later, as part of a minister's household, she was too busy with chores and family activities to do what she loved best—read. A powerful read-aloud passage starts at the top of page 11 and ends at the bottom of page 14. There we learn that female children were not allowed schooling, even when they were loved, even when they begged for it. In spite of this illiterate environment, Sampson began a diary that chronicled the American Revolution. Ironically, the poorly educated young woman became a teacher. And then she struck upon an idea for adventure. She disguised herself as a teenage boy and joined the army. This is the secret upon which this story is built. A compelling read, with many surprises, this is an easy reader to talk about.

1031. *Sequoyah: Father of the Cherokee Alphabet.* David Petersen. Chicago: Childrens Press, 1991.

Reproductions of historical artwork, photographs of historical sites, and large print provide an easy trek through the complex and frustrating life of Sequoyah, at one time called crazy for his misunderstood scratchings. This book is inspirational.

1032. *Shh! We're Writing the Constitution.* Jean Fritz. Pictures by Tomie dePaola. New York: G. P. Putnam's Sons, 1987.

The humorous dePaola illustrations poke fun at all the pomp and circumstance surrounding the company of men. Indeed, the only woman in the book is shown with her face half hidden, and the only girl is in her important father's pipe dream. And Jean Fritz's equally irreverent style of addressing the problems of logistics and personalities makes this a lively adventure back in time. The text is quite readable, without seeming simplified, and a section of notes gives an academic flavor. After that comes the actual Constitution. This is a fine teaching text. I have used it many times with ESL students and others who were preparing for U.S. citizenship.

1033. *Something from Nothing.* Adopted from a Jewish folktale. Phoebe Gilman. New York: Scholastic, 1992.

You cannot start this book without finishing it. It is a literacy book, an intergenerational book, and one about ingenuity.

1034. *Squanto: Friend of the Pilgrims.* Clyde Robert Bulla. Pictures by Peter Burchard. New York: Scholastic, 1982.

In 112 pages of simply written text, the story of a Native American named Squanto describes the friendships, betrayals, and conflicts that connected the Indians and the newcomers to the land now known as America. This is a compellingly written, historically accurate account of Squanto's life. The conversations provide excellent input for the ESL student.

1035. *Squanto: The Pilgrim Adventure.* Kate Jassem. Mahwah, NJ: Troll, 1979.

In just forty-eight pages the new reader learns of pre-European trading in the land of the Patuxet, now Plymouth, the true adventures of one young man whose bilingual skills opened the doors to world travel, the years of frustration when Squanto found himself stranded in England, a return trip on the ship of Captain John Smith, a kidnapping that placed him in slavery in Spain, and his eventual escape and return to his homeland—only to learn that his entire tribe had died. Squanto then became instrumental in helping the *Mayflower* Pilgrims settle on what had been the land of his people. There is surprising detail in the book, which has half-page illustrations on every page. An easy-to-understand map is at the front.

1036. *The Story of Admiral Peary at the North Pole.* Zachary Kent. Chicago: Childrens Press, 1988. Cornerstones of Freedom series. Focus: 1856–1909.

In its entirety, this book is an incredible read aloud of courage, adventure, physical hardship, and, finally, deceit. Born in 1856 in Portland, Maine, the adventurer made multiple expeditions into Nicaragua, and Greenland, where his daughter was born. In 1909, on his eighth expedition to the Arctic region, Peary ventured through the forbidding Northwest Passage, located at the north pole. Later, regarding that top of the earth experience, he commented, "I had passed over or very near the point where north and south and east and west blend into one." He planted an American flag atop his igloo.

1037. *The Story of George Washington Carver.* Eva Moore. New York: Scholastic, 1971.

This action-packed tale begins with the fear that Moses Carver's slaves, a widow and her two children, would be stolen. The life of George Washington Carver addresses the issues of racism, and intellectual freedom. This man eventually became a world-famous scientist.

1038. *The Story of Henry Ford and the Automobile.* Zachary Kent. Chicago: Childrens Press, 1990. Cornerstones of Freedom series. Focus: 1896–1947.

This book opens with a pictorial history of the evolution of the automobile. The fast-moving story bounces into action with an 1896 episode in which the impulsive engineer breaks down a wall to remove the vehicle that he has built too large for the doorway. The story progresses through the development of affordable transportation for most Americans and ends with the demise of Ford's unquestioned authority, and finally the 1947 death of this famous American.

1039. *The Story of Jonas Salk and the Discovery of the Polio Vaccine.* Jim Hargrove. Chicago: Childrens Press, 1990. Cornerstones of Freedom series. Focus: 1940s– 1963, 1988.

The book opens with a 1950s polio poster featuring a victim of that terrible epidemic. Paralysis, death, and the virus that causes polio are all discussed in scientific terms in this small booklet. The text leads the reader not only through history but also through the life of the scientist who found a vaccine to stop a killer from conquering the Earth.

1040. *The Story of Mississippi Steamboats.* R. Conrad Stein. Illustrated by Tom Dunnington. Chicago: Childrens Press, 1987. Cornerstones of Freedom series. Focus 1850–1950.

This book covers about 100 years on the Mississippi River and tells of capitalism and luxury and a lifestyle that is part of Americana.

1041. *The Story of Presidential Elections.* Jim Hargrove. Chicago: Childrens Press, 1988. Cornerstones of Freedom series.

This book opens to a 1789 inaugural painting of George Washington and then quickly jumps to the ballot box and the formal procedure related to it. The tumultuous evolution of this process is neatly spelled out. Included are discussions of the Amendments to the Constitution and how they came to be, the Electoral College, the emerging power of PACs, national conventions, and more. Suffice it to say, it is not just a how-to-vote booklet, though it does make a sound statement about why so many people consider the right to vote so important.

1042. *The Story of the Chicago Fire.* R. Conrad Stein. Illustrated by Richard Wahl. Chicago: Childrens Press, 1982. Cornerstones of Freedom series. Focus: 1871–1874.

This book details the life of a prosperous city in 1871, one with wooden streets and slums. A fire in the O'Learys' barn, human error that sent fire wagons in the wrong direction, and firsthand accounts of terrible loss and opportunity all make the story of this fire one of a latter-day phoenix.

1043. *The Story of the Nineteenth Amendment.* R. Conrad Stein. Illustrated by Keith Neely. Chicago: Childrens Press, 1983. Cornerstones of Freedom series.

Large print, occasionally obstructed by illustration washes, tells of women's efforts to get the right to vote. A century of struggle over this human rights issue is covered in just thirty-one pages of easy-to-understand language. Drawings of the various players in this U.S. drama make the names take on human characteristics. This book offers captivating storytelling with historical anecdotes. It is a good introductory reader for a small group or an individual who is ready to discuss or write about suffrage.

1044. *The Story of the Rough Riders.* Zachary Kent. Chicago: Childrens Press, 1991. Cornerstones of Freedom series. Focus: 1898–1904.

The First U.S. Volunteer Cavalry Regiment, known as the Rough Riders and led by Colonel Theodore Roosevelt, gave the man who would become the twenty-sixth president a spot in the limelight and a place in American hearts. The undisciplined group of soldiers were able to accomplish tremendous feats during their one hundred thirty-three day adventure. (For further information on this series, see WAR, Unit 9.)

1045. *The Story of the Spirit of St. Louis.* R. Conrad Stein. Illustrated by Len Meents. Chicago: Childrens Press, 1984. Cornerstones of Freedom series. Focus: 1927.

This book begins as a chronicle of unsuccessful flight attempts, crashes, and disasters. Then the story of the famous 1927 flight of Charles Lindbergh takes on a first-person voice, as long passages from his own pen tell of his solo flight. This is a great book for anyone interested in flying.

1046. *The Story of the Teapot Dome Scandal.* Jim Hargrove. Chicago: Childrens Press, 1989. Cornerstones of Freedom series. Focus: 1920–1933.

This is a story of the Roaring Twenties, also known as the Jazz Age, when women's skirts for the first time rose above the knee, the number of Americans who owned automobiles tripled, and the Eighteenth Amendment to the Constitution was passed (January 16, 1920) prohibiting the manufacture, sale, and transport of alcohol, and then repealed in 1933. President Warren G. Harding, one of the most popular presidents ever, was known for extramarital affairs, heavy drinking, and associations with scoundrels of all sorts, many of whom ended up as presidential appointees. The scandal was not about tea but about government-owned oil reserves in Wyoming and other areas that were exploited in bizarre and creative ways. When Harding died amid extraordinary controversy, Vice President Calvin Coolidge became president, did little to bring about reform, and won reelection with no trouble. " 'The nation wanted nothing done,' humorist Will Rogers joked about Coolidge, 'and he done it.' "

1047. *The Story of the Women's Movement.* Maureen Ash. Chicago: Childrens Press, 1989. Cornerstones of Freedom series.

This booklet opens with a photo of two English police officers arresting a woman who was demonstrating for the right to vote in front of the prime minister's house. The story begins in England in 1827 with the case study of Caroline Norton, who, as a married woman, had no right to keep her children or the money she earned from writing. Further, her husband was within his rights when he beat her while she was pregnant and when he separated her from her three sons, one of whom died of blood poisoning in his care. During her lifetime, Norton campaigned for and won some women's rights. Five years after her death, a law was passed allowing married women the same rights as unmarried ones, though not the same rights as men. Numerous other women took up the fight to change laws that were based on their assumed inferiority to men. It was difficult for them to be taken seriously by those who considered them categorically less intelligent and who passed laws denying girls entry into academic schools. "Girls were too weak, it was believed, to learn mathematics—it would make them go mad" (page 9). The story then moves to the United States, whose Constitution at that time totally ignored the rights of women, blacks, and Native Americans. Allowed to serve as emergency substitutes during wars, women in England and America continued to be denied civil rights. During the 1920s they earned the right to vote, but in the 1930s, twenty-six states passed laws prohibiting married women from getting jobs, and where they could work they were paid about sixty-five percent of what men earned for the same output. Considerable discussion is given to both sides of the Equal Rights Amendment and to statistics, including that fact that in 1987 women earned seventy cents for every dollar earned by men, and a college-educated woman can expect to earn about the same as a male high school dropout. This dynamic little history book is chock-full of facts and famous names.

1048. *Susan B. Anthony: Champion of Women's Rights*. New York: Aladdin, 1986. Childhood of Famous Americans series.

This is 196 pages of double-spaced large print. Though most of this book is about Anthony's childhood, and only a few pages at the end cover her participation in women's suffrage, this is an excellent selection for women's issues, U.S. history, or gender issues. An excellent read-aloud passage on gender inequity in a one-room schoolhouse is discussed under "Book Chapters and Strong Passages," entry 1079.

1049. *They Led the Way: 14 American Women*. Johanna Johnston. New York: Scholastic, 1973.

Each chapter is about a woman who thought for herself in ways that were inconsistent with the norms of her time. The rights to preach, tend the sick, get an education, practice medicine, break sports time records, run for mayor, run for president, and vote were all demanded by the women of this book when only men were considered able. The names are now famous enough that many books have been written at a variety of levels on each woman spotlighted. Because it is impossible to get much detail into so few pages, only an overview is provided, but more in-depth reading may occur if a student becomes interested in a particular case. Each of the chapters is a strong one for SSR. The chapters on medical women Elizabeth Blackwell and Clara Barton will contribute nicely to a science unit, too.

1050. *Thunder at Gettysburg*. Patricia Lee Gauch. Illustrated by Stephen Gammell. New York: Bantam Books, 1975. Focus: 1863.

Through the experience of fourteen-year-old Tillie Pierce, the reader discovers the terrible reality of one dreadful day in 1863. Based on an actual account, this simply told, tear-wrenching adventure gives one a strong sense of how it was as North fought South. The large print and wide margins offer a quick read. A simple map at the front assists comprehension of text that tells of how war moved from an entertaining idea to grim reality.

1051. *The United States Holocaust Memorial Museum: America Keeps the Memory Alive*. Eleanor H. Ayer. New York: Dillon Press, 1994. Focus: 1933–1945.

This book introduces the contents of the museum by leading the reader level by level through the powerful exhibits and impressions the visitor experiences there.

1052. *A Wall of Names: The Story of the Vietnam Veterans Memorial*. Judy Donnelly. Illustrated with photographs. New York: Random House, 1991.

This seemingly simple account of the Vietnam War Memorial moves progressively through the impact of the war on teenage soldiers, inhuman encounters with the elements of war in a swamp, the killings of U.S. peace protesters, veterans' return home, the memorial design controversy and compromise, and letters and gifts left at the Wall. Documented with photographs taken in the United States and Vietnam, this American perspective of "The Most Hated War" wrenches the heart while teaching details about a piece of history that is too often simplified. Of special interest may be the fact that the winning design for the memorial was done as a school assignment and earned only a grade of "B." The large text is easy to read, and the photographs support this emotionally charged account.

1053. *Who Really Discovered America?* Stephen Krensky. Illustrated by Steve Sullivan. New York: Scholastic, 1987.

This thought-provoking book does not attempt to answer the title question. Instead, it casts question on conventional givens and modern reinterpretations by starting out with unwitting settlers riding out great continental drifts.

Challenging

1054. *The Bill of Rights and Landmark Cases.* Edmund Lindsy. New York: Franklin Watts, 1989.

In just 144 pages, this little book gives the reader a brief overview of American history and politics as it is documented in our legal system. Chapter 1 describes attitudes about rights and freedoms, including biases that some members of society are more deserving than others. Chapter 2, "The First 10 Amendments," gives the actual wording of those amendments and brief discussions of their meanings. Chapter 3, "The Supreme Court," describes how that group reflects the times in which its members serve and how it influences Americans for generations afterward. Photographs of Supreme Courts of 1865, 1921, and 1957 are included. Other chapters discuss civil rights as protected under the Constitution and use specific cases to illustrate how attitudes change as the Supreme Law of the Land is interpreted and reinterpreted. Included are photographs of some of the people behind the historic cases, such as Linda Brown (Brown v. Board of Education, 1954), who, at the age of nine, became the focus of a desegregation suit that was resolved too late to accommodate Brown but opened school doors for her younger siblings and others who followed; and Walter Gobitis and his children (Minersville School District v. Gobitis, 1940), who lost a plea not to salute the U.S. flag in a public school, a case that was reversed only three years later. Also shown are a group of Amish children running from school authorities who wanted to force school attendance on a religious group that feared the influence of education on its members; a 1963 march on Washington against school segregation; Philip Lindsey, general secretary of Rotary International, after the 1987 ruling to allow women membership; Norma McCorvey, aka Jane Roe, of the 1973 abortion case Roe v. Wade; and others. Though many pages are solid print, and the vocabulary is full and descriptive, the news story style makes this interesting history book quite readable. A student might use discrete sections for SSR. And many of the cases described here would serve as read-aloud passages to launch discussion on meaningful adult topics.

1055. *Children of the Dust Bowl: The True Story of the School at Weedpatch Camp.* Jerry Stanley. Illustrated with historical photographs. New York: Crown, 1992. Focus: 1930–1940.

This book briefly describes how agricultural jobs in the Dust Bowl states declined by 400,000 between 1930 and 1940, when "nearly 50 percent of Oklahoma's farms changed hands in bankruptcy court sales" and a mass of displaced and starving people headed for California. On page 5, the Dust Bowl, 1936–1940, is depicted on a map of nine states. A dark, grainy section shows a giant teardrop shape where no rain fell on farmlands for a long time—and then the winds came. A political-topographical map of historic Route 66, "Mother Road," names the likely stopover spots, places to find day work, and trouble spots, too—Shamrock, Amarillo, Flagstaff, Kingman, Mojave Desert, Tehachapi Mountains. It has an inset U.S. map with an outline of the Route 66 area, pages 14 and 15. Another political-topographical map, page 24, shows the intersection of Routes 66 and 99 in California, again with an inset of the whole state. Kern County, Tulare County, Kings County, Visalia, Delano, Bakersfield, and Weedpatch are shown. After suffering eviction, starvation, disease, and death in the Dust Bowl, the Okies arrived in California, where residents labeled them stupid and shiftless and often told them to move on. The type is easy on the eyes, the margins wide, the historical photographs dramatic, and the prose compelling. This history book will hold the attention of any adult interested in the United States, and it readily lends itself to younger students, if used in a teacher reads aloud and class discusses format. The introduction links the Okie experience with John Steinbeck's historical fiction *The Grapes of Wrath*, but the children of the Dust Bowl are absolutely real. For background building see "The Giant Dust Bowl" under "Other Strong Passages," entry 1073.

1056. *The Civil War EXTRA: From the Pages of The Charleston Mercury and The New York Times.* Edited by Eugene P. Moehring and Arleen Keylin. New York: Arno Press, 1975.

Newspaper stories from two perspectives cover the war from 1861 to 1865, giving the reader a chance to see how the nation's journalists handled the day-to-day issues of civil war. Most of the pages have been reconstructed from stories throughout the papers, with some sections deleted simply because the print was illegible. The type is small and the language sometimes amusing, but the story of the war and the salient issues of honor and determination are reflected in both papers. This book is full of interesting read-aloud snippets, though hardly a column is without some impossible-to-decipher words. On April 17, 1861, *The Charleston Mercury* says, "Our readers know that we have repeatedly declared that we did not believe that a war between the North and the South would be the result of a dissolution of the Union by the secession of the Southern States. With the sound of our cannon still ringing in our ears, we are of the same opinion still. That the brutal fanatics who sit in the high places at Washington are ready to plunge the whole country into contest and blood, we have never doubted. It was a thorough conviction of their treacherous and desperate hatred of the South that compelled us to urge, as the only course of safety for the South, a prompt and eternal separation from their power." On the same day, *The New York Times* gave a report on the "Experience of the Times Correspondent as a Prisoner of War" as he reported, "Whenever the haze lifted, I could discover the sacred flag of our country proudly spreading itself to the breeze. Although the shot fell around it thick and fast, yet it seemed to possess an absolute power of intangibility and nothing could disturb it. The scene was solemn in the extreme."

1057. *Civil War Parks*. Rev. ed. William C. "Jack" Davis. Photography by David Muench. Las Vegas, NV: KC Publications, 1992. The Story Behind the Scenery series.

A centerfold of the Civil War area, historical paintings, a sample of Lincoln's handwritten Gettysburg Address, and clear, well-composed color photographs all serve as support for a Challenging yet intriguing text. It is the kind of book a new speaker of English or a new reader might use first as an adult picture book and revisit, gaining vocabulary and historical knowledge over time. The large, thin magazine format makes it easy to carry and allows considerable amounts of text to be large and easy on the eyes. The books in the Story Behind the Scenery series are designed by different people that yield a wealth of quality reading for all levels. I have to rate the books as Challenging because sophisticated language is used. However, these books, by virtue of their layouts and visuals, are much easier to read than some other works under the Challenging marker.

1058. *Dr. Elizabeth: The Story of the First Woman Doctor*. Patricia Clapp. New York: Lothrop, Lee & Shepard, 1974.

One hundred and fifty-six fast-moving pages without pictures give insightful details not only on the woman who lived from 1821 to 1910, but also on the gender and social issues that she faced. The biography is written from a first-person perspective through letters and journal entries, discussing her life in England and the United States. There is a reference to Florence Nightingale on page 107. The issues of censorship and the right to privacy come up in a letter from Kitty, pages 125–26.

1059. *Ellis Island*. Wilton S. Tifft. Foreword by Lee Iacocca. Chicago: Contemporary Books, 1990.

This is an oversized picture book with a rich collection of documentary photographs illustrating every chapter. Copies of passports, baggage tags, and architectural drawings also give a sense of reality to this distant time in U.S. history. On pages 55–63, "The Rise of Anti-Immigration Sentiment" explains that the U.S. Census Bureau's announcement that there were no more unclaimed frontier acres led to reluctance to admit more immigrants. The fear of many marginally established laborers that newer immigrants would willingly take even lesser wages also produced anti-immigrant sentiment. The nativist movement of the 1890s also gave rise to racism. "The fears of nativists were not restricted to the number of immigrants but focused as well on their character and origins" (page 55). The newer immigrants promised unwelcome change. "Many were Catholic. Most spoke unfamiliar languages. Many were unskilled, many uneducated" (page 55). "Anti-immigration factions sought to restrict immigrants of eastern European peasant stock . . . because it was felt they would 'pollute the young nation's bloodline' " (page 57). In 1897, promoting a literacy test as a standard for admission to the United States, Henry Cabot Lodge spoke to the U.S. Senate: "Mr. President, more precious even than forms of government are the mental and moral qualities which make what we call our race." He continued to warn that the nation was in peril of "a single danger, and that is by changing the quality of our race and citizenship through the wholesale infusion of races whose traditions and inheritances, whose thoughts and whose beliefs are wholly alien to ours and with whom we have never assimilated or even been associated in the past, the danger has begun" (page 58). The heated debate over this proposal is detailed. Close-up shots of individuals, photos of crowds on deck of a ship in harbor, and remarkable documentation of ethnic dress make this well worth the time of any student of documentary photography.

1060. *Independence National Historic Park.* Ronald Bruce Thompson. Las Vegas, NV: KC Publications, 1994. The Story Behind the Scenery series. Focus: 1790–1796, present.

The contributions of women to early U.S. history are surprisingly absent in this story. Almost as scarce are photos and references to Native Americans. It is difficult to determine the source of this bias. However, there are several interesting passages that I have not found nearly as accessible elsewhere. The large, quality photographs, a summary of "Interesting Events in Philadelphia 1790–1796," make this an informative read. See also under "Book Chapters and Strong Passages," entry 1075.

1061. *Ishi: Last of His Tribe.* Theodora Kroeber. Illustrations by Ruth Robbins. New York: Bantam Books, 1964.

Lost while searching for his homeland and driven by spirits into the land of twentieth-century white men, Ishi, the last of the Yahi of the Yana tribe, gave us a final glimpse into the spiritual, physical, and practical life of a now extinct people. Small ink drawings offer insights as an incredible tale unfolds. A map of Ishi's journey shows the lengths to which this man went to protect the spirits of his ancestors. Though written in a straightforward style, using third person and simple language, the text employs enough Yahi language to build atmosphere. I used this book in an individualized program for a Native American student who, three months earlier, had been preliterate. He recommended that I continue to use it. It would not have been effective to offer him this in the beginning. After he built background knowledge through a variety of readings, he could read, enjoy, and learn from "real" books. The point is, the materials selected must fit the individual reader.

1062. *Letters from the Promised Land: Swedes in America, 1840–1914.* Edited by H. Arnold Barton. Minneapolis, MN: University of Minnesota Press, for the Swedish Pioneer Historical Society, 1975.

This period of greatest migration from Sweden to the United States is discussed through letters and diaries of immigrants and travel accounts by Swedish visitors. Religious persecution, language difficulties, economic strife on both sides of the Atlantic, and the most difficult period—the first six months—are all detailed in these documents. There are several particularly telling passages: Foul air, cramped quarters below deck, putrid water, moldy and wormy food that was often in short supply, sickness, and death were standard during the eight- to ten-week voyage. This is so much like the slave transport, the experiences of the poor Irish, and the Vietnamese and Cambodian boat people, that it bears comparative analysis in the classroom or tutoring situation, particularly for ESL students. Note the first paragraph on page 14. Poor crops in Sweden from 1867 to 1869 are discussed on page 139. Illiteracy, spelling deficiencies, and the use of mixed Swedish and English in letters are covered in a letter of complaint to the editor of *Hemlandet* from the Swedish postmaster S. M. Korling. He also complains that addresses are often so incomplete that letters must be opened to find out who should receive them. Even then, if the letter is unsigned, it must be passed from hand to hand until someone recognizes the handwriting or contents (pages 140–41).

Language acquisition is addressed on pages 196–97 in a letter of April 10, 1888, to Sister Lotten. The letter explains what we now call the Silent Period in 1888 terms. The young writer says, "[I]t is hardest the first half year as long as you can't manage with the language, but if you only can happen to find decent folks to work for it goes well and good humor is something wherever you go." About 1902 another letter details how satisfaction with America parallels with language acquisition. That is, the immigrant experience begins with overwhelming homesickness that evolves into a love of the new country as English becomes more a part of the immigrant (page 290).

1063. *Letters from the Sand: The Letters of Desert Storm and Other Wars.* U.S. Postal Service. Washington, DC: GPO, 1991.
     Some reproduced in clear type, some in the original handwriting, letters and postcards document the history of the United States during wartime. Diary entries, children's art, stamps, and historical photographs support the text, which takes the reader on the same emotional roller-coaster ride that the writers themselves experienced. Seldom is the Spanish American War (1898–1899) covered in such detail. "The letters from Vietnam were just too sad to read," said an adult new reader. So much pictorial support is in this high-interest book that it does not really qualify for the Challenging category, yet the vocabulary and writing variety offer a lot of quality input not found elsewhere. There are actual commemorative stamps in the collector editions of this book.

1064. The Story Behind the Scenery series. Las Vegas, NV: KC Publications, 1994.
     In a large-magazine format, each book in this series covers the then-to-now story of historical landmarks. They are written by different authors and have a wide range of difficulty levels within any given text but generally are written on a high level, making the text out of reach for elementary ESL and adult new readers independently researching a topic. However, they have a lot of information in the full-color photographs that grace each page. They are a good supplement to studies of North American history and geography.

1065. *Unconditional Surrender: U. S. Grant and the Civil War.* Albert Marrin. New York: Atheneum, 1994.
     Two hundred pages of information-heavy text are supported by a generous sprinkling of historical paintings, photos, and etchings, all black-and-white, and a two-page map of the Civil War zone. Here is a storehouse of detail and drama that makes this time come alive. Although the general text is Challenging, the captions alone are a fine read. Insights into battles shed light on national icons. Popular notions about Lincoln are deftly laid to rest. And Grant's success in passing the Fifteenth Amendment, assuring blacks, including former slaves, the right to vote, is but one of many successes in the life of a master militia man. There are numerous opportunities for read alouds. This is a moving book that could spur extensive dialogue almost from any page.

1066. *Witness to an Era: The Life and Photographs of Alexander Gardner: The Civil War, Lincoln, and the West.* D. Mark Katz. New York: Viking, 1991.
     This is an oversized picture book and an extraordinary portrait of an artist's life. Gardner documented the Civil War, made numerous photographs of President

Abraham Lincoln, and photographed the conspirators to Lincoln's assassination, as well. Tribal photographs, portraits of Crow, Blackfeet, and Cheyenne people, and a lonely burial platform in a tree near Fort Laramie (1868) are in a separate collection marked "The Indians," pages 234–55. There are also reproductions of hand-written documents, complete with scratch-outs and in-process editing, of the Civil War era. The running commentary and captions make this part of history more real than does any other picture book I have seen. And the issues of battlefield agony, racism, slavery, intrigue, crime, and punishment are brought to the fore. This is an excellent book just for page-turning dialogue. It is also well written.

Book Chapters and Strong Passages

Strong Passages for Sustained Silent Reading

1067. *The Guinness Book of Records.* 1995 ed. Edited by Peter Matthews. New York: Bantam Books, 1995.

The cover reads, "The unmatched, authoritative collection of world-class facts, figures, and feats from around the globe, completely revised with all-new photos and features." One U.S. history passage: "Most Patents. Thomas Alva Edison (1847–1931) had the most patents, with 1,093 either on his own or jointly. They included the microphone, the motion-picture projector, and the incandescent electric lamp" (page 436). This is but one sample of the high-interest, adult-level short passages that are loaded with useful, everyday vocabulary written in clear, modern English—available in *The Guinness Book.*

1068. *The World Almanac and Book of Facts 1995.* Edited by Robert Famighetti. Mahwah, NJ: Funk & Wagnalls, 1995.

The table of contents is an idea prompt for thematic units: agriculture, economics, defense, anniversaries, flags and maps, taxes, elections, sports, obituaries, and much more. More detail is offered in the general index. Assassinations, for example, is broken down into attempts, international, presidents, United States, and under each of those is a list of names of the people involved. Vice President Al Gore has written an essay on the meaning of the information super-highway, pages 35–36. World War II is remembered on page 37. The attack on figure skater Nancy Kerrigan and the current status of the Menendez brothers' trial are included. Statistics of many sorts are available in narrative and column format. U.S. history is chronicled in a variety of formats, and world maps are in color. So are the flags. This book might be viewed as an encyclopedia you can hold in your hand.

Other Strong Passages

1069. *Always to Remember: The Story of the Vietnam Veterans Memorial.* Brent Ashabranner. Photographs by Jennifer Ashabranner. New York: Scholastic, 1988.

Though the entire book is worthwhile reading, the chapter "The Vision of Maya Ying Lin," pages 35–43, is profound read-aloud material and can foster dialogue on many topics. She is quoted as saying, "A memorial shouldn't tell you what to think, but should make you think." (Details are under "Thin Books," entry 998.)

1070. "Cesar Chavez: Uniting Farm Workers." In *Heroes: 21 True Stories of Courage and Honor.* Providence, RI: Jamestown, 1985, pages 36–38.

Having emerged from poverty, Chavez risked all of his hard-earned worldly goods to enter the fight for the rights of other farm workers. This is a grand introduction to Biographies, Unit 14, and U.S. history of the 1960s.

1071. *The Constitution.* David P. Currie and Joyce L. Stevos. Glenview, IL: Scott, Foresman, 1991

On page 108, an essay details the Civil War Amendments and the problems getting these laws enforced. (For details, see under "Thin Books," entry 1004.)

1072. *The Day Pearl Harbor Was Bombed: A Photo History of World War II.* George Sullivan. New York: Scholastic, 1991.

For a read-aloud discussion starter, see four pages of historical photographs that give a chilling account of the Holocaust, pages 68–71. "Early in April 1945, as a company of British soldiers advanced through Germany toward Berlin, they came upon a barbed-wire-enclosed camp. What they saw sickened them. In trenchlike open graves, piles of naked bodies were stacked like firewood. The soldiers couldn't believe their eyes."

1073. "The Giant Dustbowl." In *History's Big Mistakes.* Adam Bowett. Illustrated by Chris Mould. London: Belitha Press, 1994.

"The Giant Dustbowl," what it was and how it happened, are explained on pages 14 and 15. There is a remarkable summary of the changes in Colorado, Kansas, Texas, and Oklahoma from buffalo plains to cattle ranches to wheat farms. Then, in 1933, a five-year drought began. "High winds whipped up the dust into great clouds. These created black blizzards up to five miles high. The blizzards were so thick that the sun was blotted out and day turned into night" (page 15). The sad fact that history continues to repeat itself is also brought to light. This entire book is filled with entertaining read-aloud passages, this one relating to U.S. history.

1074. *I Dream a World: Portraits of Black Women Who Changed America.* Brian Lanker. Foreword by Maya Angelou. New York: Stewart, Tabori & Chang, 1989.

This oversized book has 167 pages of American history. On one side is a full-page, black-and-white, museum-quality photographic portrait of a famous African American woman, on the other is a full-page biographical sketch and interview, detailing her place in history. The birth date appears just below the name, and a narrow column gives an encapsulated overview of her contributions to society. There are several politicians, literary figures, and artists whose stories belong in a variety of units. Though the passages are brief and well written, this book would serve best as a read aloud and discussion piece between tutor or teacher and students. Notes: Rosa Parks and Septima Clark essays are c .d under Unit 8, Racism, Bigotry and Tolerance; Unit 1, The Arts, has the summary for photography.

1075. *Independence National Historic Park.* Ronald Bruce Thompson. Las Vegas, NV: KC Publications, 1994.

Details are under "Challenging,"entry 1060. A caption next to the portrait of John Adams gives commentary on the man, his character, and the kinds of risks taken by those who dared to voice the minority opinion regarding British rule, page 13.

1076. *The Irish Potato Famine.* Don Nardo. Illustrated by Brian McGovern. San Diego, CA: Lucent Books, 1990.

The entire book details the reasons why over 1.5 million people left Ireland during a five-year period, most relocating in the United States. Topics of emigration and immigration can be introduced by chapter 4, "Death and Flight—Ireland Depopulated," pages 46–51, or by the vignette "Where Irish Emigrants Went," page 48.

1077. *Letters from a Slave Girl: The Story of Harriet Jacobs.* Mary E. Lyons. New York: Charles Scribner's Sons, 1992.

On page 136 is a read-aloud passage concerning literacy: "We know that she had to conceal her literacy from her master. 'One day,' she recalled in *Incidents in the Life of a Slave Girl*, 'he caught me teaching myself to write.' We also know that she received notes and poems from friends. Since writing was forbidden, it is likely that she responded to them in secret."

1078. "The Shrike and the Chipmunks." In *Fables for Our Time and Famous Poems Illustrated.* Written and illustrated by James Thurber. New York: Harper & Row, 1983, pages 18–20.

Here is Thurber's satirical take on domestic strife. Bad living habits lead to unhappy lives. But in the end, doing the "right" thing gets the players eaten by a shrike anyway. Taking a whack at Aesop, Thurber has a moral at the end of his fable. But Aesop is not enough. Thurber gives a twist to Ben Franklin's Poor Richard's advice "Early to bed, early to rise makes a man healthy, wealthy, and wise." With Thurber, nothing sacred is sacred. I have used this fable to bring humor into the study of early U.S. history. It also allows examination of why, in Colonial times, it was particularly helpful to have people rising early. And the fable can be used to give dimension and character to Ben Franklin, who may appear simply stuffy at first blush. Though the fable itself is not about U.S. history, it coveys the notion that a lot of background knowledge will support comprehension of many topics.

1079. *Susan B. Anthony: Champion of Women's Rights.* New York: Aladdin, 1986. Childhood of Famous Americans series.

From pages 85 to 97 there is extensive detail on the measures taken to prevent little girls from learning math in the one-room schoolhouse. The little boys sat at the front, where the teacher's carefully guarded wisdom was rationed.

1080. *The War Began at Supper: Letters to Miss Loria.* Patricia Reilly Giff. Illustrated by Betsy Lewin. New York: Delacorte Press, 1991.

Michael's letter of February 5, pages 41–42, makes a profound read aloud. (Details are under "First Readers," entry 997.)

Magazine Article

1081. "George Washington's Patowmack Canal: Waterway That Led to the Constitution." Wilbur E. Garrett. Photographs by Kenneth Garrett. *National Geographic* 171, no. 6, June 1987, pages 716–53.

Rich photographs, skilled drawings, and foldout maps squire the reader on a voyage through time on a historical waterway. Not simple reading, this article still affords background information on early America in an intriguing way. A petroglyph, antique and modern industry and architecture, and up-to-the minute fishing reports give an understanding of the canal that would be difficult to acquire from many history books. This is an excellent supplement to units on Colonial history, geography, government, and the Constitution.

Other Events and Supplements

Readers theatre is an excellent way of reinforcing both content and language skills in a low-stress format. There are details on how to set this up in the introduction.

1082. *Paul Revere's Ride.* Henry Wadsworth Longfellow. Illustrated by Ted Rand.
    This is an excellent readers theatre selection. Consider having one person give the historical setting as an introduction and then one or more people read it aloud. It is referenced above, under "First Readers," entry 977.

Here are other suggestions for student activities:

- Write to authors of American history books for more information or just to say thanks.
- Write to historical locations for more information.
- Look for articles on topics under class discussion in newspapers and magazines.
- Draw pictures of historical people or sites and write captions.
- Collect posters of historical tourist locations and exhibit them.
- Collect maps and exhibit them.
- Go to a cemetery to look at tombstones and document dates that are linked to the period being studied.
- Make a collection of memorabilia for a particular historical period.
- Keep a journal as if you were a person living in a specific place during a specific period, such as a runaway slave in a farmhouse being used as part of the Underground Railroad. Or a bounty hunter, searching for such a person.
- Make a display using cancelled commemorative postage stamps as illustrations. Short, summary captions are an excellent framework for meaning-filled writing—at any age.

Author/Title/
Illustrator Index

Reference is to entry number. Illustrators, photographers, and other artists are noted by (I) after their names. This index includes books as well as chapters and articles mentioned in the text.

Subject Index

Reference is to entry number. Numbers followed by "n" refer to annotations. Numbers preceded by "p" refer to page numbers.

About the Author

A lifelong advocate for adult literacy, **La Vergne Rosow** teaches the Teaching English as a Second Language (TESL) practicum course at University of Southern California, is on the USC Peace Corps Advisory Board, serves as an advisor for the California State University, Long Beach chapter of Phi Delta Kappa, and is a mentor for *TESOL Journal*. Her education includes both a master's degree in Teaching English to Speakers of Other Languages and a doctorate in Intercultural Education with an emphasis in Language Teaching and Literacy. Dr. Rosow's work has led her to explore many important areas of literacy. She has researched the early childhood profile of the adult nonreader, and, in her book *In Forsaken Hands: How Theory Empowers Literacy Learners* (Heinemann, 1995), identified the phenomenon of the disempowering significant other (DSO), a person who may appear to have a vested interest in the development of the adult learner's literacy until that newfound literacy begins to threaten the power of the DSO.

In addition to producing nationally-recognized research results, Dr. Rosow has also designed language and literacy programs for small companies and international corporations, taught community college reading, writing, and ESL, established a library literacy program, and served on the needs-assessment team of a national workplace literacy project. Believing that easy access to lots of interesting reading material is essential for people who need to learn how effective English users express their ideas, Dr. Rosow has established a personal lending library for her own students, developed an adult literacy library for the new readers in her local library, and designed leisure reading libraries that serve employees of all literacy levels in numerous corporations.